GLOBALIZATION

AND

THE DEMOLITION OF SOCIETY

GLOBALIZATION

AND

THE DEMOLITION OF SOCIETY

Dennis Loo

The author gratefully acknowledges permission to reprint in near to the original form the following articles:

Dennis Loo, "The 'Moral Panic' That Wasn't: the Sixties Crime Issue in the US," in *Fear of Crime: Critical Voices in an Age of Anxiety*, eds. Murray Lee and Stephan Farrall (New York: Routledge-Cavendish, 2009).

Dennis Loo, "Creating a Crime Wave: the 1990s," *Free Inquiry in Creative Sociology*, 30(1)(2002): 40-55.

ISBN 978-0-9833081-0-2

Cover design by Michael Gerber
Book design by Arc Manor, LLC

Larkmead Press
PO Box 1173
Glendale, CA 91209

larkmeadpress.com
larkmeadpress@gmail.com

A Larkmead Press First Edition

Loo, Dennis
  Globalization and the demolition of society / Dennis Loo.
    p. cm.
  ISBN 978-0-9833081-0-2
  1. Neoliberalism 2. Globalization—Political aspects 3. Democracy
LCCN: 2011924644
LC: JC574 .L86 2011
Dewey: 320.513 .L86 2011

Printed in the United States of America

To allow the market mechanism to be sole director of the fate of human beings and their natural environment...would result in the demolition of society.

KARL POLANYI, The Great Transformation

Long is the way
And hard, that out of Hell leads up to Light.

JOHN MILTON, Paradise Lost

This book is dedicated to my father

CONTENTS

GRAPHS / FIGURES

PREFACE

A War of the Worlds

Since the 1980s, political systems across the globe have been undergoing relentless and radical restructuring. This tectonic shift in the nature and role of politics in people's lives has been and is being carried out under the signboard of installing market forces and unrestrained individualism as the director for all matters personal and public.

Reminiscent of H.G. Wells' depiction of extraterrestrial aliens invading the US in his classic *The War of the Worlds*, no arena has been spared from this full-scale assault. The proponents for free market fundamentalism bring with them not only concrete programs that they are fervently and meticulously inserting into place but an entire army of philosophers of privatization who hector us from every media outlet conceivable, generating a drumbeat of scorn for any who object. "There is no alternative, this is the panacea," this army's foot soldiers and generals tell us; nowhere and nothing is immune from their demand that they must take over and take charge. The acolytes of the invisible hand are visible everywhere we look.

This book refuses and refutes these invaders' agenda. Using market forces and individualism as the organizers for economic and political affairs is a recipe for ever-expanding inequities and the shredding of the social fabric, leading inevitably to myriad disasters on the individual, regional, and global level. It will not do to attempt to mildly modify this invasion, gesturing and gesticulating at the margins. The response to this assault that is occurring on every conceivable level requires an equally comprehensive retort, an alternative vision for our society.

To address this here on the most general level, in a highly concentrated distillation of the key themes of this book: Humans are not first and foremost individuals. Everyone and everything that exists does so only in *relationship* to other beings and to other things. Individuals and groups, in particular, are not separate from and opposed to each other but in fact different expressions of a single integrated process. Individuals cannot accomplish what they do without group support and group sustenance; groups, in turn, rely upon individual leaders to organize the group and thereby advance the groups' interests. We are not fundamentally solitary, autonomous, and exclusively self-interested individuals driven to maximize personal material rewards; we are beings who are primarily shaped by our relationships, especially those generated by our society's political and economic structures. Individuals do not principally give systems the character that those systems possess; systems and structures principally shape individuals' behavior.

Genuine freedom does not and cannot come from ignoring one's obligations to other people and by spurning necessity and material reality. Freedom can only exist on the basis of first recognizing and coping with necessity and then acting to transform it. Moreover, material wealth is not the proper measure of the worth of a person or a society. The pursuit of individual—and corporate—opulence and the downgrading or outright dismissal of the intimate and indispensible connection we have to each other and to the earth are the road to catastrophe for the people and for our planet.

This book's chapters build upon each other, beginning with the Introduction, although it is also possible to read individual chapters out of order and by themselves. I am aiming this book at two different major audiences, the academy and the wider public. The book uses the vocabulary, precision, depth, and nuance of the academy but the examples, manner, and forthrightness of argument are designed to be understandable and familiar to those who have not attended a university. I do this in order to help bridge the divide that exists between the world of theory, scholarship, and science and the broad public. Without that gap being spanned, the necessary mobilization of wide swaths of the people to directly engage in the streets, in the classrooms, in the halls, on the stage, and in all other public and private venues, to remake society from top to bottom in the face of the "invisible hand" invasion, cannot occur.

❖

I could not have written this book without the assistance and support of many others. Linda Rigas provided excellent feedback and suggestions for material in several chapters. James Lu, Lacey Palmberg, Melanie Marcell, Ellie Wood, Phi Su, Jennifer Wong, Antonina Papovolia (who has the sharpest eyes for detail I have ever seen), Morgan Love, and Brittani Washington provided me invaluable data. Michael Reibel provided some real contributions to Chapter Four. Henryka Maslowski, Peter Phillips and Debra Sweet read a full book draft and offered valuable suggestions and/or observations. Linda Swanson, copyeditor, and Michael Gerber were extremely helpful. Michael designed the elegantly evocative book cover and was always available to provide helpful advice. The folks at Arc Manor and Chandi Riaz in particular were prompt and patient and did an excellent job of designing the book. Several of my Cal Poly Pomona senior seminar classes read earlier iterations of this book and I thank them all for their feedback on how to improve the book and for reinforcing my conviction that this material could potentially find a very wide audience.

Linda Savoie gave me advice about what needed to go into the first Appendix for "those who get angry after reading this and want to do something." Adriana Scopino provided me with further editing assistance and valuable affirmation for my message. I thank Dan Simon, my first publisher at Seven Stories Press, for referring me to her. My appreciation to Larkmead Press for their support. My heartfelt thanks go to my wife for her advice and assistance in so many ways. Lastly, I owe an immeasurable debt personally and professionally to the social and revolutionary movements of the past and present, and the heroic leaders and brave followers of those movements (political, scientific, artistic, and so on), for teaching me again and again the power of what people can accomplish collectively.

INTRODUCTION

Laying a Foundation for Politics of a New Path: Contests Over What is Real and What is True

To argue with a man who has renounced the use and authority of reason . . . is like administering medicine to the dead.

THOMAS PAINE[1]

It used to be, everyone was entitled to their own opinion, but not their own facts. But that is not the case anymore. Facts matter not at all. Perception is everything.

STEPHEN COLBERT[2]

When it comes to society, deciphering what is going on and determining what to do about it are more difficult than simply stating, "Here's what is happening and here's what we can do about it." Barriers get in the way of both correctly understanding what is going on and taking action that will accomplish what you seek. The best laid plans and intentions often founder upon these barriers. This much can be

---

1   Thomas Paine, *The Crisis: Lancaster, March 21, 1778,* http://www.ushistory.org/paine/crisis/singlehtml.htm, accessed February 6, 2011.

2   Stephen Colbert, in an interview with Nathan Rabin, "Stephen Colbert," AVClub.com, January 25, 2006, http://www.avclub.com/articles/stephen-colbert,13970/, accessed February 1, 2009.

said: people act based upon what is in their heads. How people know what they know (or think that they know) therefore constitutes a fundamental issue for any efforts at social change.[3] This is true both for oneself and for those you seek to influence and mobilize. I thus begin this book by explicitly addressing certain philosophical foundational issues. If you wish to change what exists into something else, then you must first firmly and correctly understand how what exists came to be and what factors cause it to continue to be the status quo. Efforts to promote change erected upon unsound philosophical ground cannot achieve their aims; any initial gains will eventually be reversed.

One of the most dangerous forces at work in our world today, perhaps the most dangerous force, is an assault on truth coming from the Right and from some elements of the Left, bolstered by the growing power of increasingly concentrated corporate media, advertising, public relations, and government propaganda, emanating from both major political parties, all trying to convince us of what is true irrespective of actual truth. Stephen Colbert satirically dubbed this trend to downgrade truth as "truthiness"—the semblance of truth.[4] This attack on reality, on science, on reason, and on the Enlightenment is intimately connected to developments in the economy and politics, this book's core subject. Globalization and its political expression, neoliberalism, could not continue to exist and prevail without the degradation of the meaning of truth.

Since the term neoliberalism is not widely known or understood in the US, a brief explanation is in order here. Neoliberalism has nothing to do with the common meaning of the term liberalism—as in "Senator Edward Kennedy was a liberal." Neoliberalism is an ideology (and the word can also refer to public policies based on that ideology) that touts liberalism in the Adam Smith sense of the term—liberalizing or freeing market forces to do their work unimpeded, and making sure that the government's role

---

3   The study of how we know what we know is called "epistemology."

4   Nathan Rabin, "Interview: Stephen Colbert," AVClub.com, January 5, 2006, http://www.avclub.com/articles/stephen-colbert,13970/, accessed January 19, 2010:

> People love the President because he's certain of his choices as a leader, even if the facts that back him up do not seem to exist. It is the fact that he's certain that is very appealing to a certain section of the country. I really feel a dichotomy in the American populace. What is important? What you want to be true, or what *is* true? . . . . Truthiness is "What I say is right, and [nothing] anyone else says could possibly be true." It is not only that I *feel* it to be true, but that *I* feel it to be true. There's not only an emotional quality, but there's a selfish quality.

is to facilitate these market forces. (I elaborate further upon what neoliberalism is in Chapter One.)

Neoliberalism was first implemented in Chile—after fascist General Augusto Pinochet's bloody 1973 coup, backed by the US government and CIA—by point of bayonet and muzzle of gun, bloodied club and torture dungeon, massacres and assassinations. The so-called "Chicago Boys," a group of economists trained and led by University of Chicago economist Milton Friedman, engineered the draconian policies of neoliberalism in Chile.

Neoliberalism was subsequently introduced in Great Britain and the US under Prime Minister Margaret Thatcher and President Ronald Reagan respectively, at the start of the 1980s. Since that time the leaders of both the Republican and Democratic parties in the US have adhered to neoliberal doctrines and policies, even while espousing their differences with each other over how best to implement those policies. Worldwide, neoliberalism has been ascendant, displacing and replacing the welfare state wherever it previously existed.

A kind of philosophical quicksand has been expanding in the world that needs to be identified, understood thoroughly, and avoided if we are to properly grasp and deal with the threat that neoliberalism represents. In its most extreme versions, we have those who believe that "what is going on" in the world resides exclusively in people's heads. Everything, according to this view, is "discourse" or "text"; everything is interpretation and symbol. As the poststructuralist Jacques Derrida has famously put it, "*Il n'y a pas de hors-texte.* [There is nothing outside the text.]" Christian and Muslim fundamentalists both agree on one thing: that text is the Bible or the Quran,[5] which they believe, respectively, is the literal word of God or Allah. For both postmodernists and religious fundamentalists,

---

5   For a discussion of how this is being expressed in Hinduism, and the affinities between religious conservatism and postmodernism, see Meera Nanda, "Postmodernism, Science, and Religious Fundamentalism," Butterfliesandwheels.org (blog), October 28, 2003, http://www.butterfliesandwheels.org/2003/postmodernism-science-and-religious-fundamentalism/, accessed August 5, 2009. Nanda points out in reference to Science Studies, a postmodernist creation, that

> Its skepticism regarding science is so radical that it does not allow any distinctions between science and superstition . . . **having invested so deeply in anti-modernist and anti-rationalist philosophies, the academic left [of the postmodernists] has no intellectual resources left with which to engage the religious right.**

Postmodernist apologetics in both Christian and Hindu fundamentalism take aim at the naturalist methodology and worldview of science. Their aim seems to be to make room for a "theistic science" or a "sacred

nothing exists but text because no real world exists outside of text. To both religious fundamentalists and postmodernists, reason and science in pursuit of truth are anathema, or at least deeply problematic. Reason and science present obstacles—instead of indispensable tools—to literal textualists' preferred agendas for the planet. Reality, to religious fundamentalists and postmodernists, is what you make it. Reality is what you (or God/Allah) *will* it to be and *want* it to be. Postmodernists believe that the notion of truth "is a contrived illusion, misused by people and special interest groups to gain power over others." Facts "are too limiting to determine anything." [6]

Postmodernists are not fans of George W. Bush, but they share his worldview regarding empirical data and objective reality. As a Bush senior aide put it to Ron Suskind in 2002, explaining that the people in the White House and their supporters were all members of the "faith-based community" rather than the "reality-based community": "We're an empire now, and when we act, we create our own reality." [7]

For the literal textualists, winning consists of getting other people to see the world the way they do, getting others to read from the same text they do and to reach the same conclusions as they do. That is why most literal textualists believe in banning or restricting books, ideas, and words that they do not approve of. They will even mangle grammar in order to accomplish this; witness the Republican Party's bastardization of English by refusing to say "Democratic Party," and instead referring to that organization as the "Democrat Party" on the grounds, apparently, that the Democrats are not democratic.

Some literal textualists (and those influenced by them) believe that certain words should never be used because the words themselves are harmful, regardless of the context and intent of the user. They do not even think it proper to use certain terms while criticizing those very terms. In their view, words are so powerful that they surpass the context in which they are being used and the intent with which they are used. Words, they believe, have a magical power unto themselves: if you do not say it, then it

---

science" that openly brings in their conception of the divine as a cause of natural phenomena. [Emphasis added].

6   "Characteristics of Postmodernism," AllAboutPhilosophy.org, http://www. allaboutphilosophy.org/characteristics-of-postmodernism-faq.htm, accessed September 4, 2010.

7   Ron Suskind, "Faith, Certainty and the Presidency of George W. Bush," *New York Times Magazine*, NYTimes.com, October 17, 2004, http://www.nytimes. com/2004/10/17/magazine/17BUSH.html?_r= 1, accessed October 18, 2005.

will not continue to exist.[8] This is a fitting notion for people who attach such supreme and unmitigated importance to text. If you believe that the text is everything, then of course you want to make sure that the texts people are exposed to are ones that you like. In the right-wing reflection of the postmodern view, fundamentalist activists believe that they have the God-given right to use any words, shamelessly manufacturing "facts," claiming that their adversaries said something even if they did not, in order to mislead people and win them to their fundamentalist agenda. (Sarah Palin's wholly false "death panels" description of a section in the Obama Health Care Plan is an instance of this.) If enough people see things the way the literal textualists do, then the fact that they all see it the same way makes that view reality. It does not matter if what they are all saying and believing has no basis in reality: "Reality is what we say it is."

An example that demonstrates the absurdity of this position would be the belief that if you want to fly badly enough, you can will yourself into staying in the air after flinging yourself off a cliff. An alternative to this insanity, a non-postmodernist and non-faith-based response, would be to study the laws of aerodynamics and build a hang glider or airplane that *could* fly. In that instance, one creates the freedom to actually fly by taking into account the necessities and limitations imposed by objective reality—in this case, the laws of physics—using and transforming the existing conditions through design to permit one to fly.

While I was a graduate student at University of California, Santa Cruz, the graduate teaching assistants (TAs) went out on strike along with our fellow TAs at UC Berkeley. The strike's main leaders at Santa Cruz happened to be postmodernists. When the strike began to run into some difficulties and a suggestion was made that we survey the TAs of different departments to find out how many of them were still observing the strike and not holding classes, the postmodernist leadership opposed the idea on the grounds that the truth might discourage people. Better to proceed by acting as if sufficient numbers were still observing the strike than to find out that too many were not, and, in the face of that hard truth, have to decide what needed to be done. What was real, according to these leaders, was what they said and believed was real.

Postmodernists reject Enlightenment thought and the Enlightenment's legacy for pursuing the idea that truth exists independently of and outside of interpretation/symbol. Postmodernists believe, by contrast, as

---

8   One expression of this trend can be seen in K-12 textbooks where historical and/
     or contemporary events are censored or rendered more palatable by the gatekeepers
     of books on the grounds that revealing the unvarnished facts will allegedly foster
     dissension.

Jean Baudrillard states, "We are in a logic of simulation which has nothing to do with a logic of facts and an order of reasons."[9] Fundamentalist religious forces also despise the Enlightenment for their own unique reasons; fundamentally they are hostile to the very idea of reason. Science, in contrast to this, rests upon the assertion that observation, analysis, interpretation, and prediction deal with an objective reality that exists separate and apart from the observers themselves. The core and indispensable element in the scientific method is the existence of an objective reality separate and apart from consciousness, not the notion that the observer can be entirely objective. A person's consciousness, in other words, does not create the world. "If a tree falls in the forest and no one is there to hear it, has it fallen?" The answer that science gives to this classic conundrum is, yes, the tree has fallen because there are other indices of what has transpired besides human consciousness. Put another way, if you were to die this instant, would this book you are reading disappear and the world and all of its creatures cease to exist because you were no longer there to witness it and call it all into existence?

While impartiality and objectivity by observers are a traditional expectation and goal for science, impartiality and objectivity are not science's central element. Contrary to the traditional positivist view, utter impartiality by observers and scientists is impossible. The postmodernists are right about this point. Interpretation is always involved in everything we perceive. But to go beyond this, as the literal textualists of the Right and Left do, and say that no objective reality can be said to exist because it is all subject to varying interpretation (or because it is all God's doing), represents a profound and consequential error. It amounts to conflating interpretation with objective existence. Those who argue that no objective reality exists are throwing the baby out with the bathwater. And they are throwing the baby out of the window of a high-rise building.

One postmodernist author has written that

> [T]he acquisition of cultural authority carries with it the capacity to re-write history and redefine the nature of the present. . . . However, domination and disempowerment are never absolute. Even the Muslim prisoners held by the Americans at the Abu Ghraib camp. . . can protest and challenge authority.[10]

---

9   Mark Poster, ed., *Jean Baudrillard: Selected Writings* (Stanford: Stanford University Press, 2001), 178.

10   Chris Rojek, *Cultural Studies* (Malden, MA: Polity Press, 2007), 2.

Yes, the prisoners could protest and challenge and they did, but what did this elicit from their guards? More torture and even death by torture. Water being poured into your nose and mouth until you suffocate is not merely text and it is not merely symbolic. It is very, very real. We do not breathe symbols; we breathe oxygen.

To cite another example of the relationship between the empirical world and consciousness, I can objectively measure someone's weight with a scale. What that weight means—is this person dangerously thin, fat or just right?—is a matter of interpretation, but the amount of their weight is indisputable, verifiable, and reproducible.

If there is no thing or process outside of an interpretation with which to compare the interpretation so that we can determine whether it fits well with the entity or process described, then science and reason themselves fail. The world then dissolves into battles over one subjective perspective versus another with no way to judge the merits of either by an independent criterion. Truth is no longer possible because everything—and the only thing—is simply warring interpretations. That condition, without a doubt, comprises an intolerable situation that can only lead to grievous results in which might makes right and subjectivity rules. (More on this in Chapter Five especially as it pertains to democracy.)

Establishing justice and fairness in our world requires that we defend and expand the scope of reason and of science. Reason and science are under unprecedented combined assault from the Right, from some elements of the Left, and from the interests of large corporations and the major political parties. We need to handle appropriately the relationship between objective reality and interpretation without erring in either the direction of declaring that interpretation is all that matters, or the opposite. What you believe and how you interpret a situation matter greatly, but interpretation does not overcome reality. The fact that Bush and his cabinet believed that their invasion of Iraq would be greeted with flowers as a liberation and that post-invasion planning was therefore unnecessary did not make their self-induced fantasy real.

Barack Obama, for his part, while obviously more grounded in reality than the Bush team (viewing global warming, for example, as a real problem) has nonetheless contributed markedly to confounding appearance with reality. The difference between Obama and Bush is that while Bush appears to believe his own fabrications, Obama seems to know the difference. As I wrote in March 2009,

7

Yesterday *The New York Times* reported:

> The Obama administration said Friday that it would abandon the Bush administration's term "enemy combatant" as it argues in court for the continued detention of prisoners at Guantanamo Bay, Cuba, in a move that seemed intended to symbolically separate the new administration from Bush detention policies.
>
> But in a much anticipated court filing, the Justice Department argued that the president has the authority to detain terrorism suspects there without criminal charges, much as the Bush administration had asserted. **It provided a broad definition of those who can be held, which was not significantly different from the one used by the Bush administration.**

In other words, the Obama Administration is going to retain the content of what Bush and Cheney were doing but they are not going to call it by the same name.[11] [Emphasis added.]

During his 2008 campaign, Obama stated:

> We will lead in the observance of human rights, and the rule of law, and civil rights and due process, which is why I will close Guantanamo and I will restore habeas corpus and say no to torture. Because if you elect me, you will have elected a president who has taught the Constitution, who believes in the Constitution, and who will restore and obey the Constitution of the United States of America.[12]

Statements such as this are what led so many people to experience such relief when Obama was elected president. What is not so well known to people, however, is that what Obama said about respecting the rule of law and due process is at odds with his actions as president. As I wrote in February 2009,

---

11   Dennis Loo, "If You Undermine the Foundation, What Becomes of the Structure?", WorldCantWait.net, March 15, 2009, http://www.worldcantwait.net/index.php?option=com_content&view=article&id=5446:if-you-undermine-the-foundation-what-becomes-of-the-structure&catid=117:homepage&Itemid=2, accessed March 21, 2009.

12   Charles Pierce, "Absolution Without Confession," *Esquire*, June 2008, 109, citing an Obama speech during the 2008 campaign.

Contrary to his public pronouncements about taking the "moral high ground," "restoring due process," ending torture, and that "no one is above the law," the Obama administration declared on February 20, 2009 that the hundreds of prisoners in Bagram, Afghanistan being held by US forces and subjected to torture and murder since our invasion of Afghanistan, do not have the right to challenge their indefinite detentions or the fact that they have been tortured.

They are, according to this *new* White House, outside the law that the Obama team has made such a fetish of claiming that they uphold.

"This Court's Order of January 22, 2009 invited the Government to inform the Court by February 20, 2009, whether it intends to refine its position on whether the Court has jurisdiction over habeas petitions filed by detainees held at the United States military base in Bagram, Afghanistan," Acting Assistant Obama Attorney General Michael Hertz wrote in a brief filed Friday. "Having considered the matter, the [Obama] Government adheres to its previously articulated position [under Bush]."[13]

In September of 2009, Obama's administration announced that it was going to extend the right to challenge their detentions to Bagram detainees. Unfortunately, the people assigned to represent the detainees' interests were not lawyers but military personnel, and the procedures they unveiled were the same as ones that existed in the early days of Bush's military tribunals. In other words, this was more of the same and not a real extension of habeas corpus rights to the prisoners. Later in 2009, Obama further indicated that he would detain individuals if he thought that they still posed a threat. This former teacher of constitutional law was asserting that you could punish people indefinitely based on the suspicion that they might do something.

While growing numbers of people are becoming disillusioned with Obama, Obama's legitimacy continues to rest upon his ability to convincingly present a picture of where he is coming from and what he is doing that differs sharply from what he is actually doing. For many people, the fact that Obama declares that his intentions are on the side of the angels is sufficient for them to accept that he is what he says he is. (I am speaking here, of course, primarily of Democrats, not Republicans.) Many people who

---

13   Dennis Loo, "Obama: Bagram Prisoners Be Damned," WorldCan'tWait.net, February 22, 2009, http://www.worldcantwait.net/index.php?option=com_content&view=article&id=5399:obama-bagram-prisoners-be-damned&catid=128:the-war-of-terror&Itemid=30 4, accessed April 1, 2009.

are supportive of Obama's statements and actions did not accept the same rationales and actions when Bush and Cheney carried them out, underscoring further the importance of appearance. Who Obama is—an articulate black man and a Democrat—and how he says things matter more to many people at this point than what he is doing. The fact that they are satisfied with pronouncements, without questioning whether they are equivalent to actions, reveals just how much truthiness has invaded the public sphere.

We have to know what is real in all of its complexity and fluidity if we want to change reality. We have to use theoretical and conceptual tools that mirror reality well and that give us the ability to turn necessity into forms of freedom. Poor conceptual and theoretical tools blind us to what is actually going on. This book is thus not only about what is happening around us, about phenomena and the sources of those phenomena, but also about rejecting theoretical models that obscure our ability to grasp what is really happening.

"Membership Has Its Privileges:"
Where You Stand Depends On Where You Sit

Truth is not, unfortunately, self-evident. Things can get in the way of recognizing truth. Those of us in the US live in history's richest capitalist country, the greatest superpower ever seen, and the very fact of that overwhelming power and wealth clouds the truth for us. The view from the inside differs from the view from the outside; the scene from the top is very different from the scene on the bottom. The term "neoliberalism," for example, is widely used outside the US but it is not well known or well understood within the US. This is fundamentally because the US is the one of the heartlands of neoliberalism; criticizing the US and accurately naming it on its home ground are harder to do.

As former CBS anchor Dan Rather put it on *Larry King Live* in 2003,

> Look, I'm an American. I never tried to kid anybody that I'm some internationalist or something. And when my country is at war, I want my country to win, whatever the definition of "win" may be. Now, I cannot and do not argue that that is coverage without a prejudice. About that I am prejudiced.[14]

---

14   Steve Rendall and Tara Broughel, "Amplifying Officials, Squelching Dissent: FAIR Study Finds Democracy Poorly Served by War Coverage," FAIR.org, May/June 2003, http://www.fair.org/index.php?page=114 5, accessed May 1, 2007.

American media "objectivity," evidently, is limited by nationalism, even when a journalist like Rather is reporting on a war such as Bush's 2003 invasion of Iraq. That war was based entirely on lies, and because it involved attacking a country that did not initiate hostilities, it constituted the gravest war crime of all. Dan Rather, despite his admission of pro-US bias and desire for the US to "win" a war that from its very inception constituted a war crime, was deemed insufficiently subservient to the powers-that-be and was forced to retire early after his story about Bush's dodging National Guard service during the Vietnam War aired on *60 Minutes*.

Nationalism on behalf of a superpower—"USA! USA! USA!"—is a qualitatively different matter than, for example, Jamaican citizens' nationalistic pride in their country's Olympic bobsled team. The disparity between different kinds of nationalism—the nationalism of oppressed nations and the nationalism of oppressor nations—is never mentioned in mainstream and corporate media within the US, but it is not a phenomenon that Americans are unaware of in other contexts. More than a few movies about American high schools and colleges feature a split between the people who side with the already dominant (e.g., the "popular" but mean high school girls or jocks) and those who root for the underdogs (e.g., the nerds and their allies among the decent kids). In the world as a whole, most Americans see their country as analogous to the latter group, the do-gooders who sometimes mess up but whose intentions are always pure.

Most Americans do not see their country as analogous to a high school's bitchy queen bee girls or arrogant jocks who mistreat and humiliate other students; instead, most Americans think the US is more like the benevolent students in high school. That is one of the reasons why movies that celebrate the underdogs in high school (and in other arenas) are so popular. In the real world, however, the benevolent ones among the students are usually the underdogs. American Empire and its sole superpower status vis-à-vis the rest of the world does not suit us for the underdog role. Truth be told, the US has never been an underdog, except vis-à-vis the British imperialists during the American Revolution. The true underdogs in American history are the dispossessed, beginning with Native Americans and slaves. Cheering on the cavalry that routinely massacred Indians was and is an unsavory position for Americans to take. To make it palatable, the victims of genocide had to be portrayed as savages and as the real evildoers.

A current example of this is the ongoing wars on Iraq, Afghanistan, and Pakistan. "Support the troops" who are engaged in carrying out wars that constitute what the UN Charter and the American prosecutor at Nuremberg, Robert H. Jackson, define as the "supreme war crime"

—attacking a country that has not attacked you first—is very different from supporting troops engaged in a just war. In a very closely related example, those Americans who think that it is okay to torture people if it allegedly makes American lives safer (because that is what most policy-makers have falsely told them) and who do not think about the needless and immoral deaths caused by the US invasion of Iraq (over 1.2 million Iraqis[15] and conservatively more than fifty thousand American soldiers as of late 2010)[16] are looking at the world through the eyes of privileged

---

15 The prestigious British medical journal *The Lancet* published two surveys of excess Iraqi deaths (deaths that would not have occurred but for the US invasion), the first on November 20, 2004 and the second on October 12, 2006. The 2006 survey estimated that between 392,979 and 942,636 Iraqis had died as a consequence of the war. A January 28, 2008 survey by Opinion Research Business found excess Iraq deaths of over one million, consistent with *The Lancet* study. Controversy surrounds the body count, with some arguing that both *The Lancet* and ORB survey estimates are too high. If, as the VA itself admits, more than fifty thousand Americans have died by suicide alone since the 2001 invasion, then it is reasonable to assume that Iraqi deaths are at least in the high six figures. Whatever one's conclusions about these numbers in terms of magnitude, even the lowest estimates are exceedingly high for wars based on lies. See Gilbert Burnham, Riyadh Lafta, Shannon Doocy, Les Roberts, "Mortality after the 2003 Invasion of Iraq: A Cross-Sectional Cluster Sample Survey, "October 12, 2006, http://www.thelancet.com/journals/lancet/article/PIIS0140-6736%2806%2969491-9/abstract, accessed February 15, 2011. See also Tina Susman, "Poll: Civilian Death Toll in Iraq May Top 1 Million," LATimes.com, September 14, 2007, http://www.latimes.com/news/nationworld/world/la-fg-iraq14sep14,1,3979621.story, accessed February 14, 2011.

16 Armen Keteyian, "VA Hid Suicide Risk, Internal E-Mails Show," CBS News.com, April 21, 2008, http://www.cbsnews.com/stories/2008/04/21/cbsnews_investigates/main4032921.shtml. accessed May 10, 2008:

> Last November when **CBS News exposed an epidemic of more than 6,200 suicides** in 2005 among those who had served in the military, [Dr. Ira] Katz [the Veteran Administration's Head of Mental Health] attacked our report.
>
> "Their number is not, in fact, an accurate reflection of the rate," he said last November.
>
> But it turns out they were, as Katz admitted in [an email] just three days later.
>
> He wrote: there "are about 18 suicides per day among America's 25 million veterans."
>
> That works out to about 6,570 per year, which Katz admits in the same e-mail, "is supported by the CBS numbers." [Emphasis in original]

As of the end of 2010, the US war upon Iraq had been going on for more than seven-and-a-half years. The war upon Afghanistan began on October 7, 2001 and has thus exceeded nine years. Taking March 2003, the beginning of the US invasion

Americans. "The people who are being killed and roughed up are not my family or people that I know so it is all right." The unstated assumption here is that American lives are more important than the lives of people from other countries, so much more important, in fact, that torturing innocent people and even killing huge numbers of people who had nothing to do with 9/11 are seen as morally acceptable, even, and especially, by so-called Christian leaders.

In addition to the problem of being biased or blinded by superpower nationalism, what I would call "empire nationalism," we have hierarchies

---

of Iraq, as the starting point, this means that conservatively speaking, over fifty thousand American veterans or active duty soldiers have committed suicide since the Iraq war began. While not all of those suicides can be traced directly to the invasions and occupations of Iraq and Afghanistan, most of them can. The number of veterans among the overall numbers who have been committing suicide is disproportionately among those who have served in Iraq and Afghanistan and among young veterans. Veterans who kill themselves are much more likely to be those who have served in combat zones compared to those who have not, and the greatest occurrence of suicides occurs among veterans closer to their time that they served as opposed to decades later. See Armen Keteyian, "Suicide Epidemic Among Veterans: A CBS News Investigation Uncovers A Suicide Rate For Veterans Twice That Of Other Americans," CBSNews.com, November 13, 2007, http://www.cbsnews.com/stories/2007/11/13/cbsnews_investigates/main3496471.shtml?tag=contentMain;contentBody, accessed March 3, 2011:

> So CBS News did an investigation—asking all 50 states for their suicide data, based on death records, for veterans and non-veterans, dating back to 1995. Forty-five states sent what turned out to be a mountain of information.
>
> And what it revealed was stunning.
>
> In 2005, for example, in just those 45 states, there were at least 6,256 suicides among those who served in the armed forces. That's 120 each and every week, in just one year.
>
> Dr. Steve Rathbun is the acting head of the Epidemiology and Biostatistics Department at the University of Georgia. CBS News asked him to run a detailed analysis of the raw numbers that we obtained from state authorities for 2004 and 2005.
>
> It found that veterans were more than twice as likely to commit suicide in 2005 than non-vets. (Veterans committed suicide at the rate of between 18.7 to 20.8 per 100,000, compared to other Americans, who did so at the rate of 8.9 per 100,000.)
>
> One age group stood out. Veterans aged 20 through 24, those who have served during the war on terror. They had the highest suicide rate among all veterans, estimated between two and four times higher than civilians the same age. (The suicide rate for non-veterans is 8.3 per 100,000, while the rate for veterans was found to be between 22.9 and 31.9 per 100,000.)

13

within the US itself. Some people reap the benefits of enormous wealth and power, while most of the rest of us do not bask in the luxuries of great affluence. Life does not look the same to different strata. How the world looks to you depends substantially on your material conditions and life chances. Those who benefit most from the existing system in the US tend to be the fondest of the way things are, and those who benefit the least are the most likely to favor fundamental change. Exceptions to this pattern exist,[17] but they are just that, exceptions; correspondence between one's material position and one's attitudes is very strong.[18] It is one of the strongest correlations that exist in the social world. Marie Antoinette's alleged "let them eat cake" retort to a court adviser telling her that the people were without bread epitomizes this problem.[19] In a diluted version of Antoinette's famously ignorant and dismissive comment, I once overheard an insufferably smug student telling another student (who was trying to get others involved in collective political action), while strutting past him: "Your issue is not *my* concern."

Beyond one's material status and position, both as an American vis-à-vis the rest of the world and as someone within a hierarchy within the US, there is furthermore the matter and role of ideas. We see and experience the world through the lens of ideas. Everything that we experience is subject to interpretation; we respond to our environment through concepts or ideas. As an illustration of the power of concepts, consider the following anecdote of one of my students: the hosts of a party that she was at ran out of booze and rather than admit this, pretended to add alcohol to the punch. Guests proceeded to become drunk on this pseudo-alcoholic punch.

While alcohol is a central nervous system depressant and alcohol in the bloodstream will induce identifiable physiological changes, drunken behavior is a learned behavior that is culturally specific and independent of alcohol's chemical profile. Those who behaved as if drunk did so because they believed that they were drinking alcohol. As

---

17 Most notably, some artists and entertainers are exceptions in that they may be wealthy, but their views do not necessarily reflect that fact.

18 Youth and students in every country have a special and vital role to play in social movements. Their special status grows out of the fact that their basic stance is not one of being convinced that the ways things are is the way they have to be, and the fact that they have more freedom to engage in political actions and inquiry than older people.

19 A contemporary example of this was Barbara Bush's comment upon seeing the refugees from Hurricane Katrina in the Houston Superdome: "These people have it pretty good. I hope they do not stay."

described by a sociology textbook on deviant behavior, "Research identifies no universal behavioral consequence of drinking alcoholic beverages. Drunken actions are largely learned behavior sensitive to cultural and social contexts."[20]

If people lose their jobs and health insurance and end up homeless but at the same time they believe this is their own fault, they are not likely to participate in political action to address the social causes of unemployment and homelessness. If someone is unaware that the gap between the rich and the poor in the US is wider than in any other industrialized nation in the world, and if they believe that one day they might strike it rich through the lottery, they are not likely to engage in political activism to rectify or modify American society's class stratified nature. If someone heard over and over again that Saddam Hussein was harboring and colluding with the terrorists who carried out 9/11, that Hussein possessed weapons of mass destruction (WMD), and if that person was never informed that it is the gravest war crime of all to attack a country that has not attacked you first, then that person is very likely to support the US invasion of Iraq. Even after learning that the WMD story was a lie, many people developed rationales that kept them believing the original lie. Moreover, as Hitler recognized so clearly, government leaders who tell colossal lies can get away with it:

> [I]n the simplicity of their minds people more readily fall victims to the big lie than the small lie, since they themselves often tell small lies in little matters but would be ashamed to resort to large-scale falsehoods. It would never come into their heads to fabricate colossal untruths, and they would not believe that others could have such impudence. Even though the facts which prove this to be so may be brought clearly to their minds, they will still doubt and continue to think that there may be some other explanation.[21]

Facts are facts, but they are not facts to you if you do not know about them. You can be infected with AIDS and you will die from it if you go untreated, but if you do not ever learn that what you have is AIDS, you

---

20 Marshall Clinard and Robert Meier, *Sociology of Deviant Behavior* (Belmont, CA: Thomson Higher Education, 2008), 257.

21 Paul Craig Roberts, "Why Propaganda Trumps Truth," InformationClearingHouse. info, September 15, 2009, http://www.informationclearinghouse.info/article23498. htm, accessed September 20, 2009.

will likely think that it is something else and not respond appropriately to the disease.

The production and propagation of ideas within a society are consequential and powerful. The dissemination of ideas, in fact, is itself an expression of power differentials within society. To paraphrase Clausewitz's famous dictum that war is the continuation of politics by other, violent, means, ideology is the continuation of material differences by other nonviolent means. Ownership and control over the means of production of ideas is at least as important as ownership and control over the means of production of material things. Both material position and one's ideas affect one's life experiences, how one sees the world, and what one does and does not do.[22] Those with the most resources at their command to disseminate their versions of events and issues are by definition those with the most power and privilege in other respects. The ruling ideas of any epoch, as Marx put it, are the ideas of the ruling classes. People who blame the American people for the US government's policies fail to appreciate the importance of the power over public opinion exercised by the ruling groups. Those ruling groups are decidedly not the American people as a whole.

Because of the increasingly extremely lopsided distribution of resources under neoliberal regimes, the ability of the wealthy to propagate their worldviews in a way that benefits their positions is unparalleled in modern times. "What is the point of having wealth if you cannot protect it?" as the wealthy businessman in the 1976 made-for-TV movie series *Rich Man, Poor Man* told his nephew. The more inequitable things are and become, the more important it is for those on top to promote their worldviews and protect what they have.

In a world in which the gap between the rich and the rest yawns wider by the minute, convincing the non-rich to go along with this state of affairs requires convincing them to go along with policies that are not in their best interests. Reality must be distorted to bolster the growing inequity. Those who exercise power can only continue to enjoy their status if reality—as presented to and understood by the public—is altered through the presentation, advocacy, and dominance of ideas that favor the interests of the rich and powerful.

---

22 Some people (e.g., postmodernists and the Frankfurt School) argue that political power and hegemony are exercised exclusively through ideas. This is a major error that I elaborate upon in Chapter One and Three.

Paradigms

Ideas are always part of larger, coherent assemblages of interrelated ideas that necessarily involve a group of unprovable assumptions and value judgments about the nature of reality. These assemblages are known as paradigms. We all use paradigms, whether we know it or not. "My opinion" is not unique to the person espousing that opinion. Opinions do not come from out of thin air. "My opinion," in general, is one of a limited number of identifiable groups of opinions within a given society. These opinions are limited in number and can be grouped because they are born socially and socially determined.

Theories are based upon paradigms. They differ from paradigms in that theories offer explanations for phenomena. Theories and paradigms are like microscopes. They are devices through which we see the world. Optical microscopes are wonderful tools for seeing cellular-level matter and activity. But they are worthless at the atomic level. If you want to see atomic particles, you need to use an electron microscope. As far as optical microscopes are concerned, atomic particles do not even exist. In order to see society, we need the proper conceptual and theoretical equipment. That is why this book is explicitly about both illuminating what is going on, and examining what is wrong with the most influential and common conceptual tools being used to perceive what is going on.

Aren't Facts Facts?

Facts are facts, as the saying goes. And as far as it goes, the saying is true. Facts *are* facts. But what facts mean is a contested matter, and debates go on constantly about which particular facts are most meaningful. Facts can only be properly understood and perceived through the lens of theory. In fact, only through paradigms can particular phenomena even become known to exist and therefore become classified as facts. Before the invention of the optical microscope bacteria were not known to exist. Bacteria did exist, just as "date rape" existed before the term was invented in the early 1970s, but neither bacteria nor date rape was known to exist and/or was not seen as problematic before it was named. It took the development of a paradigm for the transmission of pathogens (initially involving bacteria, later on, viruses, which are much smaller and not visible via optical microscopes) before bacteria could be seen as a relevant fact. Similarly, it took the emergence of feminism as a powerful social movement for the occurrence of rape during a date to be seen as worthy of note and for it to be given a name.

To further illustrate the importance of contextualizing and interpreting facts, it is common for analysts to cite per capita income data to compare the living standards among countries. Assuming that the figures used are reliable, per capita income data are facts. A country with higher income per capita is commonly assumed to have a better standard of living than a country with lower income per capita. Other indicators besides per capita income are used, but most analysts rely heavily upon per capita income as the key indicator of living standards.

One of the problems with per capita income data is that since the data average out national income over the entire population, they do not and cannot take into account vast differences of income. A nation with a small number of extremely rich people living among a large number of very poor people would appear on a per capita basis to be a prosperous country. But most of the people would obviously not be living materially rich lives.

Occasionally, analysts use a different index as their key indicator, the Gini Index. The Gini Index is a measure of the gap between the richest and the poorest in a country. It is therefore a measure of income inequality. When the Gini Index is used and compared to per capita income, living standards look very different. Both per capita income and the Gini Index are hard numbers, but they reveal disparate pictures of reality.

When people debate one another citing dueling facts, what is generally at stake are not the facts themselves but fundamentally different assessments of reality founded in differing and competing paradigmatic perspectives.[23] The basic incompatibility of those competing perspectives usually produces an impasse between the debaters. This incompatibility grows out of the premises and the value judgments that make up the foundation of each paradigm. If your premise, for example, is that the existing system is fundamentally sound and right, then no matter how much evidence you are exposed to that contradicts this premise, as long as you do not decide that your premise is wrong and substitute it with a different premise, you will continue to see events from the prism of your existing premise. The form this takes in general is that any evidence contrary to one's paradigm is dismissed as untrue, exaggerated, taken out of context, or insignificant. In extreme cases the messengers bringing the

---

23 Theory is in turn part of a paradigm. A paradigm is how we make sense of the world. Different paradigms are possible and different paradigms exist simultaneously within society and among all of the people.

18

news of contrary evidence are suppressed by ridicule, exclusion, or, in the most extreme cases, murder or execution.

Thomas Kuhn in his pathbreaking book *The Structure of Scientific Revolutions* articulated this phenomenon in relation to the rise and eventual defeat of successive paradigms in the natural sciences. The Catholic Church's view, based on the Bible, that the earth was the center of the universe was accepted for centuries, but eventually the empirical evidence that this could not be true became too strong to dismiss and an alternative paradigm that incorporated the discordant data defeated the previous biblically-sanctioned view. This defeat involved tremendous protracted resistance by the defenders of the old paradigm; there were even threats of excommunication and torture against proponents of the new paradigm. That fight, to anyone paying attention to the views of the religious Right, still rages today, millennia later, under different guises, even though science won the fight between the geocentric and heliocentric models long ago.

Sometimes a new paradigm wins out because an experiment shows the impossibility of the existing, dominant paradigm. For example, explorers sailing over the horizon did not fall off the edge of a flat earth. Einstein's theory of relativity decisively replaced the ruling Newtonian mechanics paradigm when a solar eclipse proved Einstein's theoretical prediction correct—light traveling near large celestial bodies such as stars is bent by the star's gravitational field (a kind of depression in space the way a ball resting on a cloth pushes down on the cloth). The discovery made headline news around the world.

Nevertheless, competing paradigms still exist within the natural sciences. Even though the theory of relativity has been accepted, debates continue over such matters as whether the universe will expand indefinitely or eventually wind down. Because, for most purposes, Newtonian mechanics is close enough to correct in dealing with movement at ordinary speeds, it is still widely used, even though the theory of relativity replaced it. We find the ongoing, uneasy, and contradictory coexistence of competing paradigms even more prevalent within the social sciences than the natural sciences. Each paradigm gives different credence and weight to the meaning of particular facts. The coexistence of these competing paradigms owes much to the fact that the social sciences are more obviously and directly linked to public policies. Vested political and economic interests thus come into play in the social sciences more clearly and immediately than in the natural sciences. Research has shown clearly that welfare tends to reduce street crime, but this knowledge has not resulted in a victory for the pro-welfare position, since for ideological reasons it suits dominant interests to ignore or dismiss that research and insist on the opposite. (This difference between social science paradigms and natural science paradigms is a matter of degree, not of kind, since public policy issues also come into play with the natural sciences. Witness the stem cell research and evolution controversies.)

For individuals, adopting a different paradigm from the one that has been used is not a common occurrence. Since paradigms and their related value systems have a taken-for-granted character to them, changing paradigms is not an easy affair for people. A shift in paradigm is much more likely to happen when a person's material position stands in contradiction to the paradigm to which they had previously been adhering: for example, those who are themselves poor but who have been adopting a paradigm that best reflects the interests of the wealthy. In contrast to this, people comfortable with their lives as they are are much more likely to adopt and hold onto views that suit their current status and conditions, even in the face of a wealth of contradictory empirical evidence. "Truth," in those cases, is significantly conditioned by its comfort value to the individuals involved. This differs from the paradigms held by those whose lives are not as comfortable; their paradigm co-exists uneasily with their actual life circumstances and life chances.

Precipitants

Because those with the most social power are able to impose their paradigms (in the political context, their ideologies) upon others, a tension exists among the less comfortable between the paradigms in their heads and their lived experiences. This tension creates the potential for at least some of these individuals, under the right circumstances, with the right precipitants, to shed their existing paradigms or ideologies and adopt ones that better fit their life chances. It takes a profound crisis for this shedding of old paradigms to happen to substantial numbers of people. It requires a situation in which the way the rulers have been ruling can no longer be sustained and the people's willingness to go along with things as have they have been has ruptured.

Most people believe that the "way things are" comes about because the mass of individuals consent to and agree with the way things are. Consent of the governed, however, is exaggerated in its significance. Conformity operates more powerfully to keep people going along with the group than does consent. (See the final chapter for a more developed discussion of this.) Because we are social beings and must depend for our very survival upon our connection to the group, it is not our wont to depart from it. Most people will adopt the behavior of the group even when they know indisputably that what the group is doing is wrong.

Is this because most people are weak? Not really. It is because most people recognize that ostracism from the group is dangerous for their welfare.

Paradigms and Perceptions

Bringing to light the unstated assumptions of different paradigms and their implicit value judgments about what is right and what is wrong, what is true and what is not, what is relevant and what is not, is therefore crucial not only to becoming educated but also to being able to act in the world in a conscious and effective manner. Coming to grips with what is going on involves facts, but it also involves understanding what different paradigms are based on and the difference it makes which paradigm is used. How you see the world depends a great deal upon your viewing instrument.

In sociology there are two major paradigmatic perspectives. The first is called functionalism, sometimes referred to as the "consensus perspective." It holds that societies are best understood as held together by universal agreement about values among the people and by a division of labor that produces interdependence and therefore social solidarity; inequality is natural, inevitable, functional, and everlasting because people are not equally endowed and because the division of labor requires different levels and kinds of skill; those whose jobs are the most important to the society are more highly rewarded; the public gets the leaders and media that it deserves and wants because the leaders and media function at the pleasure of the public and reflect public sentiment; society's main and default condition is one of harmony, with the greatest harmony existing when people do their respective parts in the overall division of labor; the preservation of the whole of society is paramount and the whole functions best when everyone knows where they belong.

Sociology's other major theoretical perspective is known as the "conflict perspective." Instead of viewing societies as bound by shared values, the conflict perspective holds that society is shaped by groups with different and conflicting interests battling over resources, both material and non-material. This perspective is based on materialism (in the philosophical sense): ideas do not exist separate and apart from material interests and materiality; ideas grow out of and represent material interests and materiality; because values are based on interests, and the interests of groups are themselves in conflict, different groups possess different values; public officials and media mainly reflect the society's dominant groups rather than the society as a whole; the ideas that serve the dominant groups' interests are the most widely propagated and promoted ones in the society, but are not the ideas that reflect a society-wide consensus of shared values; the dispossessed and subordinated and those who advance the ideas of the subordinated are generally downplayed, ignored, derided, and/or dismissed; the course of history is shaped by the struggle between different interests and their corresponding ideas; revolutionary changes happen when the subordinated groups and their subordinated ideas overturn those who have been dominant, establishing a new economic and political system based on a different organization of society, especially the economy, and correspondingly different values, ideas, norms, and social relations.

Everyone adopts one of these two perspectives (including variants upon them), whether they know it or not. A consensus person *sees* the world differently from a conflict person. Both types of people could be watching the famous Rodney King video, for example, and one would see a black man being mercilessly and unnecessarily beaten and another would see the "thin blue line" of the police protecting the citizenry against a large black man, high on PCP, refusing to cooperate with authority.

Functionalism, because it advocates, naturalizes, and therefore justifies inequality, represents the dominant perspective in the US. For the American Dream of great wealth to work as a strong incentive for people to strive and work hard, there must be a wide gap between the rich and the poor. If the gap is not wide then the incentive for striving for wealth would not be strong since a standard of living that was not that much different from others could be enjoyed without having to strive for riches. Thus, those who say that the American Dream allows everyone to be prosperous are misleading people. In fact, poverty is part and parcel of capitalism and of the American Dream in particular. If no poor people existed, they would have to be created as an incentive for those at the lower rungs of society, so that those people would be afraid for their jobs and keep their noses to the grindstone lest they end up like the poor below them. The American Dream, in other words, is rather like a game of musical chairs where some must of necessity and by structural logic be left out in the cold, no matter how hard they might work or how talented they might be.

All societies need to ensure that all or at least most of their population are working and working hard. How they ensure this varies. Hunting and gathering societies demand hard work from their members (for at least part of the day, since hunting and gathering societies actually enjoy a lot of leisure time) as a precondition for being a member of the tribe/group; if you do not work hard then you will be ostracized and ejected. Slavery compelled hard work on pain of whippings and death. Capitalism offers the Hobson's choice: work or starve. Capitalism differs from feudalism in that in capitalism the vast majority of the population are systematically deprived of the means to survive independently, compelling them to work for those who own and control the means of production, that is, the means to life.

The conflict perspective regards social and economic inequality by classes and other groupings (e.g., race, ethnicity, and sexual orientation) as both very real and not desirable. Those who rule the society consequently do not generally adopt the conflict perspective because the conflict perspective challenges their own position of power and privilege.

Most people in the US have strains of both the functionalist and conflict perspectives intermingled in their views of the world. Only a minority of people are either fully consistent functionalist or conflict people. In response to the Rodney King beating, most Americans were shocked at the police brutality. They were stunned because their native worldview was/is functionalist and the video challenged that view, depicting an event that a functionalist would find hard to believe: police were not acting according to shared values; they were illegally beating a defenseless man.

If you want to fix a machine but do not know how the machine works and do not understand the principles that apply, you cannot fix it. Societies are like machines, only far more complicated; all the more reason, therefore, to study societies carefully and to draw deeply upon historical lessons. If you want to actually have an impact on a societal level—a complicated endeavor—then you need analytical tools that are up to the task. You cannot possibly get such sophisticated tools by relying on the conventional wisdom dispensed via the ordinary organs of media and public officialdom. Does the advice we get on health care over the mainstream media give us enough scope, depth and detail to allow us to treat ourselves and be our own physicians? Certainly not. Why would political advice dispensed via mainstream media and existing governmental institutions be any better? Is it reasonable to expect that reliance upon the major parties' campaign pitches and the injunction "just vote" could possibly be all you need to know to change society? The richest 497 individuals in the world have more wealth than the bottom fifty percent of the world's population. If you had such extreme wealth and power and enjoyed your luxuries more than justice, would you let your possessions be subject to the whims of the principle of "one person, one vote?" Would you let your extraordinary wealth be outvoted? You would be crazy to do so. (I go into these matters more extensively in Chapter Five.)

In every paradigm there are unstated premises that involve value judgments. Value judgments are, by definition, not refutable. You cannot prove that someone's values are wrong. Declaring someone who delights in torturing animals and people to be wrong is a value judgment. The fact that most people agree with that value judgment still does not make it the same thing as proving the person wrong. People who have lost the ability to determine right from wrong due to a brain injury but who retain the ability to reason have been found to be unable to reach conclusions, even though their reasoning capacity is intact. Vulcans of the Star Trek saga, who supposedly are purely rational and unemotional, in other words, could not exist.

You cannot reason absent value judgments. We make value judgments all the time. Those who claim not to make value judgments are simply arriving at judgments unaware (or are unwilling to fess up to the fact) that they are making value-based decisions; their decisions are hidden under the mask of "neutrality." This is not, however, the same as declaring that there is no such thing as objective reality and that there are only differing interpretations. The stance that I am arguing for here is called "postpositivism" or "empiricism." Objective reality exists outside of my consciousness. Facts exist.

The world outside of my head is measurable with objective instruments such as a thermometer and scale. Is a temperature of 88°F hot and uncomfortable? Most people think so, but some people like hot weather and find that temperature comfortable. Is two hundred pounds too heavy for a 5'6" person? That depends upon what culture we live in. Weight is a fact. What that fact means is subject to interpretation. For an NFL running back this might be a very good weight. A female of this weight in ancient Hawaiian society was considered sexy because she had access to a lot of food and was therefore privileged.

We can declare with certainty that people need clean water to live and that if they do not have access to clean water that they will surely die. We can further say that more than twenty-five thousand children die every day in the world due to diarrhea and related conditions caused by the lack of access to clean water. Some people—such as myself—would consider this fact criminal, given the state of technology today. Other people regard the more than twenty-five thousand daily deaths as perhaps unfortunate, but no cause for alarm. Better those children than their own children, they think. Still others would regard this fact as the product of karma—these children did something bad in a previous life that is now causing them to die this way. The meaning of that factoid, in other words, varies widely. The objective world, as the existentialists argue, does not contain meaning. Meaning is something that human beings impose upon the objective world.

Let Them Eat Toxic Waste

Neoliberal Michael Kinsley, in the *Washington Post* in 2008, defended former World Bank President Lawrence Summers' memo, written during his World Bank tenure, in which he suggested that toxic dumps should be exported to Third World countries:

> [Lawrence] Summers's main point was that life and health are worth less in poor countries than in rich ones. He measured that worth by the earnings lost when a person is sick or dies prematurely. But another good measure, maybe clearer, would be the amount a society will spend to save a life. Treatments that are routine in the United States, although they cost hundreds of thousands of dollars, are simply not available to citizens of poor countries. You get cancer and you die. Of course this should not be true, but it undeniably is true, and rejecting the idea of poor countries earning a little cash by "buying" pollution from rich ones will do nothing to make it less true.
>
> If an industrial plant that causes pollution is going to be built somewhere, it ought to be built where life is worth less. This sounds brutal, but it is not. Or rather, it is less brutal than reality. Turn it around: If a life is worth less, it is also cheaper to save. For what we spend in the United States to save a single life, you could save dozens or hundreds of lives in poor countries. So if the plant is going to be built somewhere, building it in a poor country will enable more lives to be saved than building it in a rich one. . . .
>
> If a city in a rich country is very polluted and a city the same size in a poor country is not, you will save lives—in the rich country this time—if some of that pollution can be moved from the rich country to the poor one. And the money the rich country pays the poor one can save even more lives in the poor country.
>
> **The general point is that clean air and other environmental goods are luxuries.** The richer a country is, the more of them it can afford. And if rich countries like the United States had had to meet some of the standards being wished upon poor countries today, we would still be poor ourselves.

Every economic transaction has two sides. When you deny a rich country the opportunity to unload some toxic waste on a poor one, you are also denying that poor country the opportunity to get paid for taking the toxic waste. And by forbidding this deal, you are putting off the day when the poor country will no longer need to make deals like this.[24] [Emphasis added.]

Is the worth of a life really measurable by a person's earnings? If this is so, then the life of Larry Ellison, who made over $330,000 a *day* in 2009, is worth far more than yours or mine. There is so much that is so wrong in Summers and Kinsley's logic here that I could write a small book untangling and tracing the threads of callous indifference in the guise of cold, hard economic logic embodied in this short passage. In fact, Kinsley's apologia could serve as the reason in microcosm for the book you are now reading.

Many people would recoil at Kinsley and Summers' assertions, as they should. The outcry against Summers was one of the reasons why Summers, who was being floated as Obama's Treasury Secretary, was not appointed by Obama to that post; instead he was appointed to head Obama's Counsel of Economic Advisors, a less visible post. Kinsley avoids the obvious point that a poor country that accepts a toxic dump from a rich country is trading dollars to supposedly save some people's lives while at the same time encouraging more deaths and injuries. How does increasing the death toll in a poor country help to lower the death toll in that country? Given the uneven trading terms between rich countries and poor countries, a "fair market value" return to a poor country for allowing a toxic dump on its turf would be disadvantageous to the poor country. This means that the tradeoff for the increased mortality and suffering from the toxins, whose long-term impacts are not well-known and difficult to measure, would not be commensurate with the damage to the poor country's people. Instead, the exporting of a toxic dump to a poor country reflects the larger trend of the dominance of poor countries by the rich.

Even if Kinsley's twisted logic were valid, it relies upon an invalid assumption, that the people in charge of using the money from the toxic dump's relocation on their land will allocate that money to save other people's lives. Anyone who knows even a little bit about how elites in Third World countries usually operate knows that this assumption is not valid.

---

24   Michael Kinsley, "Revisiting One Lawrence Summers Controversy," Washington Post.com, November 8, 2008, http://voices.washingtonpost.com/postpartisan/2008/11/revisiting_one_lawrence_summer.html, accessed November 1, 2009.

Certainly any country that would accept toxic dump material from a rich country is not going to be a country led by elites who care about their people. Finally, Kinsley states that the "general point is that clean air and other environmental goods are luxuries."

This is really quite interesting. If we did not know this comment's context and the author's intent, we could reasonably believe that his statement was meant as an indictment of industrial, capitalist society. According to his reasoning, prior to the Industrial Revolution or in some of the unindustrialized areas still left in the world, clean air and water were/are unavailable. If you do not have the bucks then you get to live like the people depicted in the Schwarzenegger film *Total Recall* in which polluted air causes people to develop physical abnormalities. As peculiar as this might sound, to capitalism's most fervent acolytes it just makes sense that life on this planet should only be non-toxic for the rich. The poor countries, as everyone knows, are surely more polluted than the rich countries. The Amazon Rain Forest, goodness knows, is famously more polluted than Houston or Los Angeles. And the waters of the spectacular Iguaçu, bordering Argentina and Brazil, are dirtier than the Hudson River. Why simply everyone knows that!

The fact that Kinsley is a regular columnist in the *Washington Post* (and not some crackpot whose extreme views are dismissed and marginalized from the mainstream discourse) and that his reasoning reflects the dominant paradigm in the US today, reveal the toxicity of the prevailing neoliberal paradigm. Kinsley, incidentally, was the designated "liberal" on CNN's *Crossfire* for many years. With "liberals" such as Kinsley, who needs conservatives? Marie Antoinette's indifference to the conditions of her people was one of the factors that led those people (whose lives were worth less than those of the monarchy) to revolt. Perhaps Summers and Kinsley's callous indifference could provoke something similar in our time? Might the revolts in Tunisia and Egypt be harbingers?

Meaning, Values and Reason

Meaning is an inescapably value-laden enterprise. Inherent in the functionalist paradigm is the premise that not all lives are equally important. Some people are more important to the society than others. To a functionalist, inequality, even extreme inequality, is only a problem if it produces disharmony in the society and if too many people come to feel that they have no chance to escape their subordinated status. This would cause people to feel that they were like a "cog in the machine," as Emile Durkheim, the "father of functionalism," put it. It is enough, Durkheim argued, that such people be told that their work is contributing to an enterprise much larger than themselves. It is not necessary for such a person to take in broad horizons; indeed, too much liberal education for working class people would be harmful because it would create dissatisfaction in them and thereby undermine harmony. They might riot or even rise up in insurrection. In contrast to Durkheim, it is my purpose in this book to bring those very broad horizons to as many people as possible and to explicitly undermine the false, paper-thin harmony that exists today. For I do not agree with Durkheim that social inequality is natural, inevitable, desirable, or eternal.

Over and above the functionalist paradigm, we also have seen, beginning in the 1980s, the revival of Social Darwinism and faith-based fundamentalist ideologies. Because functionalism lends itself to both liberal and conservative interpretations, the ideologies of Social Darwinism and fundamentalism represent the most right-wing extremist ideas on the scene. Among the Left, functionalism exerts substantial, though contested, influence as well. The battles for the future being waged today involve a battle over facts and between contending ideologies/paradigms. The forms these battles take are both abstract, in the realm of contending ideas, and literal, in the form of political struggles and physical battles between combatants. Abstractions, after all, have real and very concrete consequences. The struggle in the realm of ideas is hence a critical one. As Marx once put it: the weapon of criticism gives way to the criticism of weapons.[25]

So let the games begin.

---

25 Karl Marx, "A Contribution to a Critique of Hegel's Philosophy of Right: Introduction," Marxists.org, (Paris, 1844), http://www.marxists.org/archive/marx/works/1843/critique-hpr/intro.htm, accessed January 29, 2011. His specific words were: "The weapon of criticism cannot, of course, replace criticism of the weapon, material force must be overthrown by material force; but theory also becomes a material force as soon as it has gripped the masses."

CHAPTER ONE

The Paradox of Preeminence

[Americans] are desperate for the political-economic-social elixir that will restore our "peace of mind" or at least protect us from further harm. We definitely want those words—those exact words. But more important, we want that feeling of safety, security, and intergenerational improvement once again.

FRANK I. LUTZ, pollster[1]

It is the early years of the twenty-first century and the US stands in splendid isolation. The greatest military power and empire in history, it spends more on its armed forces than the rest of the world combined. For more than two decades its chief adversary, the socialist camp, has been absent from the scene. Since socialism's retreat, capitalism and globalization have been the triumphant marching orders of the day—unrivaled, unmitigated, and unapologetic. US military and economic might, moreover, outstrips any grouping of other national powers, notwithstanding the cavernous cracks and crevices in the US economy so glaringly evident in the last few years, and the fact that the US government continues to wage two-and-a-half wars with great difficulty upon poor and strife-ridden countries at ruinous expense, with no end in sight.

---

1 Frank I. Luntz, *What Americans Really Want... Really: The Truth About Our Hopes, Dreams, and Fears* (New York: Hyperion, 2009), xvii-xviii.

Alongside this American preeminence we also see some rather peculiar things: unprecedented levels of insecurity and fearfulness; invocations of constant danger from abroad and from within by public officials, mass media, and ordinary citizens; widening and intrusive surveillance; unparalleled abridgment of key civil liberties; and growing reliance on coercive social-control measures. As pollster Frank Luntz reported in 2009 in *What Americans Really Want... Really:* "[I]f you ask the average American what he or she *really* wants, the answer today is radically different from the heady optimism of the 1990s: *freedom from fear.*" [2]

While this juxtaposition of preeminence and insecurity has become more pronounced since September 11, 2001, these trends substantially predate 9/11 and are therefore not explicable based on 9/11 alone. A quintessential example of this, and one not well known, is that the Bush White House's warrantless wiretapping of all Americans began *seven months before* 9/11.[3] In the 1990s numerous books and articles chronicled a puzzling and widespread sense of fear and unease among the people, ever-widening

---

2   Luntz, xvi.

3   In February of 2001, the Bush team, through the National Security Agency (NSA), called all of the major telecommunications companies together and asked that they allow the NSA to tap all the nation's telecommunications traffic. All of the carriers except Qwest complied with Bush's felonious request. As former CIA analyst Ray McGovern put it in an October 15, 2007 article at ConsortiumNews.com, "NSA Spying: What Did Pelosi Know?", http://www.consortiumnews.com/2007/101407a.html, accessed on October 16, 2007:

> It turns out that seven months before the threat of terrorism got President George W. Bush's attention (despite the best efforts of then-counterterrorism chief Richard Clarke to install it on everyone's screensaver, so to speak), the administration instructed NSA to suborn American telecommunications companies to spy illegally on Americans.
>
> The general counsel of Qwest Communications advised management that what NSA was suggesting was illegal. And to his credit, the head of the company at that time stuck to a firm 'No,' unless some way were found to perform legally what NSA wanted done.
>
> Qwest's rivals, though, took their cue from the White House, and adopted a flexible attitude toward the law—and got the business. They are now being sued. Lawsuit filings claim that, seven months before 9/11, AT&T "began development of a center for monitoring long-distance calls and Internet transmissions and other digital information for the exclusive use of the NSA."
>
> For its principled but, in government eyes, recalcitrant attitude, Qwest indicates that it lost out on lucrative government contracts.

This Telecom Amnesty Bill passed Congress supported by, among others, President-Elect Barack Obama who had previously vowed to support a filibuster of the bill.

and record-breaking economic disparities, rising immiseration, increasingly punitive laws, ever-growing incarceration rates, and so on.

If victory for the American way of life and capitalism looks like this, then what must defeat look like?

Perversely, the more preoccupied the public has become with security, and the more that measures have been employed supposedly to promote security, the more insecure we in fact have become—subjectively as well as objectively. This holds true both on the national level and on the personal level. It goes beyond the question of the competence or incompetence of the US government's economic policies or its anti-terrorist and anti-disaster measures and policies. It goes beyond the matter of whether the Republicans or the Democrats are in power. It goes to the very heart of the new world order's fundamental nature.

Social systems, economic systems, political systems, and so on, are all governed by their own internal logic. Shakespeare's oft-cited line "The fault, dear Brutus, lies not in our stars / But in ourselves..." is certainly poetic, but it is fundamentally wrong when applied to whole societies or to systems within those societies. All systems have rules and inherent logic. You do not change those systems by putting different individuals in charge of them. Systems do not operate the way that they do primarily because of the nature of the people who occupy them.[4] In the Stanford Prison Experiment, for example, the "guards" and "inmates" were all Stanford students. Yet they one and all readily and quickly adopted roles that eerily mimicked real prisons' occupants and repressive atmosphere. To stop the Stanford students from behaving like prison guards and prisoners, Philip Zimbardo, the experiment's lead investigator, brought an early end to the simulated prison. You change system outcomes, in short, by changing the system.

The overarching system upon which this book primarily focuses is the political economy of capitalism-imperialism and its current political expression, neoliberalism. Capitalism is a system whose governing logic is the pursuit of profit. Neoliberals and libertarians can speak of "freedom" and "liberty" all they want, but profit as the economic system's cardinal goal inevitably generates certain outcomes.

Globalization and the Growth of Insecurity

Since the late 1970s, two powerful factors have been shaping this new world order—globalization and the dismantling of the welfare state.

---

4 I discuss this in much greater depth in Chapter Five.

The two are inversely related to each other: as globalization has advanced, the welfare state has correspondingly retreated.

Globalization has been defined in a number of different ways and it exhibits a number of different facets, but at bottom it can be summarized as the knocking down of trade and tariff barriers, the internationalization of production, the interknitting of national economies in a global economy, the triumph of the "free market" on a world scale, and the emergence of transnational corporations (superseding multinational corporations) that straddle nation-states and exceed the power of all but the nine most powerful and prosperous nations.

The welfare state within the US is known as the New Deal. It came into being in the 1930s under President Franklin Delano Roosevelt to defend capitalism against possible revolution in the face of its greatest crisis by modifying and blunting some of capitalism's and free markets' adverse attributes and expanding the ranks of those benefiting from government policies. The New Deal provided a social safety net for those that capitalism had temporarily or permanently cast off by supplying unemployment compensation, social security, welfare, and so on. The government also created jobs and carried out services that the market would not offer (for example, government works projects, public education, and opportunities for subsidized higher education).

Governments following Keynesian economic policies (named after economist John Maynard Keynes) expanded government spending in the 1930s and 1940s in order to stimulate the economy and provide more employment and social services. Through its regulatory powers, the welfare state blocked the emergence of trusts[5] since trusts, due to their size and clout, harm the public interest in self-evident ways: monopolistic pricing, production of inferior products that sell because of market dominance, planned and unnecessary obsolescence, and so on. Microsoft's word processing program Word, for example, dominates the market even though it does not have the best features and fewest keystrokes. There were many other word processing programs that were far better than Word, but they lost out due to Microsoft's nearly monopolistic position.[6]

---

5   Or it regulates aspects of the economy that are logically monopolies such as utilities.

6   See, as another example of the clout of monopolies, the case of Visa, as described by Andrew Martin, "How Visa, Using Card Fees, Dominates a Market," NYTimes. com, January 4, 2010, http://www.nytimes.com/2010/01/05/your-money/credit-and-debit-cards/05visa.html?em, accessed January 5, 2010:

"What we witnessed was truly a perverse form of competition," said Ronald Congemi, the former chief executive of Star Systems, one of the regional

Globalization requires and demands freedom from the "fetters" of welfare state measures. Globalization benefits directly from depriving the workforce of the welfare state's safety net protections because a weakened, or better yet nonexistent, social safety net enhances corporate power relative to that of workers. Antitrust regulations interfere with corporations' ability to expand and to command higher prices and more favorable conditions for profit making. For globalization to advance, the welfare state has had to be supplanted, and in its place a new paradigm has emerged: politics and policies designed to defend and promote globalization. These policies are sometimes referred to as "free market fundamentalism" and sometimes as "neoliberalism." Neoliberalism, in brief, is the political expression of globalization.[7]

Neoliberalism's Origins

The term "neoliberalism" comes from the meaning of "liberal" as advanced by the eighteenth century French free-market economists, the Physiocrats, and as popularized by eighteenth century Scottish economist Adam Smith: "*laissez-faire* (let do)," let the market decide. Everything will work out splendidly through the market's "invisible hand."[8] According to this much-celebrated "invisible hand," the best society emerges when everyone is pursuing his or her own individual interests. As Smith put it:

PIN-based networks that has struggled to compete with Visa. "They competed on the basis of raising prices. What other industry do you know that gets away with that?"

Visa has managed to dominate the debit landscape despite more than a decade of litigation and antitrust investigations into high fees and anticompetitive behavior, including a settlement in 2003 in which Visa paid $2 billion that some predicted would inject more competition into the debit industry.

Yet today, Visa has a commanding lead in signature debit in the United States, with a 73 percent share. Its share of the domestic PIN debit market is smaller but growing at 42 percent, making Visa the biggest PIN network, according to 'The Nilson Report,' an industry newsletter.

7   Gary Teeple, *Globalization and the Decline of Social Reform* (Atlantic Highlands, NJ: Humanities Press International Inc., 1995).

8   Adam Smith was personally critical of what are currently considered laissez-faire policies, such as states not regulating business. He believed that small, independent companies were ideal.

[E]very individual necessarily labours to render the annual revenue of the society as great as he can. He generally, indeed, neither intends to promote the public interest, nor knows how much he is promoting it. ... by directing that industry in such a manner as its produce may be of the greatest value, he intends only his own gain; and he is in this, as in many other cases, led by an invisible hand to promote an end which was no part of his intention... By pursuing his own interest, he frequently promotes that of the society more effectually than when he really intends to promote it.[9]

Selfishness, according to Smith, is humanity's highest and best value. The best government, according to this view, keeps its hands off the economy.

Neoliberalism's theoretical lineage can be traced primarily to Austrian economist Friedrick Hayek's writings beginning in the 1930s. Hayek argued that human rights are based on property rights and that governmental regulation of the economy was the "road to serfdom." His equating of human rights to property rights leaves out, of course, the rights of those without property. The unsurprising consequence of this is that those with property, especially a great deal of property, will inevitably distance themselves further and further from those without property in an unregulated economy.

In his 1960 book *The Constitution of Liberty*, Hayek further articulated his view of liberty:

The question of how many courses of action are open to a person is, of course, very important. But it is a different question from that of how far in acting he can follow his own plans and intentions, **to what extent the pattern of his conduct is of his own design, directed toward ends for which he has been persistently striving rather than toward necessities created by others in order to make him do what they want.** Whether he is free or not does not depend on the range of choice but on whether he can expect to shape his course of action in accordance with his present intentions, or whether somebody else has power so to manipulate the conditions as to

---

9   Adam Smith, *An Inquiry into the Nature and Causes of the Wealth of Nations*, Gutenberg.org, http://www.gutenberg.org/files/3300/3300-8.txt, accessed August 3, 2009.

make him act according to that person's will rather than his own.[10] [Emphasis added.]

By equating liberty with lack of coercion over the individual, by making a principle of individual desires and elevating individual desires over those of the group, Hayek advances a plausible but deeply flawed argument.[11] I'm going to analyze his position at some length here, as this passage represents the philosophical heart of neoliberalism.

Here is Hayek's pitch: if an individual's view differs from the views of others, then that individual is right to pursue his or her own plans. It doesn't matter, evidently, what is actually in that individual's best interests, because he or she could be wrong about what is best, including for him—or herself, and it doesn't matter what is best for the larger community of which this individual is a part. What matters is that the individual's view differs from what someone else wants him or her to do. As Ronald Reagan put it in 1964: "Recognize that government invasion of public power is eventually an assault upon your own business."[12]

Hayek in effect dismisses the idea that there is such a thing as objectivity or necessity. There is only what the individual wants and that must prevail. Hayek's hypothetically free individual declares his or her freedom, as if to say, "I care not what is right, nor what is true. I care only that it is what I want. And that shall suffice." If objective reality does in fact exist, and if science, medicine, navigation, exploration, and technology all rely upon objective reality's existence to work (a fact evident to anyone using a car or airplane, for instance), then the ongoing effort to determine at any given time in society what the best ideas are—the ones that more truly represent objective reality—is not merely an idle intellectual exercise but one with powerful material consequences. Which ideas predominate and set the terms matters to the whole of the society. Science, for example, operates through a collective process of peer review. A claim made by one scientist has to be demonstrably true for the scientific community or that

---

10   Frederick Hayek, *The Constitution of Liberty* (Chicago: University of Chicago Press, [1960] 1978), 13.

11   Ronald Reagan, "A Time for Choosing," 1964 Speech, Fordham.edu, http://www. fordham.edu/halsall/mod/1964reagan1.html, accessed January 12, 2010:

> I suggest there is no such thing as a left or right. There is only an up or down. Up to man's age-old dream-the maximum of individual freedom consistent with order or down to the ant heap of totalitarianism.

12   Ibid.

claim is rejected as untenable. If what matters more than anything, on the other hand, is that individuals should have the right to pursue their ideas and plans based on their "own" ideas, then the question of what is true and its impact on the whole of society becomes moot. Implementing Hayek's stand as a principle for the whole society would produce tremendous damage; indeed we find it doing precisely that, as this book discusses, by leading to the demolition of society.

According to Hayek, other people create necessities. However, other people do not create most necessities in life. We face necessities because, to put this succinctly, we do not now—and never have—lived in the Garden of Eden. Food, water, shelter and reproduction are some of the necessities that are met by and through social groups. Try, for example, reproducing without someone else of the opposite sex. Gravity is another example of a necessity that exists regardless of anyone's desires. If I declare that I refuse to recognize gravity, does this mean that I can now fly? Suppose I declare that my plans do not include my ever having to work for anything and that I do not recognize work as a necessity. I may have a right to do so, at least according to Monsieur Hayek, and doing so shows how much "liberty" I have, but should I?

Hayek pits individuals against groups, but individuals and groups are actually interrelated and interpenetrating expressions of the same dynamic process. We might even say that individuals and groups have an organic relationship to each other. Individuals, to begin with, can only exist because of groups. Not only is this true in the literal sense of an individual's birth via a group of two, a female and a male, it is also true throughout the life processes of all individuals. We acquire language, our brains develop, we learn social knowledge and skills, and we survive through our interdependence with others. We become human through this socialization process *and* we become individuals. Becoming human isn't something that happens by our simply being alive. We do not become humans solely or principally because of our DNA. We become human through our interaction with other humans.

Individuals are like the leaves of a tree that extend out from twigs (the family), that spring out from branches (populations) that in turn spread out from the trunk (society). The tree, for its part, cannot live without leaves. It is true that some trees shed their leaves for a season and live on their stored resources and connection to the ground. But they would not have those stored resources if they didn't sprout leaves for the rest of the year in order to collect the sun's rays and carry out photosynthesis. Leaves are a tree's way of providing for itself. Leaves, in turn, cannot survive without being attached to trees. A detached leaf, going about its own merry way, freed of its connection to and the dictates of the tree, falls and dies.

Individuals also serve as *a way for the group to express itself* and *achieve its ends*. Groups act through the mechanism of individual leaders who focus the group in action. Leading individuals are the group's cutting edge. Depraved individuals, on the other end, express the darker side of the group. There are, of course, different groups within any society, with their own respective representatives. We might compare a group's leader to an arrowhead that can penetrate an object when propelled through the air attached to an arrow and its fletching. Without the connection to the arrow shaft, the arrowhead itself could not perform properly. You could not even send an arrowhead minus the arrow shaft through the air with any real force; the arrowhead would tumble about and fall quickly to the ground.

The interaction between the individual and the group is also evident in public leaders addressing a rally or audience, athletes competing on a field of play before a stadium of fans, actors performing on stage, musicians playing before a live audience, and teachers speaking in front of a class. All of them experience the same dynamic of the interplay between performer and audience. This interplay is either strong or tepid. When the connection is strong, the audience feels that the performers in front of them are expressing their deepest sentiments and highest aspirations, entertaining them by striking a responsive chord, or perhaps stirring their darkest fears in a concentrated way. The audience members hear and recognize elements of themselves through the performer/leader.

The individual's connection to the group is also evident when you sample people's opinions about a given subject; you will find without exception that their opinions can be grouped into a fairly small number of categories. If the alpha and omega of individual opinions reside within the individual and are not traceable back to any group, then why do individual opinions constitute identifiable patterns that can be grouped? There is no such thing as an entirely unique idea or an entirely unique behavior, no matter how bizarre or outstanding. Even the most extraordinary achievers in human history, for instance Isaac Newton, achieved what they did by advancing what already existed in their time. These inventions and discoveries represented the next breakthrough needing to be made in order to allow those arenas (e.g., science, technology, art, music) to move forward. As Newton put it, "If I have seen further it is by standing on the shoulders of giants."[13] Newton invented calculus, but

---

13   Letter from Isaac Newton to Robert Hooke, February 5, 1676, quotationspage.com, http://www.quotationspage.com/quotes/Isaac_Newton/, accessed February 11, 2011.

contemporaneously Gottfried Leibniz also invented calculus. Darwin developed evolutionary theory, but Alfred Wallace was coming up with the same ideas independently and, again, contemporaneously. Einstein's startling theoretical discoveries could not have been accomplished without the work and breakthroughs of others in physics, electromagnetics, and mathematics who preceded him and/or who were his contemporaries.

Genius does not exist as something independent of and disconnected from the rest of humanity. Genius represents the cutting edge of a society, the way the tip of an iceberg rests upon the rest of the iceberg. Michael Jordan is generally considered the best basketball player of all time, but he never won a championship until a supporting cast was assembled that presented enough of an additional offensive threat that the opposing team could not win simply by containing Jordan.[14] Society, just like basketball, is a team sport, not an individual endeavor. Even individual pursuits such as chess aren't pursued separate from the community. Chess grandmasters endlessly study the games and strategies of other masters from their own and earlier times. To assert, as Hayek does, that people's conduct and sense of design are of their own creation without acknowledging the roots of that conduct in the antecedents found in people's life histories, in the influences of those who inspire them, in the groups they belong to, in the temper of their times, and so on, represents fallacious reasoning.

Individuals' ideas, behaviors, personalities, values, likes, and dislikes all occur in patterns and on a limited spectrum, because the sources of these opinions and behaviors reside in the group. An individual expression of a particular group's interests, that of the owners of capital, for instance, can be found in someone like Dick Cheney. Cheney, in fact, could be said to be the very epitome of capital at this time. Obama also personifies capital and the needs of US Empire, but he does so in a different way than Cheney; Obama has a different style that is more appealing on the surface to particular portions of the populace who find Cheney repulsive.

Leaders (as opposed to oddballs who are not followed by anyone) are compelled in important ways by the demands of the group(s) they lead. They do not have the liberty, as Hayek advocates, of going off on their own, like the sulking Achilles at Troy, pursuing their "own" plans and desires, if they wish to remain group leaders. If they move too far ahead or away from their groups, they will lose their followers. By the same token, the group needs its leaders and needs to protect, sustain, and retain them.

---

14 The same has been true for the other acknowledged contemporary basketball superstars such as Kobe Bryant and LeBron James; they need a strong supporting cast and a strong, dominant, or powerful teammate to win a championship.

Without leaders a group cannot organize itself and it cannot act. The group becomes merely a crowd. (Truth be told, even crowds have levels of organization that emerge at some point, which only underscores the interrelationship between individuals and groups.) The notion that freedom and liberty consist of following your personal desires in contradistinction to and contrary to the group's demands is a notion that does not describe how things actually operate in society. To sever the connection between the individual and the group, as Hayek advises, is to cut off a river from its source.

If Hayek's vision had actually been fully implemented and all individuals only paid attention to what they personally wanted, regardless of group needs, then the remarkable achievements of human society and human history would never have occurred. If the people who first discovered how to control fire had kept this knowledge to themselves, what would have happened to human development? The species might have even had trouble surviving. Certainly our brains would not have developed as they have done as a result of the increased nutrition made possible by eating cooked food. If the people who figured out how to cultivate and breed grains such as wheat and rice from weeds saw this as a discovery from which they alone could profit and refused to share it, how would civilization have come into being? If a society's highest principle holds individual autonomy above the significance of the group and thus privileges individuals over the group, while people *might* be free to contribute to group goals (as long as no one is forcing them to do so, since for Hayek that is verboten), the desires of individuals to adopt the interest of the group are undermined. In addition, if you do commit yourself to collective interests, then you are necessarily going to *impose* ideas on others in some fashion or another. You cannot avoid doing so, because only certain ideas and plans for a group to follow can prevail at any point in time. This means that other ideas and plans must be overruled or ignored.

If Copernicus and Galileo had decided that their discovery that the earth was not the center of universe wasn't something that others needed to know, if those who went out into uncharted waters and discovered the earth wasn't flat had never dared to venture out, if Spartacus had decided that being personally freed was all right and that all of the other Roman slaves didn't need to be freed, if the French in the late 1700s decided that starvation was less risky than revolution, if John Brown had decided that he wasn't going to jeopardize his life to free the slaves, if Susan B. Anthony decided that fighting for women's rights was not going to benefit her personally as much as staying out of the fight would, if Malcolm X and Martin Luther King, Jr. had decided that their lives were safer and better if they looked the other way in the face of savage racist oppression, if every person who had the courage to fight for change and every person who ever made a breakthrough decided that the rest of society could be damned, then human society would never have left the Stone Age. Indeed, the development of Stone Age tools and their propagation itself would have never have occurred, and we would not be having this dialogue via the printed word, and Hayek wouldn't have been able to write his books, because writing and paper and printing would never have been developed.

Moreover, what confers rightness *automatically* on an individual's desires and plans over that of a group? Does a brigade in battle do better if everyone in that brigade decides for himself or herself what is best? Does a football player do better if he decides for himself what he's going to do on the field in any given play? Could "win one for the Gipper," a slogan Ronald Reagan liked to invoke, have been uttered by one individual against a whole opposing team? Sometimes a particular individual's ideas are better than those of the group, but this isn't automatically the case as Hayek appears to presume. The neoliberal notion that becoming a rich individual should be one's life goal reflects a value that has been propagated within capitalist societies, that is, via a group. So brave and entirely autonomous individuals who refuse to be told what to do by anyone else so that they can pursue designs that only they have thought of, are actually adhering steadfastly to values and beliefs that were first thought of by others.

If you are interested in the best ideas and plans prevailing in any given situation, then you are a) committed to group action, and b) committed to the idea that there is such a thing as truth. Why is this so? To begin with, if you do not care whether the best ideas and plans prevail and only care about what you as an individual do, then you aren't interested in what the group does. Secondly, if you want the best ideas and plans to win out, then you also believe that an objective reality exists by which one can measure whether something is right, or approximately right, or at least on the right path. If you do not believe in these things, then all opinions and plans are equal because there is no independent criterion by which to measure whether one idea or plan is better than another.

Coercion and freedom from coercion are coexisting opposites: no freedoms exist without some level of compulsion attached to them. Hayek's stance makes as much sense as this: "I would like to jump into the air so as to be free of gravity without the nuisance of having to deal with the restraint of the ground." You cannot jump into the air, however, without having the *resistance* of the ground to push *against*. Jumping into the air has no meaning and isn't possible without the constraint of gravity. Necessity and freedom, in other words, make up antipodes of the same inescapable process. It is a process that will never cease. Necessities impose themselves on us regardless of whether we want to recognize them and regardless of who alerts us to their existence. The depiction of necessity as something that people arbitrarily impose on others does not conform to actuality.

Necessity and freedom are inseparable from each other just as sound and silence are opposite and necessary elements of the same process. Sound without silence is impossible, and vice versa. Light only has meaning in relation to darkness, and vice versa. Try to imagine what sound would be like if there were no silences in between the sounds. You cannot, because such a condition would be impossible. The letters you are reading on this page only exist and only make sense because of the white spaces in between the letters. If there were no white spaces then the page would be entirely black and impossible to read. Up has no meaning unless there is correspondingly a down. In has no meaning unless there is a corresponding out. The individual and the group are inseparable from each other since they are different aspects and expressions of the same dynamic or dialectic.

Coercion will never disappear in the sense that power over others will never entirely disappear as long as there are social groups. Social groups exist because there are a multitude of mutual expectations and obligations within the groups. Moreover, even if there were only one human being left on earth, there would still be compulsions that one person would have to abide by, even though there were no longer other people around to impose anything upon him or her.

Coercion in the sense of a government can and will someday disappear, but only after social classes are gone and there is no longer any division of labor and resources resulting in some being excluded from what others have in abundance. But even after government passes away, everyone will still be subject to the will of others. *It is impossible, for one thing, to have unanimity, and where there is disagreement, some people's opinions and preferences must perforce be subordinated to the opinion that holds the day, if people are to remain in groups at all.*

Compare this to Hayek:

[Freedom] meant always the possibility of a person's acting according to his own decisions and plans, in contrast to the position of one who was irrevocably subject to the will of another, who by arbitrary decision could coerce him to act or not act in specific ways.[15]

---

15   Hayek, 12.

If freedom means being able to act according to your own decisions and plans, and if the opposite of freedom is being subject to the coercive will of another, then coordinated activity with others is ruled out *except* in those circumstances in which *every single individual* in a group has *the exact same plan* and therefore the group's plan reflects every single individual's plan. Anyone who has ever worked with others on anything can recognize how impossible this is. Shall each member of a soccer team decide on the field of play that he or she is not subject to the will of any of the others on the field? Shall the players on the bench decide that they are not subject to the will of the coach and check themselves into the game regardless of the number of players already on the field? Shall players decide to ignore the coercion of the referees and do what they themselves want? What shall happen to such a team in a game? Anyone who has ever lived in a family or functioned in any group setting, even with only one other person, would recognize how impossible Hayek's vision is. If my friend wants to see a movie and I want to go to a play, do we decide we're going to split up so as not to impose upon each other's freedom?

Hayek uses the phrase "irrevocably subject to the will of another" as if to set this condition off as unacceptable. But as human beings we are inevitably and necessarily subject to the will of another most of the time, unless we are a king or queen, but even a royal has to bow to the will of others some of the time. Before we are born, while we are alive, and after we die, we are at all times subject to the will of others. The belief that one should never be subject to the will of another is called infancy or insanity.

The premise underlying Hayek's argument in a historical sense is the claim that we humans are first and foremost independent, autonomous beings instead of social beings necessarily intertwined with one another for our very survival and (personal) development. Hayek's notion is one that he shares with the social contract theorists Thomas Hobbes, Jean-Jacques Rousseau and John Locke. Social contract theory posits an original condition in which humans began as individuals, separate and apart from others, then gave up some of their autonomy in order to live together under a government and in a society. Such an original state never actually existed, since humans quite obviously are born into social groups and have lived in social groupings from the beginning. Babies, in order to survive, have to be cared for from the start by others. Even abandoned children have to be adopted by wolves or dogs or some other social creatures in order to survive. Learning a language and developing the skills to live necessarily involves social networks. The very existence of language presumes a group: you must be communicating with other people and trying to coordinate something with them, if only to coordinate a mutual understanding about something. In the absence of that need to coordinate with others, language would be superfluous and never invented in the first place.

Liberty, seen as the greatest possible absence of constraint from the will of others, would condemn human children to almost certain death, or at the very least persistent immaturity and underdevelopment; for if children could do only what they wanted, they would fail to thrive and fail to learn many of the requisite human social skills such as language and the use of tools. Their brains would not develop properly either. Since the means to survive for humans has always of necessity involved social cooperation and mutual support, the view that liberty means the near complete absence of any obligations or constraint by others constitutes the theoretical basis for the negation of society.

Anyone who asserted such a claim in a hunting and gathering society would be seen as crazy, would be ejected from the group, and would probably die a "nasty and brutish" death. In a slave society Hayek would either have been a slave (meaning that he would have no liberty) or a slave owner (in which case his liberty would have been made possible only through the enslavement of a sizable segment of the society). Nonetheless, as a member of the slaveholding class, he would still be subject to the compulsions exerted over him by the rest of the slave owners, including the fact that if he chose to free his slaves he would then face the opprobrium of his class. If he chose to try to liberate slaves he didn't own—since Hayek is such a fan of liberty—he would be subject to overt coercion by the slave owners, including probably their attempts to restrain him and, if necessary, execute him to make an example of him for betraying his class and setting a bad example that would inspire other slaves to revolt.

In a feudal society Hayek might have been a serf, in which case his liberties would have been curtailed by his obligations to his lord and the "first night" privileges of knights. If he had been a member of the church, his obligations would have been to the church hierarchy. Had he been a knight, Hayek's liberties would have been greater than those of a serf, but he would also have had obligations to protect the serfs against the predations of invaders and marauders; in addition, he would have had obligations to the aristocracy. If he had been an aristocrat, Hayek's liberties would have been greatest, but he would still have had obligations restricting his "liberty" vis-a-vis other strata of society and within the aristocracy itself.

It is only in a capitalist society where the degree of economic surplus is substantial enough and the interdependence among people more obscured (though very real nonetheless) that individuals who claim that they want freedom from the necessity of cooperation and coercion are not ridiculed as absurd antisocial jerks. And in neoliberal regimes, such individuals get to tell everyone else what to do as if their self-serving values were the very pinnacle of human development.

Behaving as if society doesn't exist doesn't alter the fact that people have to rely upon others to survive and that one's survival depends upon society itself. Hayek tries to conceal this reality under a doctrine that defends and promotes the notion that some (or all) can act as if they are free of any obligations to others. Taken to its logical conclusion, if everyone were free of the will of others, then no one would be or could be in a relationship with anyone else. Two people who are a couple, for example, exert their wills over each other. We call that "going steady," "marriage," or a "partnership." Hayek recognizes that it is impossible to be entirely free of the will of others but what he doesn't do is acknowledge the inevitable and necessary interrelatedness of compulsion and freedom. If he did recognize that, then his whole argument would fall apart since his view is premised on attempting to minimize compulsion to the nth degree, regarding, as he does, compulsion as per se undesirable.[16]

If someone knows more about something than I do, does my doing what he wants, even if my own desires and plans are different, mean that I have sacrificed my liberty? I have sacrificed some of my individualism, but what if others are right and I am wrong? I would want to be compelled to do the right thing if I were wrong (I might not like it, but this was what it was like practicing piano or learning the proper grip in tennis as a child). Being involved in a discussion about why another way of doing things is preferable is important in its own right, because just being told what to do based on faith or control doesn't help anyone learn. But getting anything done with a group of people does mean that the opinions of some individuals are not given precedence at any given time. The idea that it is wrong on principle to compel someone to do something that is different from his or her own individual assessment is obviously wrong. Freedom isn't the absence of necessity. Freedom *can* be expanded on the basis of recognizing, understanding, and on that basis, *transforming* necessity. (For further discussion of this question and its complexities, see Chapter Five.)

Capital likes to assert its independence from everything else, but first and foremost capital cannot exist without labor. Labor, in fact, creates capital. Rich people with big houses and manicured lawns may live lives of luxury, but they can only live those lives because others do the less carefree

---

16   Ibid, 12: "The task of a policy of freedom must therefore be to minimize coercion or its harmful effects, even if it cannot eliminate it completely."

labor and dirty work of tending the gardens, cars, house, swimming pool, tennis court, and children of the estate. Rich people like to think that they are free of anyone and anything, but their very lifestyles and survival depend upon the work and support of others, most of whom are low-paid laborers. Rich people's sense of self and the degree of their life satisfaction are intimately tied to others in their social networks from whom they derive their sense of belongingness (e.g., the other members of the business and social circles within which they operate). Hayek's fantasy fuels those who are either already wealthy or who aspire to wealth or to putative independence, conveniently overlooking the actual fact that their status can only exist because of mutual obligations and actual necessities. Those people of the rentier class whose worry-free lives appear to be dictated little by necessity can only live in such a way because many other people in their lives are subjected to great necessity.

Hayek's work came during a period of enormous turmoil and struggle in history: the pivotal mid-twentieth century. The whole world was very much up for grabs as proponents of fascism, capitalism, socialism (and anarchism, particularly in Spain) were fighting fiercely to determine who would dominate and which vision for society would prevail. Hayek was explicitly opposed to collectivism.[17] To advance his program, he convened a small 1947 conference at Mont Pelerin, Switzerland, inviting like-minded people such as University of Chicago economist Milton Friedman.[18] The Mont Pelerin Society that emerged from that

---

17   Thomas Sowell of the Hoover Institute, as quoted by the HayekCenter.org at "Quotes on Hayek & the Triumph of the Liberal Order," http://www.hayekcenter. org/friedrichhayek/qs-20th.htm, accessed February 6, 2011:

> The 20th Century looked for many decades as if it were going to be the century of collectivism.... Anyone who would have predicted the reversal of this trend ... would have been considered mad just a dozen years ago. Innumerable factors led to [the reversal of the rise of collectivism], not the least of which was the bitter experience of seeing 'rational planning' degenerate into economic chaos and Utopian dreams turned into police-state nightmares. Still, it takes a vision to beat a vision.... An alternative vision had to become viable before the reversal of the collectivist tide could begin with Margaret Thatcher in Britain and Ronald Reagan in the United States. That vision came from many sources, but if one point in time could mark the beginning of the intellectual turning of the tide which made later political changes possible, it was the publication of *The Road to Serfdom* by Friedrich A. Hayek....

18   Milton Friedman, as quoted by the HayekCenter.org at "Quotes on Hayek & the Triumph of the Liberal Order," http://www.hayekcenter.org/friedrichhayek/qs-20th.htm, accessed December 27, 2009:

conference sought to combat socialist and quasi-socialist trends that at the time enjoyed wide appeal internationally. In the US, GOP[19] party conservatives looking for an alternative to Keynesian economics turned to Friedman, Hayek, and Ayn Rand, the latter the well-known champion of ultra-individualism.

The General Kills the Doctor and Neoliberalism Comes to Town

Neoliberal economic policies were first attempted in Chile after General Augusto Pinochet's CIA-backed fascist coup of Dr. Salvador Allende's popularly elected socialist government in the first infamous "September 11," the one in 1973. For neoliberalism to be put into practice, masses of progressive popular forces in general and the Left in particular had to be neutralized and preferably annihilated. Neoliberalism's practical implementation was, not coincidentally, pursued on the killing grounds where 5,000 Chileans were victims of Pinochet on the very first day of his coup (with many tens of thousands more killed, disappeared, tortured and imprisoned in the years that followed).

The year 1973 not only marked neoliberalism's initial implementation but also, not coincidentally, comprised the end of the insurgencies of the 1960s (with Pinochet's coup its dramatic and bloody historical bookend) and the beginning of a sweeping counterrevolution worldwide against everything that the 1960s (and before that the social movements of the 1930s) had accomplished and symbolized. The story of that counterrevolution extends to the present day.

Bringing It Back Home: Thatcherism and Reaganism

Shortly after the Chilean experiment was launched, neoliberal policies began in earnest in the 1980s in the UK under Prime Minister Margaret

---

Over the years, I have again and again asked fellow believers in a free society how they managed to escape the contagion of their collectivist intellectual environment. No name has been mentioned more often as the source of enlightenment and understanding than Friedrich Hayek's . . . I, like the others, owe him a great debt . . . his powerful mind . . . his lucid and always principled exposition have helped to broaden and deepen my understanding of the meaning and the requisites of a free society.

19   GOP: Grand Old Party, a shorthand term to refer to the Republican Party.

Thatcher ("Thatcherism")[20] and in the US under President Ronald Reagan (the "Reagan Revolution" or "Reaganomics"). Thatcher was an overt follower of Hayek. At a Conservative Party policy meeting in the late 1970s, in response to a colleague who called for a pragmatic middle way for the party, Thatcher,

> reached into her briefcase and took out a book. It was Friedrich von Hayek's *The Constitution of Liberty*. Interrupting [the speaker], she held the book up for all of us to see. "This," she said sternly, "is what we believe," and banged Hayek down on the table.[21]

Declaring, "There is no such thing as society," there are just individuals and families,[22] and that "There Is No Alternative" (TINA), Thatcher spearheaded a relentless drive to destroy the welfare state and institutionalize neoliberalism in the UK.

Thatcher's assertion that there is no such thing as society would, of course, come as a shock to social scientists who study the dynamics of this "nonexistent" entity. But Thatcher's declaration represents merely a blunter version of what neoliberals fervently assert rhetorically: it is a war of all against all out there and it is every person for him—or herself. According to neoliberalism's proponents, government's role (and that of nongovernmental groups for that matter) isn't to support and safeguard people, unless, of course, you are already one of the elect, in which case government's role is to protect you at all costs. It is a free market for everyone except those who are already monopolists. For the monopolists, government's

---

20 As described by Wikipedia, http://en.wikipedia.org/wiki/Friedrich_Hayek#_note-1, accessed February 6, 2011:

> After winning the 1979 election, Thatcher appointed Keith Joseph, the director of the Hayekian Centre for Policy Studies, as her secretary of state for industry in an effort to redirect parliament's economic strategies. Likewise, some of Ronald Reagan's economic advisors were friends of Hayek.

21 From "Friedrich Hayek Quotes," http://homepage.eircom.net/~odyssey/Politics/Liberty/Hayek.html, accessed February 6, 2011, citing John Ranelagh, *Thatcher's People: An Insider's Account of the Politics, the Power, and the Personalities* (London: Harper Collins, 1991).

22 Douglas Keay, "Aids, Education and the Year 2000!" *Woman's Own*, October 31, 1987, quoting Thatcher: *"[W]ho is society? There is no such thing! There are individual men and women and there are families."*, MargaretThatcher.org, http://www.margaretthatcher.org/speeches/displaydocument.asp?docid=106689, accessed July 3, 2010.

role is to facilitate and protect your privileges rather than to regulate or curb your power, all the while invoking the name of the free market. This view of government would be the equivalent of arranging a basketball game in which high school athletes on one team were pitted against elementary school students on the other, and saying: "The same rules apply to everyone. Let's see who wins, fair and square." The elementary school kids can take a charging foul by standing in a high schooler's way driving the lane for a lay-up, but they do so at their own personal peril.

One of neoliberalism's pride and joys is California's Proposition 13, passed in 1978. Prop 13 froze property taxes for senior citizens (its ostensible purpose), drastically cut back business property taxes, and mandated that taxes could not be raised unless at least a two-thirds majority in both chambers of the state legislature supported it (its real agenda). As a result of Prop 13, California's K-12 school system, which until Prop 13 had been the nation's best, plummeted to second or third from the bottom, keeping company with Guam and Mississippi.

Since the late 1970s, both the Republican and Democratic parties in the US have abandoned Keynesian economics and embraced neoliberalism's free market policies. These policies have sparked alarm among those concerned about the extraordinary polarization in wealth relative to immiseration, the courting of multiple environmental disasters, militarization, increasing state surveillance, abridgment of civil liberties, and reactionary social and political trends, to name only its more prominent features. Between 1990 and 2009 the disparity between the rich and the rest of us grew at a faster rate than ever in modern times. The wealth and income gap within the US is higher than it has ever been, even higher than during the Great Depression, with, as of 2007, the top 10 percent of the population receiving 49.7 percent of the national income.

The relentless and sweeping reassertion of free market policies that began some three decades ago and the corresponding systematic dismantling of the welfare state represent in one sense capitalism's restoration to its unvarnished, truest nature. The New Deal and its welfare state cousins worldwide were seen, after all, as a temporary state necessitated by capitalism's crisis and by the Left's strength in the maelstrom of World War I and especially World War II, in which the major imperialist powers went at each other in massive blood fests.

Wars and crises tend to provoke revolutions.[23] World War I produced the 1917 Russian Revolution (the first socialist countrywide revolution in

---

23 The 1917 Russian Revolution came about as a product of, on the one hand, the tsarist autocracy's decrepitude, and, on the other hand, the acuity of Lenin and the Bolsheviks' political line. Despite being far smaller in numbers, prestige, and in

history) and World War II led to the 1949 Chinese Revolution and the expansion of the Eastern European socialist bloc.

The welfare state that emerged in the non-socialist countries represented a compromise between relatively weakened capitalist forces and the rising insurgent anti-capitalist forces domestically and internationally. Subsequently, with the 1960s' insurgent movements' ebbing and the socialist camp's retreat in the 1970s and 1980s, neoliberalism's emergence became possible and, in fact, inevitable. In the wake of the Left's decline, the capitalist camp now ruled the world roost as unchallenged champion. No longer restricted by countervailing forces such as socialist states or vibrant unions, capitalism could now slough off the welfare state's unwanted strictures and dictate terms the way a victorious army sets the terms of the peace.

Contemporaneous technological developments—especially computerization, more advanced telecommunications, and automation—also made production's internationalization more feasible and inexpensive. As a result of the Left's retreat and the emergence of these technical innovations, virtually the entire world's labor force, consumer markets, and resources were now flung wide open to capitalist expansion and exploitation. If corporations such as Walmart and Nike could pay Third World and former socialist bloc workers a fraction of what they paid US workers and still sell their finished products for the same price, what right-thinking executive with demanding shareholders and Wall Street to satisfy could resist sending their factories abroad and outsourcing relentlessly? Even if some compassionate US executives wanted to preserve American jobs and the communities that grew up around those jobs, to buck this trend meant that they were both compassionate executives *and* career suicides.

---

fluence than the German socialist party going into World War I, Lenin analyzed the approaching world war as an inter-imperialist fight in which each country's workers would have no stake in joining in to kill, and be killed by, their fellow workers of other lands for the imperial ambitions of their "own" ruling classes. While other socialist parties of the time (in the Second International) all had previously pledged not to scurry under their own imperialists' skirts when the war that everyone could see coming actually broke out, the German socialist party leaders and the rest of the Second International—except for the Bolsheviks—caved under the pressure of national chauvinism, voted for war credits, and joined in the chorus of condemning the "other" countries as the aggressors. They thus consigned their workers to the slaughter. In spite of the enormous pressures to do the same, the Bolsheviks stood firm and, to make a long story short, were able to rally people to their side and overthrow first the tsar and then the short-lived Kerensky Provisional government that betrayed its true colors when it continued the war the tsar had been carrying out.

Even in nations where social democratic parties have been the ruling parties for decades (for instance, in the Scandinavian countries) and where the welfare state has been the strongest and most extensive, the seemingly unstoppable force of globalization has compelled those governments to bend and adopt neoliberal policies. Since social democracy came into being as a sort of middle ground between capitalist rule and that of the proletariat, and since social democracy exists to mitigate, but not eliminate, capitalism's inequities and other undesirable impacts, these results should not surprise us. In countries such as France where the Left has a substantial presence historically, the government's attempts in recent times to abridge long-standing social democratic-style guarantees by, for instance, permitting the firing of young workers without explanation after two years of working, has sparked riots. But while these responses speak to the stronger tradition of mass popular political action in places like France, the writing is on the wall. If people in places where the Left and quasi-Left have much more influence and power than they do in the US have gone along with neoliberal policies, how can we expect the closest equivalent to a social democratic party in the US, the Democratic Party, to resist globalization's deadly embrace? After all, to believe in the Democratic Party's social democratic character today requires a highly developed imagination and a potent dose of wishful thinking and wistfulness.

Since the 1980s, governments in the advanced capitalist centers have obliged the interests of globalization, vigorously carrying out successive waves of deregulation and privatization, shredding the social safety net, and opening the floodgates to merger mania. Each successive merger spawned a new mind-bogglingly large corporate giant (like the crab monsters of mid-twentieth century sci-fi movies, produced inadvertently by atomic radiation and bent on ravaging the populace). During the Reagan/Bush years of the 1980s, deregulation was de rigueur. These trends continued overall under Clinton/Gore and accelerated at breathtaking speed and with a vengeance under Bush/Cheney.[24] Under Obama the trends continue. In the corporate world, downsizing employment rolls and scaling back or outright elimination of benefits packages have become the rule as globalization of production has proceeded aggressively. Disparities in income and wealth, job insecurity, income volatility, homelessness, and poverty rates have risen sharply. This stands in marked contrast to the years between the 1930s' New Deal and the 1970s

---

24 See Michael Allen Meeropol, *Surrender: How the Clinton Administration Completed the Reagan Revolution* (Michigan: University of Michigan Press, 1998).

when the income and wealth gap between the rich and the poor had actually been *contracting*.

Third World governments have been compelled by the International Monetary Fund (IMF) and the World Bank to comply with the policies of neoliberalism, producing widespread and intense immiseration. Diseases such as AIDS,[25] devastating in its impact on places such as sub-Saharan Africa, and the looming specter of avian flu that could overwhelm our medical facilities and kill tens of millions or more in the US alone,[26] are directly tied to globalization's nature.

Another way to appreciate the magnitude of these disparities is to consider a few facts about transnational corporations. Transnational corporations are the key economic figures in this new economic order. Due to their immense size and power, they dwarf most of the world's national economies.[27] The world's top two hundred transnational corporations exceed the combined economic activity of 182 countries, and are only

25   From Benardo Useche and Amalia Cabezas, "The Neoliberal Model in Times of AIDS," EnviroDigital.org, No. 289, August 2005, http://www.envio.org.ni/articulo/3029, accessed February 6, 2011:

> In recent decades, US governments and their closest allies have promoted globalization under neoliberal principles and "free trade" economic policies and imposed them on the nations of the world mainly through the international agencies under their control—the IMF and the World Bank—as a supposed panacea for all social problems.
>
> Neoliberal ideology found its perfect application in the World Bank and IMF structural adjustment programs that have devastated Latin America, Africa, Asia and the Caribbean over the last 20 years. Promoting privatization, fiscal austerity, deregulation, market liberation and the cutting back of the state, these programs have increased and globalized poverty, migration, unemployment and temporary work contracts and produced extremely polarized income and living conditions across the world to the exclusive benefit of big capital.
>
> AIDS was incubated and has been propagated in this ecosystem of social inequity and it will be impossible to prevent and combat it in any effective way without going after the conditions that are generating the pandemic and continuing its expansion throughout the world.

26   See Mike Davis, *The Monster at Our Door: The Global Threat of Avian Flu* (New York: New Press, 2005).

27   Of the top one hundred largest economic entities, as of 2000, 51 were transnational corporations, 49 were countries. GM, the world's largest corporation, was the 23rd largest economic entity in the world, larger than Denmark and bigger than 162 countries, including Poland, Greece, and Israel. Walmart was the 25th largest economic entity in the world. Sarah Anderson and John Cavanagh, "Top 200: The Rise of Corporate Global Power," Institute for Policy Studies online, December 4, 2000,

outstripped by the nine largest countries. More than one-sixth of the US's GDP comes from just thirteen of the largest US corporations. Accompanying the emergence of these megacorporations are the super rich individuals and families who, numbering in the several millions worldwide, collectively command assets of more than $17 trillion, more than twice the annual GNP of the US. In fact, the 497 richest individuals in the world today own more wealth than the bottom half of the world's six billion-plus population.[28] Four hundred ninety-seven individuals versus more than three billion people: whose needs are more important? What kind of arithmetic and what kind of morality is at work that renders these lopsided numbers reasonable or acceptable when every single day more than twenty-five thousand children die in the world from imminently preventable diseases such as diarrhea, because they do not have access to clean water?

These twin behemoths of the new order, transnational corporations and the super wealthy, are both the driving motive force behind, as well a product of, globalization. In the face of this kind of concentrated wealth and power, compared to which most nations are merely small fry, and the fact that these corporate giants and super wealthy reside in the most prosperous and powerful nations, what kind of power would you reasonably expect political institutions to exercise over these giants? The 2007/8 presidential campaign cost at least $250,000 per day per candidate for twenty-one months. Where does a serious candidate for president raise this kind of money? To whom are they inevitably beholden for those funds?

Insecurity and Coercion

The very logic of globalization dictates ever-higher levels of job and social insecurity for all but those at the very highest levels. Globalization and neoliberalism's mantra is to privatize that which has been public; outsource that which has been in-house and in-nation; deregulate so that the "free market" may be unfettered; ceaselessly downsize the workforce, cutting payroll and reducing benefits, making job security and a secure, guaranteed retirement things of the past. Not surprisingly, the inevitable outcome of these measures means that insecurity—the more, the better—is the ineluctable, inevitable, desired outcome. From the standpoint of

---

http://www.ips-dc.org/reports/top_200_the_rise_of_corporate_global_power, accessed January 30, 2009.

28 John Cavanagh and Sarah Anderson, "World's Billionaires Take a Hit But Still Soar," *The Institute for Policy Studies*, March 6, 2002 (citing 2001 data).

corporations, the more perilous the jobs and the economic status of the labor force overall the better, since this will compel employees to accept less in return for working ever harder and longer.

Leonard['s]. . . six-figure salary and benefits are all that he ever could have wanted. But . . . the pressure accompanying his twelve-hour workdays and managerial responsibilities . . . have left him feeling more like a survivor than a star. . . .

"The philosophy now is you have to squeeze more and more out of people . . . .

"Earlier this year, they laid off a hundred people in my division. The philosophy was you *probably* have a hundred people who probably aren't up to par . . . .

"We do this year after year. We squeeze. We squeeze. People are starting to feel expendable. But if you try to argue, then you are not stepping up.

"Layoffs are not good. People keep telling me, 'Len, there is a contradiction here. You tell us that things are better than ever. But the layoffs and cost cutting keep happening. Does this mean that at any time, no matter what, it could happen to me? Anything could happen to me?'" [29]

The connection between these economic changes and state policies governing business practices on the one hand, and the persistence and increasing stinginess or outright threatened elimination of governmental programs such as social security, welfare, and so on, on the other hand, has to some extent been chronicled and analyzed by others. What has not been well explored is what these dramatic economic changes imply with respect to social control and to the matter of the stability of the social order and the heightened probability of violent reaction/counteraction. Since the basis for people to cooperate, to behave normatively (for example, to abide by the law) is constantly and deliberately undermined under neoliberal regimes, and since, for the most dispossessed, even less of what was available to them in welfare states with Keynesian economic policies is now offered, governments *must* increasingly rely upon coercive means with spending on "security" (law enforcement, military, immigration control, prisons, surveillance and so on) rising inexorably. This point bears underscoring: more repression and more coercive means of social control

29   Jill Andresky Fraser, *White Collar Sweatshop: The Deterioration of Work and Its Rewards in Corporate America* (New York: W. W. Norton & Company, 2001), 7.

are not principally a policy choice in the sense that people might think of the GOP favoring more coercion and the Democrats less. The overall direction of neoliberal regimes dictates that more coercion will be required, regardless of the party in power and the individuals in office.

> A mid-level financial executive at one of the country's most successful telecommunications companies, he has held on to his post through more than a decade's worth of corporate acquisitions and divestitures, layoffs and mergers.
>
> Nick stated "people are to the point where they're keeping their lists, keeping journals of things they can use against the company when their time comes."
>
> "There is no loyalty, no faith."
>
> "When I started out, I thought I could stay forever. This seemed like such a great place to be."
>
> "I recently concluded a project that had tremendous bottom-line value for the company and its shareholders. ... I really made an impact on the company's profitability. But when it came for my annual review, I got a completely pathetic raise, which I had to be thankful for because it was zero point six percent higher than everyone else got."
>
> "I had to swallow my pride and say, *thank you.*"
>
> "Just suck it in and say thank you, while management sits and watches the stock price and exercises another fifty thousand stock options."
>
> Year after year of cost-cutting, lagging raises, declining benefits, and increased workloads have taken their toll on Nick, as they have on white-collar workers throughout corporate America. Think of him-indeed, it's the way he viewed himself-as the victim of a kind of corporate water torture, which has slowly and painfully consumed much of the energy and enthusiasm he once brought to his work life.
>
> "You have no control. It's ultimately a humbling experience to realize that you could move mountains and it wouldn't make any difference."[30]

The socialist camp's collapse by the late 1980s opened up the formerly socialist and quasi-socialist world of more than a billion and a half people to capitalist exploitation. In one fell swoop, whole sectors of the US population were thereby rendered disposable from the perspective of

---

30   Fraser, 5-6.

capital, especially transnational capital. For blue-collar workers and those in the broken sections of the proletariat for whom steady work is nearly impossible and who must survive at the margins in the gray and underground economies and through hustling, compliance with the status quo becomes increasingly problematic. What *is* to be done with these people?

For those most oppressed within the US, jail and prison are the short answer. Prisons and jails have, since at least the early 1990s, been the biggest supplier of public housing and public services to US disadvantaged youth.[31] The US leads the world in imprisoning its own people: every fourth prisoner in the world is behind bars in the US even though the US accounts for less than 5 percent of the world's population. In 2006, two million people were behind bars and another four and one-half million were under some form of custody—probation or parole. By 2010 those numbers reached 2.4 million behind bars with a total of more 7.5 million under some form of correctional supervision. Even when South Africa was under apartheid, the US imprisoned more blacks both in absolute numbers and per capita.[32] Criminal justice expenditures have been rising since the mid-1970s, rising an additional 95 percent by states in the 1980s, compared to a decline in state spending on education of six

---

31   As Currie put it in Elliott Currie, *Reckoning: Drugs, the Cities and the American Future* (New York: Hill and Wang, 1994), 19:

> Under the impact of the drug war, indeed, the correctional system has become our principal public agency for disadvantaged young men—their chief source of publicly supported housing and one of their most important sources of employment, nutrition, and medical care. We now spend considerably more on institutional housing for the poor via the jail and prison systems than we do on ordinary public housing for low-income people: eight times as much is spent on corrections as on low-rent public housing, for example, and nearly twice as much as on public housing and rent subsidies for the poor combined.

32   Becky Pettit and Bruce Western, "Mass Imprisonment and the Life Course: Race and Class Inequality in US Incarceration," *American Sociological Review*, April 2004, 151:

> Combining administrative, survey, and census data, we estimate that among men born between 1965 and 1969, 3 percent of whites and 20 percent of blacks had served time in prison by their early thirties. The risks of incarceration are highly stratified by education. Among black men born during this period, 30 percent of those without college education and nearly 60 percent of high school dropouts went to prison by 1999. The novel pervasiveness of imprisonment indicates the emergence of incarceration as a new stage in the life course of young low-skill black men.

percent.[33] In California, spending on criminal justice now exceeds its spending on higher education, with ten percent of its general fund going to prisons versus seven percent going to higher education. This has happened even while index crime rates have been falling in California and nationally since the early 1990s.

For the middle class, the answer to keeping them in line in this game of ever-ruthless musical chairs has been deception and fearmongering, about which I have more to say in Chapters Two and Six. This explains what some have observed as otherwise ironic about the GOP's rhetorical stance with regard to government: while they rail against the alleged waste of "big government" and seek to slash government programs, they have constantly bolstered state expenditures for coercion and security and moved to bail out and protect the behemoth corporations, throwing hundreds of billions of taxpayers' dollars at them when they are/were in danger of bankruptcy. Moreover, by continually outsourcing formerly governmental activities to private companies, the two major parties can continue to claim that they are reducing government while actually expanding governmental spending, except now under the auspices of private, for-profit companies.

The International Dimension: (Un)intended Consequences?

Arrayed before us are some dramatic ironies. The 2003 US invasion of Iraq offers one of the clearest examples. Invading Iraq to "fight terrorism" has provided such fertile soil for terrorism and its expansion that it is apparent that the Bush White House *needed* terrorism to accomplish its political aims as much as Osama bin Laden and al-Qaeda used Bush/Cheney to expand their ranks and support.

The CIA, in fact, concluded that bin Laden's October 2004 videotaped message just prior to the November 2004 presidential elections was actually intended to help Bush.[34] "Atiyah," a top Osama bin Laden

---

33 Tara-Jen Ambrosio and Vincent Schiraldi, "From Classrooms to Cell Blocks: A National Perspective," Justice Policy Institute, 1998, abstract cited at the National Criminal Justice Reference Service online, http://www.ncjrs.gov/App/publications/Abstract.aspx?id=189746http://www.ncjrs.gov/App/publications/Abstract.aspx?id=189746, accessed February 6, 2011.

34 Robert Parry points out: "The [Bin Laden 2004] tape had the predictable effect of giving Bush a last-minute boost in the polls, which CIA analysts concluded was precisely bin Laden's intent. Bin Laden wanted to keep Bush around as a foil for

lieutenant, stated in an intercepted December 11, 2005 letter, that "prolonging the war is in our interest."[35] In May 2007, an al-Qaeda leader released a message stating that al-Qaeda hoped that American troops would remain in Iraq longer so that they could kill enough Americans to make our invasion produce changes to our policies.

Bush and Cheney's approach was to use the fear of attacks to consolidate their power and control (witness the USA PATRIOT Act and illegal spying) rather than to take obvious steps that would truly help make America safer. In the spring of 2002, for example, the Bush White House slashed the Energy Department's requests for funding to protect nuclear plants and waste against terrorism by 93 percent. The Bush White House's priorities in response to 9/11 indicated that they were not even particularly interested in preventing another attack. Beginning in the summer of 2007, several people who supported or represented the White House made it brazenly clear that another 9/11 would in fact be good and necessary because it would justify White House policies.

Dennis Milligan, Arkansas GOP Chairman, stated on June 3, 2007: "[A]ll we need is some attacks on American soil like we had on [9/11], and the naysayers will come around very quickly to appreciate not only the commitment for President Bush, but the sacrifice that has been made by men and women to protect this country."[36]

Rick Santorum, ex-Senator from Pennsylvania, speaking on the *Hugh Hewitt Show* on July 7, 2007, stated: "Between now and November, a lot of things are going to happen, and I believe that by this time next year, the American public's going to have a very different view of this war, and it will be because, I think, of some unfortunate events, that like we're seeing

---

another four years." "Bush-Bin Laden Symbiosis Reborn," ConsortiumNews.com, September 8, 2007, http://www.consortiumnews.com/2007/090807.html, accessed October 3, 2009.

35 Ibid.:

In a letter to Zarqawi, dated Dec. 11, 2005, "Atiyah," another top aide to bin Laden, described the hard work needed to overcome the animosity of Sunni tribal leaders. In that context, Atiyah said the continued American presence was crucial.

"Prolonging the war is in our interest," Atiyah wrote in a letter captured when Zarqawi was killed in June 2006.

36 Josh Catone, "Arkansas GOP head: We Need More 'Attacks on American Soil' So People Appreciate Bush," RawStory.com, June 3, 2007, http://rawstory.com/news/2007/Arkansas_GOP_head_We_need_more_0603.html, accessed July 1, 2007.

unfold in the UK. But I think the American public's going to have a very different view."[37]

Lt. Col. Doug Delaney, War Studies Program Chair, Royal Military College in Kingston, Ontario, paraphrased by *Toronto Star* reporter Andrew Chung in the first sentence, on July 8, 2007: "[T]he key to bolstering Western resolve is another terrorist attack like 9/11 or the London transit bombings of two years ago. 'If nothing happens, it will be harder still to say this is necessary.'"[38]

A Sacramento *Democratic* strategist, paraphrased by one of the pro-impeachment Democrats at a Democratic gathering on July 17, 2007, offered the following as one of the reasons why he thinks impeachment is foolhardy for the Democratic Party: "There will be another terrorist attack between now and next November . . . the public will run into the arms of the Republicans as a cause of that, and . . . Democrats are essentially helpless to do anything about that."[39]

Jack Goldsmith, head of the Office of Legal Counsel in 2003 and 2004, quotes David Addington, Cheney's then-current Chief of Staff, in his book *The Terror Presidency: Law and Judgment Inside the Bush Administration,* as saying in a February 2004 meeting: "We're one bomb away from getting rid of that obnoxious [FISA] court."[40]

---

37   This was originally posted at Hugh Hewitt's blog, but it has been removed. A transcript of Santorum's remarks is still available at 9/11 Blogger, "Rick Santorum predicts some unfortunate events will give Americans a very different view of this war," Infowars.com, July 7, 2007, http://www.infowars.com/articles/us/santorum_predicts_some_unfortunate_events.htm, accessed February 6, 2011.

38   Andrew Chung, "Why Military Might Does Not Always Win," TheStar.com, July 8, 2007, http://www.thestar.com/News/article/233617, accessed July 20, 2007.

39   dday, "How An Insider Consultant Changed My Mind on Impeachment," DailyKos.com, July 17, 2007, ttp://www.dailykos.com/story/2007/7/17/141844/051, http://www.consortiumnews.com/2007/090807.html, accessed July 18, 2007.

40   Dan Eggen and Peter Baker, "New Book Details Cheney Lawyer's Efforts to Expand Executive Power," WashingtonPost.com, September 5, 2007, http://www.washingtonpost.com/wpdyn/content/article/2007/09/04/AR2007090402292_pf.html, accessed September 10, 2007. The FISA court [Foreign Intelligence Surveillance Act] was created in 1978 in the wake of Congressional revelations of Nixon's illegal domestic intelligence surveillance against political opponents such as the anti-war movement. FISA provided congressional and judicial oversight over executive foreign intelligence work while providing secrecy for those activities so that sensitive activities would not be compromised. If the executive branch wanted to apply a wiretap, for example, it applied to the FISA court in camera for authorization. Since its inception, FISA has only turned down two or three

Preceding these overt comments was a 2005 internal GOP memo that indicated that another terrorist attack on the US would help Bush and the GOP because it would "restore his image as a leader of the American people," and "validate" his war on terror.[41] As it turned out, no such attack occurred, but not for the lack of wishing and prognosticating by these forces. The openly expressed desire for such an incident was very revealing of the underlying political agendas. (More on this in Chapter Four.)

Bush/Cheney represented neoliberalism's most extreme and aggressive variant. Under Clinton/Gore, globalization and neoliberal policies were also pursued, albeit less unilaterally, yet generating fundamentally the same ineluctable consequences in economic and social fallout. The largest gap between the rich and poor in history occurred under Clinton, only to be exceeded subsequently by Bush/Cheney. Under Clinton/ Gore, NAFTA (the North American Free Trade Agreement) was pushed through, terrorism grew, the criminal justice system expanded, and "welfare as we know it" was eliminated. Under sanctions against Iraq some five hundred thousand Iraqi children perished. When asked about this, former UN ambassador Madeline Albright famously said that the "price is worth it."[42]

---

executive applications for covert surveillance. When it was revealed in 2005 that the Bush White House was skirting FISA approval for its massive domestic surveillance, the White House asserted that the "war on terror" necessitated their acting swiftly and avoiding FISA. FISA, however, has provisions allowing retroactive surveillance approval, a fact that the White House never mentioned. In 2008 after the revelations of the White House's illegal activities, the Democratically controlled Congress revised FISA to grant amnesty to the major communications companies such as AT&T, Verizon and so on that had illegally gone along with the White House's demands that they secretly allow NSA to wiretap all US electronic communications.

41 Doug Thompson, "GOP Memo Touts New Terror Attack As Way to Reverse Party's Decline," CapitolHillBlue.com, November 10, 2005, available as of February 6, 2011 in its entirety at http://forums.mtbr.com/showthread.php?t=143814:

> A confidential memo circulating among senior Republican leaders suggests that a new attack by terrorists on US soil could reverse the sagging fortunes of President George W. Bush as well as the GOP and "restore his image as a leader of the American people."
> The closely-guarded memo lays out a list of scenarios to bring the Republican party back from the political brink, including a devastating attack by terrorists that could "validate" the President's war on terror and allow Bush to "unite the country" in a "time of national shock and sorrow."

42 Sheldon Richman, "Albright 'Apologizes,'" TheFutureofFreedomFoundation.org, November 7, 2003, http://www.fff.org/comment/com0311c.asp, accessed on February 11, 2011.

Beyond the conditions for the labor force in the imperialist citadels, how much worse is the impact of these policies internationally as imperialist countries, led by the US, penetrate ruthlessly into every corner of the globe and batter down, as Marx put it some century and a half ago, Chinese walls and all traditions before the god of profit? In August 2006 England's Prime Minister Tony Blair (more articulate than Bush so I'm citing him) declared in a speech that the world is in a "global fight about global values"[43] and, previously in a 2001 speech, "There is no compromise possible with such people, no meeting of minds, no point of understanding with such terror," he said. "There is just a choice: Defeat it or be defeated by it and defeat it we must."[44] In a 2002 speech Blair stated, "Our values aren't western values. They're human values, and anywhere, anytime people are given the chance, they embrace them."[45]

The Brazilian favelas (shantytowns) offer another graphic example of this unity of insecurity and security. Favelas ring the glittering cities and house the dispossessed of Brazilian society, who are left to fend for themselves by political and economic policies that eschew social programs altogether and instead have protected and enriched the wealthy. The conditions have become so extreme in Brazil, so much like that of a dystopia, that cars are commonly equipped with anti-hijacking devices because of the frequency of crimes committed by the poor and by criminal gangs. In a kind of re-enactment of H.G. Wells' *The Time Machine*, the very wealthy try to avoid traveling on the ground altogether, preferring to fly by helicopter to and from the tops of high-rises.

Hurricane Katrina in 2005 offered us another instance of how "security" measures create deadly insecurity. The storm and its aftermath tore away the veil concealing the destitute in America and revealed in unmistakable terms the utter bankruptcy of Hayek's vision. For people without property, there were no human rights, just flood waters in which to drown facedown. Those who initially survived the flood waters faced days upon

---

43 "Blair: Western values Must Triumph Over Radical Islam," CNN World online, August 1, 2006, http://articles.cnn.com/2006-08-01/world/mideast.blair_1_israel-and-hezbollah-values-prime-minister-tony-blair?_s=PM:WORLD, accessed February 12, 2011.

44 "Tony Blair Says Allies Must Prevail," SFGate.com, October 2, 2001, http://www.sfgate.com/cgi-bin/article.cgi?f=/kron/archive/2001/10/02/blairspeech.DTL, accessed February 11, 2011.

45 Deseret News Editorial, "An Extraordinary Ally Across the Pond," Deseret News online, October 7, 2002, http://www.deseretnews.com/article/941098/An-extraordinary-ally-across-the-pond.html, accessed February 11, 2011.

agonizing days without food, water, or medical care; and those who were ambulatory enough, had muzzles pointed at them on bridges leading out of New Orleans, preventing their escape from the nightmare to the West Bank (a name that bears an uncanny reverse affinity to the other West Bank for the Palestinians, another internationally known people who have been rendered exiles in their own land).

The federal agencies charged with protecting New Orleans against storms and hurricanes (the Army Corps of Engineers) and rescuing those struck by disaster (the Federal Emergency Management Agency) had both been devastated by the Bush administration's prior massive budget cuts and neoliberal policies. The marshlands that act as natural protectors for the land against storm surges had been turned over to developers to drain for profit, and the levees had been allowed to languish for lack of federal money, with the Bush White House slashing the levee budget by 83 percent in fiscal year (FY) 2005, having cut the budget in FY 2004 by 73 percent.

This left the fabled New Orleans a disaster just waiting to happen. The National Guard troops who would have otherwise been available to help out were mostly in Iraq instead, allegedly to protect America from terrorist disasters, and the monies that would have gone into the levees had been diverted to the "war on terror" and to pork barrel projects of favored Congressional figures and their cronies. In the aftermath of the flooding, when troops finally were dispatched to New Orleans after unbelievable and excruciating delays, a prominent feature of this deployment was the Blackwater mercenary army whose task was to ensure that property, not human life, was protected; they actually beat US military forces to the scene.

Because of its ruthlessness towards anything that stands in its way— for example, the dispossessed in the Middle East who are held down by deeply unpopular, extremely corrupt regimes (Saudi Arabia, United Arab Emirates, Afghanistan, Iraq, and so on) and the settler state of Israel that is only sustained through US protection and heavy subsidy[46]—

---

46 Israel is sustained through massive US subsidies and US protection in the UN Security Council through which the US exercises its vetoes against UN resolutions citing Israel's violations of international law and UN resolutions.

See, for example, Richard Curtiss, Former US Foreign Service Officer, "The Cost of Israel to the American People," alhewar.com, http://www.alhewar.com/Curtiss.html, accessed February 6, 2011:

Between 1949 and 1998, the U.S. gave to Israel, with a self-declared population of 5.8 million people, more foreign aid than it gave to all of the countries of sub-Saharan Africa, all of the countries of Latin America,

neoliberalism further creates furious discontents who would rather die than go on living the way they are and who are now waging asymmetrical warfare against it.

Unbrave New World

Substantial and ever increasing insecurity is the inevitable by-product of globalization and neoliberalism's ascension. Generating more and more insecurity constitutes the fundamental logic underlying neoliberal regimes. Under neoliberalism, the curse of unintended consequences reigns supreme. Oppression breeds resistance and the more brutal the oppression and efforts to suppress, the more intense the response from the oppressed. The US invasions of Afghanistan in 2002 and of Iraq in 2003 are poster children for this.

The triumph of neoliberalism comprises the *primary* reason for this irony in the US of unmatched power alongside growing insecurity. Its international expression is analogous: as globalization marches forth, even as it enriches some segments, it immiserates many more, creating a world more and more lopsided and unstable, both socially and environmentally. While the rise of neoliberalism constitutes the major worldwide narrative and the key reason for these unwelcome developments, there are two

---

and all of the countries of the Caribbean combined—with a total population of 1,054,000,000 people.

In the 1997 fiscal year, for example, Israel received $3 billion from the foreign aid budget, at least $525 million from other U.S. budgets, and $2 billion in federal loan guarantees. So the 1997 total of U.S. grants and loan guarantees to Israel was $5.5 billion. That's $15,068,493 per day, 365 days a year.

If you add its foreign aid grants and loans, plus the approximate totals of grants to Israel from other parts of the U.S. federal budget, Israel has received since 1949 a grand total of $84.8 billion, excluding the $10 billion in U.S. government loan guarantees it has drawn to date.

And if you calculate what the U.S. has had to pay in interest to borrow this money to give to Israel, the cost of Israel to U.S. taxpayers rises to $134.8 billion, not adjusted for inflation.

Put another way, the nearly $14,630 every one of 5.8 million Israelis had received from the U.S. government by October 31, 1997, cost American taxpayers $23,241 per Israeli. That's $116,205 for every Israeli family of five.

Curtiss further points out that US aid to Israel and Egypt together accounted for many years for over half of the US bilateral foreign aid budget worldwide.

other aspects to this that merit specific attention. The subjective sense of insecurity has also been fostered by mass media for reasons that are partly due to economic changes brought on by globalization and partly due to the ideological characteristics of globalization. Lastly, certain shifts in public mood in the US, linked in part to globalization, have also been a factor in this security/insecurity dialectic.

The Hangman and the Priest

Governments everywhere rule through their use of two tools—persuasion and coercion. Were there enough resources to go around for everyone and no need to protect wealth held by some from others who do not have it, then no separate body of people with a monopoly over the means of legitimate violence, as sociologist Max Weber succinctly put it, would be required.

Neoliberal regimes rest on a process of ever-increasing inequalities. Despite rhetoric in neoliberal states about rising prosperity for all as a result of tax cuts and other benefits for the wealthy and for big business, the logic of capital versus labor engenders predictable results—more for those who already have and less for those who have not. Since the "free market" is allowed to operate without governmental restriction or regulation,[47] those who already have capital, and most especially those who already have a lot of capital, benefit disproportionately.

The "rising tide that lifts all boats" mantra of supply-side economics operates more like a rising tidal wave for some whose boats are swamped and then sunk. Some class mobility continues to operate, mostly between the working class and the middle class, with some rising and some falling. The second part of this, of course, is generally glossed over by those who talk about class mobility in the US; those who rise from the working class into the middle class (and the microscopic number who rise from the working class into upper class wealth) are featured, but the equal or greater numbers who fall from the middle class into the working class are not given the same attention.

The net results under neoliberalism are extraordinary increases in wealth for the upper class, a shrinking middle class, and swelling ranks

---

47   With the notable exceptions here of businesses that the free marketers in government favor, in which case government subsidies or no-bid contracts for them are *de rigueur*. Halliburton, Big Oil, the auto industry, defense industry contractors, and agribusiness for example, come to mind.

of the working class (who in turn find it harder and harder to find work) and of the indigent. As outsourcing of work continues apace, and in recent years as even intellectual and white-collar labor is now being exported to places like India, reversing the long-standing brain drain to the US from elsewhere (notice where the people live who are giving you most of your technical support now days), the middle class finds itself under siege in ways unprecedented in US history.

Social order in neoliberal regimes becomes more precarious because the guarantee or at least reasonable assurance of work at livable wages for people becomes more and more elusive since those jobs are increasingly disappearing. Persuasion based on actual rewards for going along consequently becomes less and less of a practical tool. Neoliberalism and globalization dictate that positive incentives will be systematically whittled away to make the workforce more adaptable and more "flexible." The so-called "Temping of America" is an illustration of this. Manpower Services, the country's largest temporary work agency, by the year 2000 became the largest domestic civilian employer, surpassing the federal government itself:

It's 10 p.m. on a cold January night in Cleveland. Work has been slow lately, and men and women have been gathered in the hall since 9 when the doors first opened. It's first come, first served, and all 40 wait, knowing that only a handful will be sent out tonight. The shift—and pay—starts at midnight. Adding in transportation and waiting, those that do get sent out will have given more than 11 hours for an 8-hour-shift's worth of pay.

Here at AmeriTemps, the dispatcher, Will, subjects the crowd to what many call the Sermon on the Mount. He stands behind a counter that—thanks to an elevated platform on the other side—makes him look 10 feet tall (whereas only the tallest workers can even rest their chins from this side), and stares down at the group. Old bearded men with worn faces shift in their seats and cast their eyes to their shoes.

"Our way or the highway.... Times are changing, and those that don't adhere will be weaned out," he says, as if possessed by the Holy Spirit. He explains how the *real world* works. Workers *will* get in line. There will be no more complaints from companies. Attitudes will be positive.

No one makes a sound while Will condescends for 20 minutes. They know that if they speak up, get up, or even stare back, they'll lose the chance for a hard night's work at $5.15 an hour.

Outside, Stephen Abnor, a laid-off welder, echoes what many in the shelter say.

"It's a new name for an old game," the 53-year-old says with a dramatic pause. "Slavery. That's all it is. How are you supposed to get paid for me working? No benefits, no hospitalization, and then they're deducting all these things.

"Let's face it, 90 percent and upwards of these people are black," he continues. "When a white boy comes in there, he fills out the application, sits down, but his seat never gets warm. Not to make this a racial issue, but I want you to know, even after years of welding, my eyes are bad, but I'm not blind."[48]

If positive incentives are being increasingly withdrawn, then negative incentives (coercion or compulsion) must of necessity become increasingly prominent. This is neoliberalism's clandestine character: the more it destroys the welfare state and undermines social welfare, the more it creates the need for coercion. Beyond this, the neoliberals' wild ambitions for perpetual world domination dictate that they *will* use torture and terror as devices to intimidate, because mere coercion is not enough to cow people before their aims of unrivaled plunder. The Democrats still insist that torture is not what the US does, but Obama's administration has retained rendition, the transporting of people to other countries where they will be "interrogated," and torture carried out directly by US personnel has continued in gulags such as Bagram and Guantanamo.

In addition, persuasion based on deceit and misdirection becomes more and more necessary and widely utilized. Fanning the flames of fear among the public is absolutely indispensable in this regard. Thus, as monstrous as it appears—and is—for conservatives to invite the prospect of another 9/11-level terrorist attack, the logic of their position within the context of neoliberalism is irrefutable. They are merely following neoliberalism to its logical end.

In the next chapter we will take a more thorough look at the rise of the neoliberal state, the fundamental fabrications that have fostered its development, the profound peril it presents, and we will lay the groundwork for promoting the conditions that could contest it and undo it.

---

48 Josh Greene, "Temporary Measures: How Temp Agencies Use Welfare-to-Work Laws to Rack Up Big Profits," *Sojourners Magazine* online, July-August 2001, http://www.sojo.net/index.cfm?action=magazine.article&issue=soj0107&artic le=010723, accessed July 4, 2010.

CHAPTER TWO

The Neoliberal State's Origins and the Rise of the Right: Wars, Revolutions and Insurgencies

The need of a constantly expanding market for its products chases the bourgeoisie over the entire surface of the globe. It must nestle everywhere, settle everywhere, establish connections everywhere.

MARX AND ENGELS, 1848[1]

To many, capitalism's triumph over socialism is captured iconically in Ronald Reagan's June 12, 1987, Berlin Wall speech in which he called for Soviet leader Mikhail Gorbachev to "tear down this wall." The wall, as we all know, came down two years later. The USSR and the rest of the socialist and quasi-socialist world, having gone toe-to-toe with the US bloc for decades, finally came apart by the close of the 1980s.[2]

---

1   Karl Marx and Frederick Engels, "Manifesto of the Communist Party," in *The Marx-Engels Reader*, 2nd ed., ed. Robert C. Tucker (New York: W.W. Norton, 1978), 476.

2   By the 1980s, the Soviet Union had for several decades not been a socialist country. Instead, it had degenerated into a state-capitalist/imperialist power. Eastern European countries had had socialism imposed from without and never really developed into authentically socialist countries. China, on the other hand, until shortly after Mao's death in 1976, was genuinely socialist. Despite these deviations, the existence of a socialist and quasi-socialist camp until 1989 presented a real point of demarcation in the world as a whole. Interestingly, when Gorbachev visited China in 1989 and the Chinese leadership was preparing to welcome their fellow state capitalist and ersatz communist, the people of China rose up in protest against the betrayal of

66

Thus ended the tempestuous and perilous Cold War. Freed of its so-cialist rivals, capitalism, like a previously pent-up dam, flooded into the former socialist camp. Undisputed "Champion of the World," capitalism battered down any barriers to its expansion and intensified its grip over resources and peoples both around the world and within its home coun-tries' turfs. Conditions for the working class soon, and predictably, wors-ened worldwide. Socialism's collapse meant that cheap labor outside of the western bloc was now to be had in abundance. "Free market" policies (deregulation, privatization, outsourcing, and so on), representing capital-ism unbound, grew like mushrooms on manure and became the norm almost everywhere.

Milton Friedman, apostle of free market fundamentalism, catapulted from outré to genius and was feted all over. "Government regulation" and "social services" (or "welfare"), indeed "government" itself, became terms of opprobrium, with Reagan governing paradoxically as the head of the very government against which he railed. In his first inaugural address in January 1981, Reagan famously declared: "[G]overnment is not the solu-tion to our problem; government *is* the problem." Reagan's denouncing of government was rather like a surgeon whispering in a patient's ear just as the patient is about to succumb to the anesthesia: "Surgery is not a solution to your problem. Surgery *is* the problem."

Reagan may as well have said: "I will use my governmental powers to curtail my governmental powers." Had he done so, his statement's illogic would have been obvious: the equivalent of a snake eating itself. If, on the other hand, Reagan used government's considerable powers to strip certain government functions to their minimum (or eliminate them alto-gether) while vastly expanding the government's role in other respects, his stance would have been possible to implement. Putting the government's considerable weight behind privatization and deregulation did not mean governmental power's dissolution. It meant governmental power would be backing private interests over public interests and public goods. (See Chapter Three for much more on this point.) The GOP has continued to pursue Reagan's path, making his message a core part of its rhetorical appeal. It is ironic that a party that incessantly assails government should seek so aggressively and insistently to be that which it ostensibly despises—the government. It is not the government itself that right-wing tax activist Grover Norquist so famously wants to shrink to a size he can "drown in

---

the fruits of the communist-led revolution in the massive Spring Uprising, popularly known in the US as "Tiananmen."

a bathtub."[3] Rather it is the public interest as manifested through public goods and public services that he seeks to drown in the icy waters of anti-government rhetoric and aggressive governmental action presented disingenuously as anti-governmental action.

Not to be outdone by Reagan and the Republicans' anti-government rhetoric, the Democrats have joined in. After all, "free trade" and the "free market" have been the only game in town since the 1980s. Bill Clinton in the early 1990s announced the "end of welfare as we know it," adopting Republican logic that welfare was a bad thing and welfare recipients scofflaws; he touted his support for the death penalty, added a hundred thousand more cops to the streets, and zealously pursued neoliberal economic policies. Clinton's Secretary of the Treasury Lawrence Summers announced in 2006: "We are all Friedmanites now," consciously reversing Republican President Nixon, who once famously declared, "We are all Keynesians now." [4] Quite a turn of events: the Democrats embracing anti-government rhetoric and neoliberal policies, replacing Republicans who had previously been forced to embrace Democrats' New Deal economic policies.

Beginning especially in the pivotal 1980s, party leaders and pundits over the airwaves and in print through the offices of increasingly more gargantuan media conglomerates proclaimed that unlimited choices and untold wealth were humanity's prerogative. No telling where we could go, we must only want it badly enough, or so went the credo of neoliberalism's dawning age. The stock market and the housing market went on a sustained boom, prompting even senior citizens' groups to gather excitedly to plot their stock buying and selling. Homeowners used their homes' rising equity values as big piggybanks and went on spending sprees. Since seventy percent of GDP in the US is devoted to domestic spending, and since real income and buying power for all but the top five percent of the population have been in decline since 1996,[5] citizens' buying on credit and beyond their

---

3 "My goal is to cut government in half in twenty-five years, to get it down to the size where we can drown it in the bathtub." BrainyQuote.com, http://www. brainyquote.com/quotes/quotes/g/grovernorq182534.html#ixzz1IfnNxUK0, accessed April 5, 2011

4 Nixon said this in 1971 when ending the international gold standard. See Roger Arnold, "We are All Keynesians Now," SwissAmerica.com, April 7, 2003, http://www.swissamerica.com/article.php?art=04-2003/200304071105f.txt, accessed February 16, 2011.

5 According to the US Bureau of the Census, *Money Income in the United States: 2000* (2001:Table A-2); *Income, Poverty, and Health Insurance Coverage, 2005* (2006:A-3),

means was the only way to keep the US economy afloat. Deficit spending, for individuals and for the government, has been the quintessential American Way of Life in the late twentieth and early twenty-first century.

Countries all over the world, even those that had been governed by social democratic parties for decades, embraced neoliberal policies. (Social democracy accommodated itself to neoliberalism readily, not only because capitalism has been setting the world economic system's overall terms after socialism's collapse, but also because social democracy came into being originally as a middle path between capitalism and socialist revolution. Social democracy seeks to mute some of capitalism's negative effects while not challenging capitalism's existence.) Deregulation, outsourcing, and privatization—the more, the better—were, and still are, the magical incantations of the times. Iceland adopted the neoliberal route hook, line, and sinker, and for a time grew at an incredible rate. In 1999, Charles Kadlec published a book entitled *Dow 100,000: Fact or Fiction?* From an Amazon book review comes this excerpt:

> [H]ow does Kadlec actually get to 100,000? First, he shoots down comparisons to previous periods of boom and bust. The cold war is over, he notes, which represents a new political paradigm. . . Kadlec also sees the worldwide trend toward freedom and democracy as a powerful economic force. . . . But he cautions that the prosperity he predicts isn't guaranteed: wars (either with bombs or tariffs) could end it pretty quickly. So could terrorism or higher taxes. . . . And a currency shock could cause untold economic mayhem. . . [I]f he's right—well, let's just say a lot of investors are going to have very comfortable retirements.[6]

We now know what has happened to those "very comfortable retirements": in the early 2000's, a mere decade after capitalism had gotten its wish with

---

as cited by Harold Kerbo, *Social Stratification and Inequality:* Class Conflict in Historical, Comparative and Global Perspective (New York: McGraw Hill, 2009), 24-25. The top quintile (twenty percent) of Americans' aggregate household income was the only one to rise of all quintiles between 1996 and 2005. The top five percent gained over fifteen percent in income and the top one percent increased by close to 63 percent in the same time frame.

6   Charles W. Kadlec, *Dow 100,000: Fact or Fiction*, (New York: Prentice Hall, 1999). The Amazon review by Lou Schuler can be found at this link: http://www.amazon. com/Dow-100-000-Fact-Fiction/dp/0735201374/ref=sr_1_1?ie=UTF8&qid=12964 85707&sr=8-1, accessed February 10, 2011.

the socialist camp's dismantling, unbridled enthusiasm for capitalism's inherent goodness and the market's unalloyed and unmatched power to fix all things came into question as the market began to unravel.

First, the US stock market crashed in September 2000, losing eight trillion dollars, a drop of 78.4 percent of its value from its all-time high of 5,132.52 achieved in March 2000. The high-flying NASDAQ in particular went down like a bungee jumper whose cord has snapped. Markets around the world shuddered and cracked. The US stock market crashed again in 2002, bringing stock exchanges everywhere down with it. It crashed once again in 2007-08. In 2008 we saw the bursting of the US housing bubble that had been fueled largely by heedless profit-taking by lenders who did not care whether borrowers had sufficient incomes for their loans. When so much money was to be made writing mortgages, why worry about the risk to homeowners who could be suckered into taking out unsustainable loans? Some homebuyers who qualified for non-subprime loans were even misled by unscrupulous lenders into taking subprime loans, since the lending companies rewarded their salespeople for using this stratagem.

Exotic financial devices such as bundled home mortgages, whose real value no one could properly ascertain but whose resales generated immediate revenue without generating any new real value, were also to blame. These "securities" subsequently resulted in the term "toxic assets" entering nearly every American's vocabulary. The housing crisis in turn provoked a massive, perilous financial crisis that spread worldwide in a New York minute. Iceland, once flying high as a poster child for neoliberal policies, went bankrupt quickly and ignominiously, the Icelandic stock exchange losing seventy-seven percent of its values in two terrible days of trading in October 2008.[7]

Unable to allow this crisis to run its course because it would mean untold and unimaginable worldwide financial disaster, the Bush White House demanded a massive bailout for the very companies that had been responsible for this debacle. The virulently anti-communist, anti-socialist Bush presidency could not wait to implement a massive "socialistic-like" bailout of big finance. The House of Representatives, more sensitive to their constituents' sentiments than the Senate, voted down the bailout plan, despite heavy lobbying from party leaders and the White House; subsequently, Treasury Secretary Henry Paulsen warned some recalcitrant

---

7   See this dramatic chart at Wikipedia, "File:OMX Iceland 15 SEP-OCT 2008. png," http://en.wikipedia.org/wiki/File:OMX_Iceland_15_SEP-OCT_2008.png, accessed February 11, 2011. Trading was suspended on October 9, 10, and 13, 2008, and reopened on October 14. The closing OMX Iceland 15 of 678.4 compares to the closing OMX Iceland 15 of 3,004.6 on October 8.

Congress members that if they did not support the bailout *martial law* would be declared.

Paulsen was named by the White House as the bailout czar and given powers befitting a dictator. Congress grumbled at this unprecedented and patently undemocratic and unrepresentative power grab; they added language to their eventual approval of Paulsen that ostensibly retained for themselves the mechanisms of oversight and approval. But the crisis was real, the mood desperate, and the warnings apocalyptic. Paulsen was a former head of Goldman Sachs who during his tenure there lobbied successfully to relax the New Deal-era restrictions regarding how much of a margin financial institutions could operate on; thus, he contributed markedly to the catastrophe he was supposed to help fix as Treasury Secretary. The proverbial fox was guarding the hen house. During his Congressional testimony Paulsen made a face at the idea that executive compensation packages should be capped in any way. This was honor among thieves indeed.

The Obama Administration then expanded the bailouts even further, approving multi-million dollar bonuses to executives of the very companies that had been most responsible for the financial debacle. When these bonuses came into the glare of media coverage, Obama expressed astonishment and made speeches decrying what his own administration had knowingly permitted. In July 2009, further evidence of even more extraordinary bonuses became public knowledge. As I wrote in my blog at the time:

> Of the $175 billion in bailout money given by U.S. taxpayers under the Troubled Assets Relief Program (TARP), **almost 19% of that money went in bonuses to employees totaling $32.6 billion.**
>
> > "When the banks did well, their employees were paid well. When the banks did poorly, their employees were paid well," [New York State Attorney General Andrew] Cuomo's office said in the 22-page report:
> >
> > When the banks did very poorly, they were bailed out by taxpayers and their employees were still paid well. Bonuses and overall compensation did not vary significantly as profits diminished.
> >
> > The report, called "No Rhyme or Reason: The 'Heads I Win, Tails You Lose' Bank Bonus Culture," comes as Congress and the Securities and Exchange Commission examine whether to limit the compensation paid to top corporate executives...

The top 200 bonus recipients at JPMorgan Chase & Co. received $1.12 billion last year, while the top 200 at Goldman received $995 million. At Merrill the top 149 received $858 million and at Morgan Stanley, the top 101 received $577 million. **Those 650 people received a combined $3.55 billion, or an average of $5.46 million.**

JPMorgan Chase had 1,626 employees who received a bonus of least $1 million last year, more than any other Wall Street firm, according to the report. Goldman Sachs had 953 employees who received $1 million or more in bonuses, while Citigroup Inc. had 738, Merrill Lynch & Co., 696, and Morgan Stanley, 428. Bank of America Corp. had 172, while Wells Fargo & Co. had 62."[8]

Meanwhile, as these entrepreneurs continue to pay themselves bonuses for their fine work, having taken their companies into spectacular insolvency only being saved by a historic bailout, ordinary Americans have been punished for their sins of not being one of the elect by losing their homes, their jobs, their retirements, their health care, their pensions, and their lives. For those of us not part of the select few at the pinnacles of high finance, our buying power during the boom years actually fell, the first time in US history when an expanding economy did not result in expanded buying power and earnings for the middle and working classes.

Now, of course, with the economic crisis, while the fat cats become ever fatter, feeding off our hides, the average person's situation gets worse. Where I work, the California State University system, the faculty were presented with a heads you lose, tails you lose choice, either accepting pay cuts on top of unpaid, overdue pay raises (even if those previously promised pay raises *had* been issued, faculty would still be lagging badly behind comparable institutions in our pay), amounting to a net pay cut of close to 20% without any real reductions in work load, or even *more* massive layoffs for lecturers and possibly also tenured and tenure-track ranks.

Meanwhile, the CSU Chancellor pays himself more than $450,000/year (more than twice what the President of the United States is paid) **on top of** a free house and free car/gas. Top administrators at the CSU system have been receiving raises every year for the

---

8   Karen Freifeld, "Banks Paid $32.6 Billion in Bonuses Amid US Bailout," Bloomberg. com, July 30, 2009, http://www.bloomberg.com/apps/news?pid=20601087&sid=a6t nHj5lPPig, accessed August 1, 2009.

eleven years I've been at Cal Poly. The students are facing yet another fee hike, another increase in class size, and the numbers of students admitted will be cut by 40,000. Draconian cuts are being carried out on top of several years of cuts.

Governor Schwarzenegger has just slashed an additional half a billion to an already savagely cut budget for California. But, of course, *we can't do anything to fix this situation like raise taxes for the rich*. Not that!

The California budget deficit, by the way, is $15 billion. This is *less than half* the bonuses paid to these financial fat cats!

As of 7/08, California's population was over 36.7 million people. In other words, to put this in perspective, *a few thousand* financial elite employees were paid *in bonuses more than twice* what more than 36.7 million people are being deprived of.

Put another way, the top 650 blood money individual recipients received $3.55 billion in bonuses, almost 25% of California's budget deficit.[9] [Emphases in original.]

Even Continents Move

Normally, the ground beneath our feet seems unshakable and solid. But every once in a while an earthquake rearranges our perceptions of terra firma, reminding us that things are more fluid than we think. If even continents move, if the stock market and long-standing, wood-paneled financial giants can crash and burn, only saved from spectacular failures by feverish and massive government bailouts, why can't economic and political systems be toppled?

How could these disasters have happened? Isn't capitalism supposed to be the cure for all ills? Its greatest rival—socialism—had departed the scene. How did the capitalist free market utopia produce such stunning evidence of fundamental structural flaws so soon? The very disappearance of capitalism's rival, it turns out, precipitated capitalism's headlong rush into a worldwide debacle. Like an animal whose predator has suddenly disappeared from the scene, the US Empire has been multiplying in an unchecked fashion, threatening to consume the very ground on which it lives.

❀

---

9   Dennis Loo, "$32 Billion in Bonuses to JP Morgan, Goldman, Merrill …," *Dennis Loo: Open Salon* (blog), July 31, 2009, http://open.salon.com/blog/dennis_loo/2009/07/31/32_billion_in_bonuses_to_jp_morgan_goldman_merrill.

To grasp what is going on we have to probe beneath the surface to the underlying forces at play. The problems of capitalism that are now being expressed are not simply the product of a few (or even a lot of) greedy, corrupt, and shortsighted business figures. They are not primarily the result of poor monitoring by the Federal Reserve and the federal government. They did not arise principally because of an inattentive media. They are not fixable through a set of adjustments or through electing one party over the other, or installing into power one individual or another. They are not mainly the fault of a mall-obsessed, savings-allergic public. These are systemic problems. Life will never again be the same as the life Americans have known for the last few generations. The limits of consumption are upon us if we will only recognize them. But recognizing what is up is not so easy.[10] Systems do not change just because you put a new face in the White House and new faces in Congress.

Capitalism's Internal Contradictions

The problems we see around us are the outgrowth of contradictions within capitalism's basic nature and logic, contradictions that were fully, openly, and convulsively expressed in the pivotal epoch of the 1930s and 1940s. Just as individuals in the midst of a crisis will either rise to the occasion or fail dramatically, systems show their fundamental characters when embroiled in crises.

It is to that critical and revealing period—the years before, during, and after World War II—that I now turn to lay bare essential elements of the roots of our present circumstances and of neoliberalism's subsequent ascension. Like *Citizen Kane's* denouement when we learn what Rosebud represents, the battles (political, military, and economic) of World War II provide a window into the soul of the forces—capitalism and its discontents—that continue to contend in the world today. These twin forces shape our present and will determine our collective futures.

---

10   The Introduction to this book addresses the major factors affecting how willing and able people are to recognize issues such as this.

Humanity's Bloodiest Period—the 1930s and 1940s

> *It was the best of times, it was the worst of times…it was the spring of hope, it was the winter of despair, we had everything before us, we had nothing before us.*

> CHARLES DICKENS, A Tale of Two Cities

For capitalism's acolytes, the 1930s were the worst of times. In the US, the Great Depression decisively ended the frivolous, partying Roaring Twenties. The depression was a disaster brought on by capitalism's fundamental cycle of boom and bust. Millions of people were thrown out of work. Because they couldn't sell their products for a profit, farmers dumped milk into rivers rather than distribute it to those in need, even as bread lines sprang up everywhere. Tent cities of the unemployed sprouted all over. Radical and revolutionary politics found increasingly wider appeal. To salvage capitalism from its greatest crisis, Franklin Delano Roosevelt intervened in capital's operations to an unprecedented degree, ushering in the New Deal. This intervention was so extensive that FDR was, and still is, seen as a traitor to his class by many other elements of the capitalist class who refused, and still refuse, to accept the concessions that FDR made to save the system from the alternative—revolution. Despite the unprecedented scale of the projects and programs of the New Deal, for the Great Depression to end other things were also required: World War II's stepped-up war production, capital assets' massive destruction through war, and the US's subsequent postwar investment and rebuilding opportunities abroad.

The US depression was matched or exceeded around the world; nearly everywhere one looked in the 1930s and 1940s,[11] one saw economic crises and wars. Since the twentieth century's rosy dawn, after all, capitalism has been a worldwide system and process. Events in one part of the world were, and are, integrated with conditions and developments elsewhere. Marx did not live long enough to see the emergence from capitalism of its highest stage: imperialism. As the nineteenth century gave way to the twentieth, extremely large capitalist corporations dominated the economies of the advanced capitalist countries, decisively ending pre-monopoly and "free enterprise" capitalism.

This concentration of capital and power in a relatively small number of hands is what characterizes monopoly capitalism, a distinct developmental stage of capitalism. Whereas industrial capital dominates in the

---

11 The Soviet Union, although not without its troubles, was an exception to this.

preceding stage of capitalism, finance capital dominates under monopoly capitalism. In most instances we do not see monopoly in the literal sense of one single company being represented in all lines of business. Instead, we have monopoly in the sense that one or a very few companies utterly dominate a particular market. Microsoft and the oil companies are examples of monopolies.

Ticketmaster is a particularly revealing example of a monopoly. Its monopoly status allows it to tack on a number of ridiculous charges over the ticket price such as "arena fees" and so-called "convenience charges." As a result, it sometimes costs more to pay Ticketmaster's add-on charges than it does to pay the face values of tickets themselves. I think of Ticketmaster's "convenience charge" as funding more conveniences for Paul Allen who was once a majority stockholder of Ticketmaster (holding eighty percent of its stock). Allen was thus an owner of two of the most prominent monopolies in the world—Microsoft and Ticketmaster. Allen is also famous for his $200 million, 414-foot yacht named, appropriately, Octopus. It "houses a crew of 60, two helicopters, seven boats, a submarine, and a remote-controlled vehicle that crawls the ocean floor, [and] costs the billionaire $20 million a year (or $384,000 a week) to keep up."[12] Since over half the world lives on less than five hundred dollars a year per person, the cost for Allen to maintain his ostentatious yacht, a ship that Goldfinger would have drooled over, would keep more than forty thousand people alive for a year. To paraphrase Hillary Clinton, it takes a yacht to support a (very large) village. With such a yacht, Allen could field a small personal army.

Microsoft is a particularly revealing example of the fraud and/or deception behind most great fortunes. Microsoft likes to tout itself as innovative and argue that its monopoly status enhances and protects this innovativeness. The extreme wealth of Allen and his co-founder Bill Gates is not so much an instance of hard work or great creativity, however, as it is the result of a one-off brilliant piece of opportunistic insight and guile. In 1980 IBM was secretly working on rolling out a personal computer but they needed an operating system. IBM approached Gates. Gates did not have the program and referred them to Gary Kildall who had created an operating software program called CP/M. For some reason—accounts vary between the parties about this—IBM and Kildall could not reach a deal. IBM returned to Gates and struck a deal for Gates to provide the operating system for their PCs. Gates did not, however, have

---

12   Irina Aleksander, "Yacht Update! Paul Allen Spends $384K a Week on His; Other Billionaires Selling Theirs Off," Observer.com, January 7, 2009, http://www.observer.com/2009/o2/yacht-update, accessed February 10, 2010.

an operating system, but he knew someone who did. Tim Paterson, a Seattle programmer, had borrowed heavily without permission from CP/M, Kildall's creation, to create QDOS. Gates then went to Paterson, bought QDOS from him for $50,000.00, not revealing to him that he had a deal with IBM, made some small changes to QDOS, renamed it DOS, and then sold it to IBM on a per PC sale royalty fee basis. IBM released their PC in 1981, becoming the standard for PCs. Gates' "innovation" was to recognize an opening when he saw it.

From Free Enterprise to Monopoly

The shift from "free enterprise" to monopoly in the capitalist citadels by the beginning of the twentieth century occurred for two reasons.

First, economies of scale undermine free market competition; big fish eat up little fish. The drive for profits impels businesses to seek competitive advantages, to expand their market shares, and to eliminate their competition, either through buying out competitors or by driving them out of business. Anyone who has played the Parker Brothers' best-selling board game Monopoly is familiar with this dynamic. After a few hours of play at most, one player emerges as the big winner and everyone else has either been bankrupted or is soon to be bankrupted. This happens in Monopoly despite the fact that all of the players start out with exactly the same amount of money, unlike the real world where resources are distributed extremely unevenly (one does not choose one's parents, after all).

It is in the nature of free markets to cease being free markets. Libertarians' belief that free markets are the solution to all ills, therefore, cannot be realized and implemented any more than a butterfly can go back to being a caterpillar. Small may be beautiful, but big is cheaper and more powerful. Small businesses can, and always will, emerge just as small saplings spring up amongst the towering pines, but the economy's key players will continue to be big businesses. Some of the big businesses will be supplanted—witness General Motors' bankruptcy plight even though for a long time it had been the world's largest corporation—but the companies that supersede their previous competitors will then assume the monopolist position themselves. The players may change, in other words, but the disparities of position between big and small remain structurally and fundamentally the same.

Second, capital seeks profit-making opportunities everywhere. This ceaseless drive for profits leads—indeed, compels—the largest companies to burst past national boundaries and roam the globe in search of still cheaper labor and resources. Sam Walton, Walmart's founder, believed that his company should sell only American-made products. His insistence on this, however, has obviously passed away like eight-track stereo. Walmart would be non-competitive today if it did not seek the cheapest labor it could find. This fact, put very briefly, is what imperialism is in the economic sense. Imperialism is a compelling and inevitable consequence of capitalism itself within the more advanced capitalist countries. It represents capitalism's underlying logic carried forward into monopoly capitalism and expressed and active on an international scale. Imperialism is, therefore, not a choice; it is not something that could be dispensed with by corporations and their governments any more than a vampire could choose to be a vegetarian.

This compelling and inescapable dynamic can perhaps be best illustrated by first comparing capitalism to the economic system that preceded it: feudalism. Capitalism differs from feudalism in one decisive respect. Under feudalism the economy's underlying logic is primarily the production of "use values"—that is, goods and services are created and exchanged primarily for their use. For example, you exchange goat's milk for shoes because you need shoes. You need the shoes to wear and walk around in because the ground is hard and rough.

Under capitalism, by contrast, production exists for the principal purpose of exchanging commodities for profit—for their "exchange value"—not for their use value. (A commodity is anything to which anyone attaches value. It could be a loaf of bread, a painting, or a handkerchief once used by Elvis Presley.) In mathematical language it would look like this: exchange value > use value. Thus, a Pet Rock, if it can be sold for a profit, serves the purpose of acquiring profit, even though a Pet Rock serves no useful purpose in and of itself (except perhaps amusement at its lack of usefulness.) While it is possible, to use a different example, to have too many bananas—you can only eat so many and make only so much banana bread before the bananas rot—it is not possible to have too much money. Money does not spoil (although it may be subject to inflationary loss). Use values continue to be important (people need to do things such as eat) but they are not as important as exchange values in capitalist systems. In a system dominated by exchange value, even eating takes second place to the production of profit, and around the world over thirty thousand people a day starve to death because of it. More than thirty thousand people. Imagine a neutron bomb being set off in downtown Los Angeles that kills all of the city's four million residents plus another one million from the immediate surrounding areas. Visualize what the city would look like with all of its people lying dead in the streets, buildings, bedrooms, living rooms, kitchens, vehicles, pools, and elevators. Imagine this happening every year. That is how many people die of unnecessary starvation every year in the world—five million people.

An economy based principally on producing use values differs fundamentally from an economy based principally on producing exchange values. As a former CEO of General Motors once correctly put it, "General Motors is not in the business of making cars. General Motors is in the business of making money." Cars are simply the incidental vehicle for the real activity—the production of profit.

Feudal economies do not experience depressions; depressions are creatures of capitalism. Depressions occur when the capital accumulation process is interrupted because the amount of profit to be made no longer suffices. No matter how useful those goods or services may be (and they could spell the difference between life and death for millions of people), if they cannot be exchanged for enough profit, then their production will cease until such time as profitability can once more resume. Moreover, if these commodities are profitable but not as profitable as some other economic activity, then the latter will win out over the former. This has nothing to do with the social or individual importance of the items in question. It has to do with profit making as the be-all and end-all of capitalist economies.

Let us suppose, to illustrate this further, that a specific capitalist decides that she will buck convention and do something very different. Imagine a new Walmart CEO who decides that she will make a change that will benefit Walmart employees and suppliers. At the next shareholders' meeting, she announces that Walmart is expanding its employee benefits program to include a living wage, pension, and medical insurance so that Walmart employees will no longer have to seek government assistance to make up for Walmart's niggardly benefits package. (Half of Walmart's full-time employees now seek government assistance, explicitly encouraged to do so by Walmart itself.) Walmart, this enlightened CEO declares with much fanfare, will also cease driving down suppliers' prices ruthlessly.

"We will henceforth pay suppliers enough," she announces with great pride, "so that their workforces will be able to live decently and have bathroom breaks and meal breaks. Walmart has a social conscience."

"This will promote goodwill among our employees," she continues, "and improve the living and working conditions for those who have been working for the subcontractors supplying Walmart products, elevating living standards in Third World countries and promoting better lives for multitudes of people."

Imagine the stockholders' shock at this declaration. Let us suppose, nevertheless, that this CEO is unbelievably persuasive and charismatic and that she convinces the shareholders that this is a good idea. She successfully fends off their first impulses to fire her, even though implementing her daring plan will cut into shareholders' dividends and profit shares. After the shareholders' meeting the financial press and the rest of the media report the dramatic developments at Walmart. How does Wall Street react at the next day's opening to Walmart's amazing initiative? The answer is obvious: Walmart's shares would get clobbered.

Walmart, after all, is not only competing for money from those who invest in retail businesses. Walmart is also competing for the investment monies for all possible investments, retail or otherwise. The new Walmart CEO would lose her job unceremoniously; perhaps she would become the inspiration for a feel-good Hollywood movie, but she would be finished and would likely be treated as insane in the corporate world.

You are not compelled to pursue greater and greater profitability within capitalism, but if as a businessperson you do not pursue profitability aggressively, then one or more of the following will likely occur: your business will remain relatively small, even marginal; you will be taken over by a bigger company; your company, or at least you, will go bankrupt. Even companies that have understood this, as did and does General Motors, are also always at risk of being surpassed. This raises the matter of the next key aspect of capitalism relevant to this discussion: capitalism's unevenness.

There are different dimensions to unevenness (such as the uneven rates of growth of different companies within the same business), but I will focus herein on the international dimension. Capitalism's uneven growth and nature means that those companies that started first possess advantages over their smaller, newer rivals, rather as the chicks that hatch first get most of the food, stunting the growth or even resulting in the demise of the chicks that hatch later.[13] These first-in-line advantages, when extended across national boundaries, mean the distortion of capitalist development in so-called underdeveloped nations; their economies are fundamentally shaped by, subordinated to, and selectively and parasitically developed based upon foreign monopoly capital's interests. Since the service of subordinated nations' economies to their domestic population is not of interest to foreign capital and is, in fact, significantly contrary to foreign capital's interests, imperialist domination renders balanced and articulated national economic development impossible.

---

13 This unevenness also means that upstart rivals (e.g., Toyota) will sometimes outstrip the formerly dominant (e.g., General Motors). Those that ascend, however, are either already or soon to be themselves monopolists. And so it goes. . . .

The American Revolution of 1776, in fact, was designed precisely to free the colonies from their disadvantaged position as a colony of British imperialism. Why is this path wrong for Third World nations under colonial domination today?[14]

From the standpoint of international capital, penetrating into China with lots and lots of McDonald's franchises is better than China's developing businesses that produce balanced, nutritious, affordable, small-carbon-footprint domestic meals. Protection of scarce resources and concern about the global environment are also externalities from foreign capital's perspective.

Foreign and monopoly capital are everywhere and nowhere at the same time; transnational corporations and finance capital straddle continents. They are more powerful and richer than most of the nation-states in the world. Within the major capitalist/imperialist citadels themselves—the US, Britain, Germany, et al—transnational corporations exert preeminent influence, matching their economic dominance within the political arena. This is not an aberration; it is what one would expect. A company like Exxon that reports quarterly profits in the tens of billions of dollars would be crazy to allow un-corporately regulated political bodies to determine its corporate fate.

Exxon makes sure that those in office and those interested in office will not curb Exxon's profitability too much, if at all, let alone threaten its very existence as a private concern. It makes sure that public opinion is influenced by a heavy investment in public relations touting Exxon's virtues and civic spirit. Finally, it makes certain that the people of oil-rich countries do not get into their heads the peculiar notion that the oil in their lands and off their shores belongs to them rather than to Exxon (with its desire to extract the oil at the lowest possible price). If that means that Exxon must interfere directly and indirectly in the politics of that foreign nation, including supporting brutal anti-labor practices, coups, assassinations, and wars, then so be it. The money at stake, after all, is immense— billions, and over time trillions of dollars. Expecting corporations and those who head such behemoth transnational corporations to think and behave differently is naïve. Believing that the US president will act to curb these illegal and undemocratic practices because he or she "represents" the American people and because "it's the right thing to do" is also naïve. Might trumps right in a system in which exchange value (profit and private interests) trump use value (social or collective needs).

---

14   For an excellent expose of this see Ha-Joon Chang, *Bad Samaritans: The Myth of Free Trade and the Secret History of Capitalism* (New York: Bloomsbury Press, 2008).

Imperialism: the Whole World Divided

Twentieth century imperialism brought with it the dividing up of the entire world amongst the imperialist powers. The First World War was a *world* war because by the early twentieth century the whole globe had been divided up amongst the imperialist powers; there was no untouched frontier remaining and future battles would be a global affair. This explains why there were no world wars before the twentieth century. Those who cling to the notion that wars are a product of aggressiveness in "human nature" need to account for why human nature somehow changed in the twentieth century and introduced a whole new level of aggressiveness in the form of global warfare.

World wars have been fundamentally fights for control over colonies. Colonies offer excessive profits to multinational and transnational corporations—profits that far outstrip those extracted from the advanced capitalist countries' domestic workforces. Foreign operations for multinational and transnational corporations account for a disproportionate share of those corporations' profits. The share of international profits for US companies has grown steadily since the 1960s, when they accounted for about five percent, and now accounts for about a quarter of all corporate profits.[15] In the era of globalization, production is increasingly being carried out abroad. Colonies are prized for their natural resources and for their "cheap" labor. They are such gigantic prizes that wars that cost immense amounts of money, involve mind-boggling levels of destruction, require the spectacular sacrifice of tens of millions of lives, and put the very systems that wage them at risk for upheaval and revolution, are not too much for imperialist powers to carry out.[16] World War I was dubbed the "war to end all

---

15   A recent Morgan Stanley study concluded that companies in the Standard & Poor's 500-stock index that receive a quarter or more of their revenue from outside the US grow faster and are more likely to beat earnings estimates than those that receive less than a quarter from outside the US. Shares of companies with a large percentage of sales from outside the US have also generally been outperforming those that are US-centric. See Timothy Aeppel, "Overseas Profits Provide Shelter for U.S. Firms," *Wall Street Journal*, August 9, 2007, A-1.

16   The war in Iraq and Afghanistan by mid-2010 surpassed $1 trillion in direct expenditures (not counting lost opportunity costs). World War I cost the US alone $334 billion, the Korean War cost $341 billion, Vietnam $738 billion, and the Gulf War $102 billion. World War II was the most expensive US war, costing $4 trillion (adjusted for inflation). From Elizabeth Bumiller, "The War: A Trillion Can be Cheap," NYTimes. com, July 24, 2010, http://www.nytimes.com/2010/07/25/weekinreview/25bumiller. html, accessed February 13, 2011. Bumiller further notes that "the annual cost

wars" because of its horrors, but of course it was merely a prelude to the much greater conflagration of World War II.

When I was young and first learned about World War I, I wondered to myself how it was possible for all of the countries of Europe as well as the US to become embroiled in a war that cost fifteen million lives. I was taught that that war was triggered by a minor incident—the 1914 assassination of one relatively unimportant blue blood, Austria's Archduke Franz Ferdinand. Attributing World War I's bloodiness to the obligations of state alliances, which is the usual explanation found in high school textbooks, does not even begin to explain the insanity of that global war.

The way forward for an ambitious imperialist country—and they must all be ambitious or else cease being imperialist—runs through the acquisition of colonies. The only way, therefore, to re-divide the colonies for imperialist powers all trying to expand their operations is for the imperialist powers to wage wars that involve multiple countries as combatants with the entire world as spoils.

Like the mafia who periodically meet to hash out conflicts among the families, imperialist countries hold periodic international and regional conferences to iron out differences: GATT (General Agreement on Tariffs and Trade), WTO (World Trade Organization), G20 (Group of 20), etc. But as with the mafia where agreements prove to be only temporary salves to inherent conflicts over turf, whole countries "go to the mattresses" to pursue politics by other violent means, declaring war upon each other with the playing field being the planet itself. Governments and big corporations, under the phony signboard of patriotism and "self-defense," thereby make the people an "offer they can't refuse."

Crises provoke revolutions and counterrevolutions. How could they not? When a system is in profound trouble, structural changes result from the existing system's obvious inability to cope with the crisis. Wars impose strains upon the populace that exceed the normal strains of peacetime conditions by orders of magnitude; wars bring with them death, destruction, and such demands as that people kill other people by their own hands (including, most horridly, the targeting of women and children in unjust wars), with all of this being carried out on a massive scale.

Economic crises induce suffering on a broad scale. When wars and economic crises are joined as we find in the World War II period, the result is a boiling cauldron. This period created the conditions in which socialist revolutions could make further dramatic and historic gains at the

---

today is $1.1 million per man or woman in uniform in Afghanistan versus an adjusted $67,000 per year for troops in World War II and $132,000 in Vietnam."

capitalist world's expense, advancing past World War I's socialist revolution—the 1917 Russian Revolution.

World War II had two "dress rehearsals": Japanese imperialism's invasion and occupation of China in 1931 and the Spanish Civil War from 1936 to 1939 (precipitated by an attempted coup d'état by fascist forces against the Spanish Republic). Over seventy million died in World War II's slaughter, the largest number of war casualties in history. Twenty-two million people perished in the Soviet Union's fight to repel Hitler's invasion, a number of lives lost from just one country that boggles the mind.

In the infamous Nazi death camps some ten million people were killed, six million of them Jews (the Holocaust), with the other four million being communists (the Nazis' first target), trade union organizers, homosexuals, Roma (Gypsies), and the disabled. Grotesque atrocities, the likes of which had not been seen since human warfare's earliest days, were achieved by the latest technical innovations; these included the attempted annihilation of "enemies of the state" by Zyklon B (a cyanide-based pesticide) that was released into ovens packed with emaciated people who were led to their horrible deaths by the Nazis promising cleansing showers.

This was by no means World War II's only sickeningly murderous rampage on a grand scale. The war finally came to an apocalyptic end with the unforgettable images of massive mushroom clouds rising over the instantaneously vaporized bodies of tens of thousands of Japanese civilians, first in Hiroshima and then in Nagasaki. Subsequently, in Hiroshima alone more than a hundred thousand more died from radiation poisoning and other related factors.

The US, under Harry Truman's leadership, thereby declared to its chief rival, the USSR, and to the rest of the world that it had a terrible new weapon that made absolutely no distinction between combatants and civilians. Truman had put the Manhattan Project into overdrive so that he could use the atomic bomb before the war was over. This rush was less motivated by a desire to save American lives in an invasion of Japan as it was by a desire to short-circuit the plan announced by the Soviets to invade Japan if the war was not over by August 5, 1945. Had the Soviets been allowed to invade Japan, they would have been in a position to dictate the peace; that was a role that the US wanted to reserve for itself.[17]

---

17   Walter Goodman, "Television Review; Behind Truman's Decision on the Atomic Bomb," NYTImes.com, July 27, 1995, http://www.nytimes.com/1995/07/27/movies/television-review-behind-truman-s-decision-on-the-atomic-bomb.html, accessed February 13, 2011:

Truman's main justification for taking the third course [dropping the atomic bombs on Japan] as shown in excerpts from a 1964 television his-

World War II was the first modern war in which both combatants and non-combatants were treated as legitimate targets by the new technologies of warfare and by the war strategists. The end-of-days' clouds over Japan announced the arrival of the Atomic Age that overshadowed an entire generation. "Duck-and-cover" drills about how to respond to a nuclear blast were insufficient in the face of mankind's anxiety about thermonuclear annihilation's all-too-literal prospect, captured so vividly in the Stanley Kubrick film classic, *Dr. Strangelove or: How I Learned to Stop Worrying and Love the Bomb.*

For the Left, in contrast to the Right, this was in certain respects the best of times despite the wars' awful toll of death and destruction. China, home of one-fourth of humanity, rose in socialist revolution; thus ending its shameful status as the "sick man of Asia" and joining the ranks of the socialist camp, a camp that for several decades thereafter accounted for close to a third of the world's population.

This best and worst of times in this most bloody epoch coexisted for a reason.

Lenin, leader of the 1917 Russian Revolution, the world's first countrywide socialist revolution, once wrote that wars mean great death, destruction, and suffering but that they did have one virtue—they revealed in naked form the true priorities of governments and of capital. What is seen only through a glass darkly in ordinary times stands out in sharp relief under the blindingly bright noonday sun of war and crisis. As a consequence, revolutionary sentiment peaks in such times in the conviction that the status quo is no longer tolerable and that one's life is worth risking, even sacrificing, in order to see that things do not continue in the old way.

In the 1930's Germany contained a concentration of the sharp contradictions present around the world. Hemmed in on all sides by rival powers and long aspiring to superpower status, Germany and its capitalist/imperialist class chafed at the bit. Germany's economy spun out of control. Something had to replace the status quo, for the center would not hold. For the German ruling class, the question of whether that new

---

tory of his Presidency, was that it saved "250,000 or 300,000 of our youngsters killed and 700,000 of them maimed." But that is contradicted tonight on two grounds: military intelligence estimates of American casualties in an invasion were a small fraction of those numbers, and an invasion of the mainland would not have been necessary at all if the Administration had relaxed its demand for unconditional surrender and allowed the Japanese to keep their emperor (as indeed they finally did).

It is also noted, contrary to some previous treatments of the subject, that Hiroshima was bombed without warning and that the bomb was aimed not at any military target but at the center of the city.

arrangement was to be led by the fascists or the communists required no time to ponder; Hitler was given the reins of power, even though his party had actually lost ground in the prior elections, proving once again that elections do not decide public policy.[18]

Germany and the other Axis powers (Italy and Japan) made an audacious and initially successful bid with the blitzkrieg—lightning war—to redistribute the global imperialist powers' colonial holdings. But beginning with the Battle of Stalingrad, World War II's turning point, the Third Reich's dreams of a thousand years of rule fell short by just a little.

---

18   See Brian Fallon, review of *Hitler's Thirty Days to Power: January 1933* by Henry Ashby Turner, Jr., *Irish Times*, November 16, 1996, Supplement p. 8:

> In July 1932, in a general election, the Nazi Party had more than doubled its support, winning 37.4 per cent of the vote and 230 seats. (This was not necessarily mass approval of fascism, or anti Semitism—then still a minor issue—so much as the desperate wish of the German people that some firm hands might seize the helm of the battered, drifting ship of state.) Various conservative interests by now had accepted that Hitler would have to be given a share of governmental power, and he had previously entered into an understanding with the shifty Franz von Papen that he would cooperate with his cabinet. Instead, Hitler went back on his word, demanding the chancellorship for himself and various key posts for his henchmen, a package deal which was rejected by President Hindenburg. His failure to enter into government antagonised many of the voters, who had hoped for a broadly rightist, nationalist alliance instead of yet another ephemeral coalition; and this reaction was reflected in the polls when another general election was held in November. This time the Nazis lost 34 seats, so that early in 1933 newspapers which supported the beleaguered republic were openly and exultantly proclaiming "Hitler's Rise and Fall;" The prestigious Frankfurter Zeititog wrote: "The mighty Nazi assault on the democratic state has been repulsed."
>
> Nazi membership declined sharply and, even worse for the party bosses, subscriptions and money donations fell off too, so that state police began to report officially that the NASDP was losing much of its old support and appeared to be facing financial and organisational collapse. Hitler himself faced open and covert rebellion among his aides, which at one stage drove him to threaten suicide if he did not get their full support and his own way.
>
> Somehow he hung on, and then at the thirteenth hour came the life belt thrown to him by Papen, who had finally talked President Hindenburg into coming to terms with "that Bavarian corporal."
>
> The rest is history: various politicians of the Right including Papen—believed that they could use him, control him when in government and 'hem him in.' Too late, they learned they were dealing with a demonic personality driven by a messianic sense of mission, who would stop at nothing and was their master in intrigue.

Stalingrad's fierce house-to-house and even room-to-room fighting was the beginning of the end for Hitler and the Axis powers. In Eastern Europe the old regimes fell to the Red Army and socialism's red flag. Many of the old order's representatives had been thoroughly discredited by their complicity with fascism's monstrous brutality (e.g., Vichy France.)

Except for the Japanese attack on Pearl Harbor in 1941, the US landmass was unscathed by the international conflagration. Because it was separated from the main arenas of conflict by two immense oceans, it was spared the scars of war that afflicted the old world. A greatly expanded American Empire, taking full advantage of its insurgent power, emerged as the other big winner of World War II; it was now contending with the new socialist bloc for developing nations' allegiances. This was not, however, an unalloyed victory for the US. World War II and concomitant revolutions brought to the scene a much larger and more powerful alternative: Russia became the USSR, Eastern Europe went under the socialist umbrella, and China added to the socialist camp what not long afterward became a billion more people. The world was now divided not between rival imperialist powers, but between the capitalist/imperialist world and the socialist world. This new division had tremendous repercussions internationally and domestically.

Ending Segregation and Brown v. Board of Education

This new, two-sided balance of forces internationally produced the famous 1954 *Brown v. Board of Education of Topeka* Supreme Court decision that desegregated US schools and declared an end to "separate but equal." *Brown v. Board,* in turn, triggered the civil rights movement that for its part inspired other movements of the 1960s. Worth reading in its entirety is this description of the circumstances that gave rise to *Brown v. Board*:

> Over a period of a few years in cases leading up to Brown, the Truman Administration filed briefs informing the Supreme Court of the international consequences of racial segregation in the United States.
>
> In December 1952, U.S. Attorney General James P. McGranery filed a friend-of-the-court brief with the U.S. Supreme Court in the Brown case telling the Court of the Truman Administration's urgent foreign policy interest in ending segregation. **At the time, the United States was engaged in an intense Cold War competition with the Soviet Union for the loyalty and friendship of nations in Asia**

with non-white populations that had newly become independent and nations in Africa that were about to become independent. In that competition, the Soviet Union was successfully exploiting racial segregation in the United States to win allies. Accordingly, *of the seven pages* of the Truman Administration brief that stated, "the interest of the United States," *five were devoted to an account of the way school segregation handicapped the United States in its competition with the Soviet Union.* "It is in the context of the present world struggle between freedom and tyranny that the problem of racial discrimination must be viewed," the Justice Department brief said. "The United States is trying to prove to the people of the world of every nationality, race and color, that a free democracy is the most civilized and most secure form of government yet devised by man…. The existence of discrimination against minority groups in the United States has an adverse effect upon our relations with other countries. Racial discrimination furnishes grist for the Communist propaganda mills." This was followed by a long excerpt from a letter by Secretary of State Dean Acheson that was described in the brief as, "an authoritative statement of the effects of racial discrimination in the United States upon the conduct of foreign relations."

. . .

In an extraordinary move, the Supreme Court reached down on its own initiative and placed the case on its own docket so that the Washington, D.C. case could be argued and decided together with the challenge to segregation in schools operated by the states. …

On May 18, 1954, the day after Brown was decided, The New York Times commented editorially that, "When some hostile propagandist rises in Moscow or Peiping to accuse us of being a class society, we can, if we wish, recite the courageous words of yesterday's opinion." The same day, The Washington Post and Times Herald as it was then called said, "It will help us to refurbish American prestige in a world which looks to this land for moral inspiration." The San Francisco Chronicle was more explicit, saying, "Great as the impact will be on the states of the South, still greater, we believe, will be its impact in South America, Africa and Asia, to this country's lasting honor and benefit." And The Minneapolis Tribune, in a statement repeated in substance in the editorial of many other newspapers, wrote that, "The words of Chief Justice Warren will echo far beyond our borders and may greatly influence our relations with dark-skinned peoples." The St. Louis Post Dispatch thought the impact of the decision on American foreign policy would be more important than at home. Its editorial said, "The greater significance is the affirmation in the eyes of millions of people in India, Pakistan and Africa, in China, Japan and Burma, in Indo-China, Thailand and Indonesia that the pledge in the United States of the worth and integrity of the humblest individual means exactly what it says. Had this decision gone the other way, the loss to the free world in its struggle against Communist encroachment would have been incalculable." African-American leaders saw it the same way. [19] [Emphases added.]

How many other Supreme Court decisions have been so explicitly determined by foreign policy considerations? The Attorney General, the White House, and former Secretary of State Dean Acheson argued for desegregation because of the US's high-stakes competition with the socialist bloc. Major newspapers hailed the decision, not because of racism's egregiousness and the need to end it; they declared instead that segregation had to end because the US was losing out to the socialist world in its wooing of the world's nonaligned nations.

What changed with World War II was not the fact that black GI's came back from the war having experienced better treatment in the military than they had gotten and were going to get from US civilian life—although this was a factor in the subsequent civil rights movement. What changed in World War II was not the attitude of American political elites towards blacks. What changed because of World War II was the emergence of a socialist bloc. Had there not been a socialist alternative, in other words, black segregation in America would not have presented such a problem for those in power in the US; their segregated system would have been the only game in town and discrimination could have gone on more or less as it had for the hundreds of years prior to that.

The US civil rights movement emerged through an opening given to blacks with *Brown v. Board*. The actions of political elites, pursuing a strategy to make US interests more appealing, opened that crack. Through this small fissure rushed blacks' long-suffering and long-suppressed aspirations and they erupted like a geyser. The civil rights movement that played a vanguard role in bringing forward the Sixties insurgencies would have, at a minimum, been indefinitely postponed absent communism's successes internationally.

---

19   Aryeh Neier, Untitled commencement address, American University Washington College of Law online, Washington, DC, May 23, 2004, http://www.wcl.american. edu/media/events/040523.cfm, accessed May 14, 2009.

In addition, without the presence in the 1930s and 1940s of a rival and alternative model to capitalist society in the form of a socialist/communist movement and camp, the New Deal would have looked quite different from what it was. It is highly likely that the New Deal would never have even happened.

Those who hold political power deeply appreciate the importance of the perspective of the international dimension, but they usually keep this knowledge to themselves. In the 1950s they temporarily pulled the curtain away to reveal this truth because the anti-capitalist forces presented a genuine threat to their colonial empires internationally.

National Liberation Struggles, the Cold War, and the Cultural Revolution

The existence of a socialist camp also acted as a midwife to the other insurgencies of the Sixties worldwide. In fact, this is an understatement: the socialist camp was a parent to the 1960's insurgencies. The right-wing bromide that these upsurges and protests were the results of "outside agitators" manipulating naïve and otherwise content citizens, that they were a product of "communist-inspired conspiracies," was not true. There was nothing conspiratorial or secretive about it.

Rather, we had the following factors:

One, socialism inspired those who wanted something different than life under capitalism. These were palpable, functioning alternatives, including ones in which white and male supremacy was not the status quo; this was particularly the case in China, where "women hold up half the sky" was an official slogan, and rebelling against authority was actually encouraged. These alternatives acted as a powerful incentive, more than the prospect of a not-yet-realized, perhaps not-even possible, alternative to capitalism because they were actually there now for most people.

Two, the Cold War standoff between the two superpowers gave Third World nations and their peoples a choice. Capitalism was no longer their only option.

Three, the socialist countries provided material and ideological assistance to the struggling Third World nations. China and Russia, for example, gave Vietnam material support in its anti-colonial struggle.

The very existence of Third World countries with dramatically lower living standards than those of the affluent, capitalist/imperialist countries was, and is, a product of capitalism's uneven development. Major advantages accrue to the already powerful capitalist countries. Marx's prediction that socialist revolutions would occur first in the most advanced capitalist countries did not prove true because imperialism—which he did not live to see—alters the dynamic of boom and bust and extends immiseration into the global arena.

Imperialism produces an extraordinarily wealthy upper class, whose privileges dwarf those of feudal monarchs and even the wealthy and comfortable emperors of Ancient Rome and Middle Kingdom China. It also produces a larger, very prosperous upper middle class, a sizable (and also by world and historic standards well-off) middle class, as well as a better-off upper stratum of the working class. People in this upper working class were so well off from the 1950s into the 1980s that they were usually incorrectly referred to as middle class. The prosperity produced by imperialism mutes class contradictions and other disparities of gender, race/ethnicity and sexual orientation. At the same time and for the same reasons, imperialism also greatly exacerbates conditions in Third World countries. Thus, revolutionary sentiment and revolutionary situations become more prevalent within the Third World, as the opposite effect occurs within the imperialist countries: imperialism produces what Lenin dubbed a "labor aristocracy," a materially very well off upper working class in the imperialist citadels, but it also expands a lower sector of the working class that makes up a key social base for potential revolution.

The Counter-Offensive to the Sixties Insurgencies: the Crime Issue

Knocked back on its heels by the Sixties' insurgencies, ruling groups fought back. Because of the strength in society and in the streets of the insurgent groups, those who resisted the insurgents' demands and vision could not launch a frontal assault. Instead, they pursued an indirect approach; they attempted to put down insurgencies by developing a discourse that treated protest and crime as essentially the same thing. Crime as a national political issue dates from this period during which conservative elites attempted to quash domestic insurgencies. The battle over crime and the battle of the social insurgencies against the Right's counter-attack gave fundamental shape to the 1960s. It is possible to see in a concentrated way in that period the relative strengths of the protagonists and the possibilities for alternative futures if the appropriate lessons are drawn.

Right-wing politics obviously predate the 1960s, but the rationale for the right-wing's dominance over public policy today rests upon the underlying logic of the "law and order" issue. Today's "war on terror" specifically owes its underlying rationale to the 1960s' "war on crime" / "law and order" campaign's logic. The 1960s' "law and order" issue is the birthplace and the birthright of a right-wing movement that by the early years of the twenty-first century exercises enormous clout. A close inspection of the 1960s' fight over crime and protest reveals the fundamental illogic and deception of this "war on crime" and its subsequent logical corollary / descendent, the "war on terror." The "law and order" / "war on drugs" / "war on terror" discourse is commonly seen as the legitimate offspring of public fears. It is, instead, the right-wing's illegitimate child. I address the first part of this in the remainder of this chapter. The second part, with a focus on the "war on terror," is the subject of Chapter Four.

The Rise of the Right

While the political right-wing enjoys unprecedented influence today, their prospects looked dismal several decades ago. Their standard-bearer, GOP nominee Barry Goldwater, the twentieth century's most far-right nominee up to that point, was buried in the 1964 presidential election, losing in a landslide to Democrat Lyndon Baines Johnson.

Goldwater's defeat was the fifth most lopsided electoral result in US history. He carried only six states, all of them in the Deep South except his home state of Arizona, and garnered only 38.5 percent of the vote nationwide. This debacle provided a kind of Scarlett O'Hara moment for extremist right-wing Americans. As Scarlett declares in the film classic, *Gone With The Wind*:

> As God is my witness, as God is my witness they're not going to lick me. I'm going to live through this and when it's all over, I'll never be hungry again. No, nor any of my folk. If I have to lie, steal, cheat or kill. As God is my witness, I'll never be hungry again.

Like Scarlett, the Right did rise again, a phoenix from the ashes. Goldwater's views regarding the national-security state, his advocacy of unapologetic and naked use of force, and his unending munificence to the military (all considered extreme in the 1960s) have become the mainstream.[20] The right-wing, Goldwater's political progeny, has drunk deeply from the flagons of power, though over time the American conservative movement has

---

20 Daniel McCarthy, "Prospecting for AuH2O," lewrockwell.com, February 17, 2006, http://www.lewrockwell.com/dmccarthy/dmccarthy58.html, accessed on April 19, 2009.

mutated and some of what the neocons represent was repudiated by Goldwater during his lifetime.

How did this dramatic shift in fortunes occur for right-wing politics and policies?

The Right exercises its disproportionate influence on the polity not principally through winning elective offices but mainly through its successful framing of public policy issues within and through the Republican Party and through the Right's media empire. The GOP and right-wing media to a substantial degree now set the terms for the mainstream media and thus for the public discourse, even when the GOP is not in the White House.

The Right's springboard to dominance dates back to an issue that Goldwater famously raised—"law and order." In Goldwater's formulation, crime was linked in a specific fashion to safety, security, and a beefed-up, unrestrained state apparatus of social control. The dictum that the American people are in favor of "getting tough on crime" forms a core justification for right-wing politics. The eventual general acceptance of this frame—and its transference to the "War on Terror"—by both major political parties and by the media, makes up a linchpin of the Right's triumph. So long as the "War on Terror" remains the defining, over arching issue in US politics, the right-wing will exert a choke hold over American politics, irrespective of whether the GOP or the Democratic Party holds the White House and the majority on Capitol Hill. A different politics can never emerge unless and until the "War on Terror" is exposed as a cover for a very real "War *of* Terror" on the people outside and inside the US.

Since 9/11, the "tough on crime" slogan has been eclipsed but not supplanted by the "War on Terror" frame. The "War on Terror" frame, after all, involves no more than substituting a new identity for the enemy. The "war on crime" laid the conceptual and practical foundations for the subsequent "War on Terror." "Cracking down," "getting tough," "taking the offensive," and so on, are phrases that frame the foremost danger facing Americans—the "Other." The implacability of this "Other" necessitates an ever-expanding national security state and the corresponding continuous contraction of civil liberties.

This bifurcation of the world into the forces of good and evil, where evil is malevolent and cannot be reasoned with, can't be bargained with, and will not stop,[21] means that the most coercive and violent measures

---

21 This mirrors a line in the film *The Terminator* in which John Connor's father, Kevin Reese, is describing the terminator to Sarah Connor. "Listen, and understand. That terminator is out there. It can't be bargained with. It can't be reasoned with. It doesn't feel pity, or remorse, or fear. And it absolutely will not stop, ever, until you are dead."

are justified against it. The "Other" represents a fatal threat to the Body (of society, of the common good, of the whole people), and anything and everything—including torture and war crimes as policy—must be done to destroy the "Other" in order to safeguard the Body. This is the Right's raison d'être, its claim to legitimacy; it is also the basis of its putative right to exercise power and to explicitly nix previously sacrosanct principles of civil liberties and constitutional guarantees.

The enemies have changed over time, but the war remains conceptually the same. This realignment of the political chessboard is fundamental and revolves around the war on crime/terror/evil. Tracing this frame to its inception means going back to the wellspring of today's configuring of the landscape of power. I turn now to tracing and analyzing that history.

The 1960s—Where It Began

The formula of social protest = crime was conservatives' answer to the Sixties' challenges (the Sixties refers herein to that period stretching from the early years of the 1960s to 1973). It provided a means by which a counterattack against social insurgency could be launched in a superficially apolitical manner, thus making it seem universal instead of reactionary. The Democratic Party, after some initial resistance, also came to adopt the GOP's basic "get tough on crime" stance. Their adoption of this frame was fateful, partly for their party but more so for the country, because it meant that the political class and "chattering classes" would henceforth speak in one voice on this question, with dissenting positions ruled off the table, ridiculed as the contemporary equivalent of World War II "appeasers." The Right has thus not only succeeded in directly taking power; they have also succeeded in setting the terms by which the Democrats govern.

The Sixties were a time of great social and political turmoil worldwide. Within the US, the civil rights, anti-war, black power, and women's liberation movements rocked the country from top to bottom. Hundreds of riots occurred (some described by critics as "insurrectionary"), along with the assassinations of a string of political leaders: Malcolm X, John F. Kennedy, Martin Luther King Jr., Fred Hampton, and Robert F. Kennedy. Powerful divisions opened up in the society and as a result, President Lyndon Johnson, who had crushed Republican nominee Barry Goldwater in the 1964 presidential election, found himself so besieged that he renounced running for reelection in 1968. The Sixties, put simply, represent a watershed—a touchstone for both the political Left and the Right. Reverberations from it are still being felt to this day, including on the topic of concern of this section—the matter of street crime.

According to collective memory and scholarly opinion, the Sixties' "law and order" issue[22] raised unprecedented levels of public concern in the US. Further, the era's social insurgencies allegedly provoked heightened fears of crime within the public, especially white Americans, and led to a number of important outcomes, including:

- The 1968 election of conservative Republican Party nominees Richard Nixon and Spiro Agnew to the White House, marking an end to the liberal policies of the Great Society under Democratic President Lyndon Johnson,

- The subsequent (and still ongoing) expansion of the criminal justice system, the growth of which became unhinged from actual changes in index crime[23] offending rates,[24]

- A shift in the public's mood towards greater intolerance, punitiveness, self-centeredness and stinginess, and

- The supplanting of the New Deal / FDR[25] class alliance by a Republican Party alliance driven by social, religious, and race issues.

In short, according to the prevailing view, the "law and order" issue originated within the public and precipitated a major shift in US public policy.[26]

---

22 It was also sometimes referred to as the "crime in the streets" issue.

23 Index crimes are the crimes recorded by police departments and then compiled and reported out by the FBI each year in the Uniform Crime Reports. Index crimes refer to what are sometimes referred to as "street crimes" such as rape, robbery, murder, theft, assault, burglary, and so on. Index crimes do not include white-collar crimes.

24 The incarceration rate in the US began its upward and still-rising trajectory in 1973, the Sixties era's endpoint.

25 President Franklin Delano Roosevelt.

26 See, especially, Thomas Cronin, Tania Cronin and Michael Milakovich, *US vs. Crime in the Streets*, (Bloomington: Indiana University Press, 1981); Tom Smith, "The Polls: America's Most Important Problem," *Public Opinion Quarterly*, 49(2): 264–74; Richard Niemi, John Mueller, and Tom Smith, *Trends in Public Opinion: A Compendium of Survey Data*, (New York: Greenwood Press, 1989); Wesley G. Skogan, "Crime and the Racial Fears of White Americans," *Annals of the American Academy of Politics and Public Policy*, 539 (1995): 59–71; Michael Flamm, "'Law and Order' at Large: The New York Civilian Review Board Referendum of 1966 and the Crisis of Liberalism," *The Historian*, 64 (2002): 643–65.

Each of the four bullets above covers core matters for political players and political terrain in the US in the early twenty-first century. They represent, if you will, the four main branches that spread out from the main trunk of the tree of their origins: the alleged shift in public mood in the Sixties over crime. One way or the other, nearly every debate in public policy circles since the Sixties comes back to this issue, like a criminal revisiting the scene of his crime.

The collective memory and scholarly consensus about the Sixties' crime issue, however, is fundamentally wrong. Sixties' poll-measured crime concerns did not show a highly aroused public preoccupied with street crime. To paraphrase Mark Twain's famous retort to reports of his death, accounts of the birth of punitive and Social Darwinist public policies as a result of a public obsessed with crime have been greatly exaggerated. Instead, elites fabricated a fictive consensus around "law and order" in the Sixties and employed it as a device to introduce momentous public policy changes. This consensus lacked a genuine popular component. It was, rather, the representation of a popular consensus. Since that time we have seen a reiteration based upon the same playbook of this fundamental falsification and manipulation of popular opinion on a succession of issues—in the 1980s' the "war on drugs;" in the 1990s' the "war on crime;" and since 2001, the "War on Terror."

Arguably the most important purveyor of the conventional view on the Sixties crime issue was James Q. Wilson's 1975 book *Thinking About Crime*, which single-handedly helped push debate about crime to the right.[27] As Jerome Miller points out, Wilson's book "came to shape the nation's policy on crime for most of the 1980s, culminating in the misinformed and destructive legislation of the 1990s."[28] Wilson claimed in his book that on *four* occasions in the 1960s crime topped the "most important problem" in the nation (MIP) polls.[29]

---

27 Jerome Miller, *Search and Destroy: African-American Males in the Criminal Justice System,* (New York: Cambridge University Press, 1996), 138.

28 The Pennsylvania Republican Party, for example, purchased Wilson's book for the entire Republican Party state legislative membership to use in planning state criminal justice policies (Miller 1996, ftn. 7, p. 272). "Sen. Edward Kennedy's support for the federal 'Omnibus Crime Bill' and its call for harsh mandatory sentences and the trying of juveniles in adults courts came out of private seminars on crime conducted by Wilson for Kennedy and his staff." (Miller 1996, 141).

29 Gallup first began polling in 1935 and offered its first "most important problem in the nation" poll that year.

Wilson states, "In May 1965 the Gallup Poll reported that for the first time 'crime' (along with education) was viewed by Americans as the most important problem facing the nation." [30] Contrary to what Wilson said, however, the May 1965 Gallup poll found only *one percent* of respondents citing crime and *two percent* citing juvenile delinquency. Wilson goes on to state, "In the months leading up to the Democratic National Convention in 1968—specifically in February, May, and August—Gallup continued to report crime as the most important issue." [31]

Wilson is wrong about these polls also, and on all counts. Gallup did not even conduct a MIP poll in February 1968. The May 1968 poll result was an artifact of a conflated category created by Gallup, with pollsters combining disparate responses into one "answer" (I discuss this later in this section, see Table 3 herein). Even as a conflated item, "Crime and Lawlessness" was far below the leading items such as the Vietnam War and Civil Rights. The August 1968 poll to which Wilson refers showed *eight percent* of the respondents citing crime and one percent citing "hippies" (see Table 3) as "most important problem" in the nation. These percentages were far below the numbers cited in other top categories on that date such as forty-seven percent for "Vietnam" and twenty percent for "Civil Rights." These were not incidental errors by Wilson and his book, based on misrepresented polls that crime was foremost on Americans' minds, played a key role in shaping US crime policy in the 1980s and 1990s.

Goldwater and "Law and Order"

Goldwater sounded the portentous theme of "law and order" and "crime in the streets" in his July 16, 1964 speech accepting the Republican nomination for the presidency:

> The growing menace in our country tonight, to personal safety, to life, to limb and property, in homes, in churches, on the playgrounds, and places of business, particularly in our great cities, is the mounting concern, or should be, of every thoughtful citizen in the United States . . . History shows us . . . that nothing . . . prepares the way for tyranny more than the failure of public officials to keep the streets from bullies and marauders.

---

30 James Q. Wilson, *Thinking About Crime* (New York: Basic Books, 1975), 65.

31 Ibid., 65-66.

Goldwater's conflating of social protest with street criminals was a not-so-subtle attempt to tar any sort of disagreement with the brush of "criminal" and provide the rationale for governmental repression of dissent.

This framing of protest as crime by Goldwater did not, at first, gain traction. His views were outré in the 1960s. Indeed, Goldwater was derided for being a warmonger and put on the defensive. (This stands in sharp contrast to the situation in recent years when the Democrat is regularly condemned as a naïve pacifist in the face of implacable danger, and some Democrats go out of their way to prove that they are just as willing to "push the button" as Republicans.) In a famous 1964 TV ad "Daisy" (the most successful political ad in history, run only once as a paid ad but repeated endlessly on news shows), LBJ's campaign warned that if Goldwater became president, Goldwater's public musings that he might use nuclear weapons in the Vietnam War could lead to a nuclear conflagration.

"These are the stakes!" Johnson says while a child picks daisy petals in a field, only to be obliterated in a flash by a mushroom cloud. "To make a world in which all of God's children can live, or to go into the dark. We must either love each other, or we must die." The narrator (sportscaster Chris Schenkel) then intones, "Vote for President Johnson on November 3. The stakes are too high for you to stay home."

Framing and Its Consequences

In order to trace and analyze the 1960s' crime issue, it is important to first make some comments about the nature of interpretative framing, or "framing" for short. Because the number of social problems—issues that need attention and intervention—that public policy potentially could address are vast, and because decisions need to be made about what things end up being addressed and how they are understood, public policy-making comes down to the framing of social problems ultimately adopted. Determining the frame, therefore, represents a level of power and influence of the first order in politics, second only perhaps to the power of having the military on your side.

To illustrate framing's importance, some examples: if we frame poverty as the result of poor people making bad decisions, then the solution to poverty would be to get poor people to make better decisions; if poverty persists, that just means that there are still too many people making poor decisions. If we frame poverty, on the other hand, as the result of poor people not having enough skills, then our solution to poverty might be to expand job training programs. If we frame poverty, alternatively, as due to capitalism's structural character in which a section of the people must remain unemployed so that wages can be kept down—the equivalent of a very large game of musical chairs—then the solution to poverty would be structural, systemic changes.

Here is another example: If we frame crime as due to evil individuals, then the solution to crime is to do whatever is necessary to isolate the evil ones from the rest of the society through incarceration, sterilization, or execution. If instead we frame crime as due to the lack of legitimate opportunities, then the solution to crime would be to expand educational and job opportunities and training. If, finally, we frame crime as the inevitable outcome of a profit-driven and highly unequal society in which resources are structurally lopsided in their distribution and where material wealth is celebrated as *the* goal, then addressing crime would have to involve altering the structural characteristics of the society and economy and the corresponding ideology of profit-making and self-centeredness.

Frames not only suggest a value system; once you adopt the language and logic of a given frame, your options are also predetermined. The diagnosis determines the prescription. If, for example, the "War on Terror" is the dominant frame in the society, then the protagonists are "Us" and "Them (those terrorists)." If "support the troops" is the dominant frame, then anyone who opposes the war(s) is consigned automatically to being against the American troops. If you protest that you are not against the troops but are against the war, you are still hemmed in by the logic of "support the troops," and the frame vitiates your opposition to the war: how can you be *for* the soldiers but against what they *are doing*? This may not be an impossible position to adopt on a logical level (it is somewhat like saying you are against the sin, not the sinner), but it is a politically vulnerable stance nonetheless. Funding the war(s) is justified automatically from the "support the troops" frame unless and until "victory" can be declared. (There can be no end to a war against a tactic such as terrorism, because you cannot eliminate a tactic anymore than you can eliminate verbs from language.) Opposing the war effectively means that you have to reject the frameworks of "support the troops" and "War on Terror" and substitute other frames such as "unjust wars" and "war *of* terror."

Frames are so powerful that every single public officeholder in the country could be from the Socialist Party, USA, but if the dominant frame for public policy on social problems were conservative, the socialists in office would be hemmed in by the constraints that those frames dictated and be unable to implement a socialist public policy. To put this succinctly: those whose frame dominates, govern.

The Sixties' Crime Issue and the War Over Crime

Goldwater is commonly credited with being the first and most notable person to characterize the widespread and growing social protest of the Sixties as no better than street crime. He was, however, actually echoing an idea that first appeared in comments by the FBI and the conservative newsweekly *US News and World Report*. Injecting a major frame into the public arena does not generally occur by individuals operating on their own. Frames are usually the product of a group or groups acting in concert. Conservatives were collectively trying to change the political balance of forces by reframing the public discourse.

On June 29, 1964, two weeks before Goldwater's nomination speech, *US News and World Report* editorialized that the country was in the midst of a "crime wave of unprecedented proportions," and suggested that much of the blame could be attributed to street demonstrations and the actions of certain civil rights leaders. The editorial read in part:

> Crime in the United States jumped 19 per cent during the first three months of this year, more than 2 ½ times as much as the increase reported a year ago, FBI Director J. Edgar Hoover said today . . . .
>
> We have . . . brushed aside something far more important than what is called 'the rights of the individual.' The key word really is 'protection'—**the right of society to take measures to protect itself**. In **this war within our gates—the war against crime**—the casualties are mounting each year. . . .
>
> We are debating . . . at the moment, whether **telephone lines should be tapped** and conversations recorded. **Theoretically, this is an intrusion upon privacy.** But if evidence is needed to convict persons suspected with good reason of having committed a crime involving human life, would not most people say that in this type of case certainly such a method of obtaining evidence would be justified?
>
> How long can society endure the **conditions of terror** which are imposed upon it—when people fear to venture out on the streets at night . . . ?[32] [Emphasis added.]

The battle in the courts and in the streets in the 1960s over what *US News and World Report* Editor David Lawrence calls the "rights of

---

32   David Lawrence, "The War Against Crime," *U.S. News and World Report*, June 29, 1964, 112.

the individual" was actually over whether the rights of groups (such as African-Americans and women) should be upheld against systematic group discrimination by the society. The dichotomy of "individual rights" versus "society's rights" is thus a distortion of the terms at issue. In Lawrence's remarks we can see many of the essential elements of the subsequent "War on Terror" being previewed: crime = terror and the terror threat is growing; it is within our "gates"; intrusions upon rights—"theoretical," he says, and therefore, he implies, not real—must give way for the sake of security.

Three months after this *U.S. News and World Report* editorial, in a report released in September of 1964, the FBI stated that the 1964 summer youth riots demonstrated an increasing collapse in respect for law and the rights of others.[33]

Goldwater, in other words, was echoing an argument that had been and was being made by a gathering number of conservative voices.

The comparatively liberal newsmagazine *Newsweek* did not blame the protesters for rising crime, as did *U.S. News and World Report*, the FBI, and Goldwater, but it did argue that social protest was provoking rising crime *concerns* among the public. The public, in other words, according to *Newsweek*, linked crime with protest. In its October 19, 1964, issue, surveying the last few weeks before the November election contest between Goldwater and Lyndon Johnson, *Newsweek* asserted that the "safety-in-the-streets" issue's real "potency could be its close association with civil rights in the minds of many voters . . . ."[34]

Echoing this view, Cronin, Cronin and Milakovich[35] argue that social upheaval, and riots in particular, produced heightened crime fears among whites." Cronin, Cronin and Milakovich state as their evidence for this claim that a "Gallup poll taken shortly before the election showed that popular sentiment [on civil rights and crime's connection] more closely resembled Goldwater's campaign statements than Johnson's." [36] Cronin, Cronin and Milakovich do not specify which Gallup poll they are referring to. Reproduced below in Table 1, however, are the results for the relevant categories from Gallup's 1964 MIP polls:

---

33   Cronin, Cronin and Milakovich, 1981:14.

34   "The Curious Campaign—Point by Point," *Newsweek*, October 19, 1964, 27-28.

35   Cronin, Cronin and Milakovich, 1981:12.

36   Cronin, Cronin and Milakovich, 1981:23

Table 1: 1964 Polls   *Source: Gallup*

Sampling Dates— Most Important Problem in Nation	Crime	Juvenile Delinquency	Civil Rights, Integration, Racial Discrimination (no reference to Demos or Riots)	Civil Rights. Demos, Negro Riots, Violence, Lawlessness connected w/ them
3/27-4/2/64	0%	1%	34%	0%
4/24-29/64	0	2	42	0
6/25-30/64	0	1	47	0
7/23-28/64	<.5	<.5	58	2
8/6-11/64	1	<.5	36	2
8/27-9/1/64	<.5	1	46	2
9/18-23/64	<.5	1	34	<.5
10/8-13/64	1	1	24	1

"Crime" and "Juvenile Delinquency," as Table 1 shows, scarcely registered in the 1964 polls. In contrast, "Civil rights, Integration, Racial discrimination (no reference to demonstrations or riots)," an indicator of those who presumably thought that civil rights was the central issue, drew numbers ranging from twenty-four percent to fifty-eight percent, the fifty-eight percent registered in July 1964.

In the poll that preceded Goldwater's nomination, "crime" registered at zero percent and "juvenile delinquency" at one percent, and in the poll that began a week after his nomination in July, "crime" ticked up from zero to less than one-half of one percent, and "juvenile delinquency" fell from one percent to less than one-half of one percent. Given the usual convention and post-convention "bump" that major party nominees and parties receive and the widespread attention that Goldwater's comments about "crime in the streets" received (along with supportive commentary in various major media), these poll results are startling.

If social protest, riots, and racial challenge were intimately intertwined in the public's mind, then we should expect that as riots increased in number and ferocity after 1964, crime concerns should have also risen. Between 1965 and 1969, however, polls indicated that few among the public were linking civil protest to crime. These data directly contradict the mass media and public officials' representations—and the subsequent conventional and scholarly wisdom—that the public was aroused about crime because of the civil protests.

At least 257 riots broke out in 1967[37] and preceding that, in 1965, the famous Los Angeles Watts Rebellion emblazoned itself in history and in headlines across the country. Despite this, poll-measured concerns for "crime and juvenile delinquency" between 1965-1967 remained low, ranging from one to four percent from 1965-1967.

White antipathy to the riots grew overall in the Sixties, but crime concerns and riots did not move together. Why did the polls not register elevated crime concerns after riots? A complete and rigorous answer to this question is beyond the scope of this chapter, but a suggestive hypothesis can be drawn based on the white reaction to the 1965 Watts Rebellion.

Watts 1965

The dominant analysis of racial attitudes in the Sixties holds that white Americans recoiled from black Americans' demands for equality as those demands became more insistent and militant. Collective memory holds that this was particularly true of the Watts Rebellion of 1965.[38] This dominant view holds out little hope that racial equity can ever be achieved because it posits that the more the privileges of white Americans are curtailed, the more they will oppose this. Without minimizing the hold that racism can exert, the historical record—the fact that white racism is neither as pervasive nor as strong as it was prior to the civil rights movement—indicates that racial attitudes can and do change.

There are two other problems with the dominant analysis. First, it overlooks the fact that white Americans are a variegated group in terms of their attitudes. There is no singular, dominant stance among all white Americans with respect to race. Certainly the history of white-skin privilege has had and continues to have an effect on white Americans as a whole. There is a taken-for-granted dimension to white-skin privilege among those it favors that makes it more difficult for whites than ethnic or racial minorities to see white racism. But to posit a more or less uniform perspective is injudicious analytically.

37 Jane A Baskin, Joyce Hartweg, Ralph Lewis and Lester McCullough, Jr., *Race Related Civil Disorders: 1967–1969* (Waltham, MA: Lemberg Center for the Study of Violence, Brandeis University, 1971).

38 It was dubbed a "rebellion" by many because it was so clearly more than an average riot.

Second, the character of a racial or ethnic group's reaction to its situation relative to other racial or ethnic groups is crisscrossed by class and other statuses, roles, life experiences, and political dispositions. Reactions by any group to other groups' actions and demands are more contingent than inevitable in the sense that political leadership—the stance that political leadership takes on a given question or set of questions—can be and usually is decisive. Put another way and with greater specificity, what is seen as the majority position matters much more than what actually is the majority position. Majority views do not hold sway as much as does the dominant presentation of what the majority view supposedly is—at least in a putative democracy where rule by the majority is the dominant shibboleth.

According to a survey (conducted by Richard Morris and Vincent Jeffries between November 18, 1965 and February 5, 1966) cited by Gerald Horne,[39] of six hundred whites in six selected Los Angeles communities that were chosen for their socioeconomic variety and range of racial integration, respondents showed a surprising degree of sympathy for the riot. Fifty-four percent of those interviewed expressed sympathy for the riot compared to forty-two percent who were antagonistic. Table 2 displays white responses to a question asking their views about the specific causes for the riot.

Reasons given for the riots are summarized as follows:

Table 2: Causes of the Watts Riot—White Respondents

Sympathetic	%	Situational	%	Unsympathetic	%
Unfair treatment	15%	Heat, Frye arrest, etc.	23%	Agitators & outsiders	14%
History of injustice	11%			Bad elements in community (troublemakers, gangs, hoodlums, delinquents, etc.)	12%
Police brutality	02%				
Just cause	28%	Situational	23%	Hostile to riot	26%

---

39   Gerald Horne, *Fire This Time: The Watts Uprising and the 1960s* (Charlottesville, VI: University of Virginia Press, 1995), 264.

As Elizabeth Noelle-Neumann points out in her study of a phenomenon she labeled the "spiral of silence," [40] people who think their opinions are in the minority will tend to silence themselves, and vice versa. If you want to have your opinion carry the day, creating the impression (even if it is false) that your opinion is the dominant one helps to make it the dominant one; or, at least, it creates a reasonable facsimile of the majority sentiment, albeit a fragile facsimile. The question before Los Angeles and the nation then was which reaction to the Watts Rebellion would come to be seen as the dominant one.

Horne observes that the widely propagated notion of a white backlash "helped to create a momentum of its own and a self-fulfilling prophecy. Though certain studies showed substantial sympathy across racial lines for the grievances of South LA, this was not the message being broadcast by acolytes of the right." [41] Right-wing radio shows, ubiquitous and dominant in the US today, were building a listenership in southern California, and helped push whites to the political Right.

The evidence from polling data about the Watts Rebellion indicates a highly divided reaction by whites, with the majority sentiment actually sympathetic to black demands. This is diametrically at odds with the dominant interpretation of the Watts Rebellion's impact on white attitudes. Extrapolating from my analysis of the data concerning Watts, I would hypothesize that the reason why riots in general did not stoke crime concerns in the polls was because, at least in part, whites were politically divided in their reactions to the riots. Whites were divided in their reaction in part because they were not uniformly hostile to black demands for equality. But it was also a fact that in the Sixties there was a powerful political "pole" countervailing the force exerted by conservative elites; this took the form of social insurgencies and the civil rights movement in particular. I discuss this factor more in the last section of the chapter.

White reaction to the Watts Rebellion (and by extension to the rest of the Sixties' rebellions) was contingent and divided. There was, in other words, no uniform white response. Summations and interpretations of the rebellions were contested. The presence of powerful and influential social movements from below affected the degree to which the dominant discourse—the discourse originating from elites—was adopted. The MIP polls record is consistent with this view. Opinion-makers, politicians, and

---

40   Elizabeth Noelle-Neumann, *The Spiral of Silence: Public Opinion—Our Social Skin* (Chicago: University of Chicago Press, 1993).

41   Ibid., 281

media outlets such as right-wing radio talk shows, played key roles in shaping and creating the elite discourse.

This perspective is, of course, quite different from the conventional one where the views of the public are believed to be the source of public policies.

1967 and After

The MIP polls following the famous 1967 Detroit riots (riots that led to tanks being dispatched down the city's streets) further illustrate respondents' abilities to distinguish crime from riots. In an August 3-8, 1967, Gallup poll taken in the immediate wake of the July 21-August 1, 1967, Detroit riots, only two percent cited crime and juvenile delinquency as their chief concerns. By contrast, thirty-five percent cited "Racial strife—arson, looting, etc." as their chief concerns. While the 1967 summer riots thus produced a large negative response in the August 3-8, 1967, poll, those polled distinguished riots from crime per se.

Respondents were allowed to choose more than one item as their top concern in the MIP polls and the tiny number citing "crime" contradicts the belief that "Racial strife—arson, looting, riots, etc." was chosen as a simple substitute for "crime." Had respondents wanted to cite "crime" as a major concern they were free to do so, and we might expect a much larger number than the two percent who did.

A bifurcated reaction was evident between the public and media/political elites after the 1967 summer riots. On the one hand, polls revealed little mass public interest in the crime issue. Gallup's August 3-8, 1967, poll showed only two percent citing "crime and juvenile delinquency," and four percent in its October 27-November 1, 1967, poll. These polls received no media attention. "Law and order," on the other hand, was the frequent topic in newspapers, on conservative talk shows, and among politicians. In October 1967, *New York Times'* columnist Tom Wicker, a liberal, predicted that "law and order" would become one of the 1968 presidential campaign's major issues.

1968: Elections and the Crime Issue

The two most prominently publicized polls in major media that supposedly showed crime to be Americans' foremost domestic concern were Gallup's May 2-7, 1968, and June 26-July 1, 1968, polls. These polls showed that fifteen and twenty-nine percent of the public respectively considered "lawlessness" the top US domestic problem.[42] Gallup created a category for these polls that they dubbed "Crime and Lawlessness (including riots, looting and juvenile delinquency)." Gallup had never used this category previously, nor have they used it since. (See Table 3.)

Table 3: Crime as the Nation's Most Important Problem 1967-1969

Date	% citing Crime/J.D.	Date	% citing Crime/J.D.
1/26-31/67	2	8/7-12/68	9
8/3-8/67	2	9/1/68	12
10/27-11/1/67	4	9/26-10/1/68	11
1/4-9/68	6	10/17-22/68	12
5/2-7/68	[15]	1/1-6/69	6
6/26-7/1/68	[29]	5/22-27/69	2
7/18-23/68	11		

[ ] indicates a conflated category: "Crime and Lawlessness (including riots, looting and juvenile delinquency)."

By combining several different items into a category that was created after the fact, Gallup created the impression that crime concerns were much higher than they actually were. Other polls publicized in the remainder of 1968 also either conflated categories—perpetuating the impression of more robust crime concerns than were actually justified by the data—or particular polls were selectively presented in a manner that generated the same impression. The polls not publicized in 1968 actually revealed crime concerns were *dropping*.

For example, Gallup's next poll, of July 18-23, 1968, recorded eleven percent citing "Crime (general), no references to juvenile delinquency, lack of respect for law and order," plus "Juvenile Delinquency—Hippies." This poll, therefore, actually recorded a fall in concerns about crime—at least as compared to the May and June 1968 conflated polls. Media did not publicize the July 18-23, 1968, poll nor did Gallup itself.

In its next poll, taken between August 7-12, 1968, Gallup found nine percent cited "Crime (looting and lawlessness)" as their first choice, down further from the results for the same choice in its July 1968

---

42   "52% In Poll Cite War As Top Issue," *The New York Times*, August 4, 1968, 45.

sampling. This was particularly low given the fact that the Republican Party convention had just nominated—on August 1, 1968—Nixon and Agnew on an explicit "law and order" platform. In addition, two major riots had just occurred—one in Cleveland between July 23-26, 1968, and one in Miami on August 7, 1968—the same day Gallup began its August 1968 sampling.

This fall in crime concerns was not reported in media either. Instead, Gallup reported erroneously that its August 1968 poll showed that twenty-one percent of respondents named "crime (including looting, riots)" as their top choice. This figure of twenty-one percent was in reality nine percent. *The New York Times* reported Gallup's inflated twenty-one percent figure in their September 8, 1968 issue, noting that "crime and lawlessness" were among the top four major worries of the electorate.[43] This was true but misleading since the Vietnam War (at forty-seven percent) and Civil Rights (at twenty percent) outdrew crime (at eight percent) and riots (at twelve percent) by a wide margin.

When disaggregated from disparate items and reported as actually answered in the poll, the "crime" figure in August 1968's polls is only nine percent vs. the twenty-one percent reported as "crime (including looting, riots)." Similarly, the figure for "crime and juvenile delinquency" as answered was six percent in the January 1, 1969 poll as opposed to the seventeen percent that Gallup reported as "crime and lawlessness (including looting, riots and juvenile delinquency)."

Gallup also administered three polls in the heat of the presidential campaign on September 1, 1968; September 26-October 1, 1968; and October 17-22, 1968. Media did not publicize these polls nor did Gallup itself. The polls recorded elevated crime and riot concerns: twelve percent (crime) and fourteen percent (riots); eleven and twelve percent; and twelve and twelve percent, respectively. While elevated, they were not comparable to the recorded concerns over the Vietnam War that were running between forty and forty-seven percent in the same polls. These data are surprising in light of the hundreds of explosive and destructive riots throughout the Sixties era, and the central status given the law and order issue during the 1968 presidential campaign.

The New York Times, despite its liberal editorial policy, publicized the following polls and did not report the fact that Gallup's September and October 1968 polls showed unimpressive crime concern levels:

---

43   "Poll Finds Most View G.O.P. As Better Able to Handle Issues," *The New York Times*, September 8, 1967, 77.

- A September 1968 Louis Harris poll that reportedly found eighty-one percent of the voters believing that "law and order has broken down."[44]

- A September 1968 Harris survey showing Nixon had a spread of twelve percentage points over Humphrey on the law and order issue.[45]

- A *New York Times* survey showing that the law and order issue was the largest single issue turning voters to Nixon.[46]

- A Gallup poll that found that people's fear of using the streets in their own communities at night strengthens the law and order issue.[47]

- A Harris survey showing fifty-two percent of blacks saying that police brutality is the major cause of the breakdown of law and order (with ten percent of whites agreeing).[48]

In sum then, with the exception of this last item of October 16, 1968, the polls that the *Times* selected to feature all conveyed the impression that the "law and order" issue was of paramount importance to the electorate and that the electorate was in a "law and order" mood.

The September 1968 Harris Poll

The Harris poll showing eighty-one percent of respondents agreeing that "law and order have broken down," published in the September 9, 1968, issue of the *New York Post* and picked up by *The New York Times* the next

---

44 "81% In a Poll See Law Breakdown," *The New York Times*, September 10, 1968, 31.

45 "Poll Finds Nixon Holds Lead on Issue of 'Law and Order,' *The New York Times*, September 13, 1968, 52.

46 Warren Weaver, Jr., "Six Lean to Humphrey, With Six Indefinite in Times Survey: Study Finds Nixon Leading in 30 States and Wallace in Eight," *The New York Times*, September 15, 1968, 78.

47 "Gallup Poll Finds Nixon is Maintaining Large Lead," *The New York Times*, October 10, 1968, 51.

48 "Poll Finds 83% of Negroes Plan to Vote for Humphrey," *The New York Times*, October 16, 1968, 26.

day[49] is very revealing. It is probably the most outstanding example of pollster misbehavior on the crime issue in the Sixties.

The *New York Post*'s headline for the piece was "'Law & Order' Top Issue Next to the War: Harris." The story began: "Next to ending the war in Vietnam, the most urgent demand of American voters in this election season is to bring back a sense of 'law and order.' By 81 to 14 per cent, a heavy majority of the public believes law and order has broken down in this country."

On August 24, 1968, 1,481 voters were asked a series of questions beginning with, "I want to ask you about some things which some people think **have been causes of the breakdown of law and order** in this country. For each, **tell me if you feel it is a major cause of a breakdown of law and order, a minor cause, or hardly a cause at all.**" [Emphasis added.]

They began by asking respondents a series of questions structured as "Many people say X has happened. Which of the following reasons would you say are responsible for causing X to happen?" Harris next asked respondents a series of questions, one of which was: "Do you think that X has happened?" In other words, the first series of questions *assume* the answer to a question asked later. Given this structure and sequence of questions, it is not surprising that eighty-one percent of respondents should then agree that "X has happened."

In summary, (a) pollsters manipulated the results of some of their surveys (either in the way in which they framed their questions, or in the way they reported the results); (b) conservative politicians, the FBI, and major media linked protest with crime; and (c) media reported the polls selectively in a manner that fostered the impression that crime was uppermost in the public's mind.

Crime concerns in the US did not rise higher than twelve percent in the Sixties. This fact does not obviate the observed fact that many Americans associate blacks with crime.[50] But the data from the MIP polls indicate that most Americans distinguished crime per se from racial challenge. Respondents who expressed opposition to racial challenge did so, but they did not also name crime in significant numbers as their choice for the nation's top problem.

Neither riots nor the rising index crime rate directly influenced the poll results with respect to crime concerns per se. The interpretation that came to be understood as dominant was both contingent on and central

---

49 "81% In a Poll See Law Breakdown," *The New York Times*, September 10, 1968, 31.

50 See, for example, Wesley Skogan, "Crime and the Racial Fears of White Americans." *Annals of the American Academy of Political and Social Science*, 539 (1995): 59-71.

to the course of public policy making. Were these riots a product of the "tangle of pathology" of disrupted black family structures?[51] Were the riots to be understood as a form of righteous rebellion? Certain state actors, major media outlets, and pollsters played critical roles in the process of generating the elite interpretation.

As Steven Spitzer points out, from the perspective of at least some social elites, street crime generates victims who are mainly members of an expendable class.[52] Social protest, on the other hand, represents "social dynamite" and is therefore much more threatening than ordinary street crime; it could lead to the system's demise. The conflating of riots and social protest with crime was, in short, an elite-sponsored social construction. Michigan Senator Robert Griffin, for example, equated the two in full in the June 30, 1972, issue of *Life* magazine, calling the then-current crime wave "a riot in slow motion."[53]

It is, of course, much easier to counter racial challenge by presenting one's self as "anti-crime" instead of as "anti-civil rights."[54] The FBI, *U.S. News and World Report*, Goldwater, and subsequently Nixon/Agnew, did exactly this, invoking the race card by playing the crime card. John Ehrlichman, Nixon's Special Counsel, admitted to this when he wrote about Nixon's 1968 campaign strategy: "We'll go after the racists. That subliminal appeal to the anti-African-American voter was always present in Nixon's statements and speeches."[55]

Polls in the Sixties and the representations of those polls were part of the production of the elite discourse. Interestingly, at times poll results were at variance with the dominant discourse. The dominant discourse,

---

51   *The Negro Family: The Case for National Action,* written by Daniel Patrick Moynihan, then Assistant Secretary of Labor, was released in August 1965. In it Moynihan, a liberal, famously advanced the view that one of slavery's legacies was the broken black family. Moynihan linked this to the persistence of female-headed black families and a consequent higher delinquency and crime rate among blacks. His argument about matriarchal-headed families being at the root of the problem and "tangle of pathology" resulting from it lent itself to adoption by right-wing and as well as mainstream voices open to explaining the riots as due to family structure failures.

52   Steven Spitzer, "Towards a Marxian Theory of Deviance," *Social Problems* 22 (1975): 638-651.

53   Tom Flaherty, "A Plan to Cut Crime," *Life,* June 30, 1972, 52.

54   See Thomas and Mary Edsall, Edsall, *Chain Reaction: The Impact of Race, Rights and Taxes on American Politics* (New York: W.W. Norton, 1991.)

55   John Ehrlichman, *Witness to Power: The Nixon Years* (New York: Simon & Schuster, 1970), 233.

in other words, did not fully replicate itself in the poll results.[56] To resolve that disjuncture—that is, to make the poll results "look like" the dominant discourse—polls have sometimes been selectively reported, and in certain instances erroneously reported, represented, or even their existence and results made up. This is as one might expect: polls, after all, make up the key part of the rationale given for public policy shifts in contemporary times.

On one level, the public relies very heavily upon the framing present in major media, on public officials' pronouncements, on well-known think tank "experts," and on pundits. Because the public relies so much upon these groups to tell them what just happened and what their reaction should be to it, the public discourse about any given issue is heavily colored by, and almost entirely, or even entirely, determined by these elite elements.

On another level, my data show that elite discourse does not entirely determine public views. The two are not fully joined and in sync. A latent public opinion exists that is almost always passed over and ignored or actively blocked from full expression by officialdom and major media. In the first year of President Obama's term, for example, a majority wanted investigations into the Bush White House's torture policies. Pundits and public officials, however, framed the issue of accountability as one of unacceptable partisanship, with many characterizing upholding the law, even those who might otherwise have thought it a good idea, as a "witch hunt."

A Southern Strategy?

On one level, the Republican Party was obviously implementing its so-called Southern strategy in the Sixties era to steal away the southern white voters from the Democrats by being boosters of the "law 'n order" issue.[57] They have been very successful in this effort. But the Southern strategy hypothesis does not go far enough. It does not explain why the Democratic Party ended up adopting the interpretive frame being pushed by the Republican Party. Why, given the polling data, did the Democrats bow to the Republican Party's misrepresentations about the level of public concern about crime?

---

56 See, for example, Anson Shupe and William A. Stacey, "Born Again Politics and the Moral Majority: What Social Surveys Really Show," *Studies in American Religion*, 5 (New York: Edwin Mellen Press, 1982).

57 Katherine Beckett and Theodore Sasson, *The Politics of Injustice: Crime and Punishment in America* (Thousand Oaks, CA: Pine Forge Press, 2000.)

A common misunderstanding about the dynamics at work between the Republicans and the Democrats is that they may best be understood by their mutual desire to defeat each other's party in elections. Winning and holding office are believed, according to this view, to be the primary motivations for both parties. While the Republican Party and the Democratic Party are certainly in partisan rivalry with each other, there are other factors at work as well. What the Republican Party and the Democrats share is their position as political elites. Anything that jeopardizes the Republican Party and the Democratic Party's mutual status organizationally and institutionally, anything that could lead to social insurgency upsetting and possibly even toppling their governing status, is to be avoided at all costs.[58] This is only what we might expect. Expecting them to act differently is unrealistic. Political parties are bureaucracies. Bureaucracies by their nature seek to maintain and expand their power and shield their decision-making from public scrutiny. Moreover, these are the two major parties of an empire.

In the 1960s, liberal elites argued that concessions (e.g., the War on Poverty) needed to be made to the insurgents lest a conflagration result. Conservatives argued that concessions would only fuel the fires of insurgency and a crackdown was what was needed. The Sixties insurgency breached the public agenda ordinarily generated by elites.[59] A society-wide debate raged over whether the key social problem was crime or social injustice. The crime issue, as authored initially by conservative elites in the Sixties, was challenged largely successfully by social movement activists who argued forcefully that social injustice, not crime, was the central social problem of the day.

This is one of the key reasons—probably by far the most important reason—that the public did not adopt the elite discourse that crime and social protest were one and the same. The Sixties' insurgencies created significant splits—for a short time—within elite ranks. The insurgencies' influence prevented crime from emerging at the top of the MIP polls during the Sixties, because the public was split in its views and its loyalties, with the majority faction favoring the insurgencies.

---

58 See Dennis Loo, "Never Elected, Not Once: the Immaculate Deception and the Road Ahead," in *Impeach the President: the Case Against Bush and Cheney*, ed. Dennis Loo and Peter Phillips (New York: Seven Stories Press, 2006).

59 David L. Paletz and Robert M. Entman, *Media, Power, Politics* (New York: The Free Press, 1981); John R, Zaller, *The Nature and Origins of Mass Opinion* (Cambridge: Cambridge University Press, 1992).

Implications and Conclusions

The data adduced and referred to here underscore the crime issue's socially constructed nature, demonstrating that the collective memory about the public's focus on the Sixties' crime issue is inaccurate. The origins of that collective memory can be attributed to the collective efforts of conservative public officials, mass media, pollsters, and conservative intellectuals such as James Q. Wilson. If we use the customary definition for a moral panic that involves the public being drawn into the panic, a moral panic around crime did not occur in the Sixties. Instead, the false impression of a panic was created.

The Sixties' insurgencies prevented the crime issue from becoming the number one domestic problem. Something similar could occur if and when a new social movement of sufficient force and influence develops and challenges the elite consensus. In that eventuality, a very fluid situation, pregnant with possibilities, would ensue. Contrary to the conventional view that the "fear of crime" exists as a kind of inevitable social fact, "crime" would then take its place among other issues that could rise or fall in prominence, depending upon the relative strength and influence of different political forces or movements.

This holds equally true of the "War on Terror" trope today. The fear of terrorist attacks upon the US is not something that exists as some kind of independent, autonomous force that predetermines how the public and public officials are going to behave. Rather, this issue is contingent on, and its power over the polity depends upon, the presence or absence and the strength of social movements that challenge the underlying logic of the "War on Terror" as it is portrayed and propagated by government, media, and interest groups.

What matters in public policy is not what the mass sentiment is. What matters is what is represented as the mass sentiment. If a public policy is not successfully marketed as the mass sentiment, then it loses any legitimacy in a nation that touts itself as democratic and based on the will of the people.

The conflation of protest and crime, as I showed in this chapter, did not actually ever even come close to a widespread sentiment. This fact, however, did not stop those who adopted and promoted the false idea that the American public in its majority was up in arms about crime and protest. It did not stop pollsters from presenting this false picture in selected polls, selectively constructed and selectively publicized. It did not stop media from making such a distorted and fundamentally false representation.

114

Neoconservatives and Neoliberals

Neoconservatives are neoliberalism's cutting edge political representatives—its most outspoken, aggressive and thoroughgoing exponents. The Democrats of today are also neoliberals, but their social base requires that they at least rhetorically support an income distribution less skewed than what neoconservatives and the GOP more generally desire.

The Bush/Cheney White House represented the triumphal installation of neocons in the land's highest offices, albeit through elections fraud. They used this power to great effect, not only spearheading unprecedented claims for unfettered executive power, but also burrowing deep into the federal, state, and local bureaucracies, leaving a legacy that their successors will have a hard time eliminating, even assuming that they were so inclined—an inclination that Obama, a centrist Democrat, has not demonstrated. Indeed, Obama has extended and deepened the trajectory begun under Reagan and continued since.

If the dominant discourse does not truly reflect mass sentiment, and a latent public opinion does exist, of what use is that latent public opinion? That is a major theme of the succeeding chapters of this book.

CHAPTER THREE

Courting Catastrophe and Sabotaging Everyday Security: Neoliberalism's Dangerous Dance

[T]he neo-conservative ideologues, who should really be called neo-liberal ideologues, are in the driver's seat at the Pentagon, the intelligence agencies and the Congress. Their agenda is global, not national, and their objective is monopoly, not free markets. This is an all-or-nothing let's-roll-the-dice group of thinkers who are nothing if not bold.

CHRIS SANDERS, 2004[1]

The likeliest and most dangerous future shocks will be unconventional... Their origin is most likely to be in irregular, catastrophic, and hybrid threats of 'purpose' (emerging from hostile design) or threats of 'context' (emerging in the absence of hostile purpose or design). Of the two, the latter is both the least understood and the most dangerous.

NATHAN FRIER, 2008[2]

---

1   Chris Sanders, "Sanders Research Associates Special Report: The US Trade Deficit," *Defence and the National Interest*, d-n-i.net, August 20, 2004, http://www.d-n-i.net/fcs/comments/c522.htm, accessed November 25, 2009.

2   Nathan Freier, "Known Unknowns: Unconventional 'Strategic Shocks' in Defense Strategy Development" (Strategic Studies Institute, US Army War College, November 2008), vii.

Finance capital does not want liberty, it wants domination.

RUDOLF HILFERDING[3]

The ocean will take care of this on its own... it's natural. It's as natural as the ocean water is.

RUSH LIMBAUGH on the BP Oil Disaster[4]

Neoliberalism's proponents' audacious agenda of unrestrained power coexists with their startling indifference to their policies' damage to people and to the planet.[5] This adds up to a devastating and historically unprecedented combination. The dangers inherent in their high-stakes gamble, a gamble they have drawn the whole world involuntarily into, guarantees not prosperity for everyone, but insecurity for all. For neoliberalism not only produces increasing endemic insecurity—troubles at the level of day-to-day life—but it also leads inexorably to episodic disasters on a regional and world scale. Perversely, the more calamities the neoliberals provoke, the more they grandstand amidst the rubble of those catastrophes, demanding even more power in their hands.

The neoliberal state's supplanting of the welfare state, for this reason, represents the single most consequential fact of our time.[6] Since states function—and continue to function—as the primary means by which society's resources are allocated within a country, the struggle over who holds state power, how that power is exercised, and in whose interests, has been the pivotal struggle for humanity for centuries. The neoliberal agenda, in both its GOP and Democratic incarnations, requires that neoliberals take

---

3   Lenin citing Hilferding in Vladimir Lenin, "Imperialism: the Highest Stage of Capitalism," in *Essential Works of Lenin*, ed. Henry Christman (New York: Dover Books, 1966), 234.

4   Russell Goldman, "Limbaugh, Environmentalists Square Off on Who Is to Blame for Oil Leak," ABCNews.go.com, May 3, 2010, http://abcnews.go.com/Technology/limbaugh-environmentalists-square-off-blame-oil-leak/story?id=10542582, accessed February 18, 2011. Who says oil and water do not mix?

5   Naomi Klein chronicles the instigation and use of disasters by the neoliberals in her book, *The Shock Doctrine: The Rise of Disaster Capitalism* (New York: Metropolitan Books, 2007).

6   The welfare state (aka the Keynesian Welfare State) is known as the New Deal in the US.

hold of and relentlessly wield state power to carry out the neoliberal vision, irrespective of any of the GOP's antigovernment rhetoric. Far from becoming less relevant, the state continues to be an arena of extremely sharp contention and a leading actor in the unfolding drama.

Much mystification and misinformation surrounds the character of politics, the making of public policy, and the nature and role of state power. I begin here then with a brief but concentrated discussion of those matters. Effecting real changes means that we must cut through the mist of misrepresentations to uncover political authority's essential elements.

The Nature of State Power: the Role of Force and the Matter of Legitimacy

Political authority, as the sociologist Max Weber put it, is the ability to get people to do what you want them to do, even when they do not want to do it. The only way to assure compliance from those who cannot be persuaded and who resist is to use force. If you do not have the ability to overcome resistance, then you lack political authority. Even in situations where force is not employed and is not necessary as in, for instance, clubs or associations, when there is not consensus, even if the majority rules, someone still has to move the activity and agenda forward. Someone has to make an executive decision. If no one does, then all activity grinds to a halt. When the stakes are as high as those in a nation-state, all the more reason why any government, so long as governments exist, has to use coercion as part of its arsenal to exercise political authority.[7]

Contrary to most conventional notions, therefore, the hard nucleus of state power is coercion, not consent of the governed. When people refuse to pay their taxes and make it clear that they will not ever pay them, the Internal Revenue Service comes knocking on their doors, backed by guns. They present the recalcitrants with a choice: pay or be arrested or die.

---

7   As long as groups exist, authority must be exercised within them. Groups are based upon, and can only continue through, the observance of mutual obligations; otherwise they could not function effectively as groups but would merely be disconnected individuals who could not thrive or survive for long. Since at any given point in time a single plan of action must coordinate a group's activities or else that group ceases to be a group, authority is inevitably exercised by that dominant plan (as directed by a dominant individual or individuals), and other plans and ideas are necessarily overruled. Those who refuse to adopt the group's plans must be compelled to do so if they are to remain within the group's sphere, and if the group's integrity as a group is to be maintained.

Another example of the state power of coercion occurred in 2000 in Miami. Miami's anti-Castro Cuban émigré community refused to allow Elian Gonzalez to return to his father (his sole surviving parent) in Cuba; so, the US government, having failed to persuade Elian's US relatives to give him up, finally came to their home and, bearing guns, extracted Elian.

On a grander scale, when a government finds itself in serious trouble with people who are demanding that the government resign, the state will bring out rifles and tanks and reasserts its authority; this is a strategy that works as long as the military remains loyal to that government. Prior to that point, states routinely—daily, hourly, and minute by minute—deploy force to lesser degrees through the use of police and other agents of social control; they also fully utilize the organs of public opinion-making in order to prevent matters from reaching a juncture where the populace is roiled into a general state of upheaval. When the state's ordinary and quotidian efforts fail, however, then the tanks roll out.

The state's use of force is not unique. The ability to impose one's will through force operates in many well-known ways on the interpersonal level as well. Robbers use a gun or other weapon, and a rapist gets what he wants through violence and the threat of more violence if his victim does not comply. The criminal underworld famously employs lavish amounts of force, intimidation, and terror. The robber, the rapist, the mafia, and the state thus share in common the fact that they use force. The difference between a state and other individuals or groups is that, as Weber put it, a state is a state because it possesses a monopoly over the means of legitimate violence. Notably, Weber does not describe a state as a body of officials who draw their power from the consent of the governed. Consent applies to his definition of a state only to the degree to which most people continue to see the state's coercive actions as legitimate. The US form of government today represents no exception to this rule.

A combination of two elements makes governmental force putatively legitimate. First, government actions are legitimate because most people see them as legitimate. Many people consider the armed forces' actions in waging war as legitimate because their country's military is doing it. Even if the war that military is waging is based on lies, the fact that it is "our" military doing it and that they are now committed to a war theatre and find themselves in "harm's way" makes that war reasonable—or at least tolerable—in many people's eyes, unless the war goes badly or drags on too long. People think (when the war is not going badly) that the government must have a good reason to do what it is doing. These are our sons, daughters, and spouses, and this is our government, they think. The government would not expend such gigantic sums, cause such catastrophic destruction, and kill people on both sides without reason. It would be unthinkable for an individual to act this way and thus it is very hard to believe that a state would knowingly do such terrible things on such a grand scale without a just cause. Even some of those who initially opposed the war can, over time, come to condone it and to believe that the military can, due to its power, rectify at least some of the damage for which it is itself responsible.

The second factor that renders governmental violence legitimate grows out of the laws that govern governmental agencies and governmental actors. State force is legitimate, in other words, *de jure*. There are rules designed to govern what government agents do and provisions in the law for handling those who abuse their authority. The very presence of those laws makes governmental force acceptable in most people's eyes, even if those rules of conduct are honored more in the breach. In a country such as the US (an example of what Weber called a rational-legal state), the existence and representation of objective rules and regulations governing the government's actions, and the codified set of procedures by which someone becomes a member of the government (through election, appointment, or credential) provide the imprimatur of legitimacy to the state's actions. Leaders are voted into office (or appointed by those who were elected) and are there—supposedly at least—to represent the people, so their actions are widely seen as legitimate almost by definition, even by those who strongly disagree with those leaders' actions. "The people have spoken and we have to accept the decisions of their elected representatives, whether we agree with those policies or not." (This applies as well to those upon whom political power is conferred indirectly, such as the nine justices of the US Supreme Court who, in a split vote in 2000, handed the presidency to George W. Bush. They did this by halting the Florida vote recount which would have shown, had it been allowed to continue and as all subsequent analyses demonstrated, that by whatever criterion one applied to the vote count, Al Gore had won.)

As is probably evident from this brief discussion, the barriers facing those who want to contest a particular government's use of force are considerable. The state enjoys a number of advantages that allow it to carry out the use of force; there is a default presumption by many people in a society such as the US that whatever it is, if the government is doing it, then it must be necessary. Beyond this, of course, a government also dominates the organs of public opinion making and can and does use that power to defend its policies and practices. Stanley Milgram (whose famous "Milgram Experiment" serves as a warning that humans are capable of doing terrible things to each other if they are told to do so by authority, even if they themselves are not cruel) has written that the authority exercised by his experiment's men in gray coats and clipboards pale in comparison to the authority that governments and military leaders exercise.[8]

When and if, however, a government's use of force comes to be seen as illegitimate in the eyes of enough people, then the government itself is in grave trouble. As seen in microcosm in the Abu Ghraib torture scandal, the My Lai Massacre during the Vietnam War, and the ruthless beating of Rodney King by the Los Angeles Police, the state's use of widely abhorred violence can create a minor crisis of legitimacy for the state.[9] In each of these cases, high governmental officials argued that the incident was due to a few bad apples and that the uncovered actions were atypical of state actions. In most cases such as these in which state violence is revealed to be excessive and/or illegitimate, a few low-level officers are convicted and must bear the burden of guilt for higher-ups and for the state as a whole. Obviously, those people who identify the most with the victims of these state-sanctioned forms of violence—because they are from that same strata/group, because of their life experiences, and/or because of their political stances—are the least likely to accept these forms of state violence as legitimate. Indeed, among the groups of people most subordinated by the status quo, the fundamental character of state force carries not so much the air of legitimacy as the air of inevitability. When the inevitability of that force comes under question (due to events such as the shocking jury verdict exonerating the LAPD officers who were caught red-handed on tape beating Rodney King), then riots or something worse become a near certainty.

When especially treasured members of the people are killed by the state—for example, the four Kent State University students gunned down by the Ohio National Guard in 1970—the scope of disaffection for the state's actions broadens. When a government fails to act, resulting in the suffering and deaths of scores of citizens—as happened in 2005 when the victims of Hurricane Katrina were dramatically abandoned by the Bush White House, or when a government in the wake of an earthquake moves too slowly to rescue those buried under the rubble , for example, during the earthquake in Haiti in 2010—its legitimacy comes under sharp criticism.

The state enjoys wide latitude for its use of force. This latitude, however, has limits. Force permits a state to overcome resistance, but when it uses that force, it risks provoking retaliatory actions and/or resentment

---

8   Stanley Milgram, "The Perils of Obedience," *Harper's*, December 1973. 62-77.

9   The Vietnam War itself eventually provoked a much greater crisis of legitimacy for the US government.

by those being coerced, and it risks the disaffection of those who witness that coercion and view that force as unjust. In other words, the fact that a state has an immense arsenal of weapons to use does not settle the matter, because if a government comes to be seen as illegitimate, no amount of repressive violence by it will protect it from being overthrown. Legitimacy, in other words, is a fairly stable but elastic factor. Weber never addressed this elastic aspect of governmental legitimacy: the fact that governmental force is subject, under the right circumstances, to fundamental challenge. Those circumstances occur very infrequently in the advanced capitalist countries; whole generations can go by without their happening. But when the right circumstances do occur, and organizational and ideological leadership is present and sufficiently influential to fulfill the potential for a revolutionary change, all bets are off. While force is a state's argument of last resort, its ability to continue to use force and the amount of force it can use are determined by whether or not its use is seen as legitimate by most of the populace.

A dramatic example of this is the event that precipitated the 1905 Russian Revolution known as Bloody Sunday. On January 22, 1905, a priest named Georgii Gapon led a peaceful march of workers and their families to the Winter Palace of Tsar Nicholas II to petition the tsar for relief of their desperate conditions. From Gapon's book, *The Story of My Life*:

> The procession moved in a compact mass. In front of me were my two bodyguards and a yellow fellow with dark eyes from whose face his hard labouring life had not wiped away the light of youthful gaiety. On the flanks of the crowd ran the children. Some of the women insisted on walking in the first rows, in order, as they said, to protect me with their bodies, and force had to be used to remove them. . . .
>
> Suddenly the company of Cossacks galloped rapidly towards us with drawn swords. So, then, it was to be a massacre after all! There was no time for consideration, for making plans, or giving orders. A cry of alarm arose as the Cossacks came down upon us. Our front ranks broke before them, opening to right and left, and down the lane the soldiers drove their horses, striking on both sides. I saw the swords lifted and falling, the men, women and children dropping to the earth like logs of wood, while moans, curses and shouts filled the air. . . .
>
> Again we started forward, with solemn resolution and rising rage in our hearts. The Cossacks turned their horses and began to cut their

way through the crowd from the rear. They passed through the whole column and galloped back towards the Narva Gate, where—the infantry having opened their ranks and let them through—they again formed lines. . . .

We were not more than thirty yards from the soldiers, being separated from them only by the bridge over the Tarakanovskii Canal, which here masks the border of the city, when suddenly, without any warning and without a moment's delay, was heard the dry crack of many rifle-shots. Vasiliev, with whom I was walking hand in hand, suddenly left hold of my arm and sank upon the snow. One of the workmen who carried the banners fell also. Immediately one of the two police officers shouted out "What are you doing? How dare you fire upon the portrait of the Tsar?" . . .

Both the [black]smiths who had guarded me were killed, as well as all these who were carrying the ikons and banners; and all these emblems now lay scattered on the snow. The soldiers were actually shooting into the courtyards at the adjoining houses, where the crowd tried to find refuge and, as I learned afterwards, bullets even struck persons inside, through the windows.

At last the firing ceased. I stood up with a few others who remained uninjured and looked down at the bodies that lay prostrate around me. Horror crept into my heart. The thought flashed through my mind, "And this is the work of our Little Father, the Tsar." Perhaps this anger saved me, for now I knew in very truth that a new chapter was opened in the book of history of our people.[10]

After this massacre of peaceful citizens, the Tsar's reputation never recovered. Sheer force, in other words, is not sufficient in and of itself. And when the scope of violence is on a grand scale—in wars, for instance, especially ones that involve mass casualties and setbacks, let alone defeats—the state's legitimacy comes under tremendous strain. Part of the reason for the 1905 Russian Revolution, in fact, was the embarrassing defeat of Russia in the 1904-05 Russo-Japanese War.

In a more recent example, as I wrote in an online essay on the situation in Iran in 2009:

Ordinarily politics everywhere in the world is carried out by a very tiny fraction of the population—the heads of state and their cabinets,

---

10   George [Georgii] Gapon, *The Story of My Life* (New York: E. P. Dutton, 1906), 180-185.

heads of the bureaucracies (ministries, etc.), public officials in the leg-islative bodies, judicial, police, etc., mass media spokespeople/pundits, and the most powerful elements of the military, business, and institu-tions (such as the clerics in Iran).

But when a legitimacy crisis occurs (in Iran a combination of widely suspected electoral fraud and youth being fed up with the IRI [Islamic Republic of Iran]), the basis exists for the usually non-involved (ritualistic voting procedures, after all, do not comprise the exercise of real political power) to take to the streets and make their presence felt.

As they come into political motion this way, the presence of naive or incorrect views of what the road forward is is very evident among the broad sections of the people. They are, after all, ordinarily not re-ally politically involved and aren't schooled in how politics really work. Spontaneously, most come into political life thinking that the solu-tion to the problems they see and experience are to be found within the existing structures and with one of the existing political leaders. In this case, former PM Mousavi is being looked to erroneously by many as the answer to their hatred for the regime under Ahmadinejad and the IRI more generally. This is one of the reasons you see green being worn by some of the demonstrators.

In addition, people's political outlook is stamped by their class background/position, which is why you can see if you look closely enough the different outlooks present among different class forces in the society.

The coming into active political life/combat that the situation in Iran manifests right now, however, creates a hothouse for people to potentially learn a great deal in a very short period of time about how politics really operates, who are your real friends and real enemies, who are your staunchest allies and who are your wavering allies, what the roots of the problem are and what the road forward is. What peo-ple may not learn over decades (or even their entire lifetime) about politics, they can learn in hours within the cauldron of a revolution-ary crisis or legitimacy crisis.

One of the extremely painful lessons that people learn comes from the ruthless violence meted out upon them by governments that, despite all of their platitudes about "the will of the people," react with repression to the people *actually* trying to exercise their will in a real way. This kind of violence shatters most people's prior beliefs that the people in charge in the government are susceptible to entreaties and to reason, and that peaceful actions like voting (and backing the "winner" who doesn't really want what the people want) will accomplish what must be done.[11] [Emphasis in the original.]

Public acceptance of governmental actions and force might be compared to the willingness of water in its liquid state to adapt to any shape into which it is put. When public opinion hardens like ice, however, icebergs can bring down mighty ships of state.

Is State Power Still Necessary?

In the face of the communist movement's reversals in the latter half of the twentieth century (with socialism being undone in the Soviet Union and China) and the egregious state of neoliberal regimes, some people (e.g., in South and Central America) have concluded that holding state power should no longer be—and does not need to be—the goal for those who want justice and fairness. While it is possible for groups to operate independently of the state (e.g., criminal gangs, slum associations, rural areas within a country with a weak state, and so on), the viability of those non-state formations ultimately depends upon their ability to defend themselves against those who would try to undo or otherwise control what they are doing. A free association of people who conduct their internal affairs free of coercion—a utopian ideal—can continue only so long as the nearest state authority tolerates it.

A movement of a free association of people that spreads widely enough in a country to become a real force for change would soon come up against the state. The state would, under those circumstances, move decisively to shut such a movement down, by co-optation and/or with force. This is why the question of state power and who holds it continues to be of undiminished importance worldwide: eschewing violence under all circumstances means that those who will not hesitate to use violence upon you will prevail, regardless of the fact that they are wrong, morally and/ or legally. Acting as if state power can be ignored also does not exempt you from the fact that those who wield state power will not recognize your dismissal of their relevance.

Even massive peaceful crowds of protestors literally comprising the majority of a country's population and calling for their government's end

---

11   Dennis Loo, "Iran: A Report from the World to Win News Service," *Dennis Loo* (blog), *Open Salon*, June 21, 2009, http://open.salon.com/blog/dennis_loo/2009/06/20/iran_-_a_report_from_the_world_to_win_news_service, accessed June 21, 2009.

cannot by themselves topple that government. For a government to fall, that state's armed forces must refuse orders from their superiors (assuming the people in power choose to stay), or must have become sufficiently unreliable that the orders to crush the popular uprising are never given. This is what happened to the Shah in the 1979 Iranian Revolution. After repeated government massacres of protestors and political opponents involving thousands of protesters killed in single incidents alone, the revolutionary struggle escalated rather than ebbed, and soldiers began to disobey their orders, in some cases, shooting their own officers instead of the people. The US, the sponsor of Shah Mohammad Reza Pahlavi since the 1953 CIA coup that brought him to power, persuaded him that his cause was lost; he fled into exile before his previously vaunted military was completely dismantled or destroyed.

In 1989, Mao Zedong's renegade successors—Deng Xiaoping, et al—demonstrated Mao's dictum that political power grows out of the barrel of a gun. The huge demonstrations against the Chinese government demanding an end to both rampant corruption and the reversals of the 1949 revolution's socialist gains were initially peopled mostly by students; in the days just before Deng's violent crackdown, the demonstrators were mainly workers. Indeed, it was the very fact that workers were joining with students and intellectuals—the alliance that spells the end of any regime historically—that provoked Deng's ordering tanks into Tiananmen Square. The soldiers used for this action were drawn from outside of Beijing because soldiers within and from Beijing could not be counted upon to fire on their relatives, friends, and neighbors.

In early 2011, the whole world witnessed the glorious and successful toppling in first Tunisia, and then Egypt, of their respective presidents. Egypt's Hosni Mubarak finally resigned and fled the country on February 11, 2011 after an eighteen-day mass uprising, unprecedented in modern Egyptian history. Egyptians were inspired and triggered into motion by what the people of Tunisia had done over four weeks of mass protests. In the initial stages of the Egyptians' popular upheaval Mubarak unleashed the police and then thugs not in uniform upon the people, killing some three hundred Egyptians. Street battles between the demonstrators and Mubarak's forces ensued. Mubarak also attempted to bribe government workers with an immediate fifteen percent raise, fired his cabinet, cut off the Internet and (undoubtedly) ordered physical assaults upon foreign and Egyptian journalists. All to no avail. His legitimacy and capacity to rule by terror were finished, with the military choosing not to come to his defense in the face of this mass rejection by the people. The Tunisian and Egyptian people have thus written a new page in history. The road ahead

126

for them now is much brighter but immensely complicated, as Zine El Abidine Ben Ali and Mubarak's departures do not by themselves change the fundamental nature of power relations in these nations. In particular, as any initial euphoria towards the Egyptian military inevitably wears off, the recognition that this is the same military that served despot Mubarak and foreign power interests faithfully for thirty years will come to the fore.

The failure to recognize the central role of force in politics has drowned many a political struggle in blood or rendered it a failure through co-optation. The uprooting of regimes of domination and plunder cannot occur without a powerful struggle that includes, without exception, at least some degree of violence. The American Revolution against the British imperialists was not accomplished through a vote. The revolutionaries did not use tea to shoot at the British soldiers; they used bullets. The British did not say in response to numerous petitions from its colony, "Oh, all right, you want to be free, you shall be free. We're leaving now. Best of luck, what?"

The end of apartheid in South Africa provides another instructive example. The white minority regime eventually ceded power in 1994 to a black majority but it did not do so without the African National Congress' prior prolonged armed struggle. The eventual peaceful transition via negotiations for multiracial elections circumvented the necessary destruction of the mechanisms that had for so long violently subordinated the black majority. In the absence of that vital restructuring that cannot occur simply through substituting who is in high office, the condition for black South Africans has not been fully transformed and much suffering continues, except now under darker-skinned leaders.

Clausewitz's famous dictum about war—"War is nothing but the continuation of policy [politics] with other [violent] means"[12]—highlights the fact that war is not something arbitrary, mad, and apart from any other human activity. Rather, wars are extensions of politics. They represent politics carried forward into the realm of the open use of massive violence to achieve political objectives. The extreme violence of wars represents a magnification of the force present in everyday politics and built into the social and economic structures of societies themselves and the choreography of everyday movements and interactions. Where there is not

---

12 Carl Von Clausewitz was a Prussian general and famous military theorist (1780-1831). In many different passages in his writings he reiterates the point that the sources of war lie in politics. For example, "War is not a mere act of policy but a true political instrument, a continuation of political activity by other means." See "Some Juicy Quotes from Clausewitz, *On War*," Clausewitz.com, http://www.clausewitz.com/readings/Cquotations.htm, accessed February 11, 2011.

explicit coercion, domination exists. Coercion, in other words, exists on a continuum. Domination and resistance to that domination assume a multitude of expressions. As a friend of mine who taught a number of years in the American South has observed, people there are extremely polite. That politeness masks and helps to forestall the eruption of open violence, given the long-standing domination there along racial, class, and gender lines. Politics and coercion are, in short, inextricably intertwined. Speaking of politics and failing to also address the role of coercion and violence is like talking about the ocean and not mentioning tides and waves. It is like discussing silk's properties and forgetting that silk comes from the deaths of silkworms. It is like striking a nail into a board without the board.

Even voluntary associations of people such as unions cannot dispense with some level of coercion over their membership. When a majority of union members votes to strike, but a few union members still want to continue working despite the strike, the workers observing the strike must exercise some pressure over their resistant union members. If everyone gets to do what they want, and some union members choose to cross the picket line, then the strike will be lost. Extended into the larger societal sphere, existing economic structures that advantage some over others cannot be changed if some compulsion is not applied upon those with privilege. Those with privilege are not, as a whole, going to willingly and voluntarily give up their privileges just because "it's the right thing to do," especially if those privileges are immense.

The notion, in other words, that you can have social change that enhances fairness and equity without resorting to some level of coercion constitutes wishful folly. Coercion is an inescapable product of the fact that, at the very least, disagreements will always exist among people over what should be done. Parents coerce their children into going to bed at a certain time and into eating their vegetables. We call that parenting. The need to get things done, whether those things are the right or best things to do or not, still means that some people must be forced to go along with things they do not agree with. The fact that coercion might be being exercised in the interests of, and with the full backing of, the majority of people and/or exercised by a wise minority in the greater interests of the community does not change the fact that coercion is being used. (I tell my students sometimes that my classes are an example of a benevolent dictatorship, suitable for a classroom, but not for a society.) As Frederick Douglass put it,

> Those who profess to favor freedom, and yet depreciate agitation, are
> men who want crops without ploughing the ground. They want rain

without thunder and lightning. They want the ocean without the roar of its many waters. This struggle may be a moral one; or it may be a physical one; or it may be both moral and physical; but it must be a struggle. Power concedes nothing without a demand. It never did and it never will.[13]

Or, as Frederick Engels said in response to those within the communist movement who thought it possible to peacefully transition from capitalism to socialism and have a revolution by ballot: "Have these gentlemen ever seen a revolution? A revolution is certainly the most authoritarian thing there is. . . . one part of the population imposes its will upon the other part by means of rifles, bayonets and cannon. . . . "[14] Real revolutions involve force. This has always been so. There are no exceptions. Speaking and advocating "revolution" without mentioning the fact that force must come into play, whether you want it to or not, claiming that a "revolution at the ballot box" can do it, amounts to misrepresentation of a high order as to how political power actually operates. If the revolution is to live up to its name as a thoroughgoing systemic change and not merely a change in who is in charge, then revolutions cannot occur wholly peacefully.

In general, the larger the material gap between those who resist a revolution and those who back a revolution, the more we can expect that violence will be required and will ensue. Put another way, the more un-equal the society, the more the mechanisms that perpetuate those ineq-uities are in place and the more likely it is that those who benefit from those inequities will fight fiercely, deviously, and tenaciously to pro-tect—or restore—their positions, as they have so much to lose. How the state's armed forces act is central to the question of how much violence will be involved. If they side with the despised regime, then violence will be greater. If the armed forces abandon the state that is under siege by the people, then violence will be less. In the 1917 Russian Revolution the soldiers en masse abandoned the government's side and the revolution it-self was therefore relatively bloodless. In addition, since the Bolsheviks

---

13 Frederick Douglass, "Letter to an Abolitionist Associate," In *Organizing for Social Change: A Mandate for Activity in the 1990s*, eds. K. Bobo, J. Kendall, and S. Max (Washington, D.C.: Seven Locks Press, [1849] 1991), cited at "Frederick Doug-lass, the Accurate 'Without Struggle/No Freedom' Quote," BuildingEquality.us, http://www.buildingequality.us/Quotes/Frederick_Douglass.htm, accessed Feb-ruary 13, 2011.

14 Frederick Engels, "On Authority," in Karl Marx and Frederick Engels, *Selected Works* (Moscow: Progress Publishers, 1973), 2:379.

immediately made good on their promises to pull Russia out of World War I, the level of violence dropped enormously. Subsequently, however, the White Armies of those who had been overthrown—joined by European and US forces—waged a bloody civil war against the revolution in an attempt to regain power.

States, it should be noted, have not always been with us. In fact, over the course of the two hundred thousand years of human societies, states have existed for less than five percent of that time. Prior to the development of an economic surplus, a state, which is in its essence an organized body of (usually) men with weapons who use force to implement state policies, was not present. Throughout most of human existence, there was no economic surplus to protect on behalf of those who controlled and enjoyed the fruits of that surplus. Put another way, states exist because classes exist.

"Power corrupts and absolute power corrupts absolutely," as the often cited quote by Lord Acton goes. This saying, however much it may perceptually describe what frequently happens, nevertheless does not uncover the source of the problem. It treats power as if it were something pursued for its own sake. Power does not exist in the abstract; it must include the ability to do something; power on a societal level means control over the distribution of material resources. Political power is, therefore, fundamentally a development linked to certain levels and configurations of material distribution and to a certain epoch of human history in which resources and services are distributed highly unevenly. When that lopsided distribution is overcome, then the need for a state and its exercise of political power will be superseded.

Acton's notion is based on the fallacy that corruption and misuse of power are products of some invariant thing called "human nature." Invoking "human nature" is a very common practice, but it fails to take into account the fact that throughout most of human existence, class oppression and classes did not exist. If "human nature" is at fault for our present troubles, then why has human nature been so strikingly different for the last five percent of our existence as compared to the previous ninety-five percent of human history, when no governments and no classes existed?

To paraphrase sociologist Robert Michels' "Whoever says organization, says oligarchy": whoever says government, says classes. What neoliberalism represents is the unapologetic assertion that classes shall exist. To paraphrase George Wallace's comments about segregation, classes now, classes tomorrow, and classes forever. And the gap between them shall grow wider and wider and wider. . . .

The End of States?

The momentous changes for which globalization is responsible are provoking varying explanations by analysts. John Robb in *Brave New War: The Next Stage of Terrorism and the End of Globalization,* for example, argues for the provocative thesis that globalization and the Internet are actually leading to the end of states. On the one hand, he says, states "are losing control over their borders, economies, finances, people, and communications. . . . They are so intertwined that no independent action can be undertaken without serious repercussions on multiple levels." And on the other hand, "a new competitive force is emerging in this vacuum of state power. Non-state actors in the form of terrorists, crime syndicates, gangs and networked tribes are stepping into the breach. . . . "[15]

Modern states and economies are highly integrated and technically advanced. Their transmission lines of collection, distribution, and communication are strung out in unprecedented ways. Modern states/economies are also for these reasons extremely vulnerable to any interruptions in this chain. Even when non-state actors are not involved, the protracted linkages of the world system and economy are subject to interruptions with far-reaching consequences. In a relatively minor example of this, but one that affected five countries and caused widespread economic injuries, an underwater telecom cable that links India and Pakistan to the West was accidentally severed in 2005:

> Service on the cable was restored on Friday [after nine days]. The cable was damaged on June 27, largely cutting Pakistan's telecommunications links with the outside world and disrupting India's connections [providing especially tech support to the West]. The problem also caused disruption in the United Arab Emirates (UAE), Oman and Djibouti.
>
> The five countries affected were linked to the undersea cable network called Southeast Asia, Middle East and Western Europe-3.[16]

---

15 John Robb, *Brave New War: The Next Stage of Terrorism and the End of Globalization* (Hoboken, New Jersey: John Wiley and Sons, 2007), 17.

16 Anthony Mitchell, "Asian Telecom Outage Leaves Widespread Call Center Damage," TechNewsWorld.com, July 11, 2005, http://www.technewsworld.com/story/44527.html, accessed July 20, 2009.

In 2008, of course, a far more serious globalized disaster threatened to bring down the entire financial system: an international financial crisis brought on initially by the popping of the US housing bubble.

Contentious non-state actors, taking advantage of both the Internet's ubiquity as an organizing tool and the ready and cheap availability of increasingly potent technology, can target the economy and state at points of vulnerability, launching actions at a relatively miniscule cost while wreaking spectacular damage. Robb points out, for example, that a PlayStation 2 console now has enough computing power to control missiles. As one expression of this, on December 17, 2009, the *Wall Street Journal* reported:

> Militants in Iraq have used $26 off-the-shelf software to intercept live video feeds from U.S. Predator drones, potentially providing them with information they need to evade or monitor U.S. military operations.
>
> Senior defense and intelligence officials said Iranian-backed insurgents intercepted the video feeds by taking advantage of an unprotected communications link in some of the remotely flown planes' systems. Shiite fighters in Iraq used software programs such as SkyGrabber—available for as little as $25.95 on the Internet—to regularly capture drone video feeds, according to a person familiar with reports on the matter . . . .
>
> The Air Force has staked its future on unmanned aerial vehicles. Drones account for 36% of the planes in the service's proposed 2010 budget.
>
> Today, the Air Force is buying hundreds of Reaper drones, a newer model, whose video feeds could be intercepted in much the same way as with the Predators, according to people familiar with the matter. A Reaper costs between $10 million and $12 million each and is faster and better armed than the Predator.[17]

Thus, a $26 device can be used against military equipment that can cost upwards of $10 million a piece. This disparity of cost is also an expression of the soft underbelly of mighty empires: the more sophisticated and therefore the more expensive their tools and weapons, the more highly integrated and hence more fragile to interruptions in the chain of

---

17   Siobhan Gorman, Yochi J. Dreazen, and August Cole, "Insurgents Hack U.S. Drones," *Wall Street Journal* online, December 17, 2009, http://online.wsj.com/article/SB126102247889095011.html, accessed on January 31, 2011.

interconnectedness the equipment becomes, and the cheaper by comparison the techniques and devices that can be used to negate or reduce the power of that advanced technology.[18] Robb forecasts that in the not too distant future the trajectory of change is going to bring us to a scenario only found in comic books—a world held hostage by a single megalomaniac.

The Only Thing We Have to Fear, Is ... the System Itself

> [T]he American failure to deal with its dependence on foreign borrowing constitutes a large and growing weight upon the international economy and is the premier source of international instability."
>
> CHRIS SANDERS[19]

Scary as the prospect of a single master criminal may be, a kind of Superman nemesis Lex Luthor writ large, Robb overlooks the fact that nonstate actors include not just criminal and terrorist groups; they also include others, such as corporations and religious organizations. Catastrophes are part of the very fabric, the warp and woof, of the globalized neoliberal world. As I wrote in a 2008 article:

In a November 2008 Department of Defense Strategic Studies Institute document authored by Nathan Frier entitled "Known Unknowns: Unconventional 'Strategic Shocks' in Defense Strategy Development," Frier points out:

The likeliest and most dangerous future shocks will be unconventional. They will not emerge from thunderbolt advances in an opponent's military capabilities. Rather, they will manifest themselves in ways far outside established defense convention.

---

18   Stan Goff, *Full Spectrum Disorder: The Military in the New American Century* (Brooklyn: Soft Skull Press, 2004), 69.

      Stan Goff also relates a similar story from 1999: the Yugoslavs induced a US F-117 stealth fighter to come close enough to shoot it down. The US fighter cost $2.1 billion (not counting maintenance) and the decoy microwave ovens that were employed to "passively track" the warplane cost $150.00 each.

19   Chris Sanders, "SRA Commentary: War As You Like It," from Sanders Research Associates, as reposted by Scoop Independent News online, May 13, 2003, http://www.scoop.co.nz/stories/print.html?path=HL0305/S00085.htm, accessed on January 31, 2011.

Most will be nonmilitary in origin and character, and not, by definition, defense-specific events conducive to the conventional employment of the DoD enterprise.

They will rise from an analytical no man's land separating well-considered, stock and trade defense contingencies and pure defense speculation. . . .

9/11 was a strategic shock. Frier warns of future such "hostile design" shocks. But what is even more dangerous, as he puts it, is the prospect of "threats of 'context'" that *arise from the very workings of the existing systems*. In other words, disasters await without anyone even trying to bring them about.

Threats of context arise, according to Frier, out of "the unguided forces of globalization, toxic populism, identity politics, underdevelopment, human/natural disaster, and disease. In the end, shocks emerging from contextual threats might challenge core U.S. interests more fundamentally than any number of prospective purposeful shocks." He goes on to say that these forces "are in—or undervulnerable to traditional instruments of U.S. power applied in predictable combinations."

What does it tell us about the nature of the contemporary and near term future world that disasters that arise *out of the very context* of our collective lives are a) certain, b) unlikely to be properly foreseen, c) extremely unlikely to be adequately prepared for, and d) more dangerous than any planned hostile actions?

It tells us at least two things.

First, the system we live in—global capitalism—is inherently unstable and dangerous whether you look at it from a local, national or international perspective. The spheres of the local, national and international are so intertwined that they cannot sensibly be separated as though events in one sphere do not impact the others.

Second, stability and security are more things of the past than of the present and, especially, the future. Massive dislocations and dramatic, startling changes to the status quo are not the stuff of science fiction but that which the DOD itself now finds it must take seriously. Granted, Frier's document is not a policy document but a think tank document. But his evaluation of the situation compels serious reflection.

Several factors stand in the way of properly grasping the reality that we face. These factors include—not necessarily in order of importance:

- Bureaucratic practice and thinking, which by definition involves the routinization of ways of doing and seeing things based on what has previously happened and not what hasn't yet happened, thus, narrowing down and aggressively *anti*-imaginative approaches trump their opposite. Bureaucracies, we should note, *run things* in the modern world. They are, in core respects, the modern world;

- Neoliberal policies—politics in service to globalization—dominate (both the GOP and the Democrats are Friedmanites) and therefore aggressive globalization which continues creating and deepening the bases for disasters and hamstringing human responses to disasters are not going to be modified or stemmed;

- Preparing for the future and hedging against unanticipated disasters are diametrically opposed to neoliberal policies of allocating resources most sparingly and cheaply for profit-making—e.g., allowing more hospital bedspace for a disaster is considered inefficient and unprofitable, devoting resources to developing flu vaccines is less profitable than drugs that require daily doses and are therefore neglected leaving us extraordinarily vulnerable to a flu epidemic.

To paraphrase (and modify) FDR, what we have to fear is the system itself proceeding along as it is. The economic crisis and the implacable wars are the most obvious conditions we confront today. But the matters which are being ruled off the table by public officials are the most perilous of all: a) re-establishing the rule of law through prosecution of its violators and b) the very logic and operations of globalization and its exacerbating of the existing economic and political inequalities and manifest threats to the planet.[20]

Nathan Frier, in an online debate at the Strategic Studies Institute in April 2009, said in his final remarks,

[F]or strategists an inescapable set of plausible worst-case scenarios [of crippling instability for "strategic states" can be readily foreseen.] Many would require rapid, comprehensive employment of significant U.S. land forces. The principal landpower mission would be stopping

---

20 Dennis Loo, "The Water Line: Morality, the Rule of Law, and Leadership," Stateof-Nature.org, Winter 2009, http://www.stateofnature.org/theWaterLine.html, accessed January 2, 2010.

and reversing hemorrhaging human insecurity in advance of irreparable harm. In many cases, pursuit of minimum essential strategic and operational objectives like this requires resources and capabilities far in excess of those available to the entire Marine Corps.

In designing future land forces, let's first be realistic about the worst-case future demand signal. I suggest it is likely to be response to a fatally broken strategic state. Then let's be realistic about what can be achieved. Here, I argue for pursuit of limited objectives that will still require significant land forces to achieve unpalatable but nonetheless manageable strategic and operational outcomes.[21]

Having laid out a convincing case that strategic shocks are unavoidable, and difficult or impossible to foresee, let alone properly prepare for, the best that Frier can offer to deal with this is the deployment of significant US land forces, beyond what the entire Marine Corps is capable of, producing unpalatable outcomes. What if this crisis occurs while the US is already engaged in one or more wars as it is currently? The incapacity of the US to police this contingency is readily apparent.

The logic of Frier's analysis conflicts with his prescription of US military responses. His analysis of "known unknowns" and the threats of "context" (shocks in the absence of hostile design or intent) points to the unmanageable and inherently dangerous, unbridled forces of globalization and movements such as ethnic warfare, fascistic nativist movements, and desperate people suffering from an epidemic, natural or man-made, that globalization spawns. In comparison to that, the deployment of military force, however large, can provide small comfort even for those who are convinced of the justness and propriety of US military action.

When Hurricane Katrina was wheeling its deadly way towards the Gulf Coast and New Orleans in 2005, the White House staff dawdled and did nothing to change their existing activities. Most Americans have known for as long as New Orleans has existed that the city lies below sea level and is therefore vulnerable to rising seas and powerful storms. Yet this fact did not alter the Bush White House's actions. It had previously demoted the Federal Emergency Management Agency (FEMA) from a cabinet level position to a subsection of the Department of Homeland Security (DHS); installed at FEMA's head people who had no background or expertise in emergency management; slashed FEMA's funds and the

---

21   Steven Metz and Nathan P. Freier, "The Army's Strategic Role: An Online Debate April 02-April 15, 2009," StrategicStudiesInstitute.army.mil, http://www.strategicstudiesinstitute.army.mil/pubs/debate.cfm?q=1, accessed August 1, 2010.

funds for levee repair and maintenance in particular (by eighty percent),[22] resulting in the Army Corps of Engineers having to abandon any levee work before the hurricane; and essentially tasked FEMA with a new mission in which disaster relief would no longer be primary.

Indeed, Michael Brown's predecessor at FEMA was his college roommate Joe Allbaugh who testified before Congress that disaster relief was an "entitlement" and that disaster relief could be handled quite nicely by Christian charities instead of FEMA. How faith-based charities could provide the necessary equipment and resources to rescue and care for people suffering from floodwaters and other natural or man-made disasters boggles the imagination. We might say, "Blessed are those who put their faith in God, for when they drown because their born-again president refused to fund levee repairs, drained marshland, and ignored warming waters due to global warming, for they shall enter the Gates of Heaven." The Katrina debacle came four years after the devastating events of 9/11 and in a global situation that the White House never tired

---

22   Andrew Martin and Andrew Zajac, "Flood-Control Funds Short of Requests," ChicagoTribune.com, September 1, 2005, http://articles.chicagotribune.com/2005-09-01/news/0509010170_1_levees-lake-pontchartrain-corps-budget, accessed on February 13, 2011:

> Despite continuous warnings that a catastrophic hurricane could hit New Orleans, the Bush administration and Congress in recent years have repeatedly denied full funding for hurricane preparation and flood control.
>
> That has delayed construction of levees around the city and stymied an ambitious project to improve drainage in New Orleans' neighborhoods.
>
> For instance, the U.S. Army Corps of Engineers requested $27 million for this fiscal year to pay for hurricane-protection projects around Lake Pontchartrain. The Bush administration countered with $3.9 million, and Congress eventually provided $5.7 million, according to figures provided by the office of U.S. Sen. Mary Landrieu (D-La.).
>
> Because of the shortfalls, which were caused in part by the rising costs of the war in Iraq, the corps delayed seven contracts that included enlarging the levees, according to corps documents. . . .
>
> Similarly, the Army Corps requested $78 million for this fiscal year for projects that would improve draining and prevent flooding in New Orleans. The Bush administration's budget provided $30 million for the projects, and Congress ultimately approved $36.5 million, according to Landrieu's office.
>
> "I'm not saying it wouldn't still be flooded, but I do feel that if it had been totally funded, there would be less flooding than you have," said Michael Parker, a former Republican Mississippi congressman who headed the U.S. Army Corps of Engineers from October 2001 until March 2002, when he was ousted after publicly criticizing a Bush administration proposal to cut the corps' budget.

of stating was one fraught with danger and one in which disasters could happen at any time.

In the years leading up to the 2005 Katrina disaster, Bush allowed private developers to drain precious marshlands that had acted as natural storm surge sponges in order to use them instead for golf courses and housing. He did literally nothing to prepare for the Category 5 storm that everyone watching the news in the days preceding landfall knew was coming. When Michael Brown told Bush in a special emergency meeting in the days before landfall that, "This could be the one we've been waiting for," Bush asked no questions and merely stated that he wanted to assure everyone that everything was under control; then he left.[23] Unlike 9/11, about which the Bush White House (falsely) claimed that they had no foreknowledge (also falsely stating that they never imagined anyone would take planes and slam them into high rises), Hurricane Katrina was known well ahead of time and Bush et al still did nothing.

Indeed, FEMA had previously concluded that there were three major disasters that could strike the US: a terrorist attack on New York City, a major earthquake in the San Francisco area, and a Category 5 hurricane striking New Orleans. Thus they knew that one of the three most dangerous scenarios was looming on the horizon. Yet they still did nothing, posting exactly one solitary FEMA employee in New Orleans before the storm hit, and preparing no assets for search and rescue beforehand. And then they ignored the fervent entreaties from that one FEMA employee who was reporting on the massive damage wreaked by the hurricane.

Why? How could this be?

Some people have concluded that the White House's actions before Katrina were so egregious and incompetent that Bush et al must have secretly wished for New Orleans' destruction so that they could rebuild it as a less "chocolate" city.[24] I find that conclusion hard to accept, not because I disagree with Kanye West's declaration that Bush "doesn't care about black people," but because the abject failures of Bush et al in the face of Katrina's destruction did tremendous damage to the White House and

---

23   Earlier that day Bush had gone on an intense bike ride and was apparently worn out from the workout. He made a practice during his eight years in office of working out for two hours a day.

24   New Orleans Mayor Ray Nagin in 2006: "It's time for us to rebuild a New Orleans, the one that should be a chocolate New Orleans." "Transcript of Nagin's Speech, *The Times-Picayune* online, January 17, 2006, http://www.nola.com/news/t-p/frontpage/index.ssf?/news/t-p/stories/011706_nagin_transcript.html, accessed on April 3, 2011.

GOP's reputations as leaders in whom the country should put their faith in a world in turmoil. This was an exceedingly high price for them to have deliberately incurred. It is one thing to claim that they were taken by surprise by 9/11; many people could and do believe that excuse. It is another thing to claim that the White House did not anticipate Hurricane Katrina's destructive power; that claim merely proves their incompetence and criminal neglect. Katrina is one of the reasons the GOP lost the White House in the 2008 election.

In another example of spectacular indifference to reason and to the anticipated consequences of their actions, the Bush White House was warned by the CIA of the ramifications of a US invasion of Iraq and the overthrow of Saddam Hussein. A US attack that eliminated Hussein, the CIA said, would unleash sectarian fighting on a grand scale. Hussein's hostility to al-Qaeda had kept al-Qaeda out of Iraq; Hussein had ordered the execution of anyone linked to al-Qaeda. Al-Qaeda in turn had a fatwa (death warrant) out for Hussein. Despite these warnings, Bush and Cheney plunged ahead. The infamous "Mission Accomplished" banner as a backdrop to Bush's triumphant declaration of victory on an aircraft carrier stands as testimony to their myopic view of the complexities of that invasion and subsequent occupation that they willfully dismissed as irrelevant.

Why?

Part of the answer lies in the philosophy of the neocons who represent the lunatic fringe of neoliberalism. Given the disconnect between neoliberal policies' negative consequences and their proponents' ardor in advocating neoliberalism irrespective of those devastating results, neoliberalism, in any of its manifestations, suffers from a singular lack of self-consciousness. With respect to the neocons, I use the term "lunatic" here not mainly as a pejorative but as a technical descriptor: their outlook and behavior fit the definition of insanity. Jane Mayer in her book *The Dark Side: The Inside Story of How the War on Terror Turned into a War on American Ideals*, writes:

> High-ranking and very conservative administration lawyers who worked closely with [David] Addington found themselves astonished by his radical absolutism. One later recalled sitting in meeting with Addington wondering, "How did this lunatic end up running the country." . . . Walter Dellinger, Clinton's Solicitor General and Duke University Professor of Constitutional Law, describing the Bush White House's theories about executive power as "insane."

Their theory of presidential power, he said, is "like Mussolini in 1930."[25]

Seymour Hersh, in *Chain of Command: The Road from 9/11 to Abu Ghraib* quoting an intelligence officer, writes: "[Senior White House officials] were so crazed and so far out and so difficult to reason with—to the point of being bizarre. Dogmatic, as if they were on a mission from God."[26] In the neocons' view, reality is what you make it, not what you have to recognize and cope with and possibly reshape. In other contexts that perspective—that reality is not something that you have to take into account—is known as living in a fantasy world.

The Bush White House did not prepare for the ensuing chaos in Iraq after their invasion because they actually believed their rhetoric that Iraqis would greet the US soldiers as liberators and shower them with garlands. But what is more disturbing than the Bush White House's mendacity and incompetence is the fact that with the very few notable exceptions of individual public officials who spoke out and acted against them (people who then resigned their positions and lost their careers), the Bush policies were not only tolerated by the rest of the American government, but their radical rupture with previous norms was also permitted and retroactively legitimized by the Congress; they were tolerated albeit with some ineffectual grumbling by certain mass media outlets, and much of it, especially with respect to "national security," has been maintained, legitimated, and carried further by the Obama White House. Bush and Cheney are gone from the White House, but the new occupants, while endorsing science and thus accepting evolution and global warming as realities, nevertheless have shielded the Bush White House from prosecution for their many crimes, including the monstrousness of torture, and moved to institutionalize the Bush Doctrine on foreign affairs and its domestic corollary—the annihilation of civil liberties.

Nowhere is this more evident than in Obama's 2009 declaration that the government may continue to hold a detainee indefinitely on the grounds that it thinks that the person may be too dangerous to release. This represents a fundamental breach of a person's right not to be indefinitely detained and their right to be released if they are guiltless of any crime. It is also a fundamental breach of the principles underlying

25 Jane Mayer, *The Dark Side: The Inside Story of How the War on Terror Turned into a War on American Ideals* (New York: Anchor Books, 2009), 77 and 67.

26 Seymour Hersh, *Chain of Command: The Road from 9/11 to Abu Ghraib* (New York: Allen Lane, 2004), 219.

jurisprudence that a person may not be considered guilty absent a court finding of guilt. The absence of habeas corpus rights in a war that Dick Cheney said will last "generations," a war waged upon a tactic, is the sign of a tyranny. Even if one likes Obama and thinks that he only suspends due process for really bad people, one day someone else will occupy the Oval Office, and they will not have any curbs or supervision upon their exercise of judgment as to who is bad and who is not. That is why the Great Writ of Habeas Corpus marked such a momentous development in human affairs and politics because it curtailed the power of an unfettered executive, making it subject to independent supervision and consideration.

The corollary to Obama's decision to use preventive detention is his refusal to prosecute war crimes and war criminals in his insistence that he is "looking forward, not backward."[27] The unnecessary deaths of more than 1.2 million Iraqis because of Bush and Cheney's 2003 invasion of Iraq is just one of their numerous crimes. Known war criminals are being shielded and people adjudicated as not guilty can be punished with indefinite detention and, in some cases, torture. What kind of society can be sustained under rules in which there is no rule of law, except that asserted arbitrarily by those in power? Adopting the wisdom of the hookah-smoking caterpillar of Lewis Carroll's classic tale of a world gone awry, our leaders tell us in essence: "Words and laws mean what we want them to mean."

Obama: Repudiation or a Continuation of Bush?

While most Americans are less than fully aware of what has been going on in their country and the world primarily because of systematic poor or misinformation from the mass media (the media themselves being impacted by, and at the same time exemplars of, neoliberal policies), the magnitude of the changes wrought by neoliberal policies has been so sweeping that even a poorly informed American public has been deeply distressed by developments. As neoliberal practices expand and deepen, and as people realize the trajectory and non-transitory nature of these changes, the dismay and outright anger grow. The level of public antipathy was enough to make Bush and Cheney's White House the most unpopular ever, despite the benefits that would have accrued to any White House that had been in

---

27   Both Bush and Cheney, for example, have publicly admitted authorizing waterboarding, a torture technique first invented in the Spanish Inquisition.

office during 9/11. Their successor, Barack Obama, gained the presidency by making "change" his campaign mantra. Even the GOP ticket of Mc-Cain and Palin claimed "change" as their theme.

The fact that a black, first term US Senator (who in other times would not have stood a chance of being awarded a legitimate candidate's stature by the media and a major party) won the Democratic nomination and the presidency is itself an illustration of just how much further the political system in 2008 had to stretch in order to shore up people's faith in it. That faith, it should be noted, was a faith premised on the belief that Obama would change what Bush and Cheney had carried out.

In 2008 the top ten highest paid corporate chiefs awarded themselves over $2.2 billion (with a B), an average of over $220 million per person, in pay and bonuses.[28] This was in a year in which corporate America had to be rescued from disaster by record-setting bailouts from taxpayers, while at the same time the share prices of these highest paid executives' companies were falling, belying claims that their stunning pay was earned by extraordinary personal performance. A quick profile of the US's wealth distribution reads:

> As of 2007, the top 1% of households (the upper class) owned 34.6% of all privately held wealth, and the next 19% (the managerial, professional, and small business stratum) had 50.5%, which means that just 20% of the people owned a remarkable 85%, leaving only 15% of the wealth for the bottom 80% (wage and salary workers). In terms of financial wealth (total net worth minus the value of one's home), the top 1% of households had an even greater share: 42.7%.[29]

If we look at income from wages in 2007, the top ten percent of Americans brought in 49.7 percent of total wages, the highest percentage since 1917 and greater than what was seen during the peak of the stock market prior to the 1929 crash. Between 1993 and 2007 the top one percent of incomes took in half of the total economic growth. Between 1993 and 2000,

---

28 "Top CEO Collected $702 million in 2008: US Survey," WasToday.com.au, August 19, 2009, http://www.watoday.com.au/executive-style/management/top-us-ceo-collected-us702-million-in-2008-survey-20090814-ekby.html, accessed August 21, 2009.

29 G. William Domhoff, "Power in America: Wealth, Income and Power," *Who Rules America? (blog)*, September 2005, updated January 2011, http://sociology.ucsc.edu/whorulesamerica/power/wealth.html, accessed January 31, 2011.

the top one percent grabbed two-thirds of income growth.[30] At the same time, immiseration continues to intensify. Between one and two percent of Americans—three to six million people—must live entirely on food stamps because they have no cash income at all.[31]

Neoliberals like to justify their economic policies as trickle-down wealth. In Hawai'i there are some waterfalls that sometimes flow uphill because of the wind. Neoliberal policies are like those upside down waterfalls in which the wealth flows up, not down. Instead of promoting general wealth, neoliberal policies promote class polarization, not only in terms of the distribution of wealth, but also in terms of the systematic and relentless undermining of the foundations upon which people live. These outcomes are not fixable through better legislation. They are the inevitable and logical outcome of the drive for profits that characterize the essence of capitalism, the expected outcome of the fact that this drive for profits results in some capitalists becoming stronger than others and outstripping their competitors. This permits them, again through the same logic of profit seeking, to use their monopolistic powers to degrade their services and eliminate or severely weaken their competition. Free market competition breeds monopoly as surely as night follows day.

Are these enormous shifts in wealth and welfare being carried out at the behest of the American people? The GOP and right-wing pundits would have us believe so, a verdict with which the Democrats collectively agree. Yet, *Business Week* and Harris found otherwise in a poll they conducted in 2000:

> In September 2000, *Business Week* magazine released a Business Week/Harris Poll which showed that between 72 and 82 percent of Americans agree that "Business has gained too much power over too many aspects of American life." In the same poll, 74 percent of Americans agreed with Vice President Al Gore's criticism of a wide range of large corporations, including big tobacco, big oil, the big polluters, the pharmaceutical companies, the HMOs. And, 74-82

---

30   Ryan McCarthy, "Income Inequality is At An All-Time High: STUDY," HuffingtonPost.com, August 14, 2009, http://www.huffingtonpost.com/2009/08/14/income-inequality-is-at-a_n_259516.html, accessed on January 11, 2010.

31   Jason Deparle and Robert M. Gebeloff, "Living on Nothing but Food Stamps," NYTimes.com, January 2, 2010, http://www.nytimes.com/2010/01/03/us/03foodstamps.html, accessed January 3, 2010.

percent agreed that big companies have too much influence over "government policy, politicians, and policy-makers in Washington."[32]

The startling economic shifts in recent decades have been accompanied by the institutionalizing of immoral and illegal practices as the norm (practices such as torture, preemptive wars and rendition), the achievement of which requires that there be an ever-widening gap between what is said to be going on and what is in fact going on. This also involves a radical reconfiguring of the basis of unity within the body politic. That new basis involves, under the cover of an unending "War on Terror," the progressive jettisoning or weakening of previously officially sacrosanct principles such as the rule of law; the right to confront your accusers; the right to habeas corpus; the right to privacy; the First, Fourth, Eighth and Fourteenth Amendments, and so on. The new rules are more rule by fiat, introduced under the cloud of the stoking of fears, than rule by consent. Emergency measures are being made permanent under the leadership of Obama, whose public persona radically differs from his actual acts. But precisely because Obama, not Bush, is president, and because Obama is much more credible than Bush to many who vigorously opposed Bush, we now see a process underway in which consent is being manufactured to measures that would have been unthinkable ten years ago.

The election of Obama may be seen as a gambit by the neoliberals. His persona promised change and offered hope at a time when the gap between the White House and the public was wider than ever. Will the neoliberals succeed in this gambit? Let us first probe the direction in which governments and the private sector have been moving for some four decades.

The Genesis of Public Order Policies

Public order policies began to emerge worldwide around the 1970s. They may be defined as a shift in emphasis by governments away from dealing with actual and discrete threats to public safety towards preparing for a putatively more generalized and ubiquitous foe. The very possibility of something untoward happening began to be treated as probable. These policies are also sometimes referred to as "risk assessments." Precluding

---

32   Sarah Anderson and John Cavanagh, "Top 200: The Rise of Corporate Global Power," Institute for Policy Studies online, December 4th, 2000, http://www.corpwatch. org/article.php?id=377#key, accessed on January 31, 2011.

the unlikely has increasingly become a guiding principle in statecraft and private enterprises. Saying it this way highlights how peculiar a practice public order policies are; devoting immense resources in an attempt to prevent the unlikely makes no sense. The zenith of this irrational approach could be said to be embodied in Dick Cheney's declaration that if a threat had a "one percent chance of occurring, then it needed to be treated as a certainty."[33] This led Ron Suskind to title his book about Cheney and Bush *The One-Percent Doctrine*. Obviously, treating remote possibilities as certainties means that probable possibilities cannot be given proper attention, since the necessarily limited resources available cannot be stretched over one hundred percent of the contingencies. Cheney's declaration is, in short, evidently a recipe for certain disasters.

Did Cheney actually mean what he said? Was it merely a cover to justify his and Bush's invasion of Iraq and their national security policy of ubiquitous surveillance? It is impossible to know for certain, although it seems wildly improbable that Cheney could have meant what he said. One could not operate on this principle in one's own life, let alone run a government based on it; one would have to become a mad recluse in a fortified house watching TV and scanning the news every day for remote possibilities and treating them as certainties. If, for example, there were a remote chance that you could trip and fall in the kitchen, you would have to take that possibility as a certainty and crawl about the house to forestall that contingency. Moreover, consider Cheney's ridiculous one percent equals certainty claim side-by-side with Bush's famous excuse after Katrina: "No one anticipated that the levees would be breached." If you think that even one-percent-probability events must be treated as certainties, then how is it that the collapse of levees that needed repairs in the face of a Category 5 hurricane was not anticipated?

Cheney's one-percent doctrine does represent the ultimate extreme of the logic of public order policies: if it is even remotely possible that someone or some group might be out to harm us, then we—the government—are justified in carrying out preemptive actions to suppress them as threats. In an example that could easily have served as a dystopian sci-fi scenario—

---

33 "'If there's a one percent chance that Pakistani scientists are helping al Qaeda build or develop a nuclear weapon, we have to treat it as a certainty in terms of our response,' Cheney said. He paused to assess his declaration. 'It's not about our analysis, or finding a preponderance of the evidence,' he added. 'It's about our response.'" From Ron Suskind, *The One Percent Doctrine: Deep Inside America's Pursuit of Its Enemies Since 9/11* (New York: Simon and Schuster, 2007), 62. According to Mr. Cheney, then, what we do is what matters, not whether what we are doing is based upon a reasonable assessment of what it is we face.

indeed, it invoked the Tom Cruise movie *The Minority Report*—in 2009 the ACLU learned from a leaked copy of the Department of Defense's (DoD) annual training course exam for all of its personnel that the DoD was instructing people that legal protest constitutes *"low-level terrorism."* (See Chapter Four for a detailed discussion of this.)

Magnus Hornqvist observed in the "Birth of Public Order Policy" in 2004:

> Over the last twenty years, the nature of the rule of law and the basis on which nation states employ force has been changing fundamentally. The distinction between what is criminal, to be dealt with by the legal and justice system, and what creates a 'perception of insecurity'—formerly to be dealt with by social policy—is being eroded at both the macro ('war on terror') and micro ('public order') levels. This paves the way for the unbridled use of state force, in the first instance, and the criminalisation of behaviours that are not necessarily illegal, in the second. Fear becomes a controlling mechanism for the maintenance of the social order and any element of non-conformity is construed as a threat. [34]

The ratcheting up of social control measures in alleged response to terrorism occurred before 9/11 and the various incidents that are commonly cited as lead-up terrorist incidents to 9/11 (e.g., the February 26, 1993, bombing of the World Trade Center; the October 12, 2000, attack on the USS Cole in Yemen; the 2001 suicide bombing murder of Afghanistan's Northern Alliance leader Ahmed Shah Massoud). The discourse of fear, the criminalization of previously noncriminal behaviors (including constitutionally protected free speech and protest), the massive covert government and private corporate surveillance of lawful activities and persons, and the increasing incarceration rate, all began in earnest before 9/11 and the "War on Terror."

Why has this happened? Hornqvist argues as follows:

> With the end of the cold war, the threat of military invasion disappeared in the prosperous nations of the world; since then, defence analysts have sought new areas in which to carry out their work and have been diagnosing new security risks. They have fastened on to

---

34   Magnus Hornqvist, "The Birth of Public Order Policy," *Race and Class* 46, no. 1 (July-September 2004), 30.

Muslim fundamentalism, poverty, the narcotics trade, streams of migration and political protest. These phenomena are at once both local and global. The illicit drugs found in every municipality are produced across great stretches of the globe, with the drug trade woven into the world economy. Refugees and asylum seekers may be found in virtually every municipality; at the same time, migration flows follow patterns of global conflict and the demand for cheap labour. As a consequence, it is judged increasingly meaningless to distinguish between internal and external security issues, to distinguish between threats and risks on the basis of whether they come from outside or inside the country.

The risks and threats on which these analyses focus are not military in nature. Neither drugs nor refugees constitute a security threat in any traditional sense. The central factor is not the potential for violence. Instead, the problem is of a more political character. ... It is a question of intent.

To determine whether an act is terrorist, one cannot merely look at the act itself; the underlying motive must also be examined.[35]

Hornqvist makes two main points in the preceding. First, the Cold War's end required military-related enterprises within and outside of government to find other justifications for their activities and expenditures. Second, the new alleged threats are simultaneously local and global in nature, and defining them as terrorist threats has to do with *who and what* these people and groups are, not their intent and their actions.

The Cold War's end has had, it is true, the effect of necessitating that military-related activities find other "threats" to justify their existence. This is in keeping with the customary nature of bureaucracies: bureaucracies do not commit suicide; they find ways to persist even when the original reason for their existence disappears. There is, however, an overarching, more important and compelling dynamic at work here: capitalism is a system that requires, but also exceeds, the specific demands of its military arm. To pursue profit and profit-making opportunities, military force is necessary, but military expenditures in and of themselves do not nearly account for capitalism's expansionist nature and aims. Wars, for example, are not waged just because or principally because some military suppliers make a lot of money from selling arms. The invasion of Iraq in 2003 did not happen mainly because Halliburton stood to gain from the invasion and occupation. Wars, in fact, create tremendous strains upon a

---

35 Ibid., 4

nation's economy as a whole and on the social fabric. (For more on this key point, see Chapter Two.)

As to Hornqvist's second point—the actors' intent—his point here would be more accurate if he had made it clear that the definition of terrorism has to do with the *definers' intent*. (He states this more clearly later: "It is more a question of who succeeds in establishing their definition of the situation and less one of what the threat really consists of. The security risks may be real or fictitious; it does not matter which—what they actually are or what they were to begin with—since they are what they have been made into and it is in this capacity that they exercise their effect.")[36]

The very fact that poor people, migrants, Muslims, drug dealers, and political protestors are all included in this list of potential "terrorists"—justifying surveillance over them all and the rousing of nativist sentiments against them—reveals a momentous and explicit shift in how public officials and opinion-makers govern. In an economy in which some must be poor because capitalism and poverty are co-occurring and mutually reinforcing phenomena—capitalism requires that some be unemployed and therefore willing to work for less in order to survive—and where migrant labor fuels economic activity like arteries keep a person alive, the criminalization of these indispensable groups reflects a deeply troubling facet of our contemporary world. The marginalized groups are told, in effect, "We need you to exist as you do, for you make us rich and comfortable, but the very fact of your existence renders you a suspect, a criminal and a possible terrorist." The poor and immigrants are therefore equally as indispensable as they are intolerable.[37]

---

36 Ibid., 40-41.

37 TV host Lou Dobbs, for example, has made anti-immigration sentiment a centerpiece of his shows. Yet this same avowed opponent of immigration relies upon undocumented immigrant workers to tend to his home and property:

> Lou Dobbs has become notorious for his hard-line stance on undocumented immigrants—and the people who hire them. Yet, as an explosive investigation released Thursday in The Nation uncovered, Dobbs has been relying on undocumented workers for years to maintain the upkeep of his homes and of the horses he bought for his daughter.
>
> In the article, "Lou Dobbs, American Hypocrite," author Isabel Macdonald spoke to at least five undocumented immigrants who were hired by Dobbs. Some were hired to help with the care and transport of the horse Dobbs' daughter Hillary, who is a champion show jumper, used in her professional career. Macdonald spoke to one immigrant, whom she called Marco Salinas:

One expression of this universalization of public order policies can be seen in the development and growth of "intelligence fusion centers." Fusion centers gather government and private intelligence in one place based on the rationale that the response to terrorism requires an unprecedented degree of data collection and surveillance. In June 2009, DHS recognized some seventy-two fusion centers nationwide. As stated by one of its advocates:

> Signs of Cold-War-era threats to national security—troops massing, submarines departing, and missile launchers where they weren't before—were easier to detect than today's more subtle indicators of terrorist activity. **Emerging terrorist threats can hide in plain sight on our own soil, scattered among millions of driver's license applications and bank transfers or amid tourists snapping photos of national icons.** In this new environment, vigilance is everyone's job, and the tasks of vetting, analyzing, and sharing information about threats can't be left to the federal government alone.[38] [Emphasis added.]

An old friend of Salinas's worked as a groom with some of the horses owned by Dobbs, and he had sent word that Salinas could be hired on as a groom at the Vermont stable contracted to care for the Dobbs Group horses.

Salinas got the job, he said, and worked at it for more than two years without documents until he was finally able to obtain a guest-worker visa designed for seasonal foreign workers (the same kind of visa denounced as a form of "indentured servitude" on Dobbs's CNN show).

I asked Salinas, still clad in his work clothes—a polo shirt and jeans—about Dobbs, the owner of the horses he cared for. But the father of three simply flashed a disarming grin, let out an easygoing laugh and politely declined to comment.

Macdonald spoke to other immigrants who worked in Dobbs' gardens, including a man named Rodrigo Ortega. Ortega told her about meeting Dobbs, who introduced himself in Spanish as "Luis." Ortega also said that Dobbs "knew very well that the majority of us didn't have papers," but that this "was never a problem."

Dobbs also neglected to pay Ortega and the other gardeners any overtime, even though they worked a fifty-hour week. Macdonald writes that this was consistent with Dobbs' overall treatment of his workers.

Jack Mirkinson, "Lou Dobbs Hired Illegal Immigrants," HuffingtonPost.com, October 7, 2010, http://www.huffingtonpost.com/2010/10/07/lou-dobbs-hired-illegal-immigrants_n_753799.html, accessed October 9, 2010.

38   Joseph Straw, "Fusion Centers Forge Ahead," SecurityManagement.com, October 2009, http://www.securitymanagement.com/article/fusion-centers-forge-ahead-006223, accessed on January 9, 2010.

This article goes on to cite the words of the New Jersey Regional Operations Intelligence Center's director Richard Kelly: "We want to be able to search everything, so we could see if Mohammed Atta ever got a parking ticket in Roselle. You can't connect the dots if you can't see them." Kelly is arguing for the viewpoint that underlies the advocates of the national security state: more information, and ideally total information, will give us the power to prevent undesirable events from occurring.[39]

In each and every known terrorist incident—beginning most famously with the tracking of the 9/11 conspirators before 9/11 through the Nigerian student Umar Farouk Abdul Mutallab's unsuccessful attempt to blow up a Northwest flight on Christmas Day 2009—there was no shortage of information. The dots were there to be connected, and in the case of 9/11 some people connected them, such as Counterterrorism Czar Richard Clarke and FBI Agent Coleen Rowley; but they were stymied by those above them and, in Clarke's case, those below him as well. As Matthew Aid, an intelligence historian, observed after the Abdul Mutallab incident, the NSA receives four times as much data every day as is held in the Library of Congress.[40] The intelligence community is, in other words, drowning in data.

In the aftermath of the embarrassing failure to bar Umar Farouk Abdul Mutallab from boarding his flight, Obama decried the failure to connect the dots and called for accountability to ensure they would be connected in the future. Obama's directive, however, does nothing more than reiterate the directives of his predecessors. The DHS and the Counterterrorism Center created after 9/11 were supposed to centralize information and allow the threads of intelligence to be recognized as patterns in order to correct the supposed failure to do so prior to 9/11. Moreover, as ex-senior CIA analyst Ray McGovern points out, the CENTRAL Intelligence Agency was supposed to do the very same thing decades ago in the wake of the surprise attack upon Pearl Harbor. "Been there, done that." More information than ever is now being collected, more agencies and personnel are charged with collecting information, redundancies have been deliberately built into the system in order to improve the likelihood

---

39   "Using programs with Orwellian names, such as Carnivore, MATRIX, Talon, Eagle Eyes, and Total Information Awareness, the administration is exercising an unprecedented level of power over citizens' lives." Barbara Bowley, "The Campaign for Unfettered Power," in *Impeach the President: the Case Against Bush and Cheney*, ed. Dennis Loo and Peter Phillips (New York: Seven Stories Press, 2006), 167.

40   As quoted in Scott Shane, "Shadow of 9/11 Is Cast Again," NYTimes.com, December 31, 2009, http://www.nytimes.com/2009/12/31/us/31intel.html?_r=3&th&emc=th, accessed December 31, 2009.

that at least one agency or even one agent will sound the alarm, agencies are sharing information a bit more, more money in the tens of billions is being shoveled into security, and civil liberties are being violated in unparalleled ways, and yet. . . they are still failing in their appointed tasks. How can this be?

"I'm Mohammed Atta." "No, I'm Mohammed Atta." "No, I'm Mohammed Atta..."

More information is not necessarily better, and in these instances there is obviously far too much irrelevant information. How can there be too much information? If you have too much data, then connecting dots becomes extremely difficult because you have too many possible threads to perceive and millions upon millions of irrelevant data points obscuring those threads. It is like trying to find multiple needles in a haystack while haystack after haystack after haystack is being dropped on you in an avalanche of hay. Obama and the bureaucracies' efforts to approach total information awareness are doomed to fail again and again because they are based on an incorrect premise.

The notion that knowing that Mohammed Atta got a parking ticket somewhere will somehow send off alarm bells assumes that you have already determined that Atta is someone to whom you have to pay particular attention. What good would it have done to know that he got a parking ticket in Roselle, even if he was already known to be a terrorist, which he was? If you have a list of more than half a million people that are possible suspects (as the US government had as of late 2010) with the list growing longer every day, this task of focusing on the next Atta becomes more difficult than ever. You have to make choices all along the way about what is relevant information and what is not. As you amass more and more irrelevant information, you make it more difficult, not easier, to determine what is relevant and what is noise.

Moreover, US policies that provoke more and more people into opposition to them are creating a cacophony of threatening noise. Public order policies that track and observe everyone as a potential suspect foster greater and greater levels of pure noise. The noise is deafening because the potential terrorists are everywhere, and by their very nature and magnitude they are impossible to identify and track. *Carrying out "national security" in this manner is like going out into a growing hurricane and trying to determine which flying objects are going to hit you and when.* If what you are doing is fostering the hurricane in the first place, as the Bush White House did in ignoring global warming and weakening New Orleans in the face of a storm, then you better stop doing those things or you are inviting disaster. The insistence that everyone is a potential problem and that more information about everything is better means that actual terrorist plots are being covered up by avalanches of useless and irrelevant information. It is like taking a gourmet meal prepared by a four-star restaurant and mixing it with tons and tons of garbage. Now, your challenge is to find the haute cuisine in that pile of stench.

The overriding problem here, however, is not the plethora of unusable and illegitimately obtained information about all of us, as insuperable as that problem is. Even if that problem did not exist, there would still be a larger problem: intelligence failures do not discredit the existing policies of ubiquitous surveillance, war, occupations, indefinite detentions, torture, assassinations, and drone attacks. Failures of intelligence promote and justify the existing policies that are supposed to prevent terrorism. The longer the US goes without another successful or abortive terrorist incident, the harder it becomes to justify the security state's measures. Thus, *the security state has a stake in having at least some anti-state terrorist incidents occur.* This is the security state's dirty little secret.

When the dominant paradigm is the "War on Terror" and when the gains to be had from continuing this war are as extraordinary as they are—booty in the trillions of dollars overall and the reins of political power of an empire—then any strategically placed individual or group could take advantage of this condition by suppressing information about an upcoming terrorist incident, by allowing an incident to happen that could have been prevented, or by manufacturing a fall guy to carry out an attack, and get away with it. The GOP, Democrats, and the mass media, after all, have ruled raising questions about the wisdom or effectiveness of the "anti-terrorist" measures out of order. The traditional safeguards, such as the separation of powers that are supposed to prevent such a cynical ploy from being carried out have been eliminated.

If this sounds hard to believe, consider the fact that Bush and Cheney were caught red-handed fabricating the WMD excuse to invade Iraq, and they were still not impeached. They were caught red-handed torturing people, at least one hundred of them to death, and they were still not impeached or prosecuted.[41] They were caught red-handed spying on every single American in felonious violation of the law, including every senator,

---

41 Glenn Greenwald, "The Suppressed Fact: Deaths by U.S. Torture," Salon.com, June 30, 2009, http://www.salon.com/news/opinion/glenn_greenwald/2009/06/30/accountability, accessed February 14, 2011.

congressperson, prosecutor and judge, and they were still not impeached or prosecuted. If these transgressive acts were not punished but were retroactively approved with their underlying excuses endorsed by both major parties, then it should be no surprise that these policies would then continue. Is it any wonder, then, that Obama has been continuing their policies and in some very important respects going even further? The wonder would be if he actually attempted to put a stop to it all.

A Disorderly New Order

Walmart's rock bottom pricing and insistence on lowering prices every year on staples forces suppliers to employ the cheapest labor the globe offers. This produces job losses domestically and hollows out the economic activity and viability of Main Street businesses around the country. It accelerates deindustrialization and the consequent rise of illicit and gray—and black-market economic activities, since licit activities are disappearing. In Detroit, for instance, real estate depends heavily for its viability upon drug dealers who represent one of the only thriving economic activities around. In China, millions of involuntary migrants undergird the country's race for economic power, even as the government treats them as hooligans. The drug trade in the US represents a highly profitable—and therefore violent—business because the drug war drives the value of the drugs up and therefore spawns drug dealers aplenty, both domestically and internationally. The drug war itself, therefore, has contributed substantially to the funding of anti-state terrorist groups that profit from the opium, for instance, of the poppy fields in Afghanistan.

Muslims' antipathy for the West grows directly out of the policies being carried out, especially by the West and the US, not by the fact that "they hate our freedoms," as Bush claimed. Neoliberalism, in other words, creates and expands the populations and activities that it then turns around to label as dire threats to its brave new disorderly order. Put another way, the forces insisting that order is under siege and that repression and extralegal measures are necessary to cope with that disorder are the same forces creating disorder in the society by dispossessing increasing ranks of the people, endangering the planet's biosystem, and provoking greater and greater levels of social insecurity.

Neoliberal regimes' ever-growing inequities produce dissension and dissatisfaction, not because the disaffected elect to feel disaffection—although the already privileged tend to see it that way, as if there is bounty for all if everyone would simply put their noses to the grindstone, there being no structural logic to the dispossession of so many for the wealth of the few. Rather, the disadvantaged's status brings them into conflict with those that the system favors. The position of the disadvantaged is what makes them criminal, dangerous, and potential terrorists. As Hornqvist correctly notes:

> [O]n the basis of the formulation contained in the [European Union] EU's definition, it is difficult to determine which motivations are not of a terrorist nature. What, for example, does it mean to intend to "unduly compel a Government or international organisation to perform or abstain from performing any act"? This will depend entirely on the political positioning of a particular observer.[42]

The breathtaking universality of this EU definition of terrorism—those who compel the government to act in a certain way are by definition terrorists—is mirrored in the US's definition, the subject of my next chapter. Government, according to this definition, can only do what it should do if the citizens do not try to influence it. A president calling on Congress to pass a piece of legislation in a State of the Union Address by this definition would constitute terrorism. Instead of Joe Wilson, Representative from South Carolina, yelling at the President, "You lie!" we could have him declare to the President: "You're a terrorist!"

Just as the meaning of terrorism has been expanded so has the larger category of "crime," so that acts that have never been considered criminal are now being proscribed as suitable for police and other social-control agents to repress. As Hornqvist puts it: "'Crime,' writes the [EU] commission, as well as 'crime in the strict sense' includes 'anti-social conduct which, without necessarily being a criminal offence, can by its cumulative effect generate a climate of tension and insecurity.'"[43] This development, by the way, is consistent with conservative James Q. Wilson's 1980's "broken windows" theory that argues that allowing windows and other physical attributes of a neighborhood to go into disrepair creates an atmosphere conducive to lawbreaking since the run-down nature of the physical surroundings shows a lack of caring that encourages offenders.

---

42 Hornqvist, 5.

43 Ibid., 36. [Hornqvist here cites Council of the European Union, "Council Decision Setting Up a European Crime Prevention Network" (26 April 2001, 7794/01), Article 1.3, 6.]

In the neoliberal world not only do physical characteristics matter, but behaviors, dress, class background, attitudes, and so on, can create a sense of "insecurity" for others, justifying clampdowns. The law no longer represents the standard that people must abide by in order to avoid having police actions and prosecutions imposed upon them. The new standard is that one can be subjected to governmental or private social control measures simply for being a perceived threat or source of discomfort to someone. This undermining of the rule of law is being carried out across the full spectrum of bureaucratic and corporate purview and policy making from top to bottom. As Hornqvist puts it: "It may seem absurd that a single area of policy should cover everything from truancy and drug sales to acts of terror. But it is absurd only because so many of us have not yet learned to proceed from a concept of security that has broken away from the logic of the law."[44] From this perspective, Bush and Cheney's express violations of the rule of law are then not unique to them. They were merely on the cutting edge of that trajectory. And Obama's perpetuation of their actions represents the further advance of that neoliberal project. *This means that attempts to restore the rule of law will not succeed as a strategy separate from a fundamental challenge to the entire logic of the system itself.*

Reinterpreting protest and poverty as terrorism is a trend that stretches across continents and that includes all of the major political parties in the world's nations. This explains what for many people is otherwise inexplicable: the perpetuation, further elaboration, and institutionalization under Democrat Barack Obama of the national security state measures that Bush and Cheney spearheaded. Obama and the Democratic Party leadership are continuing on the path that was already underway before Bush, dating back to the late 1970s. What Bush and Cheney did that was different was openly breach the wall of the rule of law.

The sensitivity and momentousness of this breach explains why Obama ran on a platform of restoring the rule of law, restoring habeas corpus, and ending atrocities such as torture: Bush and Cheney's practices had been so widely reviled and were so fundamental a rupture from the previous social contract of governments with their people that reviving people's confidence in their government had to be done lest fracturing and resultant upheavals ensued. What Obama has in fact done has been the repackaging of these practices.

When running for office and after taking office, Obama made a point of saying that he believes in, and is implementing, transparency in government:

---

44   Ibid., 37.

Just weeks after taking office, the Obama administration adopted an unprecedented policy of sunlight, directing bureaucrats across government to "apply a presumption of openness" regarding the release of documents to the public, according to a memo by Obama's attorney general, Eric Holder.

Obama's policy does not cover an important part of the White House: the Office of Administration, which oversees much of the day-to-day functions of the president's own office and staff.

In 2007, then-president George W. Bush, whose penchant for secrecy was a reliable villain in Obama's campaign speeches, became the first president to declare the White House Office of Administration off-limits to public inquiries. At the time, Bush was engaged in a heated court battle with good government groups over access to information about a massive batch of missing White House e-mails.

A federal court ruled in favor of the Bush administration, agreeing that the office was not technically an "agency" as defined by FOIA, and was not required to abide by the openness law.

Today, the Obama White House Web site announces that the Office of Administration "is not subject to FOIA and related authorities." [45]

In a May 21, 2009, speech at the National Archives, Obama said this about the "War on Terror":

We're going to exhaust every avenue that we have to prosecute those at Guantanamo who pose a danger to our country. But even when this process is complete, there may be a number of people who cannot be prosecuted for past crimes, in some cases because evidence may be tainted, but who nonetheless pose a threat to the security of the United States. Examples of that threat include people who've received extensive explosives training at al-Qaida training camps, or commanded Taliban troops in battle, or expressed their allegiance to Osama bin Laden, or otherwise made it clear that they want to kill Americans. These are people who, in effect, remain at war with the United States.

---

45   Justin Rod, "Like Bush, Obama White House Chooses Secrecy for Key Office," ABC-News.com, May 15, 2009, http://abcnews.go.com/Blotter/story?id=7589622&page=1, accessed December 12, 2009.

> Let me repeat: I am not going to release individuals who endanger the American people. Al-Qaida terrorists and their affiliates are at war with the United States, and those that we capture—like other prisoners of war—must be prevented from attacking us again.[46]

If the people he will not release cannot be released because the evidence against them is tainted—because they were tortured to obtain the "evidence"—then that is not the fault of the individual detainee; that is the result of criminal acts by the US government. This stands in direct contradiction to Obama's campaign pledge that he would restore habeas corpus because holding innocents is "not what we do." In his National Archives speech, Obama hastened to add that the decision to hold someone who has not been found guilty of any crimes should not be the action of the executive branch alone and that detention should not be open ended. "That's why my administration has begun to reshape the standards that apply to ensure that they are in line with the rule of law. We must have clear, defensible, and lawful standards for those who fall into this category. We must have fair procedures so that we do not make mistakes. We must have a thorough process of periodic review, so that any prolonged detention is carefully evaluated and justified." How does one square abridging habeas corpus with ensuring you are "in line with the rule of law?" How do you have "lawful standards" when you are breaking the law itself to do it?

This outcome was actually predictable.

First, as I have been arguing in this book, neoliberal policies have been ascendant and dominant, and both major political parties in the US operate within the overall parameters and logic of that ideology.

Second, public policy and especially public policy shifts are not ever carried out successfully by individual leaders, no matter how powerfully placed. They require movements and they require institutional support. This is true from the top of the political system and it is also true from the grassroots or from any other social or economic stratum. The widespread notion that electing a particular individual to high office will produce anything more than superficial changes reveals a lack of understanding of how politics actually operate.

Third, the elevation of an individual to the status of a viable, "legitimate," and "electable" candidate cannot occur absent the backing of

---

46 "Text: Obama's Speech on National Security," May 21, 2009, NYTimes.com, http://www.nytimes.com/2009/05/21/us/politics/21obama.text.html?_r=1&pagewanted=all, accessed February 11, 2011.

powerful organizational and institutional forces that are by their nature key players in the status quo.

Fourth, promises that public officials make are not immune from evaluation to determine what they actually intend; one does not have to wait and see until after they take office. We can, with proper analytical tools, decipher what these public officials' promises and pronouncements really mean before they take office.

As I wrote in June 2008, after Obama was nominated: "How can the same system, and the same *specific* individuals, who have cooperated in, permitted and/or legalized the outrageous and profound crimes of the Bush regime—including torture and war crimes—now tell us that the candidate that *they* endorse *is the solution* to the monstrous things that this system and these individuals have themselves *allowed and colluded in?*" [47]

The Nature of Bureaucracies

> *It's not just Katrina that caused all these deaths in New Orleans here. Bureaucracy has committed murder here in the greater New Orleans area, and bureaucracy has to stand trial before Congress now.*
>
> **AARON BROUSSARD**
> President of Jefferson Parish, New Orleans, 2005[48]

Max Weber pointed out that bureaucracies reach their highest development in advanced capitalist countries and represent the material ascension and installation of rationality, a process by which nature, society, and individual action are increasingly mastered by planning, technical procedure, and rational action. Bureaucracies triumphed, beginning in the West, because they embody a specific combination of being the most predictable, dependable, efficient, *and* controllable way of doing things. In any given situation, bureaucracies might not be the most efficient way to do something, as anyone who has had any experiences with bureaucracies knows, but over time bureaucracies' other attributes as an ensemble are almost impossible to beat. Attempting to run things by consensus for any groups

---

47   Dennis Loo, "Of Whales and Worms," Counterpunch.org, June 16, 2008, http://www.counterpunch.org/loo06162008.html, accessed June 16, 2008.

48   "Transcript for September 4," *Meet the Press*, NBC.com, September 4, 2005, http://www.msnbc.msn.com/id/9179790/ns/meet_the_press/, accessed January 31, 2011.

larger than a few people is unfeasible. The business of organizing work of any kind, be it that of a club, a political party, or a corporation, necessitates a division of tasks and specializations with the actual major work and decisions made via committees and specifically the leaders within those committees, especially the executive committee—in other words, a bureaucratic structure. The trouble with bureaucracies is precisely an outgrowth of the very things that make them so powerful and so difficult to combat and/or undo. As Weber wrote:

> This order is now bound to the technical and economic conditions of machine production which to-day determine the lives of all the individuals who are born into this mechanism, not only those directly concerned with economic acquisition, with irresistible force. Perhaps it will so determine them until the last ton of fossilized coal is burnt. In Baxter's view the care for external goods should only lie on the shoulders of the "saint like a light cloak, which can be thrown aside at any moment." But fate decreed that the cloak should become an iron cage.[49]

This "iron cage of rationality" that Weber warned of substitutes

- routinization for creativity
- formal rationality (bureaucratic logic focusing on uniform and consistent procedures for how things shall be done) for substantive rationality (the commonsense meaning of rationality—a logical goal pursued by logical means)
- orders from above (regardless of whether those orders are the best ideas and whether or not those orders are even rational) over ideas and knowledge from below or from the outside,
- specialization of tasks over big picture reasoning
- secrecy and deception in order to keep its activities obscured from scrutiny by others, including public officials and the public.

Rivalries between different bureaucracies and their reluctance to share critical information with each other—for example, between the police and the FBI, between the FBI and the CIA, etc.—even when the

---

49 Ian McIntosh, ed., *Classical Sociological Theory* (New York: NYU Press, 1997), 129-130.

consequences of this non-cooperation could be devastating, such as the terrorist attacks on 9/11, are an outgrowth of the basic nature of bureaucracies: their secrecy (not just from the public and public officials, but also from other bureaucracies) and their jealously protected turf. Their sectarianism is not, in other words, a product primarily of bureaucrats' myopia. It is a product of the narrowness that springs from bureaucracies' fundamental nature—the constant striving to guard their turf and their persistent attempts to expand further the areas under their control.

As former CIA analyst Melvin Goodman points out,

> The NSA had information on the Nigerian bomber [the Christmas Day 2009 failed terrorist on a Northwest flight from Amsterdam to Detroit] that wasn't shared with the CIA and the FBI; the CIA prepared a biographic study of the Nigerian bomber, which it didn't share with NCTC. The State Department did not pursue whether the Nigerian bomber had a U.S. visa, let alone a multiple-entry visa, in his possession.[50]

The blind spot created by bureaucracy's tendency to privilege process over results can and does produce awful consequences. In addition, the specialization of tasks that mark bureaucracies and reflect, in certain important respects, a particular strength over other forms of organization, also tends to undermine synthetic reasoning—pulling together diverse strands and seeing the larger picture. Organizational divisions, therefore, also express themselves in a tendency for bureaucracies to fail to see the big picture—a failure to put 2 and 2 together.

Finally, bureaucratic chiefs tend to suppress information that makes them look bad both before a disaster (tending to dismiss information that requires major action or that requires demoting or disciplining people they like, e.g., warnings of shoddy performance or of a catastrophe coming) and after a disaster (suppressing evidence that they failed to respond to obvious signals of trouble brewing).

Counterterrorism Czar Richard Clarke, for example, tried mightily to get the Bush White House to pay proper attention to the threat of al-Qaeda, but people higher in the bureaucracy than himself overruled him. That fact is well known. What is less well known is that Clarke was also stymied from below by lower levels of the bureaucracy, specifically by lead-

---

50   Melvin Goodman, "What's Wrong with US Intel Agencies," ConsortiumNews.com, January 28, 2010, http://www.consortiumnews.com/2010/012710c.html, accessed January 30, 2010.

ers within the FAA. As described by Nafeez Mosaddeq Ahmed, Director of the Institute for Policy Research and Development in Brighton, UK:

> The White House National Coordinator for Counterterrorism, Richard Clarke, had also given direct warning to the Federal Aviation Administration (FAA) to increase security measures in light of an impending terrorist attack in July 2001. The FAA refused to take such measures.
>
> Former Federal Air Safety Inspector Rodney Stich, who has 50 years of experience in aviation and air safety, had warned the FAA about the danger of skyjacking, specifically highlighting the fact that cockpit doors weren't secure, and further that pilots should be allowed to carry basic weapons. The FAA refused to implement his suggestions, and when it became apparent the threat was real, they blocked efforts to arm pilots, or to place air marshals on planes, among other security measures. In an extensive study of the subject, Stich observes that:
>
>> "Federal inspectors... had years earlier reported the hijacking threat and the simple inexpensive measures to prevent hijackers from taking control of the aircraft. Numerous fatal hijackings further proved the need for urgent preventative measures. Instead of taking the legally required corrective actions, arrogant and corrupt FAA management personnel destroyed official reports of the dangers and the need for corrective actions; warned air safety inspectors not to submit reports that would make the office look bad when there is a crash related to the known problems; threatened inspectors who took corrective actions or continued to make reports—even though crashes from these uncorrected safety problems continued to occur."

The *Los Angeles Times* corroborates this assessment: "Federal bureaucracy and airline lobbying slowed and weakened a set of safety improvements recommended by a presidential commission—including one that a top airline industry official now says might have prevented the Sept. 11 terror attacks...

"The White House Commission on Aviation Safety and Security, created in 1996 after TWA Flight 800 crashed off Long Island, N.Y., recommended 31 steps that it said were urgently needed to provide a multilayered security system at the nation's airports... The Federal Aviation Administration expressed support for the proposals, which ranged from security inspections at airports to tighter screening of mail parcels, and the Clinton administration vowed to rigorously monitor the changes. But by Sept. 11, most of the proposals had been watered down by industry lobbying or were bogged down in bureaucracy, a Times review found."

The U.S. government thus bears direct responsibility for this state of affairs, by consistently failing to comply with its avowed responsibility to "rigorously monitor" and enforce the required changes. Larry Klayman, Chairman and General Counsel of Judicial Watch, the Washington-based legal watchdog, comments that: "It is now apparent—given the near total lack of security at U.S. airports and elsewhere—that the U.S. government has not been forthright with the American people...

"During the last eight years of scandal during the Clinton administration, and the first eight months of the Bush Administration, reports this morning confirm that little to nothing was done to secure our nation's airports and transportation systems as a whole—despite warnings. Instead, cosmetic reform of education, social security, taxes, and other less important issues were given precedence..."[51]

Ahmed concludes that the above is "more than a case of incompetence... [indicating] wilful [British spelling] and reckless negligence of the highest order on the part of the U.S. government, rooted in sheer indifference to the potential loss in American lives." Indifference to the potential loss of American lives is, however, par for the course for bureaucracies that focus on process more than on results. It is also par for the course as businesses lobby relentlessly and successfully to weaken or avoid measures that regulators demand of them. Corporate lobbying power—both in its increasing use and in government's obsequiousness to it—has mushroomed under neoliberal regimes; market forces are, after all, to use *Star Trek's* terminology, "the prime directive." Like the elephant in the room, corporations get to do nearly anything they want.

Warnings prior to 9/11 of a pending attack were dire enough that Richard Clarke acted with tremendous urgency. The record shows that Bush, Cheney, National Security Advisor Rice, and others above Clarke behaved with criminal indifference to repeated and urgent warnings by Clarke and other members of the intelligence community. Many look at this evidence and conclude that Bush, et al must therefore have wanted

---

51   Nafeez Mosaddeq Ahmed, "Did Bush Know?", MediaMonitorsNetwork.net, May 18, 2002, http://www.mediamonitors.net/mosaddeq36.html, accessed May 2, 2009.

9/11 to happen. They may well have wanted it and they raised not a finger to forestall it. They have obviously benefited from it in spades.

But what is striking here is how much their behavior before 9/11 matches their actions prior to and after Katrina—utter indifference and criminal negligence. While 9/11 obviously served as the equivalent of a false flag attack for the Bush White House, Katrina did not. Katrina, in fact, created widespread disaffection with Bush and Cheney. At least the FAA's behavior, which was subject directly to Clarke's edicts prior to 9/11, can also very reasonably be ascribed to the power of lobbyists in a weakened regulatory environment and to the common characteristics of bureaucracies especially before a disaster strikes: "We've always done things this way, and we're damned if anyone outside of us, even if they are above us, is going to make us change what we've been doing." The worst and most alarming news here, in other words, is not that 9/11 was an inside job, a grand conspiracy hatched within the highest US government echelons. It is instead that 9/11 and other disasters such as the BP Deepwater Horizon catastrophe are due to the normal and ordinary workings of capitalism, and specifically neoliberal policies. That is much more distressing than believing that 9/11 was an inside job.

In another example of this unholy marriage of globalization and the worst attributes of bureaucracy, consider the problem of E. coli in hamburger meat. As reported by *New York Times* writer Michael Moss on October 3, 2009:

> Stephanie Smith, a children's dance instructor, thought she had a stomach virus. The aches and cramping were tolerable that first day, and she finished her classes. Then her diarrhea turned bloody. Her kidneys shut down. Seizures knocked her unconscious. The convulsions grew so relentless that doctors had to put her in a coma for nine weeks. When she emerged, she could no longer walk. The affliction had ravaged her nervous system and left her paralyzed.
>
> Ms. Smith, 22, was found to have a severe form of food-borne illness caused by E. coli, which Minnesota officials traced to the hamburger that her mother had grilled for their Sunday dinner in early fall 2007. . . .
>
> Meat companies and grocers have been barred from selling ground beef tainted by the virulent strain of E. coli known as O157:H7 since 1994, after an outbreak at Jack in the Box restaurants left **four children dead**. Yet **tens of thousands of people are still sickened annually by this pathogen** . . . Ground beef has been blamed for 16 outbreaks

in the last three years alone, including the one that left Ms. Smith paralyzed from the waist down . . . Ground beef is usually not simply a chunk of meat run through a grinder. . . . [A] single portion of hamburger meat is often an amalgam of various grades of meat from different parts of cows and even from different slaughterhouses. . . .

Despite this, there is no federal requirement for grinders to test their ingredients for the pathogen.

The frozen hamburgers that the Smiths ate, which were made by the food giant Cargill, were labeled "American Chef's Selection Angus Beef Patties." . . .[T]he hamburgers were made from a mix of slaughterhouse trimmings and a mash-like product derived from scraps that were ground together at a plant in Wisconsin. The ingredients came from slaughterhouses in Nebraska, Texas and Uruguay, and from a South Dakota company that processes fatty trimmings and treats them with ammonia to kill bacteria.

Using a combination of sources—a practice followed by most large producers of fresh and packaged hamburger—allowed Cargill to spend about 25 percent less than it would have for cuts of whole meat.

Those low-grade ingredients are cut from areas of the cow that are more likely to have had contact with feces. . . . Many big slaughterhouses will sell only to grinders who agree not to test their shipments for E. coli. . . . Slaughterhouses fear that one grinder's discovery of E. coli will set off a recall of ingredients they sold to others. . . . A test by The Times found that the safe handling instructions are not enough to prevent the bacteria from spreading in the kitchen.

Cargill, whose $116.6 billion in revenues last year made it the country's largest private company, declined requests to interview company officials or visit its facilities. "Cargill is not in a position to answer your specific questions, other than to state that we are committed to continuous improvement in the area of food safety," the company said, citing continuing litigation.

The meat industry treats much of its practices and the ingredients in ground beef as trade secrets. . . . Federal records released by the department through the Freedom of Information Act blacked out details of Cargill's grinding operation . . . . Those documents illustrate the restrained approach to enforcement by a department whose missions include ensuring meat safety and promoting agriculture markets. . . . In the weeks before Ms. Smith's patty was made, federal inspectors had repeatedly found that Cargill was violating its own safety procedures in handling ground beef, but they imposed no fines or sanctions. . . .

In the end . . . the agency accepted Cargill's proposal to increase its scrutiny of suppliers.[52] [Emphases added.]

In the case of hamburger, Cargill and the rest of the meat industry treat their practices and ingredients as trade secrets. Consider that: the food we eat, how it is processed, and where it comes from are trade secrets! The subordination of public safety and the public welfare to the dictates of profit guarantee two outcomes: huge profits for big capital and periodic disasters for the people. It is in the very nature of neoliberal policies that these two consequences will continue. That is because it is not profitable to ensure that all hamburger meat is safe. It is cheaper to allow some pathogens to be marketed on a regular basis. It costs much less money to pay lawsuit claims for incidents in which people die or are made deathly ill and left with lasting, as in Stephanie Smith's case, paralysis than it does to prevent those incidents from happening in the first place.

This was the very logic that Ford Motor Company employed with their infamous 1970s Pinto. It would have only cost them, as they calculated, $6 per car to fix the defect that caused Pintos to explode into flames upon certain kinds of impact. But it would cost less to pay for property damage and the loss of what they estimated would be a few hundred lives than to pay the $6 per car, since millions of cars had the defect. So what did Ford do? Ford executives did not fix the defect. As it turned out, Ford's estimate of the numbers who would die was low. Twelve hundred people perished. When the case went to trial the "smoking gun" memo showing Ford executives' "better idea" not to fix this deadly defect was prohibited by the judge from being entered into evidence.

As a result of Reagan's deregulation of the airline industry, large carriers have outsourced their smaller routes to regional carriers that still bear the names of the large carriers; these small regional carriers now account for more than half of all domestic flights, and they operate profitably by cutting corners on safety. As PBS's *Frontline* revealed in a 2010 show named "Flying Cheap":

Former Continental CEO Gordon Bethune was a leader in the new formula. Outsourcing helped Continental remain more competitive

---

52   Michael Moss, "The Burger That Shattered Her Life," NYTimes.com, October 3, 2009, http://www.nytimes.com/2009/10/04/health/04meat.html, accessed February 2, 2010.

and avoid another bankruptcy as they bid more routes out. "Having an independent allows an airline to bid that and have a competitive relationship and make sure they get their flying done at the lowest cost," explains Bethune. John Prater, president of the Air Line Pilots Association, says: "The major airlines created the regional industry as a way of lowering costs. They wanted to find a way of getting rid of experience. They wanted to find a way of getting rid of that expensive employee, and let's start this new industry and call it the regional industry."[53]

Bush and Cheney gambled that New Orleans would not face a major hurricane. Donald Rumsfeld decided that sending American soldiers into combat without sufficient body armor and other requisite gear and sending in far fewer troops than his generals requested would not impair the military's fighting capacity. The neocons' plans were to quickly dominate Iraq and then turn to other countries in their sights—Iran, Syria, and so on—so they did not want to commit a lot of soldiers to Iraq. American soldiers' lives, from that perspective, are disposable, just as the lives of the victims of Hurricane Katrina were disposable, as were the lives of those killed on 9/11. Lest it be forgotten, this mantle of criminal irresponsibility is not exclusive to the GOP. Clinton's administration played its part in neglecting to toughen up FAA security at airports in the face of known threats against US aircraft by al-Qaeda and others.

Threats of context, as Frier dubs them, are products of the routine, everyday workings of the existing system and that system's priorities. The system is in turn dominated and configured by bureaucracies' routine activities. How then can the organizations and institutions responsible for these threats of context deal with disasters brought on in part by themselves? That would be like asking for an invading and occupying army responsible for atrocities against a country's people to remain because they must fix the mess they created in the first place. When you are making very big profits in the present, there is a major disincentive to look to any future consequences. This is all the more true when some or all of those negative consequences are due to your own policies.

While Obama believes global warming is a danger, the measures being undertaken to slow it fall grievously far below what is necessary at this point. As James Hansen, whose proven track record on anticipating the course of global warmings' progressive danger signs makes him the most

---

53 "Flying Cheap," *Frontline*, PBS.org, February 9, 2010, http://www.pbs.org/wgbh/pages/frontline/flyingcheap/etc/synopsis.html, accessed February 21, 2010.

credible scientist around, has forcefully warned, the point of no return has already been passed and emergency measures are needed. In a 2003 report commissioned by Andrew Marshall and written by former Shell Oil Head of Planning Peter Schwartz and California think tank Global Business Network's Doug Randall, the Department of Defense (DoD) itself warned of the convulsive effects that global warming in the not distant future will wreak in the form of forced migrations of tens of millions and wars over resources critical to actual survival; the DoD described this as a threat "greater than terrorism."

> The research suggests that ...adverse weather conditions could develop relatively abruptly, with persistent changes in the atmospheric circulation causing drops in some regions of 5-10 degrees Fahrenheit in a single decade. Paleoclimatic evidence suggests that **altered climatic patterns could last for as much as a century,** as they did when the ocean conveyor collapsed 8,200 years ago, **or, at the extreme, could last as long as 1,000 years** as they did during the Younger Dryas, which began about 12,700 years ago. . . .
>
> [A]n increasing number of business leaders, economists, policy makers, and politicians are concerned about the projections for further change and are working to limit human influences on the climate. But, these efforts may not be sufficient or be implemented soon enough.
>
> Rather than decades or even centuries of gradual warming, recent evidence suggests the possibility that a more dire climate scenario may actually be unfolding. . . . [54]
>
> As famine, disease, and weather-related disasters strike due to the abrupt climate change, many countries' needs will exceed their carrying capacity. This will create a sense of desperation, which is likely to lead to offensive aggression in order to reclaim balance. Imagine eastern European countries, struggling to feed their populations with a falling supply of food, water, and energy, eyeing Russia, whose population is already in decline, for access to its grain, minerals, and energy supply. Or, picture Japan, suffering from flooding along its coastal cities and contamination of its fresh water supply, eying Russia's Sakhalin Island oil and gas reserves as an energy source to power desalination plants and energy-intensive agricultural processes. Envision Pakistan, India, and China—all armed with nuclear weapons—skirmishing at their borders over refugees, access to shared rivers, and arable land. Spanish and Portuguese fishermen might fight over

---

54 Ibid., 5

fishing rights—leading to conflicts at sea. And, countries including the United States would be likely to better secure their borders. With over 200 river basins touching multiple nations, we can expect conflict over access to water for drinking, irrigation, and transportation. The Danube touches twelve nations, the Nile runs though nine, and the Amazon runs through seven.[55] [Emphasis added.]

The response from the Pentagon's spokesperson Dan Hetlage to this report was interesting:

We did not expect any White House response to the Pentagon on this report. Andrew Marshall is our Yoda, our big thinker who peers into the future. But it's all speculation. It was very ethereal, very broad in scope. It wasn't like, "Oh, wow, that totally debunks the president's stand on global warming," because it was merely a thought exercise. We don't have a crystal ball. We don't really *know*.[56] [Emphasis in the original.]

They "don't really *know*." When astronauts go into space, the back-up systems NASA creates to protect the astronauts and their missions are multiple in nature in case the first few fail. The scenarios they run in preparation for outer space travel are diverse and complex. These efforts are protecting a handful of people in space; yet, when the entire planet is at risk, the trigger for action is based on whether or not they know *for certain* that something will happen. Of course, at the point when the dangers are manifest and present, action in response is much too late. This is the equivalent of packing the entirety of humanity into one big car and those in charge of the welfare of the passengers deciding that they are not going to put on any seatbelts because they do not know for certain that there will be an accident.

While conventional wisdom sees governments as overseeing economic players and forces, global capital (as manifested in particular by the actions of transnational corporations like Walmart and the IMF and

---

55   Peter Schwartz and Doug Randall, "An Abrupt Climate Change Scenario and Its Implications for United States National Security," Edf.org, October 2003, www.edf.org/documents/3566_AbruptClimateChange.pdf, accessed on July 30, 2010.

56   Amanda Little, "Apocalyptic Pentagon Report on Global Warming Could Spur Action on Capitol Hill," *Pentagoners* (blog), Grist.org, February 25, 2004, http://www.grist.org/article/pentagoners/, accessed on July 30, 2010.

World Bank) subordinates governments to international capital's movements and decisions. The rivalry—to the extent that a rivalry exists—between non-state actors and the neoliberal state is therefore, contrary to Robb's assessment, a unity of opposites (opposite sides of the same coin), rather than the new versus the old. In other words, the threat to our collective security comes from two ends of the spectrum, not just one, and both are outgrowths of globalization's very nature. Globalization, as it ties the entire world together more tightly, at the same time paradoxically undermines our security and subjects the parts and the whole to more and more severe disruption and grander disasters. "Too big to fail" is the corollary to "the bigger they are, the harder we all fall." The neoliberals acknowledge the growing danger and peril in society, after a fashion. They do not, of course, acknowledge their central culpability and that of late stage capitalism for this danger.

The Privatized State

Neoliberals have characterized the state as something to be avoided, an object of disdain like a grasping, lecherous, drunken uncle; it is depicted especially by the GOP as a clumsy, tax-grabbing, wasteful, intrusive, inefficient, costly Big Brother. Private and individual solutions have been increasingly offered to replace this unappealing, decrepit, sallow-cheeked state. But the GOP's anti-government and anti-bureaucracy talk represents a rhetorical conceit. They have come not to bury Caesar but to aggrandize him. The GOP, especially, has wielded governmental power to accomplish the transfer of more and more power and largesse to private interests. While the GOP has been most famously associated with this strategy and has been the most aggressive in its pursuit, the Democratic Party has also been following this path since the late 1970s.

We can refer to the neoliberal state as the privatized state, or as the "for sale" and "for profit" state. When major US investment banks such as JPMorgan and Goldman Sachs got into trouble in 2008, the government stepped in to bail them out from their own ruthless profit-raking ways—a demonstration in dramatic fashion of the primacy given to profit making by the big players; if state actions that look like "socialism" on a superficial level (the state stepping in and buying up shares of private companies) must be taken to defend and protect big capital, then this is not unjust state action according to both major parties—this is entirely necessary and appropriate.

It may come as a surprise that one of the most powerful forces driving the resurgence on Wall Street [in 2009] is not the banks but Washington. Many of the steps that policy makers took last year to stabilize the financial system—reducing interest rates to near zero, bolstering big banks with taxpayer money, guaranteeing billions of dollars of financial institutions' debts—helped set the stage for this new era of Wall Street wealth.

Titans like Goldman Sachs and JPMorgan Chase are making fortunes in hot areas like trading stocks and bonds, rather than in the ho-hum business of lending people money. They also are profiting by taking risks that weaker rivals are unable or unwilling to shoulder—a benefit of less competition after the failure of some investment firms last year.

So even as big banks fight efforts in Congress to subject their industry to greater regulation—and to impose some restrictions on executive pay—Wall Street has Washington to thank in part for its latest bonanza.[57]

Besides this, while selling synthetic collateralized debt obligations (CDO's) that resulted soon afterwards in billions in losses for pension and insurance companies, some banks and hedge funds were betting in private that these CDO's would fail and made huge profits on those bets. As *The New York Times* revealed on December 24, 2009:

Just as synthetic C.D.O.'s began growing rapidly, some Wall Street banks [such as Goldman Sachs] pushed for technical modifications governing how they worked in ways that made it possible for C.D.O.'s to expand even faster, and also tilted the playing field in favor of banks and hedge funds that bet against C.D.O.'s, according to investors.

In early 2005, a group of prominent traders met at Deutsche Bank's office in New York and drew up a new system, called Pay as You Go. This meant the insurance for those betting against mortgages would pay out more quickly. The traders then went to the International Swaps and Derivatives Association, the group that governs

---

57 Graham Bowley, "Bailout Helps Fuel a New Era of Wall Street Wealth," NY-Times.com, October 16, 2009, http://www.nytimes.com/2009/10/17/business/economy/17wall.html?_r=1&adxnnl=1&partner=rss&emc=rss&adxnnlx=1255748603-hPpsg9Xb/aMhJShp3azyqw, accessed December 28, 2009.

trading in derivatives like C.D.O.'s. The new system was presented as a fait accompli, and adopted.

Other changes also increased the likelihood that investors would suffer losses if the mortgage market tanked. Previously, investors took losses only in certain dire "credit events," as when the mortgages associated with the C.D.O. defaulted or their issuers went bankrupt.

But the new rules meant that C.D.O. holders would have to make payments to short sellers under less onerous outcomes, or "triggers," like a ratings downgrade on a bond. This meant that anyone who bet against a C.D.O. could collect on the bet more easily.

"In the early deals you see none of these triggers," said one investor who asked for anonymity to preserve relationships. "These things were built in to provide the dealers with a big payoff when something bad happened."

Banks also set up ever more complex deals that favored those betting against C.D.O.'s. Morgan Stanley established a series of C.D.O.'s named after United States presidents (Buchanan and Jackson) with an unusual feature: short-sellers could lock in very cheap bets against mortgages, even beyond the life of the mortgage bonds. It was akin to allowing someone paying a low insurance premium for coverage on one automobile to pay the same on another one even if premiums over all had increased because of high accident rates.

At Goldman, Mr. Egol structured some Abacus deals in a way that enabled those betting on a mortgage-market collapse to multiply the value of their bets, to as much as six or seven times the face value of those C.D.O.'s. When the mortgage market tumbled, this meant bigger profits for Goldman and other short sellers—and bigger losses for other investors.[58]

Sylvain R. Raynes, an expert in structured finance at R & R Consulting in New York who was quoted in the story, describes these actions aptly: "The simultaneous selling of securities to customers and shorting them because they believed they were going to default is the most cynical use of credit information that I have ever seen. . . . When you buy protection against an event that you have a hand in causing, you are buying fire insurance on someone else's house and then committing arson."

---

58 Gretchen Morgenson and Louise Story, "Banks Bundled Bad Debt, Bet Against It and Won," NYTimes.com, December 24, 2009, http://www.nytimes.com/2009/12/24/business/24trading.html, accessed December 28, 2009.

The limits of neoliberal policies are being played out before the world's eyes; as former Federal Reserve Chairman and ex-seer Alan Greenspan was forced to admit before Congress in October 2008, to his shock a fundamental tenet of his ideology had been proven wrong—the free market does not work after all:

> ALAN GREENSPAN. I made a mistake in presuming that the self-interests of organizations, specifically banks and others, were such as that they were best capable of protecting their own shareholders and their equity in the firms.
>
> CHAIRMAN WAXMAN. In other words, you found that your view of the world, your ideology, was not right, it was not working.
>
> ALAN GREENSPAN. Absolutely, precisely. You know, that's precisely the reason I was shocked, because I have been going for 40 years or more with very considerable evidence that it was working exceptionally well.[59]

Greenspan's honest admission of the bankruptcy of "free market fundamentalism" has not, however, been matched by any of the other economic or public policy-making elites still in power. Instead, the state has been enlisted to bail out big business in order to allow it to carry on more or less as it was doing before, with the regulatory measures put into place diluted to what is acceptable to the GOP, providing the basis for the next economic and/or political catastrophe.

In the years leading up to the housing bubble's bursting, investment banks and mortgage companies were raking in so much money that they did not concern themselves with what would happen when these loans and investments became unsustainable. For the people who were profiting so gorgeously from the short-term gains, considering the possible consequences down the road was unnecessary, as the government's nearly $800 billion-dollar bailout proved. As a result of the bailout, the number of financial institutions remaining has declined, making it all the more likely that they "can't be allowed to fail" in the next financial crisis. That crisis is in the offing, as the Special Inspector General for the Troubled Asset Relief Program has warned:

---

59 "Transcript of Interview with James K. Galbraith," *Bill Moyers Journal,* PBS.org, October 24, 2008, http://www.pbs.org/moyers/journal/10242008/watch2.html, accessed on September 1, 2010.

The government's response to the financial meltdown has made it more likely the United States will face a deeper crisis in the future, an independent watchdog at the Treasury Department warned.

The problems that led to the last crisis have not yet been addressed, and in some cases have grown worse, says Neil Barofsky, the special inspector general for the trouble asset relief program, or TARP. . . .

"Even if TARP saved our financial system from driving off a cliff back in 2008, absent meaningful reform, we are still driving on the same winding mountain road, but this time in a faster car," Barofsky wrote.

Since Congress passed [the] $700 billion financial bailout, the remaining institutions considered "too big to fail" have grown larger and failed to restrain the lavish pay for their executives, Barofsky wrote. He said the banks still have an incentive to take on risk because they know the government will save them rather than bring down the financial system.[60]

L. Randall Wray, Professor of Economics at University of Missouri, Kansas City, provides a broader analysis of the underlying structural problems at work:

"[F]inancialization" of the economies concurrently meant both "globalization" as well as rising inequality.

The weight of finance moved away from institutions—that were guided by a culture of developing relations with customers—toward "markets" (the "originate to distribute" model of securitizing pools of mortgages is a good example). This virtually eliminated underwriting (assessing credit worthiness of customers) and also favored the "short view" (immediate profits) of traders (you are only as good as your last trade) over the long view of financial institutions that hold loans. In addition, the philosophy of "maximization of total shareholder returns" as well as the transition away from partnerships in investment banking toward public holdings promoted pump and dump schemes to increase the value of stock options that rewarded CEOs and traders. A "trader mentality" triumphed, that encouraged practices based on the "zero sum" approach: in every trade there is a winner and a loser.

---

60 Daniel Wagner and Alan Zibel, "TARP Watchdog Neil Barofsky: Government Bailout Has Increased Risk Of Economic Crisis," HuffingtonPost.com, January 30, 2010, http://www.huffingtonpost.com/2010/01/31/tarp-watchdog-neil-barofs_n_443489.html, accessed on January 31, 2011.

As practiced, the bank would be the winner and the customer would be duped.

This transformation helps to explain why fraud became rampant as normal business practice. Competition among traders and top management to beat average returns led to ever lower underwriting standards to increase the volume of trades—with fees booked on each one—and with strong incentives to "cook the books" (record false accounting profits). Once accounting fraud is underway, there is a strong incentive to engage in ever more audacious fraud to cover the previous crimes. In the end, the US financial system (and perhaps many others) became nothing but a massive criminal conspiracy to defraud borrowers. . . .[61]

Chilling words. Professor Wray does not explain why the weight of finance capital moved towards "markets." To answer that question very succinctly, finance capital's dominance reflects the natural flow of capital into the areas where the quickest and biggest profits can be made. For a system premised on the pursuit of profit, this shift to financialization and what Wray describes as a "massive criminal conspiracy" are to be expected. Short-term logic trumps any long-term logic; profits made today override any serious considerations of longer time horizons. Arguing as some do that finance capital's focus on short-term gains is jeopardizing the system's long-term stability and viability misses the point. The system can only be governed, so long as it continues to be the system in place and is not replaced by a different system, by profit. Doing what is best for it in the long-run is not how the system operates.

The Dual Nature of the Neoliberal State

In trying to understand the neoliberal state, one at first comes up against a puzzle. On the one hand, the state seems to be shrinking. Many state functions are being increasingly farmed out to private entities, and some of the state's traditional functions are being eliminated altogether. Public services such as the military, security, criminal justice, disaster preparation and relief, public education, infrastructure maintenance and

---

61 L. Randall Wray, "Right Now, A Complete Collapse of the Financial System is Not Out of the Question," *Money Game* (blog), BusinessInsider.com, November 4, 2010, http://www.businessinsider.com/complete-collapse-not-out-of-the-question-2010-11#ixzz1CeMEnMXy, accessed on January 31, 2011.

development, information collection and dissemination, even voting machines and *speeches* in Congress are progressively being taken over by non-state actors.

On November 14, 2009, *The New York Times*, for example, revealed that more than a dozen congressional representatives of both parties delivered, orally and by submissions to the Congressional Record, speeches ghostwritten for them by lobbyists on the health care bill, the most contentious political issue of Obama's first year in the presidency. The biotech firm Genentech, a subsidiary of drug giant Roche, tailored the text to appeal to the respective social bases of the GOP and the Democrats. A lobbyist is quoted in the story saying in response to this revelation: "This happens all the time. There's nothing nefarious about it."[62] A remarkable admission—it goes on all the time and there is nothing wrong with it—given the premise underpinning this brand of democracy in America: elected representatives are not supposed to be the literal mouthpieces of corporations.

Voting machine manufacturers bar public inspection of their internal operations on the grounds that such information—their tabulating of the votes—is proprietary. The sine qua non of democracy as most people understand it can be carried out behind closed doors; the people are not allowed to confirm that their votes are being counted properly. "Virtually any asset of service that a local government owns or provides has been privatized somewhere in the United States in some manner, including fire protection, police protection, waste water treatment, street lighting, tree trimming, snow removal, parking structures, railroads, hospitals, jails and even cemeteries."[63]

The second largest military force occupying Iraq after the 2003 US invasion is not another country; it is mercenary forces, in particular Xe, the company formerly known as Blackwater. During the Bush/Cheney years, the operation of Walter Reed Army Medical Center was turned over to private interests, even though its operation had been less expensive under government auspices. The conditions there deteriorated

---

62 One of these representatives was Joe Wilson of South Carolina, infamous for blurting out "You lie!" to President Obama during Obama's health care address to Congress in 2009. Robert Pear, "In House, Many Spoke With One Voice: Lobbyists'," NYTimes.com, November 14, 2009, http://www.nytimes.com/2009/11/15/us/politics/15health.html, accessed November 14, 2009.

63 Lewis D. Soloman, *Reflections on the Future of Business Organizations*, 20 Cardozo L. Rev. 1213, 1216 (1999).

atrociously upon this privatization. As reported upon by the *Washington Post* in early 2007:

> Behind the door of Army Spec. Jeremy Duncan's room, part of the wall is torn and hangs in the air, weighted down with black mold. When the wounded combat engineer stands in his shower and looks up, he can see the bathtub on the floor above through a rotted hole. The entire building, constructed between the world wars, often smells like greasy carry-out. Signs of neglect are everywhere: mouse droppings, belly-up cockroaches, stained carpets, cheap mattresses.[64]

The management of prisons and of education has been increasingly outsourced to the private sector at both the federal and local levels. Dissemination of government information under Bush was turned over to private companies. Under the signboard of reducing government spending, the government has been outsourcing to private companies previous government activities so that it can claim to be reducing government funding. The GOP in particular has been doing this most aggressively to maintain its image as antigovernment.

Paradoxically, as the state seems to shrink because of privatization and outsourcing, it has been simultaneously expanding its social control activities and powers. This is evident in two respects. First, coercion and surveillance are being shared by the state with private entities—with the state's blessings and encouragement. The state is, in a sense, deputizing segments of the society to act as arms of the state. Second, the state is magnifying its own coercive and surveillance apparatus and declaring itself less subject to "dilution" by civil liberties, the rule of law, or competition from civil society.

Bureaucratization and Centralization

States' increasing reliance on force in neoliberal regimes and their sharing of coercive functions with certain non-state actors find expression in two dimensions. First, far-flung empires require a large and powerful bureaucracy. You simply cannot maintain an empire without a highly developed

---

64 Dana Priest and Anne Hull, "Soldiers Face Neglect, Frustration at Army's Top Medical Facility," WashingtonPost.com, February 18, 2007, http://www.washingtonpost.com/wp-dyn/content/article/2007/02/17/AR2007021701172.html, accessed July 30, 2010.

bureaucracy. While a bureaucratization trend has been evident since this country's earliest beginnings, in the most proximal and developed sense this process goes back to World War II's unprecedented total mobilization of military and industrial production and the US Empire's post-war ascendancy. President Dwight D. Eisenhower, elected primarily because of his Commanding General's role in World War II, famously warned in his January 17, 1961 farewell address to the nation of the dangers of this rising "military-industrial complex":

> This conjunction of an immense military establishment and a large arms industry is new in the American experience. The total influence—economic, political, even spiritual—is felt in every city, every statehouse, every office of the federal government. We recognize the imperative need for this development. Yet we must not fail to comprehend its grave implications. Our toil, resources and livelihood are all involved; so is the very structure of our society. In the councils of government, we must guard against the acquisition of unwarranted influence, whether sought or unsought, by the **military-industrial complex**. The potential for the disastrous rise of misplaced power exists and will persist. We must never let the weight of this combination endanger our liberties or democratic processes. We should take nothing for granted. Only an alert and knowledgeable citizenry can compel the proper meshing of the huge industrial and military machinery of defense with our peaceful methods and goals so that security and liberty may prosper together.

(In his original text, Eisenhower called it the "military-congressional-industrial complex." He dropped the congressional element in his delivered text, probably to placate the legislative branch.) Imagine Ike's words coming from the mouth of departing President George W. Bush in 2009 or the mouth of incoming President Barack Obama. People would have thought that Bush and Obama had gone crazy. Squaring the Patriot Act and massive, warrantless government surveillance over all US residents with "we must never let the weight of this combination endanger our liberties or democratic processes" makes the famous Pythagorean apostles' futile efforts to square a circle seem comparatively realistic. The fact that Eisenhower's warning is inconceivable from any contemporary US president, Democratic or Republican, is testimony to how far the military-congressional-industrial complex has come and how it now exercises supreme power that no public official who wants to be considered mainstream and taken seriously dares question.

Besides the intense bureaucratization, within the ranks of this bureaucracy power is being increasingly concentrated in the executive branch at the legislative and judicial branches' expense. This is both a natural extension of the fundamental nature of bureaucracies and consistent with the demands of running a vast empire—more power to a smaller segment holding essentially unfettered executive power. The neocons and the Federalist Society's advocacy of this unrestrained executive is called the "unitary executive" doctrine. As Marx and Engels wrote presciently in 1848 in the *Manifesto of the Communist Party*, "The bourgeoisie keeps more and more doing away with the scattered state of the population, of the means of production, and of property. It has agglomerated population, centralized the means of production, and has concentrated property in a few hands. The necessary consequence of this was political centralization."

Between the Rich and the Rest

According to Frederick Hayek, property rights are the only recognizable rights. Those with property can escape disasters (as the better-off did in New Orleans during Hurricane Katrina's approach in 2005) while those without—without enough to pay the fare and without the physical ability to get to public or private forms of transportation—can just stay and drown.

Because neoliberalism produces growing disparities within the populace inside nations, between nations, and between regions, it demands and requires the increasingly generous application of force, intimidation, and deception to defend these disparities. Because persuading people to cooperate and follow the rules based on positive incentives is less and less an option since positive incentives themselves are being sharply cut back, negative incentives are necessarily being employed more and more to maintain social control. These negative incentives take two fundamental forms: fearmongering and coercion. Frighten the people about some external and internal enemies and strong-arm them into believing that extraordinary measures must be adopted to deal with these enemies, including unconstitutional and extralegal surveillance, detention, preemptive raids and invasions, rewriting laws to suit an unrestrained state, arrests of demonstrators before they demonstrate and exercise their First

Amendment rights and charging them as "terrorists," beatings, torture, murder, and assassination. These are the new politics, endorsed and employed by both major parties; they are used more explicitly by the GOP, but the distinction between the two parties is only of tone, not overall of kind.

Convincing people that they should support (or at least not actively oppose) public policies that are against their interests via ideological and political stratagems continues to be important, and the ways in which this is being carried out deserve their own chapter (see Chapter Six). But because of the increasing gap between the representation and the actuality, and because the winners in this game grow fewer and fewer relative to the losers (with the winners a fraction of the top one percent and the really big winners almost few enough to fit into a palatial mansion), propaganda can only go so far; coercion and intimidation must assume an increasingly larger burden in the exercise of social control. Moreover, persuasion itself has more and more taken on the form of cynical manipulation through fear-mongering and more extensive lying and censorship. Playing to and feeding the public's fears fosters people's primitive emotional states that supplant rational decision-making. When you are aroused by fear, your ability to think rationally is compromised.[65]

The resurgences of fundamentalist religions in the West and in the Middle East and East that feed off of fear and anxiety and that explain what is happening on the basis of faith are a vital part of this picture, since you cannot get people to tolerate and participate in terrible things on the basis of reason. Right-wing movements are also notable for this technique. The proliferation of right-wing pundits whose shtick depends upon fear and scapegoating is clear evidence of this. Sarah Palin's "death panels" lie worked on all too many people precisely because there is an echo chamber of right-wing media outlets and the GOP that repeats blatant lies over and over again, and because the followers of the extreme Right are buffeted by unexpected and scary changes to their world—9/11, the financial crisis bringing the economy to the brink of disaster, the ongoing destruction of Main Street, downsizing, deindustrialization, globalization, the election of a black as US president—and they are desperate for certainties in an increasingly uncertain and perilous world. Fear as a method of political

---

65 Psychologists refer to this as being in your "limbic brain" where primitive emotional states such as fear and anger reside. The way out of your limbic brain and back into your frontal cortex where reason prevails on an individual level is not to be told by someone that your fears are unwarranted and that you should get rational. Coming to understand on an emotional level and rational level that you are being provoked into a limbic state is the path back to your frontal cortex.

179

control represents the closest thing to coercion that is not itself quite yet coercion. Put another way, as coercion assumes a larger and larger role, persuasion approaches coercion more and more.

There are both structural/material and subjective/political dimensions to this. On the material level, compared to the welfare state, neoliberalism offers much more job and income insecurity and volatility, social and economic polarization, and increasingly diminishing public goods and services. Individuals must rely increasingly upon their own devices (and personal resources) because the state and the economy are doing less and less for more and more people, except for the very rich who are feeding off the trough in unparalleled ways. As the security state creates a much greater need for a social safety net, it simultaneously moves to eliminate it. Contrary to what most analysts say, the public mood of fear and insecurity is not the reason for the security state's ascension. Rather, the security state's ascension is chiefly (though not solely) responsible for the public's uneasiness.

This insecurity and uncertainty, felt at nearly all levels of the society, creates fertile soil for fear to take root and thrive. On top of that, both demagogues and corporations are constantly watering and composting this soil. If social structures do not provide support for individuals, then individuals must fend for themselves. Since there is a limit to what individuals can do compared to what collectivities can do, individuals recognize that if they are to be safe and secure they must protect themselves from others who might do them harm.

Not only is the state less and less likely as time goes on to buffer you from trouble, but also globalization and neoliberal social policies ensure that nearly everyone is subject to much more economic and social dislocation. The consequences for the less privileged among us are exceedingly severe, including suffering and premature death.

But even for those who bask in prosperity's glow, neoliberalism and globalization ineluctably undermine their security. On a general level this is because income polarization produces desperation among those on the bottom. That desperation assumes various guises—street crime, drug addiction, predatory behavior, and so on. While by far the main victims of this live in poor neighborhoods and in poor countries, this income and wealth polarization also makes the well-off more vulnerable to retaliation by those made so desperate. In the US, stationary, gated communities and mobile-gated communities (SUVs) are advertised as sanctuaries from the uncertainties of the world outside your own bubble. The infamous Columbine high school massacre took place in a community expressly created for affluent whites thinking they were fleeing the crime and disorder of the cities. On a subjective level, the danger is even worse under neoliberal regimes because whether or not one actually becomes the victim of a street crime, the pervasive sense of fear of becoming a victim claims victims everywhere.

Social Darwinism, neoliberal states' ruling ethic, says that you have got to watch your own back because no one else is going to do it for you. Even those who because of their income can escape the ugly privations of neoliberal economies are both objectively and subjectively more vulnerable to retaliations from the dispossessed in the form of street crime and the schemes of corporate white-collar crime; Jack Abramoff and Ponzi-schemer Bernie Madoff who stole billions are the most famous of these white collar criminals, but the 2000 stock market collapse fueled by market analysts, investment banks, and politicos' ballyhooing the virtues of capitalism and cheerleading that "everyone's getting rich" affected far more people. As the positive incentives for co-operating with authorities diminish (jobs, income . . .) and the likelihood of non-co-operative behaviors (e.g., rebelliousness, street crime, political protest) thereby increase, the state has increasingly employed more coercion relative to persuasion as a means of social control (e.g., harsher criminal justice sentencing, criminalizing previously non-criminal behaviors, and more and larger prisons housing rising percentages of the population). This increasingly punitive criminal justice system has been in operation even as street crime rates have fallen since the early 1990s in the US.

The increasing use of fear as a propaganda device is the necessary corollary to harsher state social control policies. Fear has been generously employed as a driving force in the criminal justice system's ongoing historic expansion and in the state's antiterrorist moves (see Chapter Two). The incessant invocation of 9/11 is the most prominent example of this, but there is a plethora of others. Well before 9/11, as I pointed out in Chapter One, a culture of fear and accompanying social control policies based on risk aversion was so pronounced that it provoked a spate of books and commentaries.[66]

---

66 These include, for example, Frank Furedi, *The Culture of Fear* (London: Continuum International Publishing Group, 2005); Barry Glassner, *The Culture of Fear* (New York: Basic Books, 2000); David Altheide, *Creating Fear: News and the Construction of a Crisis* (Piscataway, NJ: Aldine Transaction, 2002).

Franchising Force and Unintended Consequences

The monopoly over the legitimate use of force, as sociologist Max Weber succinctly described the state, is being extended in the neoliberal state to non-state entities. State-authorized entities (such as private security forces, privately run prisons, and private armies) are increasingly assuming part of the mantle of legitimacy for the exercise of coercion.

There are also unintended consequences of this trend. Anti-state entities (al-Qaeda, Hezbollah, gangs, slum associations, etc.) are taking over many state responsibilities because the state is either failing to deliver on its traditional responsibilities or it has, by its actions (and inactions), become illegitimate in the eyes of growing numbers. Thus, neoliberalism, by undermining social services and fracturing the social compact, increasingly forces into being both anti-state terrorist groups and grassroots responses to take up the vacuum created by neoliberal policies.

In the wake of Hurricane Katrina that devastated New Orleans and other parts of the Gulf Coast in 2005, gang members broke into stores and distributed water and food to people whom the state had spectacularly abandoned. The two most organized forces in the disorder after Katrina hit New Orleans, in fact, were Blackwater mercenaries and gangs.

In the burgeoning slums worldwide that are growing explosively in the utter absence and/or malign neglect by the state of any regulatory, supervisory, or service offerings, residents have adopted various stratagems. As Teo Ballve relates:

> In poor cities around the world, millions eke out a living by scavenging recyclable materials from the streets that can be exchanged for fractions of a cent. They are at the lowest rung of consumer society, the very rock bottom of globalization. And they know it. "If we were any poorer, we'd be dead," said Jorge Eliécer Ospina, a trash recycler in Bogotá, Colombia.
>
> Ospina lives in a hillside slum on the outskirts of the city. Like a modern day hunter-gatherer, he leaves in the early morning to see what valuables city residents have thrown out in the trash. Ospina is part of an organization of self-employed, or informal, scrap collectors [numbering 18,000] called the Bogotá Association of Recyclers (ARB), one of the oldest waste picker organizations in the world.[67]

---

67   Teo Ballve, "Informal Trash Recyclers Go Global," Cetri.be, April 11, 2008, http://www.cetri.be/spip.php?article545&lang=en, accessed January 31, 2011.

In Lebanon, Hezbollah has gained so much power because they have been able to deliver social programs and services as well as prove themselves a determined and capable military and police force.

This transition to the privatized state has been accomplished through a combination of (a) subterfuge—much of the awarding of government contracts and services to private corporations has been out of the public eye; (b) overt, insistent, propaganda campaigns touting the supposed virtues of private business over state programs; and (c) outright fraud, accompanied at times by force.

In the former Soviet Union and Eastern bloc countries and in the formerly socialist China, for example, state assets were appropriated by private capital through theft, forming the foundational assets for both criminal underworld enterprises and legitimate, latter-day robber baron billionaires. In Moscow today the neoliberal dystopia exists: those with money can get anything they want, including illicitly obtained human organs; the mafia runs wild; and the dispossessed suffer immensely. Moscow today has been compared by a number of observers to the American Wild West.

In the US, this shift has occurred through corrupt, bloated, over-budget sweetheart deals, with Halliburton being the poster child and Jack Abramoff and Bernard Madoff its most famous disciples.

The $787 billion bailout of Wall Street investment bank giants, passed in October 2008 by Congress after doomsday warnings by the White House and by Treasury Secretary Henry Paulson et al represents one of the most spectacular examples of the passing of private debt onto the public's already overburdened backs.

Why privatize the state? According to the neoliberals, private concerns outperform the state, doing things better and cheaper. As was revealed by the Walter Reed Medical Center scandal of 2007 (in which medical care for wounded veterans was farmed out to private companies leaving the veterans in egregious conditions) savings to taxpayers is not the point. The private contractors were charging more for their services to run Walter Reed than it had previously cost the government to run it itself.

To the extent that private entities take over previously state-run activities, profit-making opportunities expand for those private entities. Rather than the revenue (sometimes out-right subsidy, sometimes partial subsidy) going back to the state, these revenues now (generally more expensively offered than when the state did them) go to corporations or to "faith-based" groups for both material and ideological profit. Thus, corporations and those favored by public officials wield ever-expanding power in the world being shaped by global capital.

And why not? If the so-called free market is The One, then why should it not directly take over the reins of power of the state? When Dick Cheney was vice-president he convened a cabal of exclusively energy company executives to draw up America's national energy policy. When some members of Congress objected, Cheney refused to acknowledge their right to supervise the Executive Branch. The Supreme Court, dominated by conservatives, upheld his defiance as "executive privilege." The Congress and the nation did not have a right to know who was writing our national energy policies!

But this is only one feature of this new landscape, albeit a remarkable one in and of itself. An even more important process at work relates to the ways in which the neoliberal state is plunging us headlong into a heartless world, what Polanyi had in mind when he warned of what would happen if "free market" measures became the sole criterion for society: the demolition of society.

Changing the Basis of Unity of the Social Compact

Because Bush and Cheney's reign provoked such widespread anger, rescuing the system's legitimacy fell to their successors. The financial debacle sealed the GOP ticket's chances and Obama rode into office with the hopes of millions. Since Obama's election two things stand out. First, Obama and the Democratic Party leadership are intent upon governing in a "bipartisan" manner, irrespective of the fact that the GOP was soundly repudiated at the polls for Congress in 2006 and for the White House and Congress in 2008. Obama and the Democrats were thus given a mandate to override what the GOP had been and what it currently stands for. Irrespective of the fact that Obama had the votes in Congress and the support of a large majority of people in the country for that agenda, and that he could thereby have effected a government single-payer health insurance plan, ended the wars, assured a woman's right to abortion, and implemented other policies regardless of Republican opposition (both because he had the votes for closure and because he could rally public opinion to isolate Republicans who stood in the way), Obama chose not to do these things and instead sought common ground with the defeated party. This strategy has only weakened the Democratic Party and strengthened the Right, most visibly in the rise of the Tea Parties and in the 2010 mid-term election results.

Second, the hue and cry against Obama by the GOP and the rest of the far Right has been vociferous and shrill (including calls for his assassination); increasingly open fascist norms are being propagated by the likes of Glenn Beck and Bill O'Reilly against Democrats (with Democrats falsely depicted as socialists and Marxists) and others with violent rhetoric, open packing of weapons, and alarming incidents such as the May 31, 2009 murder during services in his own church of Dr. George Tiller by an anti-abortion fanatic and the murderous assassination attempt upon Rep. Gabrielle Giffords in Tucson, Arizona on January 8, 2011. The blatant illogic and shameless lying—such as the ridiculous claims of the Birthers that Obama wasn't born in Hawaii and the fictitious "death panels" that Sarah Palin popularized—make the GOP look increasingly absurd and openly racist. Some people view these developments as signs that the GOP is digging its own grave as a legitimate party. This is not, however, principally an electoral strategy by the GOP. It is instead a strategy of a small minority banking on bullying and intimidation to get its way by enlisting the support of a relatively small but highly aroused social base—the Tea Parties—as a kind of shock troops strategy.

These are the early expressions of a full-blown fascist movement. They are the domestic analogue of the Bush Doctrine of preemptive war and torture. As long as the Bush Doctrine remains in place in foreign policy, its equivalent in domestic policy will and must persist because the government cannot continue those policies abroad without shoring up a xenophobic domestic base. As Paul Craig Roberts puts it, referring to Chris Hedges,

> Indeed, Hedges reports that "radical activists in the environmental, [anti]-globalization, anti-nuclear, sustainable agriculture and anarchist movements are already being placed by the state in special detention facilities with Muslims charged with terrorism." Hedges warns: "This corruption of our legal system will not be reserved by the state for suspected terrorists or even Muslim Americans. In the coming turmoil and economic collapse, it will be used to silence all who are branded as disruptive or subversive. [Syed Fahad] Hashmi [American accused of terrorism] endures what many others, who are not Muslim, will endure later."[68]

---

68 Paul Craig Roberts, "Liberty Has Been Lost," OpEdNews.com, January 5, 2010, http://www.opednews.com/articles/Liberty-Has-Been-Lost-by-Paul-Craig-Roberts-100105-429.html, accessed January 6, 2010.

These egregious policies should be exposed, isolated, and repudiated. But the Democrats and Obama refuse to do this. A new basis of unity is being configured in the US, one based on narrow nationalistic and profoundly immoral premises. In this new compact, the rule of law is subordinated to a permanent emergency condition. Security trumps liberty and freedom, and freedom is being redefined to mean the freedom of corporations and the freedom to consume. To accomplish this new compact will require silencing and neutralizing the Left and dissenters and freethinking rationalists through intimidation, repression, violence, and the Big Lie. I address this question in greater depth and detail in the final chapter of the book. I turn now, however, in Chapter Four to a specific examination of the "War on Terror" and its place in neoliberalism's Unbrave New World.

CHAPTER FOUR

The "War on Terror"
(Munchausen Syndrome by Proxy)

People with MSP [Munchausen Syndrome by Proxy] might create or exaggerate the child's symptoms in several ways. They might simply lie about symptoms, alter diagnostic tests (such as contaminating a urine sample), falsify medical records, or induce symptoms through various means, such as poisoning, suffocating, starving, and causing infection.[1]

In Munchausen Syndrome by Proxy, a parent surreptitiously harms his or her child in order to ensure that the child is entirely dependent upon them. The more ill and weak a child becomes, the more the hovering parent is "needed." The US "War on Terror" mimics Munchausen Syndrome by Proxy in its impact on the US public.

The biggest problem that we face is not the danger of anti-state terrorism, as real a problem as that is. The biggest problem is the "war" that is being justified in the name of fighting terrorism. The "War on Terror" provides by its very nature a self-generating basis for its indefinite and expanding presence, just as predatory parents create the need for their presence by slowly poisoning their children.

---

1   "What is Munchausen Syndrome by Proxy?" *Cleveland Clinic: Diseases and Conditions*, ClevelandClinic.org, http://my.clevelandclinic.org/disorders/factitious_disorders/hic_munchausen_syndrome_by_proxy.aspx, accessed January 26, 2010.

The term "terrorism" has been used so indiscriminately in public discourse and has become so freighted with purposeful fright that it needs to get a haircut, take a shower, brush its teeth, and put on a fresh set of clothes so that it can appear in decent company and be of some use. The stakes involved and the need for intellectual and emotional clarity could hardly be greater.

Let us begin with an examination of how the US government defines terrorism. Inherent in these definitions are clues to the problem we face as a people with this "War on Terror." The FBI defines terrorism as "the unlawful use of force or violence against persons or property to intimidate or coerce a government, the civilian population, or any segment thereof, in furtherance of political or social objectives."[2]

The key word in the FBI definition is "unlawful," not "coerce" or "intimidate," since governments, as well as terrorists, use force. It is not violence, intimidation, or coercion per se that makes something terroristic; it is whether or not that force can be rationalized as lawful or legitimate. If It is seen as legitimate, violence is not terroristic, no matter how unjust, excessive, or random. The question here then is, what makes something "unlawful?" The rules of engagement for soldiers in war and the procedures promulgated by law enforcement—police, FBI, Alcohol, Tobacco and Firearms (ATF), and so on—are essential to legitimizing state use of force; otherwise, the public could see the actions of soldiers and law enforcement as arbitrary and capricious. The intentional irony is that in the fog of chaos the very existence of these rules legitimates their violation.

Police use of force can be rationalized as being in the public interest since it is carried out under the color of law. Likewise, when military forces bomb and kill civilians in times of war we are told that war is a messy business and "mistakes" are inevitable. In the huge gray areas of real conflicts, the existence of tidy procedures provides a convenient fiction that justifies varying degrees of random savagery. Legitimacy or illegitimacy is not an inherent property of the act or acts; legitimacy or illegitimacy is a matter of interpretation.

The US State Department defines terrorism as "premeditated, politically motivated violence perpetrated against noncombatant targets by subnational groups or clandestine agents"—Title 22 of the United States Code, Section 2656f(d).[3]

---

2   Federal Bureau of Investigation, Albuquerque, "What We Investigate," FBI.gov, http://albuquerque.fbi.gov/priorities.htm, accessed January 19, 2011.

3   US Department of State, "Country Reports on Terrorism 2006, Chapter 7, Legislative Requirements and Key Terms," State.gov, http://www.state.gov/s/ct/rls/crt/2006/82726.htm, accessed April 6, 2011.

The State Department's definition is better than the FBI's, but it implicitly excludes state-sponsored terror since the agents of such terror are state actors.

Britannica Dictionary defines terrorism this way:

> Terrorism, n. the systematic use of violence to create a general climate of fear in a population and thereby to bring about a particular political objective. Terrorism has been practiced by political organizations with both rightist and leftist objectives, by nationalistic and religious groups, by revolutionaries, and even by state institutions such as armies, intelligence, and police.[4]

This is better still, but neither it nor the State Department's definition specifies that a key characteristic of terrorism is its *indifference* to the injury or death of innocent victims or even its deliberate *targeting* of innocents.

Finally, here is the USA PATRIOT Act's definition for a new crime dubbed "domestic terrorism": "acts dangerous to human life that are a violation of the criminal laws of the United State or of any State . . . [that] . . . appear to be intended . . . (i) to intimidate or coerce a civilian population; (ii) to influence the policy of a government by intimidation or coercion; or (iii) to affect the conduct of a government by mass destruction, assassination, or kidnapping. . . ."[5]

Obviously, by this definition any act of civil disobedience and any political protest could be readily categorized as "domestic terrorism," since they are all designed to influence government policy. Someone, after all, can always trip and get hurt in the course of an act of protest. Lobbyists, for their part, obviously intend to influence government policy. The USA PATRIOT Act's definition for "domestic terrorism" is so broad that it robs the term "terrorism" of all real meaning and makes it instead a catchall label that can be used against any dissenters or advocates of policy disliked by those in power. Environmental or animal rights activists, for example, do not target people. What they engage in might more properly be described as sabotage. Yet because a spray can might blow up while a saboteur is using it to deface a Humvee, for example, the activists could be (and have been) classified as "ecoterrorists" or

---

4   Brittanica.com, "Terrorism," http://www.britannica.com/EBchecked/topic/588371/terrorism, accessed February 14, 2011.

5   US Code, Title 18, Part I, Chapter 113B, § 2331: Definitions, reproduced at Findlaw.com, http://codes.lp.findlaw.com/uscode/18/I/113B/2331, accessed February 14, 2011.

"domestic terrorists." If truckers, to use a different example, were to engage in a strike action or demonstration in which they used their trucks to block traffic in DC for an hour or more, this could arguably be seen as dangerous to human life and a form of intimidation or coercion and treated as terrorism. Indeed, a few years ago demonstrators in Salt Lake City were prosecuted as "domestic terrorists" for interfering with the retail sales of commercial businesses on the street where they were demonstrating. Simply put, the USA PATRIOT Act's definition of terrorism renders the term meaningless except as an amorphous bogeyman.

At the 2008 Republican National Convention (RNC) in St. Paul, Minnesota, local, state and federal police—including a complement of police from a number of other cities throughout the country—carried out preemptive raids and used unprecedented covert and overt force against protestors. One observer described it as "Abu Ghraib brought home." I wrote an essay at the time entitled "Shock and Awe Comes Home to Roost:"

> *Al-Qaeda terrorists still plot to inflict catastrophic harm on America and he's [Obama] worried that someone won't read them their rights.*—Sarah Palin at the RNC

> *[T]he looser "preemptive strike" rationale being applied to situations abroad could migrate back home, fostering a more permissive attitude on the part of law enforcement officers in this country.*—FBI Special Agent Colleen Rowley.

> *We followed our [RNC] Welcoming Committee members to many cities around the country. We consulted with the terrorism task force in those cities. We received information, etc. [Did you have infiltrators?] Yes, we did. [Were they paid?] Yes.*—Ramsey County Sheriff Bob Fletcher.

> *[S]ix or seven officers came into my cell… one officer punched me in the face…And then they slammed—and I fell to the ground, unconscious. And the officer grabbed me by the head, slammed my head on the ground and re-awoke me …to consciousness. I was bleeding everywhere. … They put a bag over my head that had a gag on it. And they used pain compliance tactics on me for about an hour and a half. They pressed—they separated my jaw as hard as they could with their fingers…. They …bent my foot backwards. I was screaming for God and like screaming for mercy, crying, asking them why they were doing this.*—Elliott Hughes, member of the RNC Welcoming Committee, arrested at gunpoint days before the RNC, charged along with the other RNC8 Defendants with "conspiring to riot in furtherance of terrorism."

❂

The police state actions before and during the RNC were not the product of a dystopian America but of the real America of 2008 and were a harbinger of even worse to come. Beneath the carefully staged and tightly cordoned-off circus of "democracy" at the convention rots the corpse of the Bill of Rights:

Of what significance can a person's right to see the charges leveled against them be when there's a war on terrorists to be waged? What need do people accused of crimes have to see who has accused them— are they not guilty by virtue of being accused? What end is fulfilled to allow the accused to cross-examine their accusers? Why waste the court's time with such absurdities? What purpose does it serve to have perfectly good evidence ruled inadmissible, so what if it was extracted employing electric shock and waterboarding? These people are guilty, guilty, guilty! Why just look at them: do they not look guilty? What more evidence do we need? 9/11! 9/11! 9/11! We must wring the truth out of them, whatever it takes, the preservation of freedom demands it! Planting police undercover officers in the ranks of these protestors and provoking them into doing illegal or violent acts, even if those undercover officers have to do it all themselves, is necessary to protect the precious rights we enjoy as Americans. Country First! Anyone who dares tell us that we must not violate Constitutional rights in order to protect Constitutional rights deserves waterboarding! Strap him down! Give me that bucket of water! I'll show him who's free![6]

❖

On June 14, 2009, I wrote an Internet essay entitled: "DoD Training Manual: Protests are 'Low-Level Terrorism.'" The article hit a nerve, spread quickly, and was picked up by news sites and left—and right-wing websites and blogs. The article read in part:

The Department of Defense is training all of its personnel in its current Antiterrorism and Force Protection Annual Refresher Training Course that political protest is "low-level terrorism."

---

6   Dennis Loo, "Shock and Awe Comes Home to Roost," Counterpunch.org, September 13, 2008, http://www.counterpunch.org/loo09132008.html, retrieved September 14, 2009.

The Training introduction reads as follows:

> Anti-terrorism (AT) and Force Protection (FP) are two facets of the Department of Defense (DoD) Mission Assurance Program. It is DoD policy, as found in <u>DoDI 2000.16</u>, that the DoD Components and the <u>DoD elements and personnel</u> shall be protected from terrorist acts through a high priority, comprehensive, <u>AT program</u>. The DoD's AT program shall be all encompassing using an integrated systems approach.

The first question of the Terrorism Threat Factors, **"Knowledge Check 1"** section reads as follows:

> Which of the following is an example of low-level terrorism activity? Select the correct answer and then click **Check Your Answer.**
>
> ☐ Attacking the Pentagon
> ☐ IEDs
> ☐ Hate crimes against racial groups
> ☐ Protests

☼

The "correct" answer is Protests.

The ACLU learned of this training and on June 10, 2009 sent a letter to Gail McGinn, Acting Under-Secretary of Defense for Personnel and Readiness, objecting to their training all DoD personnel that the exercise of First Amendment rights constitutes "low-level terrorism."[7]

☼

On June 22, 2009 as a follow-up to this story, I wrote the following:

> In response to the ACLU's June 10, 2009 letter demanding that the DoD pull a question from its DoD training exam that equated protest with "low-level terrorism," which I wrote about at Open

---

7   Dennis Loo, "DoD Training Manual: Protests are 'Low-Level Terrorism,'" *Dennis Loo* (blog), June 14, 2009, http://open.salon.com/blog/dennis_loo/2009/06/14/dod_training_manual_protests_are_low-level_terrorism, accessed June 20, 2009.

Salon on June 14 ("DoD Training Manual: Protests are 'Low-Level Terrorism'")—and which was reposted and written about on scores of websites and blogs, both left and right—the DoD has removed the question from the exam.

This is good news. The problem, however, goes deeper than this one question. Before going into that, let's look at the DoD's latest actions and its explanation:

As reported by Fox News:

The Pentagon has removed a controversial question from its anti-terrorism training exam that labeled 'protests' a form of 'low-level terrorism,' calling the question 'poorly worded.'

A Pentagon spokesman said the question failed to make clear the difference between illegal violent demonstrations and constitutionally protected peaceful protests.

Civil libertarians and activist groups, interviewed by FOXNews.com for a story that appeared on Wednesday [June 17], had objected strongly to the exam question, which a Department of Defense employee had printed and given to the American Civil Liberties Union. . . .

"They should have made it clearer there's a clear difference between illegal violent demonstrations and peaceful, constitutionally protected protests," Pentagon spokesman Lt. Col. Les Melnyk said on Thursday.

Asked when a protest becomes an "illegal, violent demonstration," Melnyk said, "I'm not a lawyer. I couldn't get into the specifics of when you cross the line."

"If you're doing physical damage to people or property, that could fall into that,' he said.

There remain a number of troubling issues here.

First, how do even violent demonstrations constitute "terrorism?" Conflating the two gives license to authorities to claim with impunity that they had to act with suppressive or even pre-emptive arrests and perhaps much more violent and repressive action, including shooting demonstrators, because they feared that the demonstrations might or were showing some signs of becoming violent and therefore "terrorist." A society in which protest of any kind is officially linked to terrorism can only be described as a tyranny.

This is what in fact was done to the RNC Welcoming Committee at the 2008 RNC convention in Minneapolis-St. Paul.

Authorities carried out pre-emptive raids upon peaceful protesters prior to their even peacefully demonstrating and charged them with "domestic terrorism." In the course of this, at least one of the arrested U.S. citizen activists was brutalized in a fashion that comes very close to torture.

Second, the DoD exam question sought to define "low-level terrorism." It was not intended to distinguish peaceful and legal protest from "illegal, violent demonstration."

Pentagon spokesman Lt. Col. Les Melnyk's account for what was wrong with the question/answer choices—that the problem was that the question/answer did not distinguish between legal protest and illegal protest—is, therefore, not entirely convincing or truthful.

The Fox story goes on to say that Melnyk "added that many Defense employees work in countries where violent demonstrations are regular occurrences."

"In those situations, that anti-Americanism might be taken out on an American in the crowd," Melnyk said. This is also not entirely convincing or truthful.

The original question includes as answer choices actions that occur in both foreign locales and/or within the U.S. so it can't accurately been said that the DoD had in mind only foreign locations.

Obviously an attack on the Pentagon has to happen within the U.S. I.E.D.'s are used outside of the U.S. Hate crimes against racial groups can and do occur both within the US and outside of the US. Protests occur within and outside of the U.S.

Since the "correct" answer according to the DoD was "protests" = "low-level terrorism," they cannot accurately say that they had in mind only violent protests in foreign lands because their answer choices included activities that occur within the U.S.

The correct answer should have been "none of the above."

Third, the question and answer choices were obviously deliberately designed to lead the exam taker/DoD employee to choose "Protests" as an example of "low-level terrorism" inasmuch as the other answer choices are all obviously not low-level acts. All of the others are very violent attacks.

Finally, as I pointed out in my article, the term "low-level terrorism" appears to be a "term of art" within security agency circles given that a scholarly paper delivered in February of 2009 at an international conference incorporated it into its title as such:

Vinthagen, Stellan. "Labeling 'Low Level Terrorism:' The Out-Definition of Social Movements" Paper presented at the annual meeting of the ISA's 50th ANNUAL CONVENTION 'EXPLORING THE PAST, ANTICIPATING THE FUTURE' New York Marriott Marquis, NEW YORK CITY, NY, USA, Feb 15, 2009.

Abstract: This paper explores current state security tendency to label ordinary protests and opposition as "low level terrorism" or social movements as "terrorist environments" and the political and democratic consequences of such a politics of fear. The judic [the abstract cuts off here.]

The problem at its heart, in other words, is that this particular question in the DoD training exam is merely a glaring individual example of a larger trend and mentality—the criminalization of protest and dissent and its relegation to a category of "terrorism," legitimating the repression of dissent and free speech and assembly, ranging from declarations by public officials that dissenting ideas are "unpatriotic" and "traitorous" to training DoD employees that protest is terrorism-lite. The prospects revealed here are alarming.[8]

In Europe, the conflating of protest, immigration, drugs, and organized crime as all part of a set of risky behaviors and groups being labeled as forms of terror dates back to the 1980s:

TREVI, a discussion forum for ministers and senior officials from home affairs and justice departments within the then European Community, [was] founded in the mid-1970s. Police chiefs and intelligence officers also participated in its working groups. TREVI came to form the model for the development of European police collaboration over the following decades. Initially, collaboration was focused almost exclusively on terrorism. Then, at the beginning of the 1980s, organised crime and political protest were included as important themes, to which were added, at the end of the decade, drugs and refugees. During the 1990s, the links between various crimes, population movements and political protests were re-enforced.[9]

---

8   Dennis Loo, "DoD Deletes 'Protest = Terrorism.' Problems Remain," *Dennis Loo* (blog), June 22, 2009, http://open.salon.com/blog/dennis_loo/2009/06/22/dod_deletes_protest_terrorism_problems_remain, accessed June 30, 2009.

9   Hornqvist, p. 40.

Not coincidentally, the 1980s are what Gary Teeple has referred to as the "watershed decade," when the shift from multinational to transnational corporations took place and when neoliberal policies became the dominant ones—in Britain under Thatcher and in the US under Reagan.[10]

There is a way to parlay the term "terrorism" usefully, since terrorism does exist and is a problem. How do we prevent the use of the term as a ruse by which to repress one's political opponents? I would define terrorism in this way:

> The systematic use of force against persons or property with the intent to induce a general climate of fear in a population in order to produce a particular political objective. Such actions are carried out with either deliberate indifference to the fates of, or involve the conscious targeting of, noncombatant individuals.

I include the explicit mention of innocent civilians in my definition because terrorism differs from political violence in that it is designed to induce fear by the injury or death of innocents.

This definition bypasses the question of legitimacy since, as everyone knows, "one man's freedom fighter is another man's terrorist." Circumventing the question of legitimacy allows us to impartially define whether something is a terrorist act or someone is a terrorist or not. Of course, it is not really possible to offer a definition that everyone will accept. Some people will refuse on principle to adopt a definition that includes the actions of their own government.

The fact that governments and international organizations are now defining terrorism so indiscriminately tells us something about their assertion of independence from the people they supposedly represent. Some of those who try to affect government action are acceptable and not terrorists; corporate lobbyists, for example, have more influence than ever, while others are to be excluded and criminalized for daring to try to influence "their" governments.

❁

The US government's "War on Terror" is a very specific consequence of neoliberalism. On the ostensible grounds of fighting against terrorism, the invasion and ongoing occupation of Iraq and Afghanistan begun

---

10   Gary Teeple, *Globalization and the Decline of Social Reform* (Atlantic Highlands, NJ: Humanities Press International Inc., 1995).

under Bush II and continued under Obama, as well as the flagrant support for the state of Israel against the Palestinians, ensure constantly-growing numbers of al-Qaeda (as well as Hamas and Hezbollah and other variants) recruits and sympathizers. In the name of ending terrorism, the US government and military are producing bumper crops of terrorists who, into the indefinite future, will kill many, many more innocents without regard to age, race, income, religion, political stance, or national origin. It is almost as if the terrorists are secretly in the pay of the US government, so useful to government's policies are their attacks. We might call this the incestuous and codependent relationship between the US government and al-Qaeda et al.

The Irony of the Security State

Paradoxically, the security state makes us all more insecure. This holds true on two levels: in the microsphere of individual, everyday life and in the macrosphere of international conflict. I am going to address the macrosphere here.

The security state, because of its inherent logic and fundamental nature, creates a powerful self-fulfilling cycle of violence on the macro level. Before 9/11, the trends to "suspicionless surveillance"[11] and public order policies (of which the prevention of "terrorism" was already a part) were in clear evidence and of rising significance. The ongoing justification for the massive surveillance and the bypassing of FISA is 9/11. One of the many pieces of evidence that 9/11 was not the precipitant is the fact that the White House ordered the NSA to carry out massive warrantless surveillance of Americans' phone calls seven months before 9/11.[12]

---

11 See, for example, The Public Record Staff, "Before Warrantless Wiretaps There Was Suspicionless Surveillance," PubRecord.org, June 23, 2008, http://pubrecord. org/politics/881/before-warrantless-wiretaps-there-was-suspicionless-surveillance/, accessed February 14, 2011.

12 *USA Today* first reported on this on May 11, 2006: Leslie Cauley, "NSA has Massive Database of Americans' Phone Calls," USAToday.com, May 11, 2006, http://www.usatoday.com/news/washington/2006-05-10-nsa_x.htm, accessed January 11, 2011. Subsequently, it came to light in lawsuits and briefs that the NSA sought to initiate this illegal spying seven months *before* 9/11. Qwest Communications' CEO Joseph Nacchio states that he met with the NSA on February 27, 2001 and was asked to participate in this. He refused. AT&T et al, however, complied.

See Sarah Burnett and Jeff Smith, "Documents: Qwest was Targeted," RockyMountainNews.com, October 11, 2007, http://www.rockymountainnews.com/

War and State/Anti-state Terror

Wars are commonly depicted in bravado terms that overlook or drastically minimize any casualties, especially among civilians. Witness, for example, then Fox News' Tony Snow's cheerleading the initial, quick toppling of Saddam Hussein on April 13, 2003:

> Tommy Franks and the coalition forces have demonstrated the old axiom that boldness on the battlefield produces swift and relatively bloodless victory. The three-week swing through Iraq has utterly shattered skeptics' complaints.[13]

The toppling of Hussein and the invasion were not "relatively bloodless."

If innocents are hurt or killed or if their property is damaged and states are called to account for these happenings, their explanations are likely to be that the acts were "collateral damage" or the products of rogue individuals, or that the innocents hurt or killed were being used as "human shields" by the individual(s) the state was really targeting. States invariably respond that they had no intent to hurt, kill, or damage innocents; the harm was accidental or unavoidable through no fault of the states.

Of course, in the course of war even states that are being as careful as they can and that are not trying to deceive will sometimes inadvertently hurt innocents. The issue here is not individual acts then; it is one of state policy. Is the policy one that intends to do harm, or that reflects utter indifference and criminal recklessness with respect to civilians? If so, then it is terrorism, by design.

Anti-state terrorism and state terrorism share, at a minimum, an indifference to civilians' fates, and in most instances they both deliberately target civilians. The object in both cases is to strike fear in the population in order to provoke a particular political response. Anti-state terrorists intend for the fear and disruption they cause within the population to

---

drmn/tech/article/0,2777,DRMN_23910_5719566,00.html, accessed January 10, 2011; Steve Benen, "Did the NSA Retaliate Against Qwest?" *The Carpetbagger Report* (blog), October 11, 2007, http://www.thecarpetbaggerreport.com/archives/13201.html, accessed January 13, 2011; Scott Shane, "Former Phone Chief Says Spy Agency Sought Surveillance Help Before 9/11," NYTimes.com, October 14, 2007, http://www.nytimes.com/2007/10/14/business/14qwest.html, accessed January 23, 2011.

13 "SoundBites," Fair.org, April 2006, http://www.fair.org/index.php?page=3353, accessed February 11, 2011.

lead to public demand for the state to grant certain political concessions (possibly including the capitulation of the state to the terrorists). States use terrorism with the intention of causing their opponents and their opponents' supporters to give up their fight. State use of terror is deliberately indiscriminate: you are supposed to be terrified that you or your love ones could be the next target merely for being in the wrong place at the wrong time. This is as true of torture as it is of bombs being dropped onto civilians from planes overhead.

The Problem with the "Ticking Time Bomb" Scenario

The rationale for torture (or in the euphemistic parlance of those who defend its use "enhanced interrogation techniques") revolves around the "ticking time bomb" scenario. According to this presumed situation, someone who has been detained and who knows of a bomb that is going to go off within a short period of time (e.g., within 24 hours) must be forced by torture to reveal the plans, thereby saving the lives of a large number of people who would be killed by said bomb: one life versus many.

Let us consider the nature of this scenario. Suppose you capture a suspect and are convinced that he or she knows something about an immediately pending terrorist attack. Would you not also expect that the terrorist cell, as soon it learns that one of its members has been out of contact for an extended period, would immediately cancel its plans and all scatter to the winds or else move the timetable up for setting off the bomb? Remember that this arrest is supposed to be taking place a day or less before the bomb is scheduled to go off; this group would be very careful about staying in touch and would have signals to assure the group that none of the members has been picked up. Any missed check-in communications at previously agreed upon time intervals would trigger an automatic assumption from the group that one of their people has been picked up. They would have to expect then that their plans would be spilled within a day or less. Torturing a prisoner would therefore not work to get you the information about the location of the bomb soon enough to prevent either an accelerated detonation or to capture any of his or her co-conspirators who have now disappeared.

Furthermore, if you suspect this person to be a terrorist, or even know for a fact that this person is a terrorist, you then have a choice: Do you choose to torture this person and thereby ruin any chances of obtaining his or her cooperation in the future? Or do you try to use methods that will get you reliable information? Any information obtained through torture is not reliable because you have used torture to get it. As interrogation experts and people who have been tortured and survived agree, what someone who is being tortured will say is whatever they think that their torturers want to hear so that the torture will cease. Torture is, after all, by definition, excruciating in the extreme. Also, by torturing someone, you will have destroyed any chances of convicting him or her for any crimes, thereby putting this person and yourself in legal limbo.

This is no doubt obvious to the government itself, as interrogation experts have pointed out when they have gone public with their dissent.

So why use such a counter-productive technique as torture, leaving aside the moral issues?

The answer is because torture's purpose is not intelligence. Torture's purpose is terror.[14]

Neoliberal regimes have no choice but to rely more and more heavily upon coercion and outright terror to ensure cooperation and to forestall disruption and upheaval, because the rewards for going along with the status quo are being undercut day by day for the vast majority of the world's people; in addition, disruptions, both on the day-to-day individual and family levels and on the city/state/regional and global levels, are more the norm and not the exception. Coercion must be used more, but even coercion does not work in all instances, and in some cases sheer terror must be employed.

---

14 From Andy Worthington, "Seven Years of Torture: Binyam Mohamed Tells His Story," *andyworthington.co* (blog), August 3, 2009, http://www.andyworthington.co.uk/2009/03/08/seven-years-of-torture-binyam-mohamed-tells-his-story/, accessed January 22, 2010:

> Understandably unable to resist the effects of the torture [which included 30-40 cuts on his penis with a knife], Binyam [Mohamed] proceeded to confess to whatever wild theories were put to him by his torturers. **"They had fed me enough through their questions for me to make up what they wanted to hear," he said. "I confessed to it all.** There was the plot to build a dirty nuclear bomb, and another to blow up apartments in New York with their gas pipes." As Rose noted, "This—supposedly the brainchild of the 9/11 planner Khalid Sheikh Mohammed—always sounded improbable: it was never quite clear how gas pipes might become weapons."
>
> Binyam added, "I said Khalid Sheikh Mohammed had given me a false passport after I was stopped the first time in Karachi and that I had met Osama bin Laden 30 times. None of it was true. The British could have stopped the torture because they knew I had tried to use the same passport at Karachi both times. That should have told them that what I was saying under torture wasn't true. But so far as I know, they did nothing."

This is the underlying reason why Obama is doing what he is doing and why he is proving to be such a shocking disappointment to those who expected something very different from this charismatic and articulate black man.

Two Sides of the Same Coin

Both anti-state terrorism and state terrorism share essentially identical attitudes towards the people—people are political objects to be acted upon rather than subjects to whom we can appeal. They are best moved through the generous application of fear. Anti-state and state terrorism both evidence contempt and cynicism towards people. In that sense anti-state and state terrorism are both profoundly antidemocratic and anti-humane.

The US "War on Terror" is the obverse side of the coin from bin Laden's jihad. Osama bin Laden on a number of occasions subtly signaled his pleasure with Bush and Cheney's policies. Recruiting soldiers to his jihad was far easier with Bush and Cheney in charge than it would have been under a Kerry presidency presumably, according to bin Laden's logic, because Kerry would not have been as clumsy. (Whether bin Laden was right about this difference is impossible to know since Kerry never took office. But the events in Pakistan after the Bush White House adopted Obama's 2007 recommendation to strike at al-Qaeda and the Taliban without consulting the Pakistani government suggest that bin Laden overestimated the differences between a Democratic and Republican president.)

The US government's "War on Terror" and al-Qaeda present a unity of opposites: each needs the other and profits from the existence of the other.

On July 1, 2009, Michael Scheuer, who was head of the CIA's Bin Laden tracking unit from 1996 to 1999, interviewed by Fox News' Glenn Beck, stated: "The only chance we have as a country right now is for Osama bin Laden to deploy and detonate a major weapon in the United States."[15] The only chance this country has is if it suffers a devastating terrorist attack. Remarkable.

Or, as Nazi leader Hermann Goering put it in 1946, "The people can always be brought to the bidding of the leaders . . . tell them they are being

---

15   This is available in transcript form and also on YouTube, for example, here: http://vodpod.com/watch/1840866-beck-guest-only-chance-us-has-as-a-country-is-for-bin-laden-to-detonate-a-major-weapon, accessed February 14, 2011.

attacked, and denounce the peacemakers for lack of patriotism and expos-
ing the country to danger."[16]

The corollaries of rights violations and illegal surveillance by the Bush
and Obama White Houses in the US are the violations of the rules of war
that constitute state terror abroad. As seen in Abu Ghraib and at GITMO
and in their assault on Fallujah[17] (where they specifically suspended international rules of war by aiming phosphorous missiles at people and shooting at anyone who moved), and Hilla[18] (which had the misfortune of being
on a direct path to Baghdad), the US military today rules in substantial
degree through generous uses of terror. In the case of Hilla, where the
US used cluster bombs on densely populated civilian areas, the objective
was to quickly crush any resistance to their drive to Baghdad because they
did not think that American public opinion would tolerate a protracted
war campaign. (This is a core part of the [Colin] Powell Doctrine that
grew out of the Vietnam War experience). In Fallujah's case, the point was
to punish the people of Fallujah for their support of the insurgents. The
use of drones upon Pakistan not only results in deaths to innocents, it is
warfare waged on a nonbelligerent sovereign nation's territory, violating a
basic tenet of international law.

A state that uses terror reveals itself to be on particularly precarious footings because it must resort to means that exceed those normally
employed by states to carry out their policies and/or retain their power.
The so-called "War on Terror" cannot be won the way it is being waged.
Indeed, current methods only guarantee the spread of anti-state terror and
its growing virulence indefinitely. It is like fighting a fire by drowning
it with barrels and barrels of gasoline. As the conflagration grows ever
higher, the US government calls out: "We need more gasoline here!"

---

16   Gustave Gilbert, *Nuremberg Diary* (New York: Farrar, Straus, 1947), 255–256. From
     a conversation Gustave Gilbert held with Goering in his cell on the evening of April
     18, 1946.

17   See Dahr Jamail, "The 'Free Fire Zone' of Iraq," *in Impeach the President: the Case
     Against Bush and Cheney*, eds. Dennis Loo and Peter Phillips (New York: Seven Sto-
     ries Press, 2006).

18   See Howard Friel and Richard Falk, *The Record of the Paper: How the New York Times
     Misreports US Foreign Policy* (New York: Verso, 2004), 127: "The decision, then, to
     continue the march to Baghdad without troop and supply-line reinforcements was
     both politically and militarily risky. To reduce such risks, the Bush administration
     made the additional decision to proceed to Baghdad using maximum force, which
     turned the eighty-mile corridor from Najaf to Baghdad literally into a US warpath."

The Bigger the Failure, the Greater Their Success

A vicious paradox characterized the Bush White House: the more they failed, the more they succeeded in getting what they wanted all along, and the more grounds they marshaled and spun to justify their continued leadership. After Katrina ravaged an unprotected New Orleans, Bush stated that he wanted to overturn the Posse Comitatus Act—the Civil War law that prohibits the use of military forces in domestic affairs. Soldiers are ill suited by training and mission to handle domestic matters. The "grave and deteriorating" situation in Iraq where American and other forces are charged to a large extent with handling domestic affairs is further living evidence of this.

Bush got his wish in the John Warner Defense Authorization Act of 2007. He signed that bill into law in a private ceremony on the anniversary of his signing of the Military Commissions Act of 2006 the previous October.[19] The Warner Act, unbeknownst to nearly the entire US population, gives the president the power to declare a "public emergency" and take control of National Guard Units (the National Guard is ordinarily under the control of state governors) to conduct mass roundups, arrests, and detentions. The Warner Act, in other words, is a martial law-enabling act.[20] The Act calls for the president to inform a handful of Congress members of what he's doing and why he's doing it if he does declare a "public emergency." In his signing statement Bush declared that he reserved the right not to tell anyone in Congress the reason for any declaration of martial law or the precise nature of any steps he might take to impose it.[21] In other words, any president could declare for

---

19   "Public Law 109-364, the 'John Warner Defense Authorization Act of 2007', (H.R. 5122)," Bill of Rights Defense Committee online, http://www.bordc.org/threats/hr5122.php, accessed August 23, 2009.

20   Frank Morales, "Bush Moves Toward Martial Law," TowardFreedom.com, October 26, 2006, http://www.towardfreedom.com/home/content/view/911/, accessed November 3, 2008.

21   George W. Bush, "President's Statement on H.R. 5122, the 'John Warner National Defense Authorization Act for Fiscal Year 2007,'" October 17, 2006, *Presidential Signing Statements: 2001-Present*, CoherentBabble.com, http://www.coherentbabble.com/ss2006.htm#a200616, accessed May 12, 2009.

   The executive branch shall construe sections 914 and 1512 of the Act, which purport to make consultation with specified Members of Congress a precondition to the execution of the law, as calling for but not mandating such consultation, as is consistent with the Constitution's provisions

unscrupulous reasons that they were imposing nationwide martial law and not have to tell anyone in Congress why or what he or she was doing.

A tragically all-too-plausible and all-too-possible scenario whereby the president might invoke the Warner Act would be a nuclear device being set off in a US city, killing tens or hundreds of thousands immediately and endangering millions more. Bin Laden, as Scheuer has pointed out, has already received permission to use nukes.

> "You've written no one should be surprised when Osama bin Laden and al Qaeda detonate a weapon of mass destruction in the United States," says Kroft. "You believe that's going to happen?". . .
>
> "I think it's pretty close to being inevitable," says Scheuer. . . .
>
> "[Bin Laden] secured from a Saudi sheik named Hamid bin Fahd a rather long treatise [a fatwa issued in May 2003]... that [bin Laden] was perfectly within his rights to use [nukes]. Muslims argue that the United States is responsible for millions of dead Muslims around the world, so reciprocity would mean you could kill millions of Americans."[22]

What would happen in case of another 9/11? Imagine the chaos that would ensue after a nuclear (or chemical or biological) attack. The president would most likely declare martial law, suspend civil rights and civil liberties, and muzzle the press. Both major political parties would undoubtedly join the chorus in demanding the most draconian anti-terrorism measures possible in order to "prove" their patriotism. The country would stand

---

concerning the separate powers of the Congress to legislate and the President to execute the laws.

A number of provisions in the Act call for the executive branch to furnish information to the Congress or other entities on various subjects. These provisions include sections 219, 313, 360, 1211, 1212, 1213, 1227, 1402, and 3116 of the Act, section 427 of title 10, United States Code, as amended by section 932 of the Act, and section 1093 of the Ronald W. Reagan National Defense Authorization Act for Fiscal Year 2005 (Public Law 108-375) as amended by section 1061 of the Act. The executive branch shall construe such provisions in a manner consistent with the President's constitutional authority to withhold information the disclosure of which could impair foreign relations, the national security, the deliberative processes of the Executive, or the performance of the Executive's constitutional duties."

22 *60 Minutes* interview, Cbsnews.com, November 14, 2004, http://www.cbsnews.com/stories/2004/11/12/60minutes/printable655407.shtml, accessed May 16, 2008.

"united in outrage" and at one with the martial-law president who would promise us, against the (video) backdrop of a major American city in ruins, to find and punish the perpetrators of this terrible act and to wage an unremitting, indefinite war against terror. All bets would be off; all prior "normality," all pretenses of "checks and balances" and due process would be quaint and increasingly distant memories.

Should this scenario come to pass, no one can say that we were not warned. Warnings of the 9/11 attacks were numerous, dire, and ignored. The most blatant of these was the August 6, 2001 Presidential Daily Bulletin (PDB) that warned Bush that bin Laden might be planning to hijack commercial airliners. The PDB was entitled "Bin Laden Determined to Strike in US." [23] It specifically mentioned the World Trade Center.

Despite what they knew before 9/11, the Bush White House did nothing to alert the North American Aerospace Defense Command (NORAD) of a potential hijacking, nor did they step up security at the airports. Suspects were not followed up on, despite repeated and urgent requests to do so from FBI field agents who were shocked to find Arabs taking flight lessons with no interest in learning how to land.

Condoleezza Rice, in spite of the foregoing, declared on May 16, 2002, to the 9/11 Commission: "I don't think anybody could have predicted that they would try to use an airplane as a missile, a hijacked airplane as a missile." Rice insisted that nobody knew whom, when, or where, and that therefore the US government's inaction was appropriate; they did not have Mohammed Atta's exact itinerary after all.

As Thomas Kean, former Republican Governor of New Jersey and 9/11 Commission Chairman, concluded, 9/11 "was not something that had to happen.... There are people that, if I was doing the job, would certainly not be in the position they were in at that time because they failed. They simply failed," Kean said.[24]

---

23   "Transcript: Bin Laden Determined to Strike in US," *Politics*, CNN.com, April 10, 2004, http://news.findlaw.com/hdocs/docs/terrorism/80601pdb.html, accessed April 7, 2008.

24   Joel Roberts, "9/11 Chair: Attack Was Preventable," CBSnews.com, December 17, 2003, http://www.cbsnews.com/stories/2003/12/17/eveningnews/main589137.shtml, accessed December 23, 2008.

The Losing War on Terror: Is It Cultural Myopia?

Scheuer attributes the counter-productiveness of the "War on Terror" to cultural myopia. Cultural myopia certainly helps to explain the disastrous wars on Afghanistan and Iraq—an arrogance and laziness of mind that sees everything and everyone in the world through the lens of American values, practices, and behaviors. "With regret," the Russian official said, "I have to say that you're really going to get the hell kicked out of you [in Afghanistan]."

Cofer Black, Director of the CIA's Counterterrorism Center, responded: "We're going to kill them," he said. "We're going to put their heads on sticks. We're going to rock their world."[25] This kind of grotesque arrogance can explain much about why we are losing the wars in Afghanistan and Iraq, but it does not explain why the neocons wanted to invade Afghanistan and Iraq prior to 9/11 in the first place. It does not explain their outsourcing the pursuit of bin Laden and their willful exchanging of bin Laden as "Public Enemy Number One" with Saddam Hussein. Cultural myopia and arrogance can account for tactical blunders but they do not explain the overall strategy.

Bush and Cheney knew when they launched their campaign to parlay the anger and fear of Americans as a result of 9/11 into an invasion of Iraq that Saddam Hussein and Iraq had nothing to do with 9/11.[26] Bush and Cheney elected to go after Iraq under the signboard of the "War on

---

25 Bob Woodward, *Bush at War* (New York: Simon and Schuster, 2002), 103.

26 In September 2000 the Project for the New American Century (PNAC), a neoconservative think tank, published a ninety page report entitled "Rebuilding America's Defenses: Strategies, Forces, and Resources For a New Century" (RAD). PNAC's members included, among others, William Kristol, Richard Cheney, Elliott Abrams, Gary Bauer, Donald Rumsfeld, Paul Wolfowitz, Steve Forbes, Jeb Bush, and William J. Bennett. "Rebuilding America's Defenses" quoted extensively from PNAC's June 1997 "Statement of Principles" and called for expanding upon US military preeminence. On page 26 RAD states: "While the unresolved conflict with Iraq provides the immediate justification, the need for a substantial American force presence in the Gulf transcends the issue of the regime of Saddam Hussein." In other words, Hussein is the pretext but the real agenda is US dominance in the Gulf. On page 63 RAD states, "the process of transformation [of ratcheting up US military might], even if it brings revolutionary change, is likely to be a long one, absent some catastrophic and catalyzing event—like a new Pearl Harbor." That catalyzing event came a year later. As Bush wrote in his diary on September 11, 2001, "The Pearl Harbor of the 21st century took place today." (Dan Batlz and Bob Woodward, "America's Chaotic Road to War—Bush's Global Strategy Began to Take Shape in First Frantic Hours After Attack," *Washington Post*, January 27, 2002, A1.) RAD

Terror" knowing that al-Qaeda was elsewhere. Incompetence and cultural arrogance do not comprise the central reason for the bungling of this "War on Terror." As Scheuer points out, Bush and Cheney (and for that matter Obama) need their putative enemy al-Qaeda just as much as al-Qaeda needs its foil in the US government.

The anti-terrorism measures employed by the White House are not just dramatically counter-productive; their anti-terror measures appear to be designed primarily to repress and control the US population and the people of other countries. As PBS's 2007 *Frontline* show, "Spying on the Home Front" chronicled,

> On New Year's Eve weekend [2003] the FBI demanded records from all hotels, airlines, rental car agencies, casinos and other businesses on every person who visited Las Vegas in the run-up to the holiday. Stephen Sprouse and Kristin Douglas of Kansas City, Mo., object to being caught in the FBI dragnet in Las Vegas just because they happened to get married there at the wrong moment. Says Douglas, "I'm sure that the government does a lot of things that I don't know about, and I've always been OK with that—until I found out that I was included."
>
> A check of all 250,000 Las Vegas visitors against terrorist watch lists turned up no known terrorist suspects or associates of suspects.[27]

Here is the problem with this event: If you were a terrorist planning a dramatic terrorist attack upon Las Vegas, would you register in a hotel or rent a car in your real name in the days leading up to New Year's Eve? Would you not place some people in the Las Vegas area months or even years ahead of time and have them working and/or living in the town under pseudonyms? Does the FBI not realize this? Of course they do. That is why the unconstitutional demand for all of the names of all of the visitors to Las Vegas that weekend was in all probability a test—to see if the FBI could obtain the compliance of Vegas businesses to their demands, and to set a precedent for future incursions into business and private records. As another segment in the *Frontline* show relates, "Peter Swire, a law professor and former White House privacy adviser to President

---

can be found online at NewAmericanCentury.org, www.newamericancentury.org/RebuildingAmericasDefenses.pdf, accessed on February 14, 2011.

27 "Spying on the Home Front," PBS: *Frontline*, PBS.org, May 15, 2007, http://www.pbs.org/wgbh/pages/frontline/homefront/view/, accessed October 11, 2011.

Clinton, tells FRONTLINE that since 9/11 the government has been moving away from the traditional legal standard of investigations based on individual suspicion to generalized suspicion. The new standard, Swire says, is: 'Check everybody. Everybody is a suspect.'"[28]

Bush openly mused while president that a dictatorship would be fine, as long as he was the dictator.[29] On May 9, 2007, with little fanfare and no protests from the Democratic Party, Bush issued two new presidential directives, the National Security Presidential Directive/NSPD 51[30] and Homeland Security Presidential Directive/HSPD–20. These directives allow the president to decide on his own say-so when and if a national emergency has occurred, and they also give him the power to carry on governance absent a role for Congress or any other branch of government whatsoever. The Bush White House's shocking actions and policies were not, however, an aberration. They were actually a continuation and acceleration at a higher level of policies begun in earnest under Reagan and carried forward with somewhat different attributes by Clinton.

Since taking office, Obama has retained the apparatus created by his predecessors and gone even further, insisting, for example, on a new principle his Department of Justice (DOJ) calls "sovereign immunity" with respect to the government's ubiquitous surveillance: the executive government is not subject to supervision unless it can be shown that private information about someone was deliberately released in order to harm that person. As Glenn Greenwald described it:

> [T]he Obama DOJ **demanded dismissal of the entire lawsuit** [brought by the Electronic Freedom Foundation in October 2008 against the government for its warrantless spying on Americans] based on (1) its Bush-mimicking claim that the "state secrets" privilege bars any lawsuits against the Bush administration for illegal spying, and (2) a brand new "sovereign immunity" claim of breathtaking scope— never before advanced even by the Bush administration—that the

---

28 Ibid.

29 Bush said this out loud at least three times. See "If Only I Were a Dictator, by George W. Bush," Buzzflash.com, October 29, 2002, http://www.buzzflash.com/analysis/2002/10/29_Dictator.html, accessed May 23, 2008.

30 George W. Bush, "National Security and Homeland Security Presidential Directive," WhiteHouseArchives.gov, May 2007, http://georgewbush-whitehouse.archives.gov/news/releases/2007/05/20070509-12.html, accessed February 15, 2011. Bill Weinberg, "NSPD-51: Bush Prepares Martial Law," *World War 4 Report* (blog), May 24, 2007, http://www.ww4report.com/node/3940, accessed August 27, 2009.

Patriot Act bars any lawsuits of any kind for illegal government surveillance **unless** there is "willful disclosure" of the illegally intercepted communications.

In other words, beyond even the outrageously broad "state secrets" privilege invented by the Bush administration and now embraced fully by the Obama administration, the Obama DOJ has now invented a brand new claim of government immunity, one which literally asserts that the U.S. Government is free to intercept all of your communications (calls, emails and the like) and—even if what they're doing is blatantly illegal and they know it's illegal—you are barred from suing them unless they "willfully disclose" to the public what they have learned.[31] [Emphases in original.]

In 2010, Obama publicly targeted an American citizen, Anwar Al-Aulaqi, for assassination. The ACLU, on behalf of Al-Aulaqi's father, filed suit attempting to prevent his son's assassination and to reverse the precedent that allowed a US president to act as judge, jury, and executioner of someone who has merely been accused. The Obama DOJ replied that Al-Aulaqi's father's fear for his son's life was not credible: the allegations that Al-Aulaqi had been targeted for killing are "entirely speculative and hypothetical [and] plaintiff cannot demonstrate that he faces the sort of real and immediate threat of future injury,"[32] that the evidence against Al-Aulaqi could not be examined because the president declared it to be "national security secrets," and that the executive branch's decision to

---

31 Glenn Greenwald, "New and Worse Secrecy and Immunity Claims from the Obama DOJ," Salon.com, April 6, 2009, http://www.salon.com/news/opinion/glenn_greenwald/2009/04/06/obama, accessed February 14, 2011.

32 "[T]he relief he [Plaintiff] seeks is based on unfounded speculation that the Executive Branch is acting or planning to act in a manner inconsistent with the terms of the requested injunction. Because such allegations are entirely speculative and hypothetical, plaintiff cannot demonstrate that he faces the sort of real and immediate threat of future injury that is required in order to seek the relief he is requesting. Moreover, the declaratory and injunctive relief plaintiff seeks is extremely abstract and therefore advisory—in effect, simply a command that the United States comply with generalized standards, without regard to any particular set of real or hypothetical facts, and without any realistic means of enforcement as applied to the real-time, heavily fact-dependent decisions made by military and other officials on the basis of complex and sensitive intelligence, tactical analysis and diplomatic considerations." From "Opposition to Plaintiff's Motion for Preliminary Injunction and Memorandum in Support of Defendants' Motion to Dismiss," pp. 2-3, at Scribd. com, September 25, 2010, http://www.scribd.com/doc/38129561/Aulaqi-v-Obama-DOJ-Main-Brief, accessed February 16, 2011.

target Al-Aulaqi was a "battlefield" decision and should not be subject to supervision by the judicial branch:

> "It would be intolerable that courts, without the relevant information, should review and perhaps nullify actions of the Executive taken on information properly held secret." *Chicago & Southern Air Lines*, 333 U.S. at 111. "Judges deficient in military knowledge, lacking vital information upon which to assess the nature of battlefield decisions, and sitting thousands of miles from the field of action" cannot reasonably review the lawfulness of a an alleged military or intelligence operation. *Dacosta*, 471 F.2d at 1155; *see also Schneider v. Kissinger*, 412 F.3d 190, 196 (D.C. Cir. 2005) ("Unlike the executive, the judiciary has no covert agents, no intelligence sources, and no policy advisors. The courts are therefore ill-suited to displace the political branches in such decision-making."). That resolution of plaintiff's claims would put at issue the Executive's confidential military, intelligence, and diplomatic information, including information concerning the threat posed by a foreign organization against which the political branches have authorized the use of all necessary and appropriate force, whether that threat is imminent or concrete, whether there are reasonable alternatives to lethal force, and how such actions may affect relations with a foreign state, is further evidence that plaintiff raises non-reviewable political questions. . . .
>
> It should therefore be apparent that to litigate any aspect of this case, starting with the threshold question of whether plaintiff has in fact suffered any cognizable injury that could be remedied by the requested relief, would require the disclosure of highly sensitive national security information concerning alleged military and intelligence actions overseas. For this reason, the Secretary of Defense, the Director of National Intelligence, and the Director of the CIA have all invoked both the military and state secrets privilege, and related statutory protections, to prevent disclosures of information that reasonably could be expected to harm national security. Absent the privileged information, the case cannot proceed.[33]

---

33 "Opposition to Plaintiff's Motion for Preliminary Injunction and Memorandum in Support of Defendants' Motion to Dismiss," in the Matter of Nasser Al-Aulaqi, on behalf of Anwar Al-Aulaqi v. Barack Obama et al, Civ. A. No. 10-cv-1469 (JDB), filed September 25, 2010, in the US District Court for the District of Alabama, available at Scribd.com, http://www.scribd.com/doc/38129561/Aulaqi-v-Obama-DOJ-Main-Brief, accessed February 16, 2011.

These are the words of the administration that came into office claiming that Bush and Cheney were violating the Constitution and promising to change that.[34] Let us assume for the sake of argument that Al-Aulaqi really is a bad guy. Allowing a president to order someone's assassination, even a really bad individual, without any trial and without any supervision, means that any president, those that you like and those that you do not, those that you trust and those that you do not, those who have no problem with you and those who regard you as a dire political opponent, can simply order you eliminated. That is why the legal system's philosophical linchpin is that no one is above the law.

Consider the following highly abbreviated list of what has happened since Bush II took office: the legalization and ongoing practice of torture; the doctrine and practice of preemptive attacks; the targeting of civilians during war; the open and ongoing violation of the 1978 FISA law through the warrantless surveillance of hundreds of millions of Americans; the stripping of habeas corpus rights and the consequent indefinite detentions; the Warner Act, NSPD-51, the USA PATRIOT Act, the Protect America Act of 2007, and hundreds of signing statements that override the laws passed by Congress. The breaching of long-standing civil liberties and fundamental beliefs in American governance risks generating severe fissures in the social compact.

❁

As instances of terrorism break out, frequently in retaliation for the inequities and repression that neoliberal policies create and exacerbate, neoliberal regimes trumpet the need to further intensify government clampdowns on dissent and dissenters, on civil liberties, and on free speech and association. It is not inevitable that anti-state terrorism should follow on the heels of state terror. Anti-state terror is neither the correct nor the effective way to respond to state terror. But state terror does tend to produce its mirror opposite in anti-state terror, as they are opposite poles of the same perversity.

---

34 Obama's pledge to assassinate Al-Aulaqi has been reported by numerous mainstream media outlets such as *The New York Times* and *ABC News* and confirmed by Obama's Director of National Intelligence Adm. Dennis Blair in Congressional testimony. Glenn Greenwald summarizes this in his column, "Confirmed: Obama Authorizes Assassination of U.S. Citizen," Salon.com, April 7, 2010, http://www.salon.com/news/opinion/glenn_greenwald/2010/04/07/assassinations, accessed April 7, 2010.

The two, after all, share fundamentally the same anti-humanist stance: people are to be acted upon as objects rather than appealed to and engaged with on the basis of reason and justice. Terror, whether state sponsored or anti-state in nature, represents the deliberate use of unbounded violence, including the use of torture and the deaths of innocents and many of one's opponents. The indiscriminate use of violence upon others, indeed, is a necessary and inevitable component of terror. It is one of the sources of its efficacy (such as it is): one is supposed to surrender to those who use terror because one could easily be the next arbitrarily and capriciously chosen victim.

Terror's indiscriminateness is a major source of its counter-productiveness as well. People who are collateral victims of state and anti-state terror will turn against terrorists, whichever one they are the victims of.

> [I]nstead of confining terrorists, Guantanamo often produced more of them by rounding up common criminals, conscripts, low-level foot soldiers and men with no allegiance to radical Islam—thus inspiring a deep hatred of the United States in them—and then housing them in cells next to radical Islamists. . . .
>
> Guantanamo became a school for jihad, complete with a council of elders who issued fatwas, binding religious instructions, to the other detainees.[35]

Alberto J. Mora, Former General Counsel, United States Navy, in testimony before the Senate Armed Services Committee on June 17, 2008, stated as follows:

> Mr. Chairman, our Nation's policy decision to use so-called 'harsh' interrogation techniques during the War on Terror was a mistake of massive proportions. It damaged and continues to damage our Nation in ways that appear never to have been considered or imagined by its architects and supporters, whose policy focus seems to have been narrowly confined to the four corners of the interrogation room. This interrogation policy—which may aptly be labeled a 'policy of cruelty'—violated our founding values, our constitutional system and the fabric of our laws, our over-arching foreign policy interests, and

---

35 Tom Lasseter, "Day 3: Militants Found Recruits Among Guantanamo's Wrongly Detained," McClatchy Newspapers online, June 17, 2008, http://www.mcclatchydc. com/detainees/story/38779.html, accessed March 3, 2009.

our national security. The net effect of this policy of cruelty has been to weaken our defenses, not to strengthen them, and has been greatly contrary to our national interest. . . .

All of these factors contributed to the difficulties our nation has experienced in forging the strongest possible coalition in the War on Terror. But the damage to our national security also occurred down at the tactical or operational level. I'll cite four examples:

First, there are serving U.S. flag-rank officers who maintain that the first and second identifiable causes of U.S. combat deaths in Iraq—as judged by their effectiveness in recruiting insurgent fighters into combat—are, respectively the symbols of Abu Ghraib and Guantanamo. And there are other senior officers who are convinced that the proximate cause of Abu Ghraib was the legal advice authorizing abusive treatment of detainees that issued from the Department of Justice's Office of Legal Counsel in 2002.[36]

Terrorism's indiscriminateness is not a product of poorly trained personnel or something that could be adjusted with the proper motives and leadership; it is a fundamental characteristic of anti-state and state-sponsored terrorism and an extension of its logic.

The Impossibility of "Surgical Strikes"

The viciously counter-productive effects of the security state's policies have their analog in medicine: the application of antibiotics to kill bacteria produces bacteria that mutate into more virulent forms to negate the antibiotics. Our bodies' own immune systems and abilities to cope with the ubiquitous presence of unfriendly bacteria are hampered and weakened by the overuse of antibiotics and antiseptics that kill friendly and unfriendly bacteria alike. For unfriendly bacteria, as Nietzsche famously stated more generally, that which doesn't kill you makes you stronger. And as Israel learned (or, more correctly, still has not learned) from its brutal invasion of Lebanon in 1982, their efforts at wiping out the Palestine Liberation Organization (PLO) once and for all, in the course of which they unleashed the massacres of Sabra and Shatila in which defenseless Palestinian men,

---

36 Ali Frick, "Mora: Abu Ghraib and Guantanamo are 'First and Second Identifiable Causes of U.S. Combat Deaths in Iraq,'" ThinkProgress.org, June 17, 2008, http://thinkprogress.org/2008/06/17/mora-abu-ghraib-and-guantanamo-are-first-and-second-identifiable-causes-of-us-combat-deaths-in-iraq/, accessed July 2, 2009.

women, and children were systematically slaughtered, only succeeded in creating a more militant and more intransigent opposition in the form of Hezbollah. Israel, in other words, inadvertently created Hezbollah and fostered their suicide bomber tactic.

Bush and Cheney's failure to heed the explicit, urgent, and repeated warnings of a coming terrorist attack before 9/11 (perhaps due to inattention and tunnel vision, perhaps due to something more sinister), resulting in that day's devastating attacks, gave them a blank check for instituting policies that they were in the process of covertly implementing anyway.

The US government's invasion and occupation of Iraq opened wide the doors for al-Qaeda to enter Iraq, a country where al-Qaeda had previously been successfully suppressed under Hussein's militantly anti-Wahhabist regime. In the name of fighting terror, Bush and Cheney handed al-Qaeda a gift that keeps on giving. The more Bush and Cheney failed to stem anti-state terrorism, in other words, the more they succeeded in advancing their agenda, an agenda that Obama has continued and intensified to a substantial degree.

In state and anti-state terrorism we find a unity of opposites. They mirror each other even as they appear to be mortal enemies, existing like MAD comics' Spy v. Counterspy characters. They meet only to try to annihilate each other. Like gas thrown onto a fire to supposedly drown the fire, however, the measures taken to eradicate only succeed in fueling the conflagration. The only possible solution is to break out of the fundamental logic that underpins the vicious cycle of violence: anti-state and state terror are both Wars *of* Terror.

CHAPTER FIVE

Why Voting Isn't the Solution:
The Problem with Democratic Theory

It doesn't matter who you vote for, as long as you vote.

Common saying in the US at election time

When, as a teenager, I first heard the injunction that a person should vote but that it did not matter who or what they voted for, I asked myself: "How come it doesn't matter how I vote? If my choice doesn't matter, then what's the point?" The answer that most people would give to such a question is that voting embodies the essence of democracy. "Democracy!" is our times' indispensable political slogan or shibboleth[1]—rule by all the people, as opposed to rule by the few.

According to the vast majority of people in the US—and perhaps the world—the popular will, the sine qua non of democracy, expresses itself by and through the vote. The majority of commentaries on governance reflect this, making the central question whether or not votes are being honored—how *universal* is the right to the franchise, how extensively is the populace *exercising* its right to vote, how correctly and *fairly* are the

---

1 "Shibboleth...**1 a** : a word or saying used by adherents of a party, sect, or belief and usu. regarded by others as empty of real meaning <the old shibboleth*s* come rolling off their lips—Joseph Epstein> **b** : a widely held belief <today this book publishing shibboleth is a myth—L. A. Wood> **c** : **truism, platitude** <some truth in the shibboleth that crime does not pay—Lee Rogow>" from *Merriam-Webster's Collegiate Dictionary*, 11th ed., s.v. "shibboleth."

votes being counted, and how much are public officials *abiding* by the vote. In addition, public opinion polls are now frequently treated as the between-elections expressions of public sentiment.

Yet somehow something is lacking in all of this. How can voting in and of itself shoulder the entire weight of authentic popular rule? How can voting satisfy "the people" if we take the phrase "of the people, by the people, and for the people" seriously? Actual popular rule—it does not take much to see this—eludes us the way the pot of gold at the end of the rainbow recedes as we pursue it. There is always something: a corrupt officialdom, a non-vigilant press, an overly powerful corporate world, an apathetic populace. The list goes on and on, and the shortcomings continue as surely as sunsets follow sunrises. Winston Churchill's "it has been said that democracy is the worst form of government except all those other forms. . . ." is supposed to placate us: you may think you have it bad now, but see what awaits you if you leave!

The truth is it is not that fallible human beings keep messing up a wonderful idea. It is not principally a matter of perfecting the franchise; the problem grows out of the *theory* being implemented. When the practice and experience of implementing a theory fall short of expectations, we can generally find an underlying problem in the theory itself; democratic theory, as a theory, contains critical—in fact, fatal—flaws.

Theories are built, after all, upon their premises. Premises are assumptions and assertions about the world. Democratic theory therefore, like any other paradigm, paints a picture of the world via the prism of its premises. Several of democratic theory's baseline assumptions about how things work are theoretically unsound and, as practice reveals, clearly wrong.

Yet paradigms tend to persist even in the face of substantial contradictory evidence, like a habit that is hard to break. Dominant paradigms enjoy the privileges of incumbency and the security of the familiar, but they can be powerful traps, obscuring uncomfortable and ineluctable realities, and dooming their adherents to futility if they attempt to rectify inequities while still clinging to the paradigm that is itself part of the problem.

The momentous changes going on in the US and in the world cannot be properly understood and addressed by those who seek a different world if we do not possess the analytical and theoretical tools to see clearly what is afoot. These times urgently demand a different paradigm.

This chapter consists of two parts. In the first part, I explore key problems with and in democratic theory. In the second, based on this critique I suggest the basic principles and, to a limited extent, the concrete practices of an alternative path towards actually approaching authentic popular rule.

Democratic Theory: Confounding Leaders With the Led

Classical democratic theory holds that political leaders and the mass media are the people's servants; leaders and the media mirror what the people want.

There are two variants on this perspective. In the first variant, political leaders and opinion-makers do what they do because leaders are responding in the same way the public does to the same stimuli; both the broad public and the leadership are guided by what sociologist Emile Durkheim dubbed the "conscience collective," a commonly held, diffuse sentiment.[2]

The other variant on classical democratic theory holds that political leaders are bound by the strictures of citizens' votes, while mass media—society's key opinion-makers—are guided and constrained by their audiences. The "power of the people," in other words, fundamentally determines what political leaders and mass media do through the paired powers of the ballot and the wallet. According to this variant, leaders and the media are not necessarily understood as identical in their sentiments to those of the mass populace; they can depart from the mass public's sentiments. But if and when leaders and the media stray too far from public sentiment, the mass populace, because it allegedly holds the trump card, can and does bring officials and opinion leaders back to reflect mass desires.

This notion that public officials and opinion makers reflect, or at least respond to mass sentiment, expresses itself in different ways. When people complain about the media today—for example, their tendency to employ cheap sensationalism or their vulnerability to government manipulation—critics are customarily told that media disseminate what the public wants and what sells. If they did not reflect public interest and demand, they would not be on the air or in print. If you do not like them, blame the people who watch or read them. If you want something better, boycott what you do not like and support what you do.

Similarly, manifestly bad public policies are routinely attributed to public stupidity and superficiality. Those who complain about a public official's performance are counseled that a majority voted the offending official into office in the first place—hence, *the voters* made a bad choice—and, in any case, constituents can vote this official out of office in the next election. If constituents do not vote the scoundrels out, the public must

2   In social problems theory, a subdiscipline within sociology, this approach is known as "structural strain."

217

be one or more of the following: irredeemably gullible, tolerant of that which it should not tolerate, or it secretly wants to be lied to or misled. Ex-Senator Lowell Weicker, explaining why he was not supporting the impeachment of George W. Bush, put it this way: "Bush obviously lied to the country and the Congress about the war, but we have a system of elections in this country. Everyone knew about the lying before the 2004 elections, and they didn't do anything about it . . . Bush got elected. The horse is out of the barn now."[3] That Bush and Cheney actually lost both the 2000 and 2004 elections and that fraud delivered them the White House does not even enter into apologists' retorts.[4]

Those who do not vote are said to be even more blameworthy for public officials' actions because they did not bother to cast a ballot.[5] Getting politically involved in the US, in other words, means one thing: vote! The will of the people, we are told, ought to be understood as the equivalent of consumer choice. This is rather like seeing the people—and popular rule—through the wrong end of a pair of binoculars. This miniaturized view of what constitutes popular rule lies at the heart of the multifaceted problems within democratic theory.

According to conventional wisdom then, the responsibility for bad media and bad public policies rests squarely upon the public's shoulders. If something is wrong in the media world or in the state, look to the people. This perspective reflects a fundamental misunderstanding—or misrepresentation—of the actual relationship between the leaders and the led. Briefly put, democratic theory misconstrues the relationship between leaders and those they lead by confounding the two and either obliterating the actual differences between leaders and led or improperly attributing primary power to the led.

An illustration of this error can be found in a May 22, 2007 *Salon. com* essay by Gary Kamiya entitled: "Why Bush Hasn't Been Impeached." After correctly stating that the main reason he had not been impeached was because the Democrats refused to press for it, Kamiya went on to articulate his essay's main theme:

---

3 David Lindorff and Barbara Olshansky, *The Case for Impeachment: The Legal Argument for Removing George W. Bush from Office* (New York: St. Martins Press, 2006), 9.

4 See Dennis Loo and Peter Phillips, eds, *Impeach the President: The Case Against Bush and Cheney* (New York: Seven Stories Press, 2006), 29-58.

5 Among those who do recognize that media represent the interests of elite elements that there is a gap between public officials and the populace, most still believe that a solution to both of these problems can be found through the ballot box—which indicates how strongly held the belief is that voting can right wrongs.

"[T]here's a deeper reason why the popular impeachment movement has never taken off—and it has to do not with Bush but with the American people. Bush's warmongering spoke to something deep in our national psyche. The emotional force behind America's support for the Iraq war, the molten core of an angry, resentful patriotism, is still too hot for Congress, the media and even many Americans who oppose the war, to confront directly. It's a national myth. It's John Wayne. To impeach Bush would force us to directly confront our national core of violent self-righteousness—come to terms with it, understand it and reject it. And we're not ready to do that.

The truth is that Bush's high crimes and misdemeanors, far from being too small, are too *great*. What has saved Bush is the fact that his lies . . . tapped into a deep American strain of fearful, reflexive bellicosity. . . . Congress, the media and most of the American people have yet to turn decisively against Bush because to do so would be to turn against some part of themselves. . . ."[6]

He goes on to cite as evidence of this:

"[L]arge numbers of Americans did not just give Bush carte blanche but actively wanted him to attack someone [after 9/11]. They were driven . . . by primordial retribution, reflexive and self-righteous rage. And it wasn't just the masses. . . . Pundits like Henry Kissinger and *The New York Times* columnist Thomas Friedman also called for America to attack the Arab world. Kissinger . . . said that "we need to humiliate them;" Friedman said we needed to "go right into the heart of the Arab world and smash something." . . . For many Americans, who Bush attacked or the reasons he gave, didn't matter—what mattered was that we were fighting back.[7]

Kamiya's essay provoked scores of letters in response, many agreeing with him that the fault lies with the American people. Kamiya's argument, however, contains major flaws. To begin with, he cites no evidence from the masses to support his claim that the public did not *want* Bush and Cheney impeached. In fact, he actually cites evidence to the

---

6   Gary Kamiya, "Why Bush Hasn't Been Impeached," Salon.com, May 22, 2007, http://www.salon.com/news/opinion/kamiya/2007/05/22/impeachment, accessed May 22, 2007.

7   Ibid.

contrary—polls showing that for years large numbers, in several instances, a majority, had wanted impeachment. (See Appendix 2.)

All of the specific individuals he cites to support his characterization of the public mood differ distinctly from the American public as a whole. John Wayne was a popular movie star, but in at least one respect he was not a typical American. Wayne's defense of the war, the widely panned film *The Green Berets*, was a flop because the American people had turned against the Vietnam War.

And unless you conflate elite policymaking and public opinion-making figures with the public (which democratic theory does conflate), Henry Kissinger and Thomas Friedman also cannot be said to fairly represent the American people. The 2003 Iraq War was predicated on lying to the American people repeatedly, persistently, and ubiquitously about a connection between Iraq and 9/11. Without those half-truths, untruths, and deceits, a popular basis for the war would have been impossible to assemble. If Kamiya is right and Americans just wanted revenge, then Bush and Cheney would not have had to lie about a 9/11-Iraq connection and the liberal *New York Times* would not have had to make the case for war. Bush and Cheney could have said: we're blaming Hussein—all those Arabs are alike after all—and let's have at them. Good ole boys would have been persuaded by that caliber of argument, but they would have been vastly outnumbered by the rest of the country who are neither as gullible nor as xenophobic.

Vanilla Ice Cream Anyone?

Aside from Kamiya's unfortunate choice of whom to cite, the traction of Kamiya's argument and the reason it resonated with so many of his readers arise from his voicing an exceedingly widespread, unexamined, taken-for-granted, and cherished belief: leaders are simply expressing what the public wants. We are, after all, a democracy, aren't we? This view confuses policy makers and opinion leaders' *initiatives* with public *receptivity*.[8] Just because the public (or some segment of the public) responds favorably to something proffered to it by leaders does not mean—and is not the same as—the public's initiating attention to the issue. If someone offers you vanilla ice cream and you eat it with relish, this does not mean that you decided that you would rather have vanilla than, say,

---

8   I owe this distinction between initiative and receptivity to sociologist Katherine Beckett.

chocolate. It merely means that you respond favorably to vanilla and are willing to eat it.

You could hold out and say: "I will not eat anything at all until what I really want is put in front of me," but if you are not the cook in the kitchen and you have to choose either to eat what is handed to you or not to eat, the fact that you eat the vanilla does not prove anything other than that you would rather have vanilla ice cream than nothing at all. Furthermore, if the cook offers you a choice of vanilla, chocolate, or strawberry and you select chocolate, this means only that you prefer chocolate to vanilla or strawberry and to not eating. It does not mean that you would not really have preferred a hamburger (or a soy burger if you are a vegetarian).

The Difference Between Consumer Choice and Popular Sovereignty

Ameriprise has a TV ad in which actors portraying Joe and Jane Q. Public declare that once they signed up with Ameriprise and could effect their stock market trades without an intermediary sales agent, they were in charge, as if this conferred upon individual traders control of the stock market—a world notorious for its volatility, insider advantages, and un-certainties. This is similar to a toddler in the woods declaring (assuming he could talk) that he was in charge because his wandering about was entirely up to himself. Capital One's "Freedom Card" advertising declares that its credit cardholders are "Free! Free! Free!" because they get reward points redeemable for commodities from their credit charges. The idea that greater spending and more indebtedness render you freer exists only in Madison Avenue's Alice in Wonderland world.

Corporations, mass media, and public officials tell us that the fact that we get to choose what cell phone, what kind of sweetened cola, which pain reliever, what cut of denim jeans, what type of car, and which major party nominee for office we will vote for, means that we are in charge. As Todd Gitlin points out,

> Capitalism would work to present consumer sovereignty as the equiv-
> alent of freedom. . . . ("If you don't like TV, turn it off." "If you don't
> like cars, don't drive them." "If you don't like it here, go back to Rus-
> sia." "If you don't like Crest, buy Gleem." "If you don't like Republi-
> can, vote Democratic.) The assumption that choice among the givens

amounts to freedom then becomes the root of the worldwide rationale of the global corporation.[9]

We may as well say that if a Nevada brothel prostitute gets to choose which John she will have sex with next, this means that she is in control.

When Henry Ford introduced the Model T Ford in 1908, he famously declared that consumers could have any color Model T they wanted, as long as it was black. Ford is also famous for introducing what was subsequently dubbed "Fordism"—an assembly-line process that involved speeding up production tremendously (cutting the average time to finished car from twelve hours down to one-and-a-half hours); standardization of product (everyone got the same car); and at its heart a compact between capitalist owners and workers in which workers would be paid better than they had been in the past in return for which they would become the major prop holding up the capitalist economy by buying more heavily. Domestic spending as a result of Fordism grew to make up what is today more than two-thirds of the Gross National Product (GNP) of the US.

Fordism operated in the US from the last decade of the 1800s to the middle of the nineteen seventies. Its eventual supersession by neoliberalism and the proliferation of consumer choices has meant that you no longer only have access to a black car. You can get a lot of different colors and features—as long as it is an internal combustion machine. But the fundamental relationship between capital and the populace delineated by Ford's statement "you can have any color as long as it's black" remains: more color choices has not made the consumer into the producer, still less has it made us into the ones who are "in charge." The process by which corporations decide what they will produce and the shaping of state public policies remain at least once removed from the realm that the consumer and the public occupy. Moreover, the vast expansion of consumer options—you can find what seem like dozens of kinds of pain relievers in a drug store—masks an ever-deepening decline in the degree of influence and power that consumers, workers, and the citizenry actually exercise in the economy and polity. Consumers—to put this most cogently—are not the equivalent of citizens. Exercising choices about what to consume is a far cry from the duties and potentialities of being a citizen. More to the point, still less is a citizen—in the best and most elevated sense of the term within democratic theory—the source of political sovereignty.

---

9   Todd Gitlin, "Media Sociology: The Dominant Paradigm," *Theory and Society* 6, no.2, (September), 245.

Confusing Public Sentiment With Public Policies

To return to Kamiya's argument, he conflates a specific policy (the invasion of Iraq) with an alleged generalized sentiment (wanting revenge for 9/11). He argues, in other words, that the sentiment itself gave rise to the policy. This represents a major oversimplification of how public policy and media coverage are determined and a reversal of the causal order. Kamiya's approach here is not unique. It is, in fact, exceedingly commonplace; nearly all scholarly and lay commentators commit this error by confounding sentiment with policies.

Shock, anger, and grief gripped the American people after 9/11, but 9/11 did not on its own mean that Americans hungered for a war. The events of 9/11—even accepting the official government version of events—actually lent themselves more readily and logically to a hunt for al-Qaeda and criminal prosecution. Had the Bush White House handled 9/11 as a horrible crime rather than as a declaration of war, does anyone seriously believe that Bush and Cheney would have encountered major resistance from most of the American people?

A popular sentiment is by definition diffuse and unfocused. If it is widespread, it will of necessity adopt different forms and vary in intensity from person to person and group to group. While a specific public policy must reverberate with a popular sentiment in some fashion or other[10] (if it does not, then that policy will meet overwhelming public disinterest or opposition), a particular popular sentiment does not guarantee or even necessarily lead to any particular policy outcome. Pointing to a specific public policy and tracing it back to an alleged American cultural sentiment as its certain source reflects post-hoc reasoning: event A occurred, then event B occurred, therefore A caused B.

In this case, not only did event A (a desire for retaliation against the 9/11 perpetrators) occur before B (the invasion of Iraq), but also a whole host of other responses could have followed from event A: B2, B3, B4, and so on. The White House and a cooperative mass media shaped public outrage and harnessed it to the specific "solution" of attacking Iraq. New Yorkers, in the immediate wake of 9/11, were not, after all, walking about the streets in the dust cloud of the Twin Towers muttering, "We gotta get that damn Saddam Hussein." As self-evident as this point may seem, this kind of false attribution of cause occurs constantly in scholarly accounts, journalistic explanations, and person-in-the-street conversations. Its prevalence comes from a fallacy that resides within democratic theory itself:

---

10   Ford Motor Company's Edsel, for example, never found an audience.

that the media and the state—and public policy more generally—reflect the will of the people.

Even if a single, internally consistent, universal sentiment did exist among the people that was not countered by any other contrary sentiment—a situation that does not exist—that sentiment would still need to be focused, harnessed, and organized to become a public policy. The public cannot become this unified without leadership. Leadership can either come, on the one hand, from among the existing political leaders—the Democratic and/or Republican Parties (and, under certain circumstances, from third parties)—or, on the other hand, from mass media or the grassroots. For it to come from the grassroots, however, the grassroots need to be organized into a mass movement. This represents a major challenge for grassroots/mass movements, which is why grassroots-initiated policies succeed so infrequently. (How they can succeed and what factors need to be present for success I discuss in Chapter Seven.)

Sunflowers and Sunny Sentiments

Back in the 1960s, a popular anti-Vietnam-War poster hung on my bedroom wall for a while. It had a picture of a big sunflower and it said: "What if they gave a war, and nobody came?" Nice sentiment (I was young and naïve after all), but very misleading. Wars do not end because one day everyone decides not to participate. Governments can, where necessary, press-gang people into serving in their armed forces. The very definition of government is that it has the power to make people do what they do not want to do. As the sociologist Max Weber put it succinctly, political power consists of the ability to get your way, even against resistance. Weber was a conflict theorist and his dictum cogently sets forth state power's essence, in contrast to the much more nebulous and naïve conception of political power set forth by democratic theorists. Even if governments did not have the power to make people do things that they do not want to do, the whole population of a country would never unanimously decide simultaneously to do or not to do something. Social dynamics do not operate that way. Major social changes always begin with micro-changes originating in sub-groups. In other words, leaders and the led continue to exist as a dialectical unity; the two are in dynamic interaction with each other.

When wars are ended by the people (and not by governments) this happens because refusals to serve in the military start to become a significant phenomenon and, even more importantly, soldiers already in uniform begin to refuse to fight and start to turn on their own officers. This results in the destruction of the government's key lever of political power, the one thing that more than anything else gives it the ability to make people do things they do not want to do—government's monopoly over the means of legitimate violence (Max Weber also described this in his analysis of political authority). The breakdown of the military as a governmental tool does not happen often. Indeed, it is extremely rare. It takes an extraordinary amount of conflict, strain, and challenge to the status quo to produce this result.

Historically, the military's collapse as a state weapon has occurred when a war or other crisis engulfed a government, and the government's credibility and legitimacy came under fire, metaphorically as well as literally. The 1917 Russian Revolution, for example, was precipitated by a series of military debacles for the Tsarist and Kerensky governments, beginning with Russia's embarrassing defeat in the 1905 Russo-Japanese War. Its later inability to even outfit many in its army with boots during World War I (a major disaster in a Russian winter!) also contributed to its overthrow. The 1949 Chinese Communist Revolution was preceded by the failure—and refusal—of the Kuomintang (KMT) to fight off the Japanese imperialist invasion of China. The KMT under Chiang Kai-shek was more interested in trying to destroy the Chinese Communist Party (CCP) and workers' organizations than in fighting the Japanese invasion. The KMT, in fact, class-collaborated with the Japanese in significant ways. To make a very long and extremely interesting story short, Chiang lost credibility among the Chinese masses as compared to the CCP whose credibility was exceedingly high. Eventually Chiang had to flee to Taiwan.

Soldiers' resistance to unjust wars, like any other social phenomenon, does not occur spontaneously. Some brave individual soldiers must lead the way. The dissident individual soldiers are in turn catalyzed by political resistance within the domestic population and by military setbacks incurred by the armed forces. What starts small—sometimes with just one person—ripples out and becomes a wave, or even a tsunami, engulfing the government.

The Vietnam War in the 1960s and 1970s finally ended due to the combined impact of the fact that (a) the Vietnamese were winning, (b) the antiwar movement at home and abroad was persistent and widespread (both in numbers of direct participants and in the antiwar movement's exceedingly broad influence), (c) the US government faced a "credibility gap"—people broadly disbelieved what the government was saying, and (d) US troops began to resist orders, even going so far as to, on occasion, frag—kill—their superior officers. Even though President Nixon wanted desperately to continue the war, the US military was in danger of internal collapse, and soldiers in growing numbers could not be counted on to fight.[11] Nixon, a staunch Republican, had no choice but to withdraw or else face the very real possibility of the further contagion of rebellion.

Horses and Drivers

Class-divided societies might be very roughly compared to horse-drawn buggies: the horses are the people and the political and opinion leaders are the drivers. (The metaphor has obvious limitations but it does highlight some useful aspects of the dynamic at work.) Horses under harness can refuse to move even if whipped, but whips are pretty persuasive tools. Horses can also engage in runaway behavior, but such refusals are rare. If horses could freely declare their preferences, they probably would do more than decide which driver is going to put them in the harness and under the whip every few years. They probably would throw off their harnesses and choose to roam freely on the plains. Some horses, it is true, would choose to remain under harness—the ones who fear the open plains.

In the US especially, where the tradition of mass struggle and protest in the streets is weak compared to that of other countries, and where faith in representative government is particularly strong, even those sectors of the public that strongly desire change and want to demonstrate and mobilize themselves against government leaders face major hurdles. Majority sentiment against the existing government is not by itself enough. Sentiment must be organized, focused, and turned into a material force. Organization, in turn, means perforce, leadership. If no segment of the existing leadership (in the US the Republican and Democratic Parties and mass media) chooses to provide leadership to this mass sentiment, then a competing, alternative leadership to replace the existing leadership must be constituted. Accomplishing such a feat—and it is absolutely a feat—constitutes a task of an order or two of magnitude greater in difficulty than the public's swinging its support to a section of the customary leadership. (I discuss this much more in Chapters Six and Seven.)

That Bush and Cheney escaped impeachment and removal from office despite record levels of dissatisfaction was not principally the fault of the American public. Mass sentiment was recorded in favor of an end to

---

11   This stands in stark contrast, of course, to the mythology, embodied in films like *Rambo*, that cowardly politicians tied the military's hands and that if they'd just been allowed to do their jobs they'd have beaten the Vietnamese into submission.

Bush and Cheney and an end to the war on Iraq (a majority of the people wanted a full withdrawal from Iraq at least as early as 2005).[12] But there was a formidable barrier in the stance of mass media and the Democratic Party who adamantly refused to seriously entertain the possibility of impeachment. On the rare occasions when the mass media and the Democratic Party actually brought up the idea of impeachment, it was, with almost no exceptions,[13] to dismiss or deride the idea and pass off those who were advocating it as out of touch with reality and/or seeking partisan revenge. The numbers wanting impeachment found by the pollsters, therefore, were remarkably high given the fact that all prominent political leaders in the government and in media opposed the simply outlandish idea of invoking the Constitutional remedy of impeachment.

As an indication of just how monolithic this stance was, consider the following which represents the entire list of exceptions to this pattern over the Bush White House's eight years: the *Washington Post* ran exactly one op-ed piece from former Senator George McGovern advocating impeachment ("Why I Believe George Bush Must Go") on January 6, 2008. Bill Moyers broadcast one show about impeachment on PBS ("Tough Talk on Impeachment") on July 13, 2007 (which elicited hundreds of letters in support).[14] Keith Olbermann editorialized for impeachment on his MSNBC show on June 11, 2008 ("Impeachment of George W. Bush"). Seven well-written, lively, closely argued, thoroughly (indeed, profusely) researched, and documented books on impeachment were published by prominent individuals, including one by former U.S. Representative Elizabeth Holtzman (who sat on the House Judiciary Committee that

---

12   See, for example, Kenneth Barzinet, "Bush Not Swaying Opinion on War," *New York Daily News*, December 7, 2005, 6, which cited 60 percent wanting the U.S. to withdraw and 40 percent who thought the troops should "get out immediately." Susan Page, "Poll: Majority of Americans Want Withdrawal Plan for Iraq," June 26, 2006, USAToday.com, citing a USA TODAY/Gallup Poll showing 57 per cent wanted US troops to withdraw from Iraq within a year, http://www.usatoday.com/news/world/iraq/2006-06-26-iraq-poll_x.htm, accessed February 4, 2011. Washington Post-ABC News Poll, cited in Michael Fletcher and Jon Cohen, "Poll Finds Support for Obama's War Views: Less Pessimism on Iraq, but 70% Back Pullout," WashingtonPost.com, December 16, 2008, http://www.washingtonpost.com/wp-dyn/content/article/2008/12/15/AR2008121502103.html, accessed February 4, 2011.

13   The only exceptions to this were Rep. Dennis Kucinich, Robert Wexler, Cynthia McKinney and, until the Democrats regained the House majority in the 2006 election, Rep. John Conyers.

14   "Tough Talk on Impeachment," PBS: *Bill Moyers Journal*, pbs.org, July 13, 2007, http://www.pbs.org/moyers/journal/07132007/profile.html, accessed August 1, 2007.

drafted impeachment articles against Nixon), and one by Congressman John Conyers, but not a single one of them received a review or even mention in a major mass media outlet.[15] The only authors to breach the TV boycott of the impeachment books were John Nichols, who appeared on Moyers' show, and Elizabeth de la Vega, who made a brief appearance on *The Colbert Report*.

In 2008, several times best-selling author and former prosecutor Vincent Bugliosi (famous for his prosecution of Charles Manson) published *The Prosecution of George W. Bush for Murder*. Despite his track record of blockbuster books and fame, Bugliosi had trouble finding a publisher, and even once his book was published it never got better than a single reference in a *New York Times* article. His book was never reviewed in major media.

Democratic theory's premise is that public officials and media are the servants of the people; they are supposed to be, therefore they are. This is, of course, circular reasoning and reasoning by assertion rather than by evidence. The truth is far more complicated. Underlying the question of whether democracy is possible or not rests a deeper dynamic between leadership and those they lead.

The Decisive Power of the State and Media

Leaders and those they lead operate in a dialectical relationship to each other; they interact and interpenetrate. But their interaction, as in all dialectical relationships in which opposites dynamically play off of each other, is a weighted one. One end of the dialectic in general exercises overall dominance until it is replaced by a new dialectic, precipitated by the opposites changing positions in a revolutionary reconstitution of the dynamic, creating a new set of opposites and dynamic tensions. Leaders play crucial and decisive roles in determining what the groups they lead end up doing,

---

15　Center for Constitutional Rights, *Articles of Impeachment of George W. Bush* (Brooklyn: Melville House, 2006); David Lindorff and Barbara Olshansky, *The Case for Impeachment: The Legal Argument for Removing George W. Bush from Office* (New York: Thomas Dunn Books, 2006); Elizabeth Holtzman with Cynthia Cooper, *The Impeachment of George W. Bush: A Practical Guide for Concerned Citizens* (New York: Nation Books, 2006); Dennis Loo and Peter Phillips, eds., *Impeach the President: The Case Against Bush and Cheney* (New York: Seven Stories Press, 2006); Elizabeth De La Vega, *The U.S. v. Bush* (New York: Seven Stories Press, 2006); John Nichols, *The Genius of Impeachment* (New York: New Press, 2006); John Conyers, compiler, Anita Miller, ed., *George W. Bush Versus the U.S. Constitution: The Downing Street Memos and Deception, Manipulation, Torture, Retribution, Coverups in the Iraq War and Illegal Domestic Spying*, (Chicago: Academy Chicago Publishers, 2006).

even in thoroughly and genuinely democratic situations in which the leaders are conscientiously and successfully serving the people they lead.

I remember one of the first times I went hiking with a high school friend who was a devoted hiker. He took the lead on our path, and we trudged along at his pace. At some point we switched positions and I picked up the pace, surprised at the fact that we were going significantly faster now that I was the pacesetter. No aspersion on my hiking partner, but the pace is determined by the lead person. The people behind can grouse that the pace is either too slow or too fast, but unless they assume the lead themselves, they are confined by what the lead person is doing.

Democratic theory fails to give proper weight to the initiating and decisive power of the state and media relative to the populace. Under normal circumstances, media and the state possess virtually all of the advantages—and dominate the process—by which the public agenda gets set. They set the table. The public must decide what to eat from the offerings placed there by the media and state, and in that sense the public "democratically" chooses what it likes, but *the public does not decide what will be on the table in the first place.*

In the case of the media, the decision about what gets airtime or column inches lies with executives who do not choose solely—or even mainly—on the basis of what they think the public would like. The prevalence of "reali-TV" programs such as *Survivor, America's Next Top Model, The Great Chase,* and the preceding reali-TV cop shows such as *COPS* and *America's Most Wanted* that date from the late 1980s is commonly ascribed to public demand. A more accurate way to explain these shows' ubiquity, however, can be seen by considering the networks' perspective. While sitcoms such as *Friends, Seinfeld,* and *Cheers* drew huge audience shares, their production costs were also high, with each of the stars of these ensemble shows earning $750,000 or more per episode. While the audience shares for reali-TV shows do not even begin to approach the levels of these smash hit sitcoms (with the sole exception of *American Idol*), their production costs are miniscule. The return on investment for reality shows, the profit-to-cost ratio, is very high. The shows could not exist without drawing decent audiences, but they do not have to draw very large audiences to make economic sense. The TV audience, in short, did not initiate the onslaught of reality programs. Network executives did.

The bromide that media present what gets them the biggest audience does not conform to the media businesses' actual dynamics. Media must satisfy four major audiences: consumers, advertisers, their owners (including Wall Street if the company is not privately held), and the government. Advertisers are a more important audience for media companies overall than consumers. Obviously, having no readers or viewers (or too few) would consign a media corporation to bankruptcy, but what media companies are interested in are: (a) which market segments they can draw, with bigger-spending consumers the preferred target, and (b) avoiding any conflict with big money and with the government.

When CBS' *60 Minutes* got the explosive insider's account of how big tobacco company executives had known decades earlier that nicotine caused cancer but suppressed this information, the head of the network and of the show tried to suppress that information out of concern that it would hurt their bottom line due to advertisers' ire. The story's producer, Lowell Bergman, put his job and his career on the line to get the story aired. He finally succeeded and the tale of his triumph became the film *The Insider* starring Al Pacino as the courageous newsman Lowell Bergman and Russell Crowe as the disillusioned tobacco insider Jeffrey Wigand. What struck me in watching this film was how hard it was to get this explosive story—which undoubtedly drew a large audience—shown, and how Bergman had to go to the mat and risk his career to get it aired. How many other stories that we never hear about die quiet deaths because they would or might offend corporate America or the government? How many journalists avoid even looking into stories that they suspect might get them into trouble?

Many companies have had to close shop at the very time that their subscribing audience was its highest ever, e.g., *Life* and *Ms.* magazines. In the period leading up to and after the 2003 Iraq invasion, MSNBC's highest rated and most popular show was *Donahue,* hosted by Phil Donahue, which outdrew Chris Matthews' influential, long- and still-running *Hardball.* Had the network been solely interested in Nielsen ratings, it would not have cancelled *Donahue.* Instead, MSNBC executives canned Phil Donahue, citing disappointing rating. But, as Rick Ellis wrote, referring to an internal NBC memo, the main reason was political:

> That report—shared with me by an NBC news insider—gives an excruciatingly painful assessment of the channel and its programming. . . . [T]he harshest criticism was leveled at Donahue, whom the authors of the study described as "a tired, left-wing liberal out of touch with the current marketplace."
>
> The study went on to claim that Donahue presented a "difficult public face for NBC in a time of war. . . . He seems to delight in presenting guests who are anti-war, anti-Bush and skeptical of the administration's motives." The report went on to outline a possible

nightmare scenario where the show becomes "a home for the liberal antiwar agenda at the same time that our competitors are waving the flag at every opportunity."[16]

When the WMD hoax and other Bush White House lies about Iraq and 9/11 (that the media nearly unanimously passed on uncritically) became known to everyone, MSNBC could have proudly pointed to *Donahue* as evidence of their network's uniqueness and courageous pursuit of the truth. MSNBC chose not to take this chance because their executives were more afraid of being seen as insufficiently red, white, and blue than they were eager to be honored for doing accurate reportage—in other words, doing the jobs most people think journalists are supposed to do.

Donahue, interviewed in October 2003, after being fired, told Fox's Sean Hannity:

SEAN HANNITY (co-host). What happened at MSNBC?

DONAHUE. Well, we were the only antiwar voice that had a show, and that, I think, made them very nervous. I mean, from the top down, they were just terrified. We had to have two conservatives on for every liberal. I was counted as two liberals.[17]

Politics and ideology, in other words, frame and affect corporate decisions. They make up a crucial part of corporations' bottom lines. Money in the narrow sense is not, in other words, corporations' only concern. The notion that media are only interested in profits does not take this critical factor into consideration.

In the case of the two major political parties, the vetting process to determine who the "viable" candidates are is carried out principally by party leadership and mass media, not by the party rank and file, and still less by the broader public. Deciding who gets to participate in debates and who gets the backing of the party's apparatus are two major ways this sleight of hand trick gets carried out. To eliminate a candidate from the race, even a front-runner, is remarkably easy. Witness the manipulated soundtrack

---

16   Rick Ellis, "Commentary: The Surrender of MSNBC," allyourtv.com, February 25, 2003, http://www.allyourtv.com/0203season/news/02252003donahue.html, accessed August 10, 2009.

17   "Phil Donahue on his 2003 MSNBC firing: 'We had to have two conservatives on for every liberal. I was counted as two liberals.'" MediaMatters.org, October 29, 2004, http://mediamatters.org/items/20041029000 4, accessed September 5, 2009.

of Howard Dean's after-primary speech during the 2004 presidential race in which the loud noise from the crowd over which Dean was shouting was deleted from the soundtrack, making Dean sound like a raving lunatic. Being excluded from debates and party backing spells doom to virtually any candidate's political career, no matter how capable or potentially popular he or she may be.

One illustration is this: the League of Women Voters (LWV) sponsored the presidential debates from 1976-1984, but in 1988 they withdrew in protest; the major party candidates—George H. W. Bush and Michael Dukakis—demanded the right to micromanage every detail of the events. In their October 1988 press statement announcing their withdrawal, the LWV scathingly stated,

> The demands of the two campaign organizations would perpetrate a fraud on the American people. It has become clear to us that the candidates' organizations aim to add their debates to the list of campaign-trail charades devoid of substance, spontaneity and answers to tough questions. The League has no intention of becoming an accessory to the hoodwinking of the American public.[18]

Since 1988, the hoodwinking has been carried out by the Commission on Presidential Debates (CPD), a neutral enough sounding name that masks the fact that it is made up wholly of GOP and Democratic Party representatives and funded by corporate contributions. In keeping with its membership's desires, the CPD's role has been to tightly control the parameters of acceptable debate, discussion, and participation. In 2000 the CPD issued a rule that in order to be included a candidate had to be polling at least fifteen percent across five national polls, thereby excluding Green Party candidate Ralph Nader from the debate. Had Nader been allowed to appear in the debates between Al Gore and George W. Bush, the dynamics of the presidential race would have been dramatically altered. Nader, an articulate and exceptionally well-informed lawyer, would have undoubtedly made Bush look even more ill informed and inarticulate than he has eventually come to be known for.

A graphic illustration of what the CPD was set up to avoid can be seen in the stunning 1998 election of former professional wrestler Jesse

---

18   "News Release: For Immediate Release—League Refuses to 'Help Perpetuate a Fraud' Withdraws Support from Final Presidential Debate," lwv.org, October 3, 1988, http://www.lwv.org/AM/Template.cfm?Section=Home&template=/CM/HTMLDisplay.cfm&ContentID=7777, accessed July 1, 2009.

Ventura as Minnesota's governor on a third party ticket. Ventura, despite high name recognition and a regular talk show gig, was polling in single digits in the months leading up to the election. The Democratic nominee, Hubert Humphrey III, enjoyed a twenty-point lead on the field as late as mid-September. Humphrey, however, calculated that libertarian Ventura would siphon off votes from his GOP rival Norm Coleman and insisted that Ventura be included in the debates—a fatal decision for both his and Coleman's candidacies. Ventura so impressed voters with his candor in the debates that after the debates he began gaining rapidly on the GOP and Democratic candidates and ended up being elected, drawing record numbers of voters who would have otherwise sat out due to their antipathy for both major parties.[19]

The mere act of being included in a debate confers credibility upon a candidate: "This is someone who is viable." The sheer act of excluding people from debates turns them into fringe candidates and single-handedly dooms their chances. In the 2008 race the CPD and CNN excluded Dennis Kucinich and Michael Gravel from major debates. If you look at their actual platforms, Kucinich and Gravel were more closely aligned with majority sentiment in the US than were any of the other so-called "major candidates." If majority sentiment determined who won, then Kucinich and Gravel would not have been forced to the sidelines; they would have been the leading Democratic candidates!

The cost to run a minimally viable presidential campaign in the 2007-08 race—the longest race in US history—was $250,000 per candidate per day over the course of twenty-one months. As impressive as the dollar amounts raised by candidates through the Internet were, this kind of money demand cannot help but make a candidate beholden to big money. Hillary Clinton, the nemesis of the health insurance industry when Bill Clinton was president, made her peace with the Health Maintenance Organizations (HMOs) by the time she decided to run for president as a

---

19   David Beiler, "The Body Politic Registers a Protest: Jesse Ventura's Stunning Victory in Minnesota was More Than a Fluke," highbeam.com, February 1,1999, http://www.highbeam.com/doc/1G1-53889303.html, accessed July 1, 2009:

> Another big factor in Ventura's favor was Minnesota's unusual election law. It gives voters the right to register at the polls on Election Day. That made Ventura's impact particularly hard to gauge, especially for pollsters who never showed the full force of the Reform [Party] surge.
>
> In the end, voter turnout hit 61 percent of the voting age population (the highest in the country) and 16 percent of the total election day electorate had registered at the polls, a figure unseen since the law's inception in 1974. Analysts estimate more than three of every four new voters opted for Ventura."

precondition for being in a position to vie for the Democratic nomination. While running for president she was in fact being paid by the very HMOs that she took on while serving as First Lady.

Deciding to include or exclude someone from debates and from other forms of legitimacy is a power exercised by a small number of people in leading positions. It is not a decision arrived at by the public as a whole. This fact alone makes a mockery of the conventional view that the people control the government through their voting choices.

Thus, much like TV executives who decide what shows will be broadcast on their stations, the major political parties' national leaders along with representatives of the corporate media decide which candidates will be given the attention necessary for nomination. Candidates who pass their test represent the "finalists" from among whom the party faithful and broader public are permitted to choose. This selection process, internal to the party leadership and news organization mavens, by itself undercuts the "one person, one vote" principle, rendering it largely irrelevant—a rhetorical claim rather than a real exercise of citizens' choices.

The Contradictoriness of Public Sentiment

Even if a single, undifferentiated, and internally consistent sentiment existed among the people, one that was not contradicted by any other sentiment, that sentiment would still need to be focused and harnessed. But such consistency never exists. Sentiments of varying intensities, many of which contradict other sentiments, course through the body politic, with clashing ideas coexisting even within the same individuals. Even the much-observed cultural strain of American individualism—as strong a sentiment as any among the American people—exists alongside sentiments that contradict it. During the 1960s, for example, the "War on Poverty" and the "Great Society" agendas of President Lyndon Johnson foregrounded a clashing idea: that assistance to those in need was as necessary and equally as "American" as rugged individualism. The widely subscribed-to belief in "equal opportunity" fits equally as well into American individualism as do Social Darwinist notions of cutthroat individualism. Indeed, given the multiple diverse and contradictory strains within public sentiment, any number of very different policies could find a large appreciative public audience.

As much as Americans are individualistic, they also (mostly) want to do the right thing. As Daniel Ellsberg (the former Pentagon official

234

who released the famous "Pentagon Papers" during the Nixon presidency that helped to bring the Vietnam War and the Nixon Presidency to an end) told Greg Palast: "What's good about the American people is that you have to lie to them. What's bad about Americans is that it's so easy to do."[20]

Americans do not as a general rule like to think (and do not believe) that the US plunders and oppresses other people. When they are finally convinced that our foreign policies are doing just that, most Americans are alarmed and shocked. To cite a domestic equivalent, when white Americans saw the 1991 videotape footage of Rodney King being beaten, the most common response was shock. (Black Americans' responses in general were "Finally, they got it on tape!") The fact that many Americans are shocked to find that our government officials are not doing what they say they are doing means two things: (a) Americans are unusually naïve as compared to citizens of other countries about what their government does, and (b) Americans as a rule (there are, of course, significant exceptions among a significant minority of Americans) want to do good things in the world.

Cultural values, in other words, do not by themselves dictate which public policies are adopted. They instead operate as a conditioning factor. Effective leadership succeeds in foregrounding some elements within the pool of cultural values and backgrounding other elements. While grassroots sentiments can develop in ways that impact what leaders do, the initiative lies overall with leaders and not with the grassroots. There is no inevitable or invariant way that a culture will "read" an event. How the culture reacts to an event will depend to a significant extent on the spin that opinion leaders propagate. This is precisely why spin has become such a highly prized and emphasized activity.

Moreover, as neoliberalism proceeds apace and the state and media transform themselves into the neoliberal image—the extraordinary concentration of media ownership in literally a handful of oligopolies and the state operating more and more openly and thoroughly as a facilitator to, rather than a regulator of, megacorporations—the public's ability to affect the media and state (within the parameters of electoral politics and normal channels such as lobbying) diminishes from even the modicum of influence that it had in the past. To be clear, even the amount of influence the public had in the past never approached the standard of "democracy"

---

20 Greg Palast, "The Downing Street Memos, Manipulation of Prewar Intelligence, and Knowingly Withholding Vital Information from a Grand Jury Investigation," in *Impeach the President; the Case Against Bush and Cheney*, eds. Dennis Loo and Peter Phillips (New York: Seven Stories Press, 2006), 132.

as people customarily understand it. Today, it is a mere shadow—and a diminishing shadow—of even that.

Ordinary channels available to the public to set the public agenda provide little relief from this picture. As I detail in Chapter Six, media and corporate interests have largely replaced citizens as the actual constituencies that legislators and executives must please, particularly on the state and national levels. Media, in other words, are today's surrogate electorate. In 2002, when the resolution to authorize the use of force against Iraq—the blank check for war that the Bush White House was seeking—was being considered in Congress, citizens flooded their Congressional representatives' offices with messages that were overwhelmingly against war. The range of opinion reportedly ran from 50:1 to as much as 300:1 against the authorization to use force. Congress, nevertheless, voted for the authorization. Had they been more worried about being punished at the ballot box than they were about the reaction from the White House and the media, the resolution would never have passed.

In 2007 hundreds of citizens petitioned their Congressional representatives through mass, in-person lobbying efforts to impeach Bush and Cheney. These lobbying efforts were backed by popular opinion as reflected in polls taken since summer 2005 that had shown massive sentiment (in a number of these polls, majority sentiment) for impeachment, as well as by very many large protest demonstrations. These citizen-lobbyists were told by Congressional staffers that their representatives or senators already knew that a majority of Americans wanted impeachment, but the public officials wouldn't represent that sentiment because they were "listening to what their party leadership told them [i.e., Speaker of the House Nancy Pelosi and Senate Majority Leader Harry Reid]." Did the supposed fear of being punished by voters in the next election strike fear into the Democratic Party leadership and cause them to bend to the majority's will? Obviously not. Did the franchise mean much of anything here? Clearly not.

As I wrote in July 2007, in an Internet posting entitled "Why the Democrats are Acting This Way,"

> Many people say they wish the Democrats would "grow a spine" and "show some courage." They also say things like: "Don't the Democrats realize that they're throwing away the chance to stand with the majority of Americans? Don't they know that failing to do so is going to hurt them?" There are, of course, other variants on these themes, with some people saying: "Throw out the lot of them. Elect some people

who will do the will of the people." All of these responses, while understandable, miss the point.

The Democrats HAVE been showing a REMARKABLE amount of spine—it's just that they are directing their strong backs AGAINST the will of the people.

Think about this: their approval ratings are even lower than those for Bush and Cheney (or at least Bush!) because they aren't doing what people elected them to do in the 2006 election. Yet they won't end the Iraq war, won't stand up against Bush and Cheney's plans to attack Iran, and insist that impeachment is "off the table."

They know that a large majority of Americans want Bush and Cheney gone.

They know that they are shamelessly and transparently lying when they say that they haven't seen any impeachable offenses.

They know that they are violating the Constitution and international law through the bills they've passed (e.g., the Military Commissions Act and the John Warner Defense Authorization Act) and by allowing Bush's hundreds of signing statements and executive orders that violate their acts and the law.

They know that their failing to act according to the law, Constitution and the will of the people runs a huge risk that they will be punished by the people.

They know that if they were to impeach and were to hold hearings in the course of impeachment that this White House's crimes would come spilling out like an avalanche and that this would bury the GOP for a generation and the Democrats would thereby earn the gratitude of the vast majority of the people.

YET they are determined NOT to do these exceedingly popular things. They are showing tremendous fortitude in resisting doing the right thing and resisting the American people.

Why?

It's quite simple. They don't represent the people. The U.S. is the biggest, strongest imperialist power to ever exist on this earth. Why would you expect that the two major political parties in the most powerful empire to ever exist would be ANYTHING ELSE but fundamentally representatives of the most wealthy elements and fundamentally representatives of the extraordinary power and wealth concentrated in a small number of transnational corporations?

What kind of leaders of corporations that make BILLIONS in QUARTERLY profits would you be if you allowed "the people," poor and rich alike, to have one vote each? Would you turn over your power and wealth to "the people?" You'd be crazy to do so. You'd make sure the system worked in your interest. You'd make sure that elections turned out the way you wanted them to and that the people who get elected do what you want them to do.

Someone made a button once that I really like. It went something like this, "If elections meant anything they'd make them illegal."

The truth is that elections don't decide public policy. Democrats and Republicans are part of the same system. They have more in common with each other than what distinguishes them. Even independents and third parties, should their people get elected, have to operate in the same structure. The only way that we can take on and defeat Bush and Cheney and everything they stand for and the whole direction that they are leading us down (and the Democrats are cooperating and colluding in) is through the people's mass, independent actions in our millions.[21]

As I detail in Chapters Two and Seven, mass movements from below do offer the public a way to breach the public agenda-setting process—at times. What theory regarding public participation can actually provide a guide through this unexplored forest of increasingly dense trees and pesky vines that are choking off our path and threatening to condemn us indefinitely to a jungle of irrelevance, dependence, and dramatic insecurity? Clearly, a model is needed that better explains how the public agenda is set—a model that offers a better explanation than is offered by the democratic theory model.

The power to set the agenda (which includes the power to reject, accept and/or modify any items put before them by the public for the public agenda) gives media and the state extraordinary powers that classical and pluralist democratic theorists[22] are unable to appreciate or convey. Indeed, democratic theory oversimplifies the relationship between leaders and the led, downplaying leadership's importance theoretically and rhetorically, and thereby undermining the role that democratic participation by the led can actually play. Ironically, as I will shortly argue in this chapter, contrary to conventional wisdom, the more active a role leadership plays, the

---

21 Dennis Loo, "Why the Democrats Are Acting This Way," WarIsACrime.org, July 31, 2007, http://warisacrime.org/node/25271, accessed February 4, 2011.

22 Put most simply, pluralist theory holds that democracy is maintained and expressed through the different lobby groups appealing to the state.

greater is the role for the led. But this requires a particular kind of leadership.[23] I now turn to consider more closely why.

Democracy: An End in Itself or A Means to an End?

The central question in politics is who wields power and in what/whose interests? Both parts of this are significant—*who* is doing it and in *what/whose* interests. The *who* does not necessarily tell you the *what*. And vice versa.[24] The fact that someone in office is from a working class background, for example, does not tell you whose class interests he or she is pursuing. The fact that someone is an ethnic minority or a female is worthy of note (and if the faces of the rulers are all homogenous in a heterogeneous society then this by itself tells you that there is a problem of inequality in the society), but one's demographics do not by any means tell the whole story.[25] The relationship between the *who* and the *what* merits close attention. First: the question of who?

Democracy in its broadest potential expression differs from other political systems—on the most basic level—because it involves a substantial degree of participation by the people in political decisions. So-called liberal democracy involves many other dimensions such as subordination to the law, an independent judiciary, separation of powers, and so on, but what I will discuss here revolves around the conceptual essence of the question: public participation.

Karl Popper provides an apt summary of democratic theory this way: "democracy, the right of the people to judge and to dismiss their government, is the only known device by which we can try to protect ourselves

---

23 This way of distinguishing leadership and led comes out of Lenin's work, especially in *What is to be Done?*, and as discussed by Bob Avakian in *Democracy: Can't We Do Better Than That?* (Chicago: Banner Press, 1986).

24 The fact that someone is from the working class, for example, and grew up poor does not tell us whether they are exercising political power in the interest of the downtrodden. Some of the worst leaders in history—for example, the USSR's Nikita Khrushchev who openly betrayed socialism and shamelessly hungered for Disneyland—came from humble backgrounds.

25 Consider the cases of Condoleezza Rice who went shopping when New Orleans was hit by Hurricane Katrina in 2005 or Wilson Goode, former mayor of Philadelphia, who bombed to death most of the members of the African-American group, MOVE, in their home in 1985.

against the misuse of political power; it is the control of the rulers by the ruled." [26]

Popper here lays out explicitly the commonplace meaning of democracy—first of all that it is representative not directly participatory, and second, that in a democracy the very most that the people can do politically is determine which public officials will exercise political rule over them. The very idea that the people might eventually exercise all-around political rule themselves Popper excludes from consideration. This is rather remarkable if you think about it. If democracy means rule by the many, then dismissing out of hand the notion that authentic rule by the many can ever happen, except in a highly truncated and indirect form, means that the version of democracy that is possible can only be something strangled of its fullest expression. If we rule out the possibility now or ever of the people politically ruling themselves, then we are, of course, left with no alternative but to assert that the essence of democracy is representative government supervised via elections.

The franchise, then, must shoulder the entire weight of popular rule. It is, according to this view, the sole way for the people to exercise any influence politically. Representative democracy, which is what the vast majority of commentators mean when they say "democracy," is in fact, therefore, but one version, rather like an expurgated *Reader's Digest* version, of popular political rule.

Popper further claims that the ruled exercise "*control* of the rulers" (italics added) by their votes. "Control" seems highly overstated in this context. How do you exercise control over the rulers if you are one of the ruled? Is something not obviously wrong with the terms themselves: "ruler" and "ruled"? How do the people manage to exercise control if they can only decide which individuals will be their political representatives every two to six years? What happens during the intervals between elections? At best do the people have to wait two, four, or six years to oust their elected officials from office if they are unhappy with what those officials have done? That certainly does not sound like very much control. Imagine you are in charge of steering and therefore controlling a car, but you are only able to actually take the wheel every several years. If in the in-between times you have no control over the steering wheel, are you really in control of the car? If a car salesman tried to sell you a car on that basis you might

---

26   Sir Karl Raimund Popper, *Open Society and Its Enemies*, vol. 2, *The High Tide of Prophecy: Hegel, Marx, and the Aftermath* (Princeton, NJ: Princeton University Press, rev. first ed., 1966; Princeton, NJ: Princeton University Press, first Princeton pbk. printing, 1971]), 127.

look elsewhere for a car, or perhaps you would decide to adopt a different mode of transportation altogether.

Representative democracy overwhelmingly confines public participation in political affairs to voting for or against one's representatives. Even in the best of all possible scenarios, if voting comprises the best and highest political role that the people can play, then the people will never have any real power over politics. Karl Popper's view of democracy, in which the most significant role that the people can play is as a check upon the unrestrained power of the state, reflects a dismal view of what the people are capable of doing. What kind of foundation for society's political affairs does this constitute? Popper's perspective forever consigns the people to subordinate status, leaving intact long-standing inequalities among the people without even considering any way to bridge these inequalities. Saviors from on high—benevolent dictators—are sorry and, at the very best, temporary salves.[27] Charity is not the same thing as genuine equality. As long as the people remain in a politically passive position vis-à-vis the rulers, democracy will remain an unrealized rhetorical device, fit for masking the true sources of political power in the hands of the few.

If one is inclined to assume that voting itself confers real power upon the people and that choosing from among the candidates allows the voters to select the candidates whose promises they like best, one must know not only that campaign promises often do not predict what candidates will end up doing once in office, but also that candidates not infrequently end up doing the exact opposite of what they promised. Lyndon Johnson won in a landslide against Barry Goldwater in 1964 to a large degree because he ran as the "peace" candidate. He then proceeded to escalate the Vietnam War, resulting in the deaths of two million Indochinese and 58,000 Americans. George W. Bush campaigned in 2000 against "nation building." After he invaded Afghanistan and Iraq, nation building was precisely what he set out to try to do—spectacularly unsuccessfully. Obama campaigned on a promise of "change," specifically promising to restore habeas corpus, end torture, end the Bush White House's self-serving and dangerous invocations of state secrets, close Gitmo and pull out of Iraq. Since taking office not only has Obama not kept these promises,[28] but he has also followed Bush and Cheney even further down the road they were so despised for taking.

---

27 Max Weber resorted to this forlorn hope—a charismatic leader occasionally arising who could rally the people to shake up the "iron cage" of bureaucracy.

28 He has drawn down troops from Iraq but has stated that he will indefinitely keep a force of some 50,000 soldiers, a still larger contingent of mercenaries, and an

Bureaucracies are indispensable to all forms of government, "democracies" among them. Yet the bureaucratic impulse and the bureaucratic mode are at odds with the democratic impulse and objective. "Democracies" cannot do without bureaucracies, but their need for bureaucrats as well as the inherent nature of bureaucracy undercut democracy itself. As Max Weber pointed out in his close study of bureaucracies, bureaucrats by their very nature try to shield what they are doing from public scrutiny. Secrecy and deception are synonymous with bureaucracy: "The concept of the 'official secret' is the specific invention of bureaucracy, and nothing is so fanatically defended by the bureaucracy as this attitude."[29]

One need only attend a legislative committee hearing once or a few times to see that bureaucrats, brought before the committee routinely dodge, misrepresent and depending on which bureaucracy, not infrequently outright lie before legislators. The activities of the Pentagon, the CIA, the NSA, and others are masked even from the putative people's representatives. Even some members of the White House itself, including the President, have been regularly excluded from knowing the full activities of segments of the government bureaucracy.

Max Weber and his best-known student Robert Michels offer an instructive angle on the preceding. Weber was the foremost theorizer of the rise and triumph of bureaucracy in the modern state. He observed that bureaucracies would prevail and dominate because they are, as an ensemble of characteristics, the most efficient, predictable, dependable, and controllable way of doing things; but he also saw that their very nature would create an "iron cage of rationality," stifling freedom of thought, creativity, and liberty.

Weber's solution to this inevitable and inescapable dilemma was a hope that a charismatic leader would periodically emerge from within the ranks of the existing major political parties and shake up the iron cage for a time. Because charismatic leaders derive their power from their personal followings and from outside of bureaucratic-legalistic procedures and channels, a leader can, for a time, use that appeal to bring into motion efforts that can suspend or bypass bureaucracy's established power. The operative phrase

---

embassy that measures some eighty football fields in size and that costs $1 billion per year to maintain. See Steven Thomma, "Obama to Extend Iraq Withdrawal Timetable; 50,000 Troops to Stay,"McClatchyDC.com, February 27, 2009, http://www.mcclatchydc.com/2009/02/27/62930/obama-to-extend-iraq-withdrawal. html, accessed April 1, 2009.

29 Max Weber, "Bureaucracy," in *Classical Sociological Theory: A Reader*, ed. Ian McIntosh (New York: NYU Press, 1997), 151.

here, however, is "for a time," because inevitably the bureaucracy (since it is the most powerful means of carrying out "societal action" and since mass action, e.g., social movements and rebellions/riots/revolutions, can only sometimes and only for a while overcome bureaucracies) will reassert its "iron cage" and have the last word.

Weber prescribed that the charismatic leader should come out of the ranks of the existing major political parties because he was not, after all, a socialist or a revolutionary. In an 1895 speech entitled "The Nation State and Economic Policy," Weber declared: "I am a member of the bourgeois classes. I feel myself to be a bourgeois, and I have been brought up to share their views and ideals." Owing to the nature of major, established political parties and their requisite bureaucratic character, a person with enough charisma to actually challenge the existing bureaucracy is highly unlikely to survive the journey up the party hierarchy where charisma is regarded with suspicion and as a shortcoming rather than as an asset.

Michels, who started out as a socialist, came to the conclusion that no matter how democratically an organization or a society starts out, it will inevitably and ineluctably become an oligarchy—that is, ruled by a few. He dubbed this the "Iron Law of Oligarchy." As a result of this chain of reasoning, Michels ended up becoming a fascist.

Anyone who has been in an organization of more than a handful of people knows that most of the time organizational decisions cannot realistically be arrived at through consensus. In groups—be they clubs, sororities/fraternities, political parties, associations, legislative bodies, and so on—the actual work takes place in committees. The group's membership as a whole may come together periodically to consider what the committees have recommended and, while on occasion the body as a whole may reject something coming out of committee, in general committee recommendations are ratified. Within the committees themselves, leadership devolves to one person or to a few people who are aligned with the one leader. If there is a sharp and equal division of loyalties within the committee between two leaders, sooner or later this division is resolved in favor of one or the other through defections, departure of the dissident(s), or elimination of the dissident(s).

Anyone in a group who has had to issue a group statement on any issue knows that the statement itself cannot practically be drafted by the body as a whole and that its drafting ends up being placed in the hands of an individual or two. An expression of the resulting problem in common parlance is "too many cooks spoil the broth." The initiative always rests with a few individuals operating in committee, either formally or informally. The act of ratification, it should be noted, differs very substantially from the act of initiating something. Ratification is commonly presented as equivalent to initiative, whereas in fact the two differ substantially, sometimes dramatically.

Groups that have attempted to run their affairs by consensus run up against two major problems. One, it is virtually impossible to get everyone to agree, so if consensus is necessary the group members quickly get bogged down and get little done. Two, even if majority rule is adopted, originating ideas and following through on them within the body as a whole falls, for practical reasons, before the more effective and efficient mode of delegating nearly all matters to committees where most of the organization's work actually occurs. Committees, and especially the executive committee, then end up running the organization's affairs. As anyone knows who has ever been on a committee, one person leads each committee, with the greatest power residing in the hands of the person who runs the executive committee. This is as true in the US Congress as it is in any other organization. As Michels put it: "Whoever says organization, says oligarchy."

Was Michels right? Is authentic popular rule doomed to fail?

The answer to this question is "not necessarily." But the problems that Weber and Michels point to are real and the answer to their pessimistic prognoses involves very large challenges and a protracted struggle within and across multiple generations, at the very least. For these problems to be overcome, determined, popular struggle in an ongoing way would be indispensable. The nature of that struggle and its particular features I will address shortly herein and also develop further in the final chapter, but first it is vital that we delve further into the actual conditions that face the people in societies.

Money, Class, and Coercion

The role of money and lobbying in politics results in political power tilting decisively into the hands of those who already have a great deal of money and power. As the gap between those who are wealthy and those who are not grows ever more extreme, there is simply no realistic hope that public officials would be able to overcome these inherent differentials, even if they wanted to. Congress and state legislatures can pass all the laws they want to supposedly curb these inequities, but those laws and regulations will not do much more than provide window dressing to conceal the fact that wealth differentials still rule. Political egalitarianism cannot be achieved in the absence of economic equality. To think otherwise represents pure utopianism disconnected from any reality. To promote the hope that such a thing can be achieved under current arrangements misleads people. Yet democratic theory does precisely this, in whatever variant of it is being offered, and whatever the conscious intent may be of those who advocate on its behalf.

Consider a scenario in which socialist politicians, constituting a majority, are elected to office in the US but with no mass movement present other than the one that funneled people into an electoral solution. In such a scenario, the president would also be one of the lefties, given the preponderance of public opinion that produced a legislative socialist majority. What impact would this have on the economic and political landscape of the US? What might we expect to happen? For one thing, the political system would now be dominated by politics at odds with the current economic organization and institutions. What would happen if this political system, now dominated by socialists, moved to curb the extant huge disparities of economic power?

During Franklin Delano Roosevelt's administration (his White House was not even remotely socialist but it did carry out reforms), prominent economic elites actually plotted a military coup modeled after Germany and Italy's fascist regimes. As Alan Nasser relates, based on the recent release of data from the National Archives,

> The owners of Bird's Eye, Maxwell House and Heinz, among others, totaling about twenty four major businessmen and Wall Street financiers ["including Prescott Bush, George H.W. Bush's father. Bush, along with many other big businessmen, had maintained friendly relations in 1933 and 1934 with the new German government of Chancellor Adolph Hitler, and was designated to form for his class conspirators a working relationship with that government"] planned to assemble a private army of half a million men, composed largely of unemployed veterans. These troops would both constitute the armed force behind the coup and defeat any resistance this in-house revolution might generate. The economic elite would provide the material resources required to sustain the new government.
>
> The plotters hoped that widespread working-class discouragement at the stubborn persistence of the Great Depression would have sufficiently disenchanted the masses with FDR's policies to make the coup an easy ride. And they were appalled at Roosevelt's willingness after 1933 to initiate economic policies that economists and businessmen considered dangerously Leftist departures from economic

orthodoxy. Only a fascist-style government, they thought, could enforce the kind of economic "discipline" that would reverse the Great Depression and restore profits.

Interestingly, it was a military man, a prominent retired general assigned the task of raising the 500,000-man army, who blew the whistle after pondering the grotesque implications of the undemocratic installation of a fascist dictatorship in Washington. FDR was thus able to nip the plot in the bud.[30]

Nasser notes that FDR declined to reveal the plot publicly and punish the fascist coup conspirators, despite their treasonous plans, out of class solidarity and concerns that if the plotters were broadly exposed it would produce a victory—at a particularly sensitive time—for anti-capitalist sentiment. The coup's failure, it should be noted, turned on the decision of just one man—the general who was picked to lead the coup.[31] The conspirators themselves, key figures of this country's economic elite, cheerleaders at every opportunity for "freedom," "democracy," and "the American way of life," were not at all reluctant, when their fortunes appeared to be even mildly attenuated, to override the putatively sacred principles of what America claims to be all about.

In Chile in 1970, a socialist president, Dr. Salvador Allende, was elected—the first Marxist to assume power through the electoral process. Allende proceeded to nationalize industries that had previously been

---

30 Alan Nasser, "The Threat of U.S. Fascism: An Historical Precedent," Commondreams. org, August 2, 2007, http://www.commondreams.org/archive/2007/08/02/2933/, accessed July 10, 2009.

31 This was U.S. Marine Major General Smedley Butler, who stated in a 1933 speech: "I spent thirty-three years and four months in active military service as a member of this country's most agile military force, the Marine Corps. . . . And during that period I spent most of my time as a high class muscle man for Big Business, for Wall Street and for the Bankers. In short, I was a racketeer, a gangster for capitalism. . . . I helped make Mexico, especially Tampico safe for American oil interests in 1914. I helped make Haiti and Cuba a decent place for the National City Bank boys to collect revenues in. I helped in the raping of half a dozen Central American republics for the benefit of Wall Street. I helped purify Nicaragua for the international banking house of Brown Brothers in 1902-1912. I brought light to the Dominican Republic for American sugar interests in 1916. I helped make Honduras right for the American fruit companies in 1903. In China I helped see to it that Standard Oil went its way unmolested. . . . Looking back on it, I feel that I could have given Al Capone a few hints. The best he could do was to operate his racket in three districts. I operated on three continents. . . ." From "War Is A Racket," twf.org, September 11, 2001, http://www.twf.org/News/Y2001/0911-Racket.htm l, accessed February 14, 2011.

dominated by foreign businesses. The US government in conjunction with multinationals such as Anaconda Copper conspired to overthrow the Allende government. The coup's approach in the weeks and months before it happened on September 11, 1973, was apparent to everyone in Chile. The masses demanded of Allende that they be armed in order to defend the government and to have a chance to fight off the coup. Allende wavered and ended up staking his hopes on the military upholding the Constitution, declaring repeatedly in public pronouncements that the army was "patriotic" and would not participate in a coup. Why would he do this when it was clear that this was foolish in the extreme? To a significant extent, Allende did so because he adhered to the USSR's political line— securing a compromise with the US imperialists for a piece of the action, but not a genuine revolution. Allende and thousands of Chileans paid for this halfway version of socialism with their lives.

This highlights a critical point. In Mao's pithy phrase: "Political power grows out of the barrel of a gun." Or, as one American Congressional member in 2007 said candidly when asked by some of his constituents why he was not moving to impeach Bush and Cheney: "They have the guns."[32]

Any serious attempt at structural and dramatic political change must confront this reality. You can elect all of the sympathetic politicians you want, but if you do not command the coercive apparatus, you will lose the (political and economic) war sooner or later. A gun placed against one's temple, after all, makes a very persuasive argument. An amply equipped and trained military force facing a larger, unarmed, untrained, and relatively unorganized mass assemblage nearly always carries the day.

As I wrote on September 8, 2008 in an online essay:

> Two items in the news offer us rare glimpses into how public policy is actually arrived at and what differences there really are between Democrats, even progressive Democrats—let alone centrists such as Obama—and Republicans. The first item concerns the Minneapolis City Council's role in the police state tactics used at the St. Paul RNC [Republican National Convention] and the other item concerns foreign policy and Pakistan in particular. Both are related directly to the so-called war on terror: what both major parties call the central issue of our time.
>
> It is clear that the fulcrum for today's politics involves the "war on terror" and whether the dominant paradigm about it that both major

---

32 Two individuals who spoke to the quoted representative in his office related this to me in person.

parties subscribe to will carry the day, or a different paradigm wins out that originates from among the people.

First item: At OpEd News on September 11, 2008 Michael Calvan reported the inside dirty dealing in the all progressives Minneapolis City Council in which the council gave the green light to the police to use the storm trooper tactics before and during the RNC. I quote from the piece at some length as follows:

"In the months before the Republicans came to town, there had been a flurry of activity. Local activists were keeping a close eye on their local elected officials. Initially, there had been a so called Free Speech Committee set up, supposedly to look at how authorities could allow free speech during the RNC and keep order. We found out that the Free Speech Committee did not allow any members of the public to add our input. Only City Council members on the committee and lawyers were allowed to speak. There was no free speech allowed at the misnamed Free Speech Committee. Nonetheless, activists followed the Committee's actions closely and were present during each meeting.

The City Council of Minneapolis is almost 100% Democratic. In fact the only real opposition in Minneapolis is the Green Party which currently has one Green on the City Council, Cam Gordon, who was a small light in a very dark room. But, we were to discover, even that light was to be extinguished. The so called Free Speech Committee would change the time and locations of its meetings. There was also discussion on protest groups being required to register themselves and even their members, to be 'allowed' to protest. At these times, Cam Gordon spoke eloquently on behalf of the community and in opposition to these repressive measures.

Then suddenly [after months] we found out that the Free Speech Committee had their last meeting, July 16th. The meeting itself was unannounced, unlike the other meetings which at least had a pretense of openness and public inclusion. At the next Minneapolis City Council meeting July 25th, the recommendation of the misnamed Free Speech Committee was announced. The Free Speech Committee Resolution passed unanimously, even by our one small light, Councilman Cam Gordon.

The Minneapolis Police were given 'legal' authority to shut down any protest or group of 25 people or greater. They were also authorized to use rubber bullets, mace and the other array of non-lethal weapons on innocent, peaceful demonstrators, practicing our First Amendment Rights. Also violated repeatedly was the Fourth Amendment Right protecting us citizens against illegal search and seizure. Police violated the laws of assault and battery and destruction of evidence of their crimes, as evidenced by their targeting journalists."

Calvan notes, probably correctly so, that even if the city council had not approved these fascistic tactics that they would have been bypassed and the police and various state and federal officials would have done it anyway.

Despite months of efforts by grassroots activists and even a Green on the City Council—making grand speeches about protecting free speech—despite the people doing the very best that they could to monitor, participate and speak out, the fix was in and democratic participation was merely a charade for the real power being exercised, even on the nearest thing to local control as you can find in the government—at the City Council level—and even in one of the most left-influenced places in the country.

Second item: As reported by *The New York Times* on September 11, 2008, in July 2008 Bush secretly approved Spec Ops forces to launch ground military attacks inside Pakistan without prior approval from the Pakistani government. The NYT essay notes: "It is unclear precisely what legal authorities the United States has invoked to conduct even limited ground raids in a friendly country." It's unclear because such actions are blatantly against international law. (During the Vietnam War when President Nixon announced on April 30, 1970 that he had begun bombing Cambodia and thereby expanding the war, a fury broke out in America. During the widespread protests that followed, four students were famously shot and killed by National Guardsmen at Kent State University in Ohio on May 4.)

The Times article continues: "Pakistan's government has asserted that last week's raid achieved little except killing civilians and stoking anti-Americanism in the tribal areas. " "Unilateral action by the American forces does not help the war against terror because it only enrages public opinion," said Husain Haqqani, Pakistan's ambassador to Washington, during a speech on Friday. "In this particular incident, nothing was gained by the action of the troops."

What gives this story even more resonance is the fact that the Bush regime is now finally embracing the tactics that Obama had called for back in August 2007. At the time, Bush, John McCain and the other Democratic presidential hopefuls including Joe Biden and Hillary Clinton derided Obama for offering such a bellicose proposal. Bush said: "he's going to attack Pakistan" in disbelief.

As Reuters reported on August 1, 2007: "Obama said if elected in November 2008 he would be willing to attack inside Pakistan with or without approval from the Pakistani government, a move that would likely cause anxiety in the already troubled region. "If we have actionable intelligence about high-value terrorist targets and President Musharraf won't act, we will," Obama said."

So there you have it: the reactionary Bush White House has now adopted a plan that it previously publicly described as overly aggressive—can you imagine this White House thinking anything is too aggressive?—a plan offered up by the Democratic Party's standard bearer, Obama, the man that many progressives pin their hopes on.

This reminds me of the line from a comic who wondered what the world is coming to when the world's best golfer is black and the best rapper is white.

What is the world coming to? The labels certainly don't tell you the story. You have to look carefully and critically at what people are actually saying and what they are doing. And you have to examine carefully how political policy is actually made, not how you might have learned about it in civics class and not how it is presented everyday in the news.

Obama himself has said—correctly so—that people should pay attention to what he's saying. He does not oppose all wars, just "dumb wars." He approves of the war on terror. His differences are over tactics and whether the goals of the "war on terror" are being best pursued. In other words, is the US imperialist empire doing what is in its best interests? This is like campaigning for Godfather and saying that the existing Godfather isn't being efficient enough in his extortion, racketeering, drug running, torture, brutality and death dealing.

If the city that may be second only to Berkeley in the degree to which progressives hold political office colludes, conspires and co-operates with the police state, even while some of the progressives make fine sounding speeches but vote with the gendarmes when push comes to shove, and if the one "realistic" choice on the national level that the people are being given to oppose the Bush regime's reign of terror is a man whose foreign policy is now being adopted by the very

250

same hated Bush regime that Obama says he is a "change" from, then what's realistic now? What good does your vote do? Just what kind of democracy is this?[33]

While widespread belief in a state's legitimacy must be present for a state to carry out its functions over any appreciable period of time, the bottom line is, no state will lose power as long as it has a military force capable of and willing to suppress its opponents. "Men with guns" would be the most concise way of describing what a government is in its essence. A government performs many different functions, and all governments that stay in power for any real duration must have some level of legitimacy in the eyes of its citizens, as there are not enough cops and soldiers to force the populace to do what the government wants on a day-to-day basis. But boiled down to its very elemental and indispensable parts, a government consists, to indulge here in some alliterative play, of guys with guns.

Political power is exercised via both persuasion and coercion. The goal for those genuinely interested in popular rule should not be popular participation per se. The goal should be that there be authentic popular rule. The two are not synonymous and the latter cannot be achieved simply through mass voting. The path to authentic popular rule, therefore, does not involve handing over the key decisions to others. Instead it must involve the masses of people increasingly becoming engaged, informed, and involved.

How can the people exercise real political power over decisions that affect their society and world? Since representatives are a necessity for many decisions, the nature of such a real democracy would have to include at least two specific elements in order to amount to something more than what we ordinarily (or invariably) see in governments: first, the pay and privileges of representatives would have to be the same as that of ordinary citizens (so that the privilege of public service would be not one that can be pursued for personal gain); and second, the populace would have to be consistently well-informed about the cardinal issues of the society so that they could exercise choices sensibly rather than being objects to be manipulated. Both of these outcomes are unimaginable short of a revolutionary change in the society. This point bears repeating: short of a revolutionary reconstitution of the society that directly involves the

---

33 Dennis Loo, "To Those Who Put Their Faith in Progressive Democrats and Obama," WorldcantWait.org, September 8, 2008, http://www.worldcantwait. net/index.php/organizers-mainmenu-223/steering-committee-mainmenu-276/ dennis-loo-mainmenu-255/5029-to-those-who-put-their-faith-in-progressive-democrats-and-obama, accessed September 8, 2008.

masses of people in effecting such change, talk of democracy will carry as much real meaning and accurately describe the policy-making process as well as the myth of Santa Claus explains the appearance of gifts on Christmas morning.

Why Democracy? To What Ends?

People should have a say-so over their lives and over their society. This is something with which most people, though by no means all, agree. If we assume that democracy—in this sense—is a good for this reason, then we still need to settle a corollary question before we can proceed. Is democracy an end in and of itself? Or is it best understood as a means to an end?[34] Let me take the first instance first.

If democracy is an end in itself, then it does not matter how ill-informed the populace or what decision (wise or foolish, effective or in-effective) the populace arrives at. Participation is what matters, not the results of that participation. Participation *is* the result sought. As the saying goes: it doesn't matter whether you win or lose, it's how you play the game. The philosophical principle undergirding democracy as an end in itself is agnosticism: —the view that truth is not knowable.[35] If truth is not knowable, and facts can all be disputed such that no decision can be made about their veracity, then it does not matter what one's opinion is because we cannot determine what is real anyway. Hence, all opinions are equal because there is no independent criterion of truth.

I often pose this example in my university classes to illustrate this point: if democracy is an end in itself, shall we vote on what time it is? If mass participation were an end in itself, then what would have been the verdict on whether the earth was round or flat during the Middle Ages in Europe? If democracy is an end in itself, should surgeons about to perform a delicate procedure on someone's brain poll the hospital staff and patients to decide what procedure is best? It does not take long before people all agree that expertise and knowledge make a big difference, and that at least some things are not and should not be subject to a vote.

This objection might be raised here: expertise of course is necessary and those with expertise should be given prominence for their views, but

---

34 I owe this distinction to the work of Bob Avakian. See Ibid.

35 Agnosticism comes from religion originally and refers to those who are undecided on the existence or nonexistence of God. Agnostics think that it is not possible to determine whether God exists or not. See Ibid.

experts almost never agree and the decision should and must ultimately still be made by the populace. An informed populace is the key; the problem of lack of information or expertise can be addressed.

However, how is information communicated to the public, and which experts get to have their views aired? In a world without vested interests and differentials of power based on clashing material interests, information and expertise might be provided readily, extensively, and fairly to the public; however, we do not live in such a world. To get to a world such as that would have to involve a radical transformation of the economy. Political egalitarianism cannot be sensibly pursued whenever wider and ever-expanding economic inequality provides the driving logic for our economic system and political policy. To think otherwise is to deny the most obvious fact, demonstrated over and over throughout history: huge economic disparities produce political inequalities. The more unequal the economy becomes, the more unequal the public policies have been (they helped produce this economic inequality, after all), and the more unequal the public policies will therefore be (since the political system will adjust to the economic more than the other way around). That is, unless some dramatic change that involves a fundamental reworking of the economic system's dynamics occurs.

To overcome the expertise problem, some of democracy's greatest defenders cite the American people's inherent wisdom or goodness. Lincoln's often-cited dictum is invoked in connection with this: "You can fool some of the people all of the time and all of the people some of the time, but you can't fool all of the people all of the time." Lincoln's epigram is undoubtedly true. But fooling enough of the people enough of the time means that an unacceptable amount of fooling goes on. As the 2003 invasion of Iraq demonstrates, well over a million Iraqis and tens of thousands of Americans have died based on conscious lies by the Bush White House.[36] This provides terrible testimony to the government and a compliant media's ability to mislead the people. The White House's lies were so ubiquitous and the media's credulity and active participation in perpetuating those lies so great that even now a large percentage of the American people still believe incorrectly that Iraq had something to do with 9/11 and many (mostly Fox News viewers and Rush Limbaugh dittoheads) think that WMD were found in Iraq. Lincoln's dictum pales in power compared to this.

Moreover, a basic problem arises from the fact that the US is an imperialist superpower, indeed, the sole imperialist superpower. Imperialism

---

36 Armen Keteylan, "VA Hid Suicide Risk, Internal E-Mails Show," CBSNews.com, April 21, 2008, http://www.cbsnews.com/stories/2008/04/21/cbsnews_investigates/main4032921.shtml, accessed June 1, 2008.

means dramatic inequalities in the world—in essence, the economic plunder of other countries. The American people benefit economically from these savage inequalities; one cannot help but benefit from them merely by living in the US. This means that absent a conscious decision to try to redress these gross inequalities, the spontaneous tendency among many Americans, particularly those who are more materially privileged by these inequities, is going to be to support policies that, at the very least, maintain these inequities, and at worse, exacerbate them. You do not have to be an evil, conscienceless person. You merely have to do what comes naturally. You just have to follow the path of least resistance.

Thus the inherent wisdom or goodness of the American people—to whatever degree it exists—is subject to this ineluctable material fact. Relying on the people's wisdom/goodness means relying on a population that is vulnerable in substantial degree to political leaders who play upon Americans' fears of terrorism, promote ethnocentrism, and expand and intensify the tendencies of a populace to spontaneously favor what benefits them personally in the narrowest sense. The social base for the politics of plunder and domination of other countries exists in the US for material reasons. The social base is not itself the source of such politics (elites are the source), but the social base constitutes the fraction of the population for whom such politics resonate most strongly.

As I discuss in Chapter Six in greater detail, the organs of public opinion making are increasingly concentrated in smaller and smaller numbers of hands, and the corresponding and related increasing concentration of wealth in fewer hands means that the informed citizenry that underpins the rationale of democracy continues to diminish, rather like Lewis Carroll's Cheshire Cat's disappearing body, with only the smile remaining, and the smile itself now fading away as well.

While the Internet and alternative media are providing the public with greater access to competing outlooks and facts, the challenge to the ability of even those who are well informed to break through the barriers that mainstream media and the two-party oligarchy present is formidable. Witness the previously cited fact that for over three years a majority or near majority of the public (the numbers varied depending upon how the question was asked) wanted Bush and Cheney impeached. A majority wanted the Iraq war to end.[37] Yet despite a Democratic majority being elected on those very issues in 2006, Congress continued to fund the war at levels that actually exceeded what Bush requested, and the Democratic leadership absolutely refused to move towards impeachment in the face of a veritable

---

37   See Appendix 2.

flood of the most egregious and most blatant violations of the rule of law and core principles of the Constitution imaginable. The mass media, for its part, refused to legitimate the majority's desires for impeachment and accountability, scarcely uttering the dreaded word "impeachment"; when they did utter it, almost without exception they summarily and disdainfully dismissed the idea as unthinkable or misrepresented impeachment as a partisan vendetta.

Democracy as a Means to an End

While democracy as an end in itself grows out of agnosticism, democracy understood as a means to an end originates philosophically in empiricism—the view that truth and reality are knowable. An informed opinion means more than an uniformed opinion, and expertise and experience matter. But running a society solely by "experts" would not result in a good society because of what this would mean: the subordination and dependence of the broad ranks of the people. Mass participation in the cardinal questions of society represents something vitally important in and of itself, because popular participation means that people are involved in the processes that affect them. Moreover, their involvement is necessary if the historic inequalities between those in leading positions and those who are the ruled are to be eventually overcome.

How do we handle the contradiction between those who lead and those who are led? Having explicitly acknowledged the distinction between leadership and the led, you must still confront the problem of how you can prevent those who lead from using their positions to deceive the led and perpetuate and even expand the gap between themselves and those they lead. Simply declaring that "the people" are in charge and creating all kinds of institutions and procedures that are supposed to ensure that they are "in charge" do not prevent privilege and domination from occurring. Declaring that a pit bull is kid friendly does not make it so. De facto power can override de jure power at any time.

The two terms of Bush and Cheney during which they repeatedly, openly, and flagrantly flouted the "rule of law," and the mass media and the Democratic Party's collusion in these criminal acts, are vivid testimony to this contemporary fact. As Cheney's chief of staff David Addington put it: "We're going to push and push and push until some larger force stops us." It is a strategy that has worked remarkably and dramatically well. Addington and his colleagues knew that the larger force was not the Bill of Rights, the Constitution, the judiciary, the mass media, or the Democratic Party; and they have bet that the American people would follow their customary leaders—especially the "opposition" party and the mainstream media—and not rebel in the face of their outrageous acts and constitute that "larger force."

The contradiction between leadership and the led actually expresses an underlying, more fundamental dialectic—the tension between freedom and necessity. Freedom is not the absence of necessity; it is based on the recognition of necessity. Paradoxically, the deeper one's understanding of necessity, the more freedom one can express. Ignoring necessity, acting as if it does not exist, does not produce freedom; it produces disappointment at best and disaster at worst. If you are at the edge of a wide, deep river with a strong current, necessity dictates that to get across the river you need to understand either how to build a watercraft to ford the river or how to build a bridge. In either instance, necessity requires that you create a vessel or bridge that can stand up to the rigors it will confront. You are free to pretend that the river does not exist, and you can create a fanciful-looking but unstable bridge, but you *will* drown. Likewise, if you want to fly, you have to deal with the compulsions of gravity and learn the principles of aerodynamics, control and thrust. You cannot jump off a cliff and will yourself to fly. Building a bridge across a raging river and flying in the air are wonderful accomplishments that can only be achieved at the price of dealing with the strictures of necessity first.

Gymnasts can do amazing physical feats, but they can only do them by training enormously hard and dealing with the cold realities that such athleticism demands. Due to their discipline, they are able to achieve things with their bodies that people who do not put their bodies through those rigors cannot possibly approach. To put this in social terms, people who live lives of luxury in oversized homes with manicured lawns only do so because there are other people who must deal with tending the gardens, cleaning the houses, and making the meals and beds. The person who can afford to live high on the hog does so only by sloughing necessities off onto the backs of others who must correspondingly live lives filled with much less freedom. The beautiful people of Orange County, California, live lives that are sustained through the sweat, toil, and low wages of largely immigrant laborers who face intense necessity.

Democratic theory glosses over the gap between leaders and led. The theory in principle suffers from two problems. The first has to do with the nature of organization itself which democratic theory glosses over. The second has to do with the fact that economic inequality and the means of coercion are part and parcel of power exercised in and through the state.

The Nature of Organization

As a practical matter, barriers to democratic participation arise even among those who are more or less equal in their abilities, experience, and knowledge. No two people have equal voices in the face of an organization's exigencies. Robert Michels' "Iron Law of Oligarchy" underscores this problem. This would happen regardless of the participants' intentions because by its very nature participatory democracy is cumbersome, inefficient, and especially ill suited to groups larger than twenty or thirty. Indeed, even in groups as small as two, when a basic disagreement exists between the individuals and compromise is not possible, one person's say-so has to determine what the group does if the group is not to remain at a standstill.

While Michels and Weber put their fingers on a very real contradiction, their "iron law" and "iron cage" are not necessarily inevitable. Overcoming these tendencies is not easy; it is exceedingly difficult. But if we understand the dynamics at work, we can address the problems; a path exists towards resolving them. To explain why that is, we need to explore further the nature of the relationship between leadership and the led.

Leaders and the Led: A Unity of Opposites

Groups cannot operate without group leaders. Without leaders groups are no more than aggregations of individuals. The strength of a group cannot be realized without organization, and organization means and requires leadership. For those who think that a division of labor with everyone adopting a specific task can eliminate the need for a hierarchy of leadership, I would point out that specialization involves some whose role in the division of labor involves leadership. Moreover, no group absent leadership can organize itself. Consensus policies, if taken to their logical ends, produce group paralysis because there will always be disagreements about what needs to be done. Someone eventually, given the inevitable dissensus, will have to make an executive decision. As anyone who has ever worked in a group knows, trying to please everyone results in pleasing no one.

Leaders and the led operate in a dialectical relationship to each other, when handled properly. Leadership and the led exist as a unity of opposites; they co-occur, and one does not and cannot exist without the other. Contrary to those who argue against leadership and regard leadership as an imposition on the collectivity's rights and powers, the collectivity

257

cannot realize its greatest potential without leaders. To expect otherwise is naïve. The obverse of this is also true and self-evident: leaders do not lead in a vacuum. For the gap between leadership and the led to be overcome, the actual and material nature of this gap needs to be deeply understood and addressed rather than ignored.

The material roots of this gap grow out of the historic separation of mental from manual labor. Owing to their privileged access to information as well as networked connections to others in leading positions and experience in exercising leadership, mental laborers have advantages over manual laborers that cannot be undone overnight. These differences must be addressed systematically and in a protracted fashion to bridge and eventually overcome those differences.

By contrast, Durkheim's functionalism, in some respects the theoretical grandfather of democratic theory, adopts a more nebulous assessment of the workings of a polity. The public's sentiments, or what he dubbed the "conscience collective," reigns supreme, with the political institutions and public officials, along with the media, reacting to and fundamentally reflecting the public's sentiments. Functionalism thereby conflates leaders and the led. And, as happens when two distinct ends of a polarity are conflated, one pole is in fact given primacy over the other, except that it is the wrong one. By downplaying leadership's role and exaggerating the role of the led/group, functionalism ends up paradoxically creating a situation in which leadership ends up dominating the populace. The public, correspondingly, ends up being unable to play its fullest possible role.

The public, in fact, in modern societies with large populations and a highly developed division of labor, becomes increasingly impotent in the face of bureaucratic leadership. Weber's observation that bureaucracies inevitably triumph over community action (the actions of mass movements would be the most notable of community actions) holds true because bureaucracies systematize and routinize the allocation of responsibilities and tasks. They are, in other words, highly organized, and the skill set of bureaucrats is developed through practice and/or training. Mass movements, while much larger than bureaucracies in general, do not have this level of specialization and rationalization of tasks. There is no getting around the fact that if an oligarchy is to be avoided, the led must step up and monitor and increasingly participate in self-governance. Benevolent saviors cannot obliterate these fundamental problems.

Surpassing Democracy

People do not know what they do not know. Leaders, virtually by definition, unless they come forward as leaders because of nepotism or another
vehicle that has nothing much to do with real qualifications, understand
what is going on better than the led. What they do with their leadership,
what its actual content is, is up to them to a significant degree. Due to
organizational factors, this holds true even in groups made up of equally
qualified individuals. How much more true should this be then in situations where substantial differences in experience and knowledge exist?
Proper leadership commits itself to raising the level of understanding of
the led so that the led can increasingly become leaders themselves. For a
kind of mass participation to prevail that will eventually supersede the
very word "democracy," two things must happen: leaders must play a larger role in leading others in ways that raise the led's grasp of what is going
on in the society as a whole, and the led must resist the temptation to settle
into lives of indifference. Instead, the led must themselves become masters
of their and our collective fate.

Democracy as a political stage in history reflects a particular division
of labor. When the divisions between mental and manual labor, between
those at the center and those at the periphery, and between those whose
material interests rest on the continued subordination of others and those
who are exploited, are overcome, then democracy too will be overcome
and become itself insensible as a term.

The underlying issue here is not that democracy is being distorted by
corrupt officials, overly aggressive lobbyists, lazy media watchdogs, or a
disengaged citizenry. The central problem grows out of the shortcomings
of democratic theory itself and the underlying material conditions that
produced democratic theory and that make representative democracies a
sham for real popular participation.[38]

---

38 A very brief reflection here on a basic division of opinion within the Left over the
role of the masses: Some within the Left see that the masses of people need to
be mobilized, but their vision for the masses' role is fundamentally that of a pressure group to those in public office. Their strategy amounts more to a participatory
form of lobbying and not one in which the people are being called forward to play
increasingly active autonomous roles politically. The people's role is seen as one of
convincing the Democrats to vote against the empire's imperialist interests and to
fund domestic social programs.

CHAPTER SIX

Media: the New Faux Public

If men define situations as real, they are real in their consequences.

W.I. THOMAS[1]

There is something terribly wrong when Americans know more about Martha Stewart's prison stay than they do about the torture scandals at Abu Ghraib and Guantanamo Bay.

ROBERT MCCHESNEY[2]

On two occasions I have been asked,—"Pray, Mr. Babbage, if you put into the machine wrong figures, will the right answers come out?"... I am not able rightly to apprehend the kind of confusion of ideas that could provoke such a question.

CHARLES BABBAGE[3]

---

1   This is also true for women! W.I. Thomas and D.S. Thomas, *The Child in America: Behavior Problems and Programs* (New York: Knopf, 1928), 571-572.

2   Robert McChesney, "The Moment Has Come for Media Reform," Common-Dreams.org, January 5, 2005, http://www.commondreams.org/views05/0105-20.htm, accessed January 5, 2007.

3   Charles Babbage, *Passages from the Life of a Philosopher* (London: Longman and Co., 1864), 67.

B ecause of media's central role in determining what the people see, know, and think about current events, their power to determine our collective condition has never been more pronounced. This shows up in two respects. First, media today reach and influence more people, hold our attention longer, and pervade our social and physical environments more extensively and intensively than at any other time in history. Media's presence and intrusions into our lives defy escape: television monitors, music, ads, and so on, hector us everywhere we go, whether we are filling up our gas tanks, waiting in a doctor's office, driving down the road, or sitting in the airport. The news no longer comes to us as something we read over morning coffee and watch at six o'clock; it is now available 24/7.

Second, media mediate our interactions and our information about what others think and are doing to an unprecedented degree: information and impressions about what the public thinks today come less from among and between the people than secondhand via media. This function of media has received comparatively little attention, yet it represents a critical aspect of media's role. "What the people think" occupies a central place in any contemporary nation since putatively democratic states depend on at least the semblance of popular support for their ongoing legitimacy. Since opinion must be mobilized to effect and justify any public policy, as detailed in Chapter Five, what we know and what we think we know about others' opinions matters enormously to those who would consider instigating any social change, whatever the nature of that change may be—whether to the Right, the Middle, or to the Left, and whether the people interested in the change sit at the top of the social ladder (e.g., public officials), in the middle strata, or at the grassroots.

People act, after all, based upon what is in their heads. Events and objective conditions matter, but we can only understand the meaning of those events and conditions through a process of interpretation. What we think is going on, why we think these things are happening, and what we think others think, are all shaped powerfully for nearly all of us by media.

More is Less

Does media's ubiquity mean that the public knows more about current events than ever? The more pervasive media have become in our lives, the less the average person knows about matters critical to his or her life and that of their society. This is not a product of the growing proliferation and presence of media and its use, a kind of dilution of content by virtue of sheer quantity. It is a product, instead, of the following factors: the content and framing by media of what they present; the extreme concentration of media ownership in but a few hands; the relentless logic of bottom-line profitability that today dominates media conglomerates' choices of what to cover, how to cover it, and what not to cover; and the right-wing's powerful and expanding presence and influence within the media universe.

Most people do not realize how badly misinformed and under-informed we have collectively become. How can we be suffering from a paucity of critical information by which to make decisions when we are swimming in a sea of what passes for information? We see and hear multiple voices beamed at us from the multiplex media. But, as in a multiplex cinema, the profusion of choices masks the scant substantive differences among the major voices and the few and increasingly homogeneous owners and interests behind the cacophony. As Bruce Springsteen put it in his song of the same title regarding TV, "fifty-seven channels and nothin' on."

Why so little awareness about so much ignorance? The problem here, put simply, is that *you do not know what you do not know*. If you think you already know what is going on and are not exposed to a competing explanation or set of facts, then you do not go looking for an alternative perspective. Why would you, if you do not even know that a legitimate alternative perspective exists and that crucial facts have been withheld from you, especially when the surface appearance of things makes it seem as if plenty of voices are being heard? If you have been trained to be skeptical and to seek out more information, then you might broaden your search for solid information and illuminating analysis, but comparatively few people have received that training and most of society cannot reasonably be expected to act so diligently. Even those who do seek out alternative views cannot do it about all things and are not always sure what to do with competing explanations. "How do I know," they wonder, "what is true?" It is a very good question, and one that I address further in Chapter Seven of this book.

Since the main way that people in a society learn about current affairs is via mass media, then what media are doing and what they are not doing constitute something extraordinarily important. Even those who do not pay much attention to the news garner their views via media from what might be termed "headline impressions:" they take what the headlines say as their point of orientation to the big stories and issues of the day and add to those media headlines the comments of others around them (with those others around them also having received their take on current events from the media). Headlines and lead stories are the snapshots that most people absorb from the news and tabloids, and it is the frame of that story/

issue that is decisive. Because of this, the dominant news/issue frame determines the perspective of the large majority of even those who consume a lot of news from diverse sources (e.g., professionals and intellectuals) as well as the people who only go by "headline impressions."

As Shanto Iyengar, a leading expert on framing, explains, referring to the well-established phenomenon that people will give very different answers to questions depending upon how the questions are worded, "Question wording effects are not symptomatic of weakly held preferences or naïve respondents. To the contrary, these effects emerge across a wide range of subject-matter sophistication and expertise."[4]

In other words, it is not just the ignorant or easily swayed that are seduced by framing effects. This effect applies equally to people of very varied political persuasions. A story's framing determines the boundaries of acceptable discussion and debate. Thinking outside those boundaries is invariably labeled "unrealistic," rendered irrelevant, and designated as impossible or outlandish in the arena of "legitimate" public debate.

The main problem for our society is not, therefore, that too few Americans pay close enough attention to the news or that too many Americans are gullible, even though both of these phenomena exist and contribute significantly to the problem. Through a combination of, on the one hand, the media's failure to cover—or censorship of—vital facts and issues and, on the other hand, their framing of issues in ways that predetermine what may or may not be considered, what the people of this country do not know about public policy and what falsehoods they believe have never been more extensive, extreme, and consequential. In the parlance of computer science: GIGO—Garbage In, Garbage Out. If the people are not being given reliable and fair representations of current events and issues, and if in addition they are being systematically told outright falsehoods, then there is no way that they can make sensible and wise decisions; they are being fed a steady diet of garbage. Mushrooms grow well on manure, but people do not make good decisions on a steady diet of it, as the quote from Babbage at the beginning of this chapter illustrates.

All of us, all of the time, are interpreting the sense impressions that come to us. Framing, that is to say, interpretation, is, therefore, inevitable. What are not inevitable are the particular frames that the media choose. The process by which those frames are chosen now constitutes the key arena of political power in society. It even trumps the use of state or non-state violence, since both those who use guns or other weapons and

---

4   Shanto Iyengar, "Framing Responsibility for Political Issues: The Case of Poverty," *Political Behavior*, Vol. 12 (1990), No. 1, 20.

those who choose to either acquiesce to weapons or actively resist those weapons do so based upon what is in their heads. Guns do not settle political disputes in the final analysis, even if in the short run they can be decisive. If the people who use the guns are seen as doing so illegitimately, there are not enough guns and people to put down a determined and broadly aroused people, composed in part of a significant minority within that majority who are willing to die if necessary to change what has become an intolerable situation.

(A) Six (Pack of) Lies

To illustrate this point, consider the power exercised by six utterly false claims that media have propagated in recent times. The first three falsehoods justified the war upon Iraq and the other three turned the 2009 town hall meetings on health care into fracases and played key roles in precipitating the Tea Party movement. The first item in this list is a lie by omission. The rest are direct lies.

1. Media have failed to inform the people that according to the Geneva Conventions, the United Nations (UN) Charter,[5] and the Nuremberg Principles,[6] attacking a country that has not first launched armed hostilities, regardless of whether they possess "weapons of mass destruction" or not, constitutes the supreme war crime.

2. Iraq has weapons of mass destruction (WMD).

3. Saddam Hussein aided and supported the 9/11 terrorists.

---

5 Article 2, paragraph 4 of the United Nations Charter reads: "All Members shall refrain in their international relations from the threat or use of force against the territorial integrity or political independence of any state, or in any other manner inconsistent with the Purposes of the United Nations." Article 51 states in relevant part: "Nothing in the present Charter shall impair the inherent right of individual or collective self-defense if an armed attack occurs against a Member of the United Nations...." From UN.org, http://www.un.org/en/documents/charter/index.shtml, accessed December 12, 2010.

6 At Nuremberg, the chief American prosecutor Robert H. Jackson stated: "To initiate a war of aggression, therefore, is not only an international crime; it is the supreme international crime differing only from other war crimes in that it contains within itself the accumulated evil of the whole." Wikipedia, "War of Aggression," http://en.wikipedia.org/wiki/War_of_aggression, accessed May 4, 2010.

4. Obama's health care plan calls for "death panels" for the elderly.

5. Obama is a Muslim/Socialist/Communist/Nazi.

6. Obama was not born in the US.

Notably, the first three falsehoods were propagated by all major media, including the esteemed "paper of record" *The New York Times*, and not just the right-wing media. To this day, *The Times* has not once mentioned that international law bars the invasion of a country that has not first initiated armed hostilities.

While it is true that Bush and Cheney originated and perpetrated the first few deceptions, the media had the ability to expose them as lies and instead legitimated the trumped-up "facts." As one of those in the anti-war movement who spoke out during the pre-war period about why these were demonstrably lies and sins of omission, I found it painful to watch as these fabricated "facts" were allowed to go uncontested in major media, resulting in the launching and perpetuation of an unjust war, the unnecessary deaths to date of more than a million Iraqis and tens of thousands of Americans, and trillions of dollars in direct war and lost opportunity costs, contributing mightily to the budget crises that fill the news and impact our lives in alarming ways.

The fact that falsehoods such as these can be propagated, and the fact that the perpetrators of these falsehoods and distortions retain or are even increasing their credibility and influence, mean that the media, and therefore the polity, are in deep trouble. Certainly gullibility makes people more vulnerable to manipulation, but the people propagating these lies (ranging from Sarah Palin to other Republican Party leaders as well as Fox News anchors) know that they are lies; they have promoted them in a cynical campaign to stoke people's fears, anxieties, and prejudices.

The first three lies in my list, however, did not depend on credulousness. They were bought wholesale by most of the populace because all of the major media and public officials repeated them over and over. Indeed, many people still believe these lies, despite the fact that the second two—"WMD" and the linkage of Hussein to 9/11—were eventually exposed as fabrications. (The right-wing media are now claiming by an audacious feat of revisionist history that Bush and Cheney never uttered those lies in the first place.)[7] The truth about the first lie by omission is probably still

---

7   See, for example, Karl Rove's assertions that Bush did not know that his claims about WMD were false: "[D]id Bush lie us into war? Absolutely not." (Ed Hornick, "Rove: Bush didn't 'lie us into war,'" CNN.Com, March 6, 2010, http://articles.cnn.com/2010-03-06/politics/karl.rove.book_1_rove-then-cia-director-george-tenet-

unknown to perhaps ninety to ninety-eight percent of the people because no one has informed them of it; that is the weighty responsibility of the "watchdog" media. (See Chapter Five for a discussion of the question of why more Americans who *do* know that they have been lied to have not acted in response in more visible and effective ways.)

What good can come to a nation whose government and media get away with perpetrating major falsehoods, leading tens of millions to hundreds of millions of people to believe outright lies and remain unaware that they are lies? What will be the fate of the world when that misinformed nation is the most powerful and influential country on earth? The consequence of these lies not being exposed in a timely fashion and their perpetrators not being held to account has been the warping of the American soul. The condition and role of the media today are a concentrated expression of much of what is wrong with neoliberalism. Media have been harnessed as the key instrument in the promotion and perpetuation of neoliberalism—at least in the US. Outside of the US, media and government distortions and lies are perhaps less important in relative terms than the use of undisguised violence to intimidate and suppress the people and more craftily disguised misleaders posing as the people's representatives.

---

wmd?_s=PM:POLITICS, accessed February 19, 2011. By contrast, as Greg Palast points out in "The Downing Street Memos, Manipulation of Prewar Intelligence, and Knowingly Withholding Vital Information from a Grand Jury Investigation," in *Impeach the President: the Case Against Bush and Cheney*, ed. Dennis Loo and Peter Phillips (New York: Seven Stories, 2006), 131:

> The top-level government memo. . . dated eight months before Bush sent us into Iraq, following a closed meeting [at 10 Downing Street with Tony Blair and close advisers] with the President, reads: "*Military action was now seen as inevitable. Bush wanted to remove Saddam Hussein through military action justified by the conjunction of terrorism and WMD. But the intelligence and facts were being fixed around the policy.*"
>
> Read that again: "The intelligence and facts were being fixed. . ."

See also "Claims and Facts: Rhetoric, Reality and the War in Iraq," AmericanProgress.org, http://www.americanprogress.org/kf/priraqclaimfact1029.htm, accessed February 19, 2011. For some specific statements, see for example:

> Dick Cheney, August 26, 2002: "Simply stated, there's no doubt that Saddam Hussein now has weapons of mass destruction. There is no doubt he is amassing them to use against our friends, against our allies, and against us."
>
> George W. Bush, March 17, 2003, while issuing an ultimatum to Saddam Hussein: "Intelligence gathered by this and other governments leaves no doubt that the Iraq regime continues to possess and conceal some of the most lethal weapons ever devised."

Lies, Damn Lies, and Statistics of Media Ownership

There are three major dimensions to media's nature and role today. In addition to the unprecedented influence of all forms of media, two other factors contribute to media's dominance over the political landscape. The first of these is the highly concentrated corporate ownership of media (there are now only six major media companies).[8] This situation is a product of media moguls' unquenchable search for profits, encouraged by neoliberal policies that eschew regulation—a recipe for uniformity and corporate supremacy. The second factor is the right-wing media's disproportionate and powerful influence over all public policy discussions.

As a net result of these two factors, the media's traditionally-assumed and exclusively-relied-upon mission of adequately informing the people and acting as vigilant watchdogs over the government is now almost never fulfilled; it has been subdued by the double blows of mega-corporate, bottom-line profitability and militant, aggressive, right-wing agendas that declare that those who disagree with their views are at best unpatriotic and at worst, traitors who should be prosecuted and/or bullied into submission or even killed. As just one example of the latter, see this fatwa declared by right-wing pundit Jonah Goldberg, *National Review* editor-at-large and American Enterprise Institute Fellow, in the October 29, 2010, issue of the *Chicago Tribune*:

---

8   The six are: Time Warner, Disney, Rupert Murdoch's NewsCorp, Viacom, Bertlesmann and NBCUniversal (Comcast/General Electric/NBC). In 1983 there were fifty mass media corporations. As former *Washington Post* editor Ben Bagdikian put it in 1997 in his book, *The Media Monopoly*, 5th ed. (Boston: Beacon Press, 1997), ix:

> In the last 5 years, a small number of the country's largest industrial corporations has acquired more public communications power-including ownership of the news than any private businesses have ever before possessed in world history.
>
> Nothing in earlier history matches this corporate group's power to penetrate the social landscape. Using both old and new technology, by owning each other's shares, engaging in joint ventures as partners, and other forms of cooperation, this handful of giants has created what is, in effect, a new communications cartel within the United States.
>
> At issue is not just a financial statistic, like production numbers or ordinary industrial products like refrigerators or clothing. At issue is the possession of power to surround almost every man, woman, and child in the country with controlled images and words, to socialize each new generation of Americans, to alter the political agenda of the country. And with that power comes the ability to exert influence that in many ways is greater than that of schools, religion, parents, and even government itself.

I'd like to ask a simple question: Why isn't Julian Assange dead?

In case you didn't know, Assange is the Australian computer programmer behind WikiLeaks, a massive—and massively success-ful—effort to disclose secret or classified information. In a series of recent dumps, he unveiled thousands upon thousands of classified documents from the wars in Afghanistan and Iraq. Military and other government officials insist that WikiLeaks is doing serious damage to American national security and is going to get people killed, in-cluding brave Iraqis and Afghans who've risked their lives and the lives of their families to help us.

Even Assange agrees. He told the New Yorker earlier this year that he fully understands innocent people might die as a result of the "collateral damage" of his work and that WikiLeaks may have "blood on our hands." WikiLeaks is easily among the most significant and well-publicized breaches of American national security since the Rosenbergs gave the Soviets the bomb.

So again, I ask: Why wasn't Assange garroted in his hotel room years ago?

It's a serious question.[9]

As Glenn Greenwald accurately observed, such sentiments, echoed by other right-wing pundits and GOP leaders, reflect a society in which the torture and assassination of those believed to be on the wrong side of the "War on Terror" are ordered from the very top—by the president (previ-ously covertly by Bush and now openly by Obama).

While media still continue to do some limited informing for the pub-lic, they have overall become an instrument for the few to manipulate the many and a device to insulate elites from the oversight of the many.

Media serve today as a surrogate electorate, trumping the roles of the citizenry and of election results; even assuming that the elected represen-tatives running for office on a "change" platform actually did mean this and did in fact represent a real difference from the present rule by the rich and powerful. Regardless of who is in the White House and which party controls Congress, a small minority of far right-wing voices now hold the upper hand overall via their powerful presence in the media, exceeding Barry Goldwater's wildest dreams. Whoever sets the commonly accepted frame of reference for public policy determines the outcome. Although the

---

9   Jonah Goldberg, "Why Is Assange Still Alive?" *Chicago Tribune* online, October 29, 2010, http://www.chicagotribune.com/news/opinion/ct-oped-1029-goldberg-20101029,0,5734943.story, accessed November 3, 2010.

frame that dominates may be contested by other sectors of the "chattering classes," the right-wing's frame exercises extraordinary influence.

Despite the Democratic sweep of Congress in 2006 and 2008 and Obama's victory in 2008, for example, the national debates on major political issues such as the wars, detention, health care, the economy, abortion, and national security matters have all taken place on terms dictated by the right-wing. In sports this would be the equivalent of the far Right having home court advantage; noisy, pumped-up, aggressive, and violent fans packing the auditorium; and partisan referees officiating in favor of the home team.

Consider the "War on Terror." If the "War on Terror" is treated as the nation's foremost concern, and if the enemy cannot ever be eliminated (since by definition "terror" is a tactic, not a person, organization, or country), then all else must perforce be indefinitely subordinated to that war. Once the nation's foremost public issue is framed in such a way, anything is justifiable, including unilateral, secret and not-so-secret executive action, torture, assassination, and repeated violations of the Constitution and the rule of law. Once you accept the "War on Terror" frame as proper, then you are always going to be vulnerable to those to your right who claim that your stance on any policy or practice undermines the "War on Terror" and gives comfort to the enemy. As Bush put it: "You're either with us or you're with the terrorists." You are trapped in the logic of the "War on Terror" unless you challenge the phrase with a different framing of the issue altogether and succeed in making your frame at least as powerful and adhered to as "War on Terror." Ominously, a different frame has not been substituted either by the mainstream media's major outlets or the Democratic Party leadership. Their collective failure—or refusal—to do so is fateful.

Consider similarly the "Support the Troops" formulation, also initiated by the GOP. People who seek to challenge the wars and occupations but who accept the frame "Support the Troops" are compelled to support the wars; anything they do to challenge the wars such as restricting or cutting off funding can be characterized as failure to support the troops. So the war critics who accept "Support the Troops" are once again vulnerable from their political right. When the Bush White House was preparing the groundwork for its invasion of Iraq, they carefully built the case based on phony claims of WMD. If the media had pointed out that it did not matter whether Iraq had WMD because Iraq had not attacked us and was not even threatening to attack us, the White House would have had a much harder time winning support for their elective invasion.

A little-known fact, because it was barely publicized in the media, is that a majority of Americans on the eve of the 2003 Iraq invasion were opposed to a US invasion without UN authorization. (Once the invasion began, however, a majority rallied around the flag and the president, as could be expected.) The UN, as many may know, refused to endorse the US invasion. At the last minute Bush and Cheney had to pull together their Gibraltar "summit" involving Great Britain and Spain, and coined the term "coalition of the willing" for their tiny assemblage. As a comedian put it at the time, the US's "coalition of the willing" included three other major countries—Great Britain, England, and the United Kingdom. (And let us not forget: Poland, Guam, and Spain.) The difficulties that Bush and Cheney had in putting together their war alliance stemmed directly from the tens of millions of people demonstrating worldwide against the pending war; these multitudes played a major role in the UN's refusing to endorse the illegal invasion.

Consider further the "debate" about torture. To begin with, it is a frightening fact that there is even a debate over torture in the US. Prior to the Bush years, torture was unquestionably understood to be illegal and immoral and explicitly against international and national laws; it was the infamous tactic of tyrants, dictators, and serial murderers. (This did not prevent the US government from using it on occasion, as it did, for example, during the Vietnam War in the Phoenix Program. Before Bush the government had almost always used proxies to carry out torture. Torture had not been turned into a common, everyday practice carried out by hundreds of American personnel, and the US government had never officially endorsed it, as they were setting out to do.) In their quest for unchallengeable world supremacy, the neocons proceeded to drive a Mack Truck through this legal and moral barrier; they began a campaign of secretly implementing torture as a policy while initially, and even for several years thereafter, denying that they were doing it. When their practices became widely known as a result of the Abu Ghraib photographs, they blamed a "few bad apples" and continued to deny that they were systematically torturing people, even as they continued to build the case that "national security" (protecting American lives) required extraordinary measures, including torture and a number of other extremely egregious activities and policies.

When it was revealed that waterboarding was a common practice and that it was being used in American prisons such as Bagram and at dozens of secret black sites, the Right, led by Cheney, claimed that waterboarding was not torture and that it was, as Cheney put it, a "no brainer." While voices within various mainstream media outlets have spoken out forcefully against torture (and waterboarding in particular), they have never challenged the underlying premise—that American lives are more precious than non-American lives. Indeed, none other than a liberal human rights spokesman, Michael Ignatieff, Director of Harvard's Carr Center for Human Rights, argued in *The New York Times Magazine* on May 2, 2004, that preventing another attack like 9/11 justified torture:

> To defeat evil, we may have to traffic in evils: indefinite detention of suspects, coercive interrogations, targeted assassinations, even pre-emptive war. These are evils because each strays from national and international law and because they kill people or deprive them of freedom without due process. They can be justified only because they prevent the greater evil.[10]

It apparently occurred to no one at *The New York Times Magazine* that this "greater evil" of another 9/11 was being "prevented" by carrying out the atrocities that Ignatieff endorsed upon Iraq, a country and a people that had had nothing to do with 9/11 in the first place. Ignatieff's argument, in other words, even if accepted as valid for use against guilty parties, was absurd when defending and advocating policies to be used on completely innocent parties. Could *The New York Times Magazine*'s editorial staff be so blind as to not see this? Could a human rights director like Ignatieff fail to see the gigantic hole in his argument? What was a human rights advocate doing advocating express violations of human rights?

The publication of Ignatieff's essay was an exemplar of (a) the blind spot shared by the media and public officialdom over the sacredness of American lives as compared to the lives of people from other countries, even entirely blameless people and countries; and (b) the manner in which the right-wing's frames were now in control. Ignatieff's essay echoed Dick Cheney's famous statement on *Meet the Press* in which he said that the US government would have to work on the "dark side" to counter terrorists.

The May 2, 2004, Ignatieff essay appeared two days before the infamous revelations of Abu Ghraib by CBS's *60 Minutes*. When confronted by the graphic photographs of torture, *The New York Times Magazine* and Ignatieff backed off a little from their earlier, now embarrassing, advocacy. Ignatieff wrote another essay for *The New York Times Magazine* on June

---

10   Michael Ignatieff, "Lesser Evils," *The New York Times Magazine* online, May 2, 2004, http://www.ksg.harvard.edu/news/opeds/2004/ignatieff_less_evils_nytm_050204. htm, accessed January 23, 2008.

27, 2004, criticizing the "legal memoranda by lawyers in the Bush administration that appeared to justify" the torture at Abu Ghraib,[11] thus backtracking from his earlier stand. Unfortunately, the Bush lawyers, John Yoo and Jay Bybee, advocated what Ignatieff himself had only a few weeks earlier justified. *The New York Times Magazine* also ran an essay by Susan Sontag on May 23, 2004, condemning torture in no uncertain terms. The damage, however, had already been done. If other people's lives are less important than the lives of Americans, then the torture of some people, even innocent people, or even deaths by torture, can continue to be justified in ways that all too many Americans will now accept.

If the reputedly liberal and most esteemed publication in the country could, via Ignatieff, provide support for preemptive wars, assassinations, and torture, then can anyone be surprised that the US government is still, now under Obama, continuing to torture people, publicly ordering assassinations (including as of 2010, assassination of American citizens), and that torture is now being openly advocated in polite company?

Sen. John McCain and Sen. Joe Lieberman introduced a bill (Enemy Belligerent Interrogation, Detention and Prosecution Act of 2010, S. 3081) on March 4, 2010 to permit the government to *indefinitely detain Americans without charge and without trial* on the grounds of their allegedly being terrorists, and that those so labeled would be barred from being read their Miranda Rights. Howard McKeon, a Democrat from California, then introduced a similar bill in the House on March 19, 2010. With the exception of the *Atlantic Magazine*,[12] the mainstream media did not deem it worthy of note to even tell the American people about the introduction of these explicitly fascist laws. The mere fact of their introduction by two of the most prominent senators in Congress, one who had run for president and the other who had run for vice-president, was worthy of news. Liz Cheney and Bill Kristol took out ads in 2010 accusing Justice Department lawyers of treason for representing, as lawyers are obligated to do under

---

11   Michael Ignatieff, "Mirage in the Desert," *The New York Times Magazine*, June 27, 2004, 151.

12   Marc Ambinder, "A Detention Bill You Ought to Read More Carefully," March 5, 2010, TheAtlantic.com, *Enemy Belligerent, Interrogation, Detention, and Prosecution Act of 2010*, http://www.theatlantic.com/politics/archive/2010/03/a-detention-bill-you-ought-to-read-more-carefully/37116/, accessed February 18, 2011: "Why is the national security community treating the 'Enemy Belligerent, Interrogation, Detention, and Prosecution Act of 2010,' introduced by Sens. John McCain and Joseph Lieberman on Thursday as a standard proposal. . . . A *close reading of the bill suggests that it would allow the U.S. military to detain U.S. citizens without trial indefinitely in the U.S. based on suspected activity*." [Emphasis in original.]

our system of jurisprudence, detainees in the "War on Terror." All of this is made possible by the framing of the "War on Terror" that privileges American lives over anyone and anything. These egregious actions are the logical extension of the logic of that frame. The slope is a steep one and there are no stopping points along the way, no points beyond which it can be said "No Farther." The fact that torture has been and is still being touted as justifiable, even a source of pride, by people at the highest levels of government speaks loudly to this fact.

The media's failure to cite a central tenet of relevant international law on even one occasion, let alone their failure to refute in a timely way the flimsy WMD hoax has, therefore, had major, disastrous, and ongoing repercussions. As I have argued previously in this book, the exercise of political power is surprisingly tenuous compared to conventional understandings of it. It all turns on a small set of facts and fairly subtle interpretive moves. The framing of public issues, a process in which media play a major role, determines what gets done and how it is done. Framing determines whether actions are seen as legitimate and whether the actors advocating the actions are themselves seen as acting legitimately.

Legitimacy is fundamentally the be-all and end-all of political rule. When leaders come to be seen as illegitimate, there are not enough guns and soldiers to hold back the people. Governments can suppress people for a time with violence, but they cannot win if enough of the people see them as illegitimate. The swing votes on this question, figuratively speaking, are from the middle strata of society. In general, the working class and oppressed minorities tend to be much more cynical about government and corporate America, carrying on their lives without a strong belief in the legitimacy of the status quo. The lower strata go along with the program largely because they know that every day "the Man" uses violence to keep them in line and will deploy more force on short notice. They recognize that rebelling against the status quo has no chance of success on an individual or small-group level in ordinary times; it only has a chance when very large groups of people act in concert.

When the middle strata and the intelligentsia break ranks with the people who wield societal power, then these ruling groups, who are a very tiny minority to begin with, are in deep trouble. The use of violence by a government against its adversaries only forestalls the inevitable at that point. Indeed, violence will usually accelerate the inevitable, because by using violence, leaders further expose their fundamental character and shock ordinarily quiescent people from the middle strata, as well as intellectuals, into political opposition.

Pols and Polls

In the past, public sentiment was primarily expressed via elections, citizens' visits to public officials, letters, phone calls, petitions, unions, grassroots organizations, demonstrations, strikes, riots, rebellions, revolutions, and so on. Even before Reagan, Clinton and Bush flung open the doors to major media consolidation, another development helped to neutralize these older public forms of expression: polls. Since the mid-twentieth century when polling first became popular, media and public officials have increasingly substituted polls (selectively reported and presented) for demonstrations and other organized expressions of grassroots sentiment.

Polls have been used increasingly by both public officials and media as *the* evidence of what the public wants and thinks (between elections), at the expense of the traditional forms of public expression that were more the province of political forces and grassroots groups on the Left. These groups, as Benjamin Ginsberg has pointed out,[13] had the credibility to speak because they were close to and spoke with and on behalf of the dispossessed and middle and lower strata through their presence and leadership in unions and community organizations.

Polls' ascension has given governments and well-heeled interest groups the ability to claim that they "know better" what the public thinks, eclipsing to a significant degree the power of Left and community-level groups. Media's dominating presence in social affairs and life, with their use of polls only a part of their impact, means that their representations of what is going on, and why, essentially determine the ruling consensus. (The misuse of polls in this way is something that I addressed in detail in Chapter Two.) Demonstrations matter less than they have in the past because public officials, and frequently media, cherry-pick the demonstrations they approve of, frequently counter-posing demonstrations they do not like with letter writers or with polls that allegedly show that most other Americans do not agree with the demonstrators.[14]

The ultimate expression of public sentiment is supposed to be an election. Why elections are not in fact good indicators of public

---

13 Benjamin Ginsberg, *The Captive Public: How Mass Opinion Promotes State Power* (New York: Basic Books, 1986).

14 Polls, as ordinarily employed, do not distinguish those who feel strongly about an issue from those who are less engaged. Unorganized mass opinion, therefore, can be cited to dismiss the people who are highly aroused and actively engaged in advocating for their views.

sentiment and not the be-all and end-all of "democracy" I discussed in greater detail in Chapter Five. The problem with polls I pursue further later on in this chapter.

Media *are* the new public. The reverse is not true: the public is not the media, the proliferation and increasing popularity of media such as Twitter and Facebook notwithstanding. Twitter and Facebook are not yet, nor will they ever be, a match for major media outlets' reach, influence, and presumed legitimacy. Today, public officials and others are more concerned about how they themselves will appear in the media and how media interpret their actions than they are about the voting public's reactions or sentiments. (This is also true, by the way, of those who seek their fifteen minutes or more of fame, ranging from Paris Hilton to the latest reality TV participant, and from a confessor on any number of daytime TV talk shows to the millions who reveal their personal lives to the world on Facebook and MySpace.)

Media audiences are far more segregated now than they have ever been, with tens of millions of people almost exclusively seeing, hearing, and/or reading media that mirror what they already believe or wish to believe. This situation is primarily a result of the 1987 abolition under Ronald Reagan of the Fairness Doctrine; since then media outlets may bar dissenters from engaging directly with the outlets' own spokespersons, leaving their untrue pronouncements unchallenged.

Changes in the Economics and Politics of Media

Over the last few decades, there has been a melding of economic and political/ideological objectives in the media business, some of it purposeful, some of it incidental. This coalescing of the narrowly economic and the broader political is highly consequential to not just the media world but more importantly to the society and the planet.

Changes in media ownership (merger mania), the proliferation of diverse media outlets (cable, video, the Internet, et al), and the intensification of competition among an increasingly tiny number of gargantuan players have together led to news operations being governed in unprecedented ways by bottom-line logic, resulting in more sensationalism, the news being produced more inexpensively, a preponderance of crime news (since crimes stories are cheaper to run and easier to obtain), and the pronounced ubiquity of fear frames. The bottom-line logic is manifest in many ways: outlets are cutting back on the number of journalists on the payroll; reducing the overall amount of coverage and investigation; cutting back sharply on international news; becoming more reliant on government news feeds and private-corporate, special interest, and disproportionately deep pocketed right-wing groups;[15] and increasing the share of lightweight or "fluff" news, such as the endless parade of the latest celebrities' doings or alleged doings.

Celebrity/Fluff news and fear frames have assumed an increasingly important and pervasive presence for several different and overlapping reasons. Celebrity/Fluff news serves two purposes: first, it promotes the Horatio Alger Myth (see how rich you, too, might become!) necessary in a time of Social Darwinism; and second, this kind of non-news news is cheap and readily available.[16] As for fear frames, their prevalence predates 9/11, though 9/11 escalated their use and created a shift from a predominant fear of crime to a predominant fear of terrorism, and from the realm of neighborhood fears and community fears to the much larger realm of fear of perceived threats to the entire planet.

Strong-arming as Journalism

Since the 1970s, the radical right has invested tens of billions of dollars in creating their own outlets (Fox News and AM talk radio, think tanks, publishing houses, magazines, etc.) that have exerted a sharp right-wing pull on the media and, in turn, on public opinion. Talking/shouting heads such as Glenn Beck and Rush Limbaugh can only operate as they do in the absence of any real opposing viewpoints that would offer a fair and civil debate. As former right-wing propagandist David Brock revealed in his 2004 book, *The Republican Noise Machine: Right-Wing*

---

15 "Long before the current recession and radical cutbacks, many newspapers had lost their community watchdog function, no longer bothering with the expensive and time-consuming work of investigative reporting. A 2005 survey by Arizona State University of the 100 largest U.S. dailies found that 37 percent had no full-time investigative reporters, and the majority of the major dailies had two or fewer."

From Katharine Mieszkowski, "Spare Change for News," Salon.com, April 13, 2009, http://www.salon.com/news/feature/2009/04/13/nonprofit_journalism/index.html, accessed April 13, 2009.

16 I owe this observation about celebrity news to sociologist Karen Sternheimer. In asking her in the spring of 2010 about her book on celebrities and the news, *Celebrity Culture and the American Dream: Stardom and Social Mobility*, I discovered that her assessment of the tremendous growth of celebrity news paralleled my own observations about media's increased attention to crime stories.

Media and How It Corrupts Democracy, the radical right recognized early on that in order to turn the tide of public opinion in their favor—they were taking it on the chin during the 1960s era—they needed to first eliminate the Fairness Doctrine in order to build their media empire. The Fairness Doctrine was a Federal Communications Commission (FCC) policy introduced in 1949 that dealt with controversial issues. It sought to ensure that licensed broadcasters presented contested issues of public importance and gave equitable and honest coverage to those issues. Through the deep pockets of radical right-wing interests, the Fairness Doctrine was eliminated in 1987, opening the door to the self-referential world of right-wing media where truth and falsehoods live indistinguishably side by side, with falsehoods overshadowing the truth by far. The phenomenon of millions of listeners believing absurdities (the Birthers' claims about the place of Obama's birth or the speculation by some that Obama is a socialist and/or Muslim) are emblematic of the power of a large media universe that does not have to provide viewpoints opposing its own on the air.

In the 2000 Presidential race, when the major TV networks retracted their earlier and correct projection that Florida was going to Gore, thus making him President, Bush's cousin John Ellis, who was brought into Fox's studios to act as the head of their "decision desk," called Florida for Bush. Jack Welch, head of NBC/GE, who was in the NBC studios while this unfolded, asked the NBC elections desk chief why NBC was not also calling Florida for Bush. NBC listened to their boss and put Florida in Bush's column; they later retracted it, but they had nevertheless helped to set into motion the impression that Bush was the winner and that Gore's subsequent insistence that all the votes be counted were the actions of a sore loser.[17] The rest of the major networks then followed suit, again without any new data about the actual vote count.[18] As David Podvin and Carolyn Kay describe it:

---

17   See Robert Parry, "Price of the 'Liberal Media' Myth," ConsortiumNews.com, January 1, 2003, http://www.consortiumnews.com/Print/123102a.html, accessed January 5, 2009.

See also Dan Kennedy, "Jack Welch's Journalistic values (II)," *Media Nation* (blog), October 28, 2006, http://www.dankennedy.net/2006/10/, accessed February 11, 2009.

18   Michael I. Niman, "Bush Cousin Calls Presidential Election," *Buffalo Beat*, MediaStudy.com, December 14, 2000, http://www.mediastudy.com/articles/jellis.html, accessed May 23, 2009.

Shortly after George W. Bush declared his candidacy for president in June of 1999, General Electric Chairman and Chief Executive Officer Jack Welch was contacted by Bush political advisor Karl Rove. Welch later informed associates that Rove told him a Bush administration would initiate comprehensive deregulation of the broadcast industry. Rove guaranteed that deregulation would be implemented in a way that would create phenomenal profits for conglomerates with significant media holdings, like GE. Rove forcefully argued that General Electric and the other media giants had a compelling financial interest to see Bush become president.

Welch told several people at GE that the conversation with Rove convinced him that a Bush presidency would ultimately result in billions of dollars of additional profits for General Electric. Welch believed that it was his responsibility to operate in the best interest of GE shareholders, and that now meant using the full power of the world's biggest corporation to get Bush into the White House.

Toward that end, Welch said that he would finally deal with a longstanding grievance of his: the ludicrous idea that news organizations should be allowed to operate in conflict with the best interests of the corporations that own them.

Since the beginning of the country, it has been considered appropriate for the business community to exercise its right to aggressively support the candidate that best represented its interests. The new dimension that Welch introduced was the concept that the mainstream media should aggressively advance the political agenda of the corporations that own it. He did not see any difference between corporate journalism and corporate manufacturing or corporate service industries. Business was business, and the difference between winners and losers was profit, whether you were selling nuclear power or ads on the network news. From Welch's perspective, it was insanity, not to mention bad business practice, for the corporate owners of the mainstream media to restrain themselves from using all of their assets to promote their financial well being.

In general, he saw corporate news organizations as untapped political resources that should be freed from the burden of objectivity.

Specifically, NBC News was an asset owned by the shareholders of General Electric. It existed to make profits and to serve the interests of those who owned GE stock. Period.

Anything else, Welch told associates, was "liberal bullshit."

In 1988, NBC News president Lawrence Grossman insisted to Welch that news was a public trust and should not be subjected to the same pressure to make profits that was applied to other GE units. Welch fired him.

In 1999, the GE chairman decided that it was no longer good enough for NBC News to just be profitable. Seven years of a frequently uncooperative Democratic Administration, combined with the Rove-inspired vision of spectacular profits through deregulation, now motivated Welch to take action.

He began to aggressively, but very discreetly, evangelize the gospel of corporate media as corporate lobbying tool. It was not a new concept; in the opinion of many, it was already the status quo. But from Welch's point of view, the corporate news organizations were not living up to their potential.

The mainstream media could make George W. Bush president.

That would be good for Americans who believed in free markets and the merit system, Welch said[19]

In 2004, in a story that parallels the NBC/Jack Welch tale, Viacom chief Sumner Redstone explained how his corporate identity trumped his personal politics. From *The Asian Wall Street Journal*, September 24, 2004, "Guess Who's a Bush Booster? The CEO of CBS's Parent Company Endorses Bush":

Sumner Redstone, who calls himself a "liberal Democrat," said he's supporting President Bush.

The chairman of the entertainment giant Viacom said the reason was simple: Republican values are what U.S. companies need. Speaking to some of America's and Asia's top executives gathered for Forbes magazine's annual Global CEO Conference, Mr. Redstone declared: "I look at the election from what's good for Viacom. I vote for what's good for Viacom. I vote, today, Viacom."

"I don't want to denigrate Kerry," he went on, "but from a Viacom standpoint, the election of a Republican administration is a better deal. Because the Republican administration has stood for many things we believe in, deregulation and so on. The Democrats are not bad people. . . . But from a Viacom standpoint, we believe the election of a Republican administration is better for our company."

---

19   David Podvin and Carolyn Kay, "Media Coverup Part IV," MakeThemAccountable. com, December 31, 2009, http://makethemaccountable.com/coverup/Part_04.htm, accessed January 3, 2010. A source for the Podvin and Kay article is a former GE media executive who wishes to remain anonymous.

Sharing the stage with Mr. Redstone was Steve Forbes, CEO, president and editor in chief of Forbes and a former Republican presidential aspirant, who quipped: "Obviously you're a very enlightened CEO."[20]

Mirrors to the Public?

The common wisdom about media's relationship to the polity holds that media wholly—or at least largely—mirror public sentiment. The people, we are often told, want sensationalism—the more blood and gore the better! They want to be entertained and/or scared: thrills and chills! "Give the people what they want," and "If it bleeds, it leads," are two frequently employed dictums, in the news business especially, asserting this accepted truth. "No one ever went broke underestimating the intelligence of the American people," circus magnate P. T. Barnum once famously said. If the media are reprehensible, narrow, or philistine, blame the people.

I have heard comments such as the following more times than I can remember: Americans care more about *American Idol* than they do about foreign or even domestic policy. Apathy, complacency, and cynicism rule. The people are either responsible for the commission of war crimes such as torture and illegal invasions of countries that did not threaten us because they voted for Bush, or they are responsible for tolerating it all because they failed to rise up in sufficient numbers and determination to put an end to it. In either case, it's the people's fault. The media may have misrepresented the facts about WMD and so on, but if they did, this is only because they are telling the people what the people want to hear.

What a fine mess of a country we must be if this is so!

What *is* the relationship between the media and the people and what is the nature of media itself?

To state the argument most directly: the accepted wisdom about media and the polity, while containing partial truths, is fundamentally wrong, especially—and increasingly so—in the midst and context of neoliberalism's ascent.

---

20   This article is no longer available on the *Wall Street Journal*'s website. A copy and paste version of the entire article, however, can be found at GamingForums.com, http://igamingforums.com/iGaming/ViacomSetsRecordStraight/dnqjn/post.htm, accessed February 19, 2011.

Isn't It All About Audience Share?

While it is obviously true that no media outlet could afford to stay in business if it was not appealing to its audience enough to draw their attention away from competing sources for news and/or entertainment while also holding that attention enough to convince its advertisers to continue their financial underwriting (or subscribers to continue subscribing, in the case of publicly-supported outlets such as National Public Radio), the media do not operate in as simple-minded a fashion as the common wisdom asserts.

"Give the people what they want" would be closer to the truth if it read: "Give the people what they want from among the options that we are willing and able to offer them." The people are not dictating what is offered to them. They are choosing from among preselected choices. Those preselected choices are determined by the owners of media operating with a careful eye to the corporate world and to the strictures of the government and the society's dominant ideology.

Media's most important audience is not its readers/viewers. Their most important audience is actually their advertisers (or underwriters). They do not make most of their money from subscribers or viewers/listeners; they make most of their money from ads/underwriters. Mainstream media outlets attract advertisers and can charge higher rates by demonstrating that they have the desired audience, which is not necessarily the largest audience numerically. There are instances, of course, of smash hit shows such as *Friends* or *Seinfeld* that draw very large Nielsen ratings and permit the networks to charge more for ads. But the overall direction of television, and the media more generally, is towards the bottom line of profitability and towards niche marketing. Investment in network television has moved decisively away from sitcoms and towards reality-show programming mainly because a sitcom requires an ensemble cast and much, much higher costs than a reality show.

The time when there were just a few, well-known and heavily read magazines such as *Life* and *Look* is gone. In their place we now see an explosion of magazines (and of cable stations) targeting special interest or specific-demographic audiences. As Joel Kramer (CEO and editor of *MinnPost*, and former editor, publisher, and president of the *Minneapolis Star Tribune*) put it in 2009: "The pricing power of publishers for advertising is dramatically deteriorated. That is the core issue [behind the demise of many newspapers and the threat to the rest], not whether readers love the stuff."[21]

If advertisers are media's main audience, then media are most beholden and influenced by advertiser's desires and outlooks, along with the outlooks and desires of the media outlet's owner(s). (I speak here of major media players, not the far smaller media outlets that are not as subject to these pressures from advertisers.)

What matters most for media outlets *with respect to their audiences* is what segment of the public is being reached. In many instances the more affluent the audience the better. In other instances the target audience has a special perspective or interest; for example, it may represent a chunk of a particular part of the political spectrum. Right-wing radio's core audience, for instance, consists largely of right-wing listeners—with a healthy helping of people who are not self-consciously political but who are drawn to Rush Limbaugh and others like him because they find them entertaining, newsworthy, and so on, and also because the offerings of radio are so heavily weighted to the right-wing. The skewing of newspaper and magazine coverage to appeal to upscale readers reflects the desire of their advertisers to appeal to those with bigger wallets; the more this segment spends, the better.

To underscore media's power over public opinion and public policy making, I now turn to a case study media's role in creating the notion of a crime wave in the US in the early 1990s.

The 1990s' "Crime Wave"

When we attempt to track how various public issues are prioritized by public policy, we are fundamentally tracing how political power is exercised. Because social problems demand a large share of public resources, retracing the process by which an issue reaches "social problem" status constitutes an important task for any who want to understand how public policy is made. Within the realm of sociology, the sub-discipline most directly concerned with this is called "social problems." Social problems theories, and in particular social constructionism,[22] which is the dominant

---

21 Katherine Mieszkowski, "Spare Change for News," Salon.com, April 13, 2009, http://www.salon.com/news/feature/2009/04/13/nonprofit_journalism/index.html, accessed April 16, 2009.

22 See, for example, Malcolm Spector and John I. Kitsuse, "Social Problems," *Social Problems* 21 (1973): 145-159; Joel Best, *Threatened Children: Rhetoric and Concern*

theory within social problems, tend to treat media coverage of social issues as generally originating from mid-range advocacy groups. Mid-range advocacy groups sit halfway between the grassroots and public officials/media. An example of a mid-range advocacy group would be Mothers Against Drunk Driving. In trying to account for why one issue becomes a social problem (and thus is given resources) and another does not, Lowney and Best[23] assert that one issue wins out over another in the social problems game due to three factors: (a) the *drama* of the claim pressed by claims-makers, (b) the extent of *resources* mobilized on the claims' behalf, and (c) the degree to which the claim *resonates with cultural themes.*[24] A claims-maker is anyone or any group that makes a claim that their issue should receive attention and resources to be remedied.

The Lowney-Best schema cannot, however, fully account for one social problem's ranking over another. This is because first, the social issue that ultimately predominates in the social problems contest does not necessarily constitute the most dramatically presented problem.[25] Second, resources mobilized by claims-makers may not always decide the issue; instead, media and/or public officials may decide unilaterally to pay more attention to an issue. Finally, any number of claims might resonate with cultural themes. The victorious social issue does not necessarily resonate any more powerfully with cultural themes than the also-rans.

Lowney/Best underplay the active role media play in selecting an issue for social problem status. They do not take into account the fact that media do not simply legitimate the claims-makers who "make the best case" to them. Legitimating an issue and giving it recognition as a social problem constitute as active and decisive a step in the social problems

---

about Child-Victims (Chicago: University of Chicago Press, 1990); Ray Surette, "News from Nowhere, Policy to Follow: Media and the Social Construction of 'Three Strikes and You're Out,'" in *Three Strikes and You're Out: Vengeance as Public Policy*, ed. David Schichor and Dale Sechrest (Thousand Oaks, CA: Sage, 1996), 177-202.

23 Kathleen Lowney and Joel Best, "Stalking Strangers and Lovers: Changing Media Typifications of a New Crime Problem," in *Images of Issues: Typifying Contemporary Social Problems*, 2nd edition, ed. Joel Best (Hawthorne, NY: Aldine de Gruyter, 1995).

24 Lowney and Best also note the role of contingency in the emergence of a social problem. For example, the drug-induced death of basketball player Len Bias played a contingent role in the launching of the crack scare.

25 That is, as presented to media outlets. Media outlets do not merely choose from among contestant issues, selecting the most dramatic one from the group. Media themselves take an active part in *shaping* the frames within which issues are presented.

game as any other. Furthermore, media themselves play an active, often predominant, role in deciding which story or issue frame will hold sway. For an issue to achieve social problem status, it must, of course, resonate with some dimension of popular experience or sentiment. But resonance is not the same thing as initiative. Diverse story frames may resonate with themes manifest within popular culture.[26] A specific story frame is consequently not inevitable.

While social constructionists' accounts of specific social problems commonly emphasize the manner in which media exaggerate the significance of an issue, media's impact is nonetheless viewed in these accounts as secondary to that of other claims-makers. Thus, a lacuna (a gap or hole) within social problems theory exists because social problems theory treats media inaccurately as passive actors.[27]

In August 1993, US news outlets began running stories about a so-called crime wave. By 1994, coverage of this alleged crime wave occupied center stage across all major media outlets. Polls recorded an unprecedented proportion of Americans citing crime as their choice for the country's number one problem. However, the index crime rate during this period was actually falling; understanding how this phenomenon came about, therefore, offers an important insight into how the media can affect social opinion and influence social policy.

Tracing the precise role of various protagonists (media, advocacy groups, mass sentiment, political officials, and so on) in a social problem's evolution has been done infrequently, in part because it presents difficult methodological problems.[28] The failure to satisfactorily resolve those methodological problems has severely limited the advance of social problems theory and media effects studies regarding the analysis of social problems. Furthermore, the implicit and unexamined ideological assumption within classic social constructionism of pluralism precludes the recognition that, at times at least, media can act as initiator of social

---

26 Katherine Beckett, "The Politics of Law and Order: the State and the Wars Against Crime and Drugs, 1964 to the Present" (PhD diss., University of California at Los Angeles, 1994).

27 See Appendix 3 for material that I have removed from this chapter that would have begun in this section. The material in the appendix focuses on methodological issues that are of the most interest to scholars and not as interesting to the general reader.

28 Vincent Price, *Public Opinion* (Newbury Park, CA: Sage, 1992).

problems.[29] If, as in this case study of the 1993-94 crime wave, record levels of public monies are devoted to the criminal justice system in the name of public demand, then a demonstration that that public demand was manipulated challenges the validity of those public expenditures.

Several observers of journalistic practices (Cohen;[30] Gans;[31] Fishman[32]), as well as professional journalists themselves (e.g., Steffens;[33] Winerip[34]), have noted that journalists regularly decide what is "newsworthy" by monitoring what stories competing media are covering. Fishman[35] notably observed first-hand that New York newspapers were fueling a fictive crime wave against the elderly as they vied with one another to come up with more crimes-against-the-elderly incidents. The newspapers did this even though they knew that, according to police statistics, crimes against the elderly were actually in decline. The story was just too "juicy" to pass up (Fishman[36]).

The drive to avoid being scooped by competing news organizations operated in the 1990s (and since) more intensely than in previous decades. John Kueneke, Pulitzer Corporation Vice-President, made this point explicitly. Asked why media companies do not carry more reasoned and less sensationalistic local news broadcasts, Kueneke stated: "We're a publicly-owned company and we have to pay attention to *what our peers do* and *what analysts on Wall Street expect.*"[37] [Emphasis added.] In other

---

29 Beckett, "Politics of Law and Order," and Katherine Beckett, "Culture and the Politics of Signification: The Case of Child Sexual Abuse," *Social Problems* 43, no. 1 (February, 1996), 57-76.

30 Bernard C. Cohen, *The Press and Foreign Policy* (Princeton: Princeton University Press, 1963).

31 Herbert J. Gans, *Deciding What's News: A Study of CBS Evening News, NBC Nightly News, Newsweek and Time* (New York: Pantheon, 1979).

32 Mark Fishman, *Manufacturing the News* (Austin: University of Texas Press, 1980).

33 Lincoln Steffens, *The Autobiography of Lincoln Steffens* (New York: Harcourt Brace & Co., 1931).

34 Michael Winerip, "Looking for an 11 0'Clock Fix," *The New York Times Magazine,* January 11, 1998.

35 Mark Fishman, "Crime Waves as Ideology," *Social Problems,* 25 (1978): 531-543. Fishman, 1980.

36 Fishman, 1978.

37 Winerip, 1998, 40.

words, news organizations monitor and compete against other media outlets' coverage, and must pay attention to finance capital's dictates. For today's media organizations, media "peers" range from tabloids, to the Internet, to more respected publications such as *The New York Times*. In today's twenty-four-hour news cycle, unlike in the past when the number of news media outlets was smaller and *The New York Times* and, to a lesser degree CBS news, were the litmus tests for newsworthiness, it no longer matters what media credentials—or audience share—the original story-breaker possessed.

The 1990s' Crime Alarms

In a January 28-30, 1994, national Gallup poll, forty-nine percent of respondents cited "crime" in the "most important problem" (MIP). This forty-nine-percent reading capped an unprecedented escalation in poll-measured crime concerns—a rise of forty-three points over the span of four months. This represented the first spike in crime concerns since 1977. See Table 1.

Table 1: Crime in Most Important Problem Poll 1962-95

Survey Date	JD, teen probs	Survey Date	C+ JD	Survey Date	Crime +JD	Survey Date	C + JD
4/6-11/62	2%	9/25-28/70	5%	10/27-30/78	2%	11/11-14/93	21%
6/28—7/23/62	2	10/9-14/70	7	2/23-26/79	3	12/2-5/93	25
8/23-28/62	2	2/19-22/71	4	5/4-7/79	2	12/4-7/93	30
	C + JD	6/4-7/71	4	8/10-13/79	3	12/5-7/93	15
1963	0	8/27-30/71	4	10/12-15/79	2	12/13-14/93	22
3/27-4/2/64	1	11/19-22/71	5	1/25-28/80	1	1/3-5/94	22
4/24-29/64	2	2/4-7/72	5	11/7-10/80	4 (C + Vio)	1/15-17/94	28
6/25-30/64	1	4/28-5/1/72	5	1/30-2/2/81	2 (Crime)	1/15-17/94	19

7/23-28/64	<.5	6/16-19/72	3	10/2-5/81	5	1/15-19/94	25
8/6-11/64	1	7/14-17/72	6	4/2-5/82	3	1/20-23/94	31
8/27-9/1/64	1	9/22-25/72	6	7/22-25/83	2	1/28-30/94	49
9/18-23/64	1	10/13-16/72	5	8/10-13/84	4	2/15-17/94	27
10/8-13/64	2	1/12-15/73	5	5/85	4	2/24-27/94	31
3/18-23/65	2	2/16-19/73	6	7/11-14/86	3	3/16-21/94	32
5/13-18/65	3	5/4-7/73	5	4/10-13/87	3	4/16-19/94	34
9/16-21/65	5	5/11-14/73	2	9/9-11/88	0	4/21-23/94	24
11/18-23/65	2	9/7-10/73	4	4/5-8/90	2	6/23-26/94	17
1/26-31/67	2	5/21-6/3/74	4	7/19-22/90	1	7/12-25/94	26
8/3-8/67	2	8/16-19/74	2	11/1-4/90	2	7/14-17/94	19
10/27-11/1/67	4	9/27-30/74	4	1/30-2/2/91	0	7/15-17/94	21
1/4-9/68	6	10/11-14/74	3	4/25-28/91	0	7/23-26/94	24
5/2-7/68	15*	2/28-3/3/75	5	9/5-8/91	4	8/1-3/94	24
6/26-7/1/68	29*	7/18-21/75	5	3/26-29/92	5	8/8-9/94	24
7/18-23/68	11	10/17-20/75	4	1/8-11/93	3	8/15-16/94	52
8/7-12/68	9	1/2-5/76	8	1/12-14/93	3	8/16-17/94	28
9/1/68	12	10/8-11/76	5	4/1-4/93	5	9/6-9/94	33
9/26-10/1/68	11	3/18-21/77	15	5/18-24/93	7	9/8-11/94	26
10/17-22/68	12	7/22-25/77	6	6/12-14/93	6	10/16-18/94	20
1/1-6/69	6	10/21-24/77	6	9/9-15/93	15	10/22-24/94	27
1/15-20/70	5	2/10-13/78	4	9/10-12/93	16	1/16-18/95	19
5/21-26/70	8	4/14-17/78	0	9/16-19/93	10	C/Gangs/CJS	
7/31-8/2/70	3	7/7-10/78	3	9/25-28/93	6	4/6-9/95	23

*Composite figures for crime plus other items: "Crime and Lawlessness (including riots, arson and juvenile delinquency)." Source: Roper Center—Certain percentages vary on the same date due to different polling organizations' results. (JD = Juvenile Delinquency. C = Crime. Vio = Violence).

Remarkable as these polls were, the polling data of 1993-94 have escaped scrutiny in journalistic accounts. Why? The assumption that crime concerns have frequently dominated the polls is so prevalent as to constitute accepted wisdom. Contrary to this notion, however, "crime" has not commonly been an uppermost concern in the polls. Indeed, an examination of the MIP poll record, from its inception in 1935 through 1995, shows that until late 1993, "crime" had never even approached being the number one problem cited. The prior high for "crime" before late 1993 was only fifteen percent reached in one poll in 1977.

Prior to 1993, "crime" averaged in the low single digits (see Table 1). The two time periods in which "crime" is commonly believed to have been especially high are the 1960s and the 1980s-90s. Close examination of the record belies that belief. In four polls in 1968 Gallup combined a number of disparate items and reported them in a larger category: "Crime and lawlessness." When disaggregated, "crime" and "juvenile delinquency" together registered no higher than twelve percent. If one assumes that during the 1980s "drug abuse" acted as a surrogate for "crime," it should be noted that only in 1989 and part of 1990 did the "drug abuse" category draw significant responses. In 1989, three percent of respondents cited "crime" as their choice for number one problem, while twenty-seven percent chose "drug abuse." "Drug abuse" drew thirty percent in an April 1990 poll, and then dropped by November 1990 to eight percent. "Crime" fluctuated between one and two percent in the same time frame.

The belief that crime has frequently topped the polls probably accounts for the absence so far of any social constructionist analyses of the 1993-94 poll data. Yet the rapid and sudden escalation of poll-measured crime concerns in that period bears all the indicators of a classic moral panic: (1) a folk devil (a specific deviant such as a criminal); (2) a disproportionate level of concern; and (3) huge fluctuations in the degree of concern from one period to another.[38] What spurred this alarm over crime?

Conventional Explanations

One of the most frequently cited explanations for heightened public attention to crime holds that the public was or is in an especially punitive

---

38   Erich Goode and Nachman Ben Yehuda, *Moral Panics: The Social Construction of Deviance* (Cambridge, Massachusetts: Blackwell, 1994), 103.

mood, either because of a generalized public anxiety extraneous to crime[39] or because of putative increases in criminal incidence and prevalence.[40]

These explanations, however, do not explain satisfactorily the events of 1993-94 because they cannot account for the late 1993-94 polls' extreme and time-delimited pattern as depicted in Table 1. If crime concerns can be explained by generalized anxiety, then the polls should not display such extreme volatility.

The data do not support the changes in crime rates explanation either, since prior to January 1994's forty-nine percent poll reading, overall index crime rates had been *falling*. In 1993 and 1994, street crime dropped slightly by any standard measure, either the Uniform Crime Reports (UCR) or the National Crime Victimization Survey. Between 1973 and the mid-1990s, robbery dropped seventeen percent, forcible rape fell thirty percent, and murder remained stable.[41] Thus, at precisely the time that crime concerns rocketed upward, index crime rates were falling.

One subcategory of index crimes, however, did rise between 1985 and 1993—juvenile homicide. Some observers explain the exceptional levels of crime concerns registered in the 1990s' polls on those grounds. Juvenile homicides fell from 1980 until the mid-1980s at which time they began a steep rise. In 1992, 2,428 minors were killed in index crimes. In 1993, 2,697 were killed. This represented an increase of 11 percent between 1992 and 1993 (or a total of 167 more victims). There does not seem to be any doubt that the growth of child murders and child murderers, or "kids killing kids," between 1985 and 1993 was a significant factor in 1990s' crime worries.

As displayed in Figure 1, however, juvenile homicides had been rising at alarming rates for seven years before polls registered a change in public concern about crime. At the point where polls took off, juvenile homicides had actually stopped rising, and had begun to fall a bit.

39 Edward Luttwak, "The Middle-Class Backlash," *Harper's*, January 1996. Stuart Scheingold, "Politics, Public Policy and Street Crime," *Annals of the American Academy of Politics and Public Policy*, Vol. 539 (1995): 155-168.

40 Richard Niemi, John Mueller and Tom W. Smith, *Trends in Public Opinion: A Compendium of Survey Data* (New York: Greenwood Press, 1998).

41 Stephen Donziger, ed., *The Real War on Crime* (New York: Harper Collins, 1996), 65-66.

Fig. 1: Homicides 18 y.o. and under v. Percent Naming Crime in MIP poll

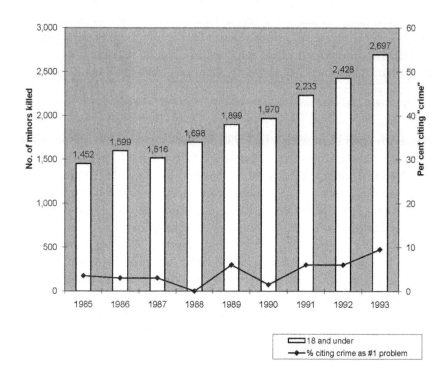

The fact that more and more juveniles were dying violently was evidently not by itself enough to spike the polls. If juvenile homicides do not account for the crime alarm, then what can?

Could a few spectacular incidents have fueled crime fears? The most spectacularly publicized incidents of 1993, the kidnapping and murder of Polly Klaas in California and the Long Island Commuter Railroad killings by Colin Ferguson were reported in December of 1993, prior to the peak recording of crime concerns in January 1994. But these crimes occurred after the dramatic rise in poll-measured crime concerns was already underway beginning in September 1993 and continuing through the end of 1993 and into 1994. Thus, while it seems very probable that the Klaas and Ferguson cases played a role in the forty-nine percent reading in January 1994, they do not help to explain the early stages of the crime scare in the fall of 1993.

Further, crime rates continued to fall throughout 1994. Subsequent to the Ferguson shootings in December of 1993, no criminal incidents of comparable magnitude, nature, or attention marked the months of

January through September 1994. (Nicole Brown Simpson and Ron Goldman were murdered on June 12, 1994, but this case was not treated, nor was it perceived by the public, in the same manner as a "random" killing.)

Could it be that crime perceived as a social problem rose so high in 1994 because of the end of the Cold War and the absence of an international conflict? Undoubtedly the MIP poll has in the past been and will in the future be affected by international events. Public concern with international events had historically been fairly low in the MIP polls up through the mid-1990s, with the clearest exception being the Vietnam War up to that point. Moreover, the 1990-1991 Gulf War launched by George H. W. Bush had been over for nearly two years before crime showed a sudden increase of concern in the MIP poll. Hence, contrary to conventional wisdom, the crime issue's emergence at the top of the polls in late 1993-94 cannot simply be attributed to the Cold War's end.

What, then, was happening in the period before and during the ratcheting up of crime concerns at the end of 1993-94? A review of news media in that time period reveals a crime news coverage wave of exceptional proportions across major news outlets, initiated by the newsmagazines and not by the activities and influence of any mid-range advocacy groups. Politicians and various public officials assumed significant secondary roles in this news coverage wave; as analyzed later on in this chapter, their pronouncements, particularly in August 1994, received substantial news media attention. Taken as a whole, this media-driven coverage wave preceded the changes in poll-measured crime concerns.

Turning Point: August 1993

A turning point in media coverage of crime came in August 1993 when the three major newsmagazines ran a total of four crime cover stories. All three newsmagazines simultaneously opened the month with crime covers. *Newsweek*'s August 2, 1993, cover was entitled "Teen Violence: WILD IN THE STREETS." The sub-headline (kicker) read: "Murder and mayhem, guns and gangs: a teenage generation grows up dangerous—and scared." *Newsweek* cited law enforcement and public health officials who reportedly described "a virtual 'epidemic' of youth violence in the last five years, spreading from the inner cities to the suburbs."

On the same day, *Time*'s cover also raised the youth and guns issue: "Big Shots: Guns. An inside look at the deadly love affair between kids and their guns." Finally, *US News and World Report*'s August 2, 1993, cover was entitled: "Super cops: Can they solve America's crime problem? The FBI's tough new chief [with a picture of LAPD's new chief Willie Williams]."

Then, in its August 23, 1993 issue, *Time* followed up with a dramatic cover story: "AMERICA THE VIOLENT: Crime is spreading and patience is running out." The cover graphic featured a menacing figure done in collage style, wearing stereotypical gang attire. The cover story featured Clinton's crime bill and began:

> President Clinton could not have known, of course, that the week he picked to talk about crime would be the week crime was what everyone was talking about. On Tuesday, there was the man in fatigues who shot up a McDonald's in Kenosha, Wisconsin. The same day in Kansas City, Missouri, a 15 year-old went to the movies with his mother—and shot her as they watched the film. 'I don't know why I did it,' he said. On Thursday in Burlingame, California, a man walked into a real estate office, shot one broker and wounded another before trying to kill himself. He had just been evicted from his home.

The next paragraph in the story noted the murder of Michael Jordan's father, James Jordan.

Mark Fishman discusses this thematic style of reporting—taking disparate incidents and pulling them together to create the appearance of a trend.[42] In this case, none of these incidents involved a gang member, despite the fact that a gang member was portrayed on the cover. What the incidents did have in common, however, was that they all occurred in places commonly considered safe—places frequented by the middle class: McDonald's, the mall, and a professional office. The story of the fifteen year old who shot his mother at the movies pushed a number of powerful emotional buttons. These acts were depicted as random, senseless, rising, and expanding in their targets. Certain central themes and narrative structures rather than incidents themselves played the key role in crime news during this crime coverage wave. As Joel Best put it, speaking more generally about contemporary crime coverage:

> Random violence is a central image in the construction of contemporary crime problems. This imagery ignores the patterns in criminal activity, implies collapse in the social order, and denies rational

---

42 Fishman, 1978.

motives for criminals. These images are consequential; they promote intense public concern while fostering punitive social policies.[43]

These themes were very clear in the August 23, 1993 *Time* issue. One of the accompanying stories in the issue was headlined: "DANGER IN THE SAFETY ZONE: As violence spreads into small towns, many Americans barricade themselves." The theme sounded here was that urban crimes were now invading the previously safe sanctum of the suburbs and small town America: "The broadening of targets to include suburban and rural preserves—and the savageness of the crimes that fill the news—has left far more Americans feeling vulnerable." However, index crimes in the suburbs and rural areas did not increase in the 1990s. This story derived its punch from the perception that small towns and the suburbs were previously safe from crime and were only now being invaded by the type of crime seen in the inner city. This perception was contradicted by crime statistics. In 1994, suburban murders were actually down by two percent as compared to 1993, and rural murders were down by ten percent over the same time period.

Crime Cover Stories in the Newsmagazines

This attention to crime on the covers of newsmagazines in the 1990s, particularly in 1993 and 1994, was unprecedented. By way of comparison, throughout the whole of the 1960s (1960-1969), there was only one cover story devoted to crime among all three newsmagazines. In the decade of the 1970s, there were a total of eight crime cover stories among the news-magazines. In the 1980s there were also only eight crime cover stories. In 1990 there was one crime cover. In 1991 there was one. In 1992 there were four crime covers. In 1993 there were eleven crime cover stories, with nine of them concentrated between August 1993 and December 1993. And in 1994, there were sixteen crime cover stories (three of them in January 1994). Thus between the years 1960-69, a cumulative total of 0.0006 percent of the three newsmagazines' covers were devoted to crime compared to eleven percent of their covers in 1994 alone. Clearly, in the 1990s, and especially beginning in 1992, crime became a hot topic for newsmagazine cover stories.[44]

---

43 Joel Best, "Random Violence in the Construction of Contemporary Crime Problems," paper (not presented) at the American Society of Criminology's Annual Meeting, Chicago, November 1996.

44 What if I had counted the number of covers during the 1960s that were about social disorder? Would this have made the contrast between the amount of attention given

Changes in Newspaper Crime Coverage

The dramatic August 1993 newsmagazine cover stories did not go un-noticed. Two major events followed. First, public opinion polls registered the first spike in crime concerns since 1977. The numbers citing crime more than doubled from the June 1993 figure of six percent to fifteen or sixteen percent in September 1993, the month immediately following the four newsmagazines' crime cover issues (MIP polls were not taken in August 1993). Second, after the newsmagazines' August coverage spike, both newspapers and TV followed beginning in October 1993. Newspaper stories on the crime issue in the four papers examined leapt upward some 250 percent in one month, going from twenty-one stories in August 1993 and twenty-two stories in September 1993 to fifty-five stories in October 1993. Then in November, newspaper coverage rose still further to seventy-one stories and stayed high through the next year, peaking at 202 stories in August 1994, an increase of over 900 percent compared to September 1993's crime news. See Figure 2.

---

to the crime issue by newsmagazines in the 1990s as compared to the 1960s less dra-matic? Yes, a bit, but with a very important caveat. The issue of crime in the 1960s had a different character than had the same issue in the 1990s. That is, "crime in the streets" was a contested matter in the 1960s in which the liberals (e.g., most no-tably President Lyndon Johnson and members of his cabinet such as Vice-President Humphrey and Attorney General Ramsey Clark) attacked the conservatives (e.g., notably, Barry Goldwater, Richard Nixon and Spiro Agnew) on the express grounds that those touting "law and order" were using crime as a code word for race. This debate at the highest levels was also seen in the streets where the social movements of the day argued that civil rights was the key issue. In this view, crime was, by com-parison, at best a secondary issue, and at worst a red herring. The media coverage at that time reflects that debate, and as a result the street crime issue did not attain the levels of attention in the polls or in the media that it did in the 1990s. There is, unfortunately, not room here to fully pursue these points.

**Fig. 2: Newspaper Crime Stories 1/92-1/95
(LA Times, NY Times, Wall SJ & Wash Post)**

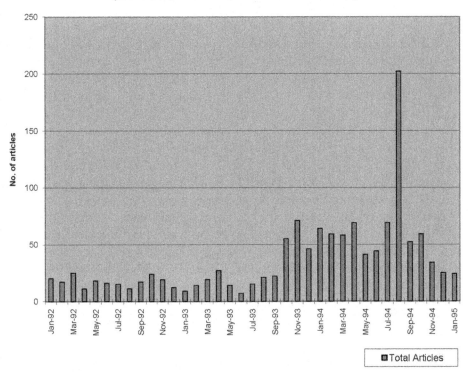

Crimes Stories in Newsmagazines After October 1993

On November 8, 1993, *US News and World Report*'s cover story was en-titled: "Guns in the Schools: WHEN KILLERS COME TO CLASS. Even suburban parents now fear the rising tide of violence." In their next is-sue, November 15, 1993, *US News & World Report* stated: "The voters' cry for help: Clinton, governors and mayors try to respond to the wave of crime fear gripping Americans." The article asserted "Fear of crime has become the most urgent issue in the country." *Newsweek*'s November 29, 1993 cover featured rapper Snoop Doggy Dog. The cover read: "When is rap 2 violent? His album hit the top of the charts this week. Last week, he was indicted for murder."

Time's December 20, 1993 cover featured a handgun with Colin Fer-guson's eye staring back through the trigger hole. The headline encapsu-lated the thrust of media's crime news coverage with the big bold letters:

"ENOUGH! The massacre on a suburban New York train escalates the war on handguns. Colin Ferguson, who shot 23 people, killing five, on the 5:33 train from Penn Station to Hicksville, Long Island."

Newsweek's January 10, 1994 cover reiterated the children, guns, and violence theme: "Growing Up Scared: How our kids are robbed of their childhood." The headline kicker read: "Guns for Toys: the new anti-crime crusade." Then on January 17, 1994, both *Newsweek* and *US News and World Report* ran crime covers. *Newsweek's* had a close-up of the agonized face of ice skater Nancy Kerrigan: "First Monica Seles, Now Nancy Kerrigan: 'WHY ME?' The new fear of stalking."

US News and World Report's cover marked a kind of high point in newsmagazines' crime covers: "The Truth About VIOLENT CRIME: [in red:] What You Really Have To Fear." The cover graphic was of a bullet-ridden windshield seen from the driver's perspective. This article and accompanying pieces totaling fifteen full pages were the archetype of this genre of reporting. The articles were rife with contradictions sitting beside each other, and were deliberately alarmist in tone. "The drumbeat of news coverage has made it seem that America is in the midst of the worst epidemic of violence ever. That sense is not supported by the numbers. The latest evidence is that crime levels actually fell last year. But that does not mean that last year wasn't the scariest in American history." It thus began with an acknowledgment of media's role, and followed by stating that the data did not support widespread crime fears. Then it immediately contradicted itself by asserting that the previous year was the "scariest in American history" because "[o]verriding the statistics is the chilling realization that the big crime stories of recent months have invaded virtually every sanctuary where Americans thought they were safe: their cars (James Jordan's murder); their public transit (the Long Island Rail Road murders); even their bedrooms (the kidnap and murder of young Polly Klaas in Petaluma, Calif.)." Inasmuch as some forty thousand people die annually in auto accidents, compared to some twenty thousand or so who die from street crimes (during the 1990s),[45] the car does not actually seem that safe. And for children and women especially, their home is the least safe place of all.

The article went on to point out that random killings such as those in the Long Island Rail Road massacre and post office shootings were not increasing sharply. Cases where four or more people were killed in a single incident varied from 10 to 30 ten to thirty victims annually between 1976 and 1991. Criminologist James Fox was quoted as stating that "[m]

---

45   Homicide rates have been falling in the US since the early 1990s.

ost mass murderers do not kill at random in public places." Further, it was noted that mass killings at workplaces were relatively rare and "'hardly at epidemic proportions.'" The authors noted that child-snatching incidents in 1993 would probably come in at the low end of the average. Finally, they stated: "Family strife. This is one problem that does not get the attention it deserves. There are eight hundred thousand 800,000 or more violent incidents within families each year, but the terror of living in many homes is largely overlooked. . ." After noting how overlooked this domestic violence was, the report did not elaborate, essentially repeating the sin of omission they had just identified. None of the three graphs in the articles, for example, included those eight hundred thousand or more violent incidents in the family.

Changes in Television Crime Coverage

A word of explanation will help to clarify the startling data that follow. Late 1993-94 witnessed a major shift in the number of stories by networks on the crime *issue*. There began to be more stories about crime-as-social-problem as opposed to stories about specific criminal incidents. While criminal incidents were mentioned in these crime issue stories, the specific incidents were employed more as illustrations of crime as a larger problem than as the point of the story itself. What the reader will see displayed in Figure 3 will look, therefore, surprisingly low initially. (Since these network stories were about the crime issue and not specific crimes per se, the numbers I cite here *do not* include any O. J. Simpson stories.)

Fig. 3: TV Crime Stories v. "Crime" in MIP polls 92-93

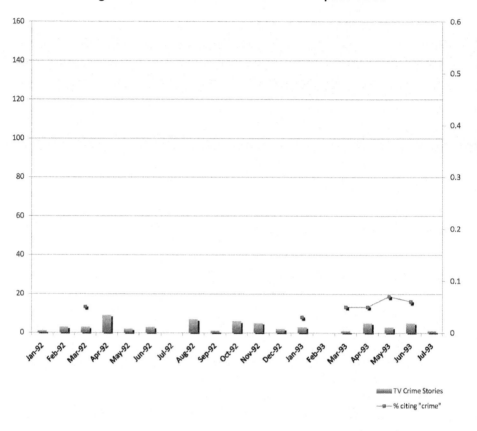

Network crime issue news increased tremendously beginning in October 1993, as did crime news in the four surveyed newspapers. Network news coverage of the crime issue had been relatively low throughout 1992 and into 1993 (see Figure 4). These crime issue stories up until October 1993 were almost invariably reports about the latest national crime statistics—usually the FBI's Uniform Crime Reports.

Fig. 4: TV Crime Stories v. "Crime" in MIP polls 93-94

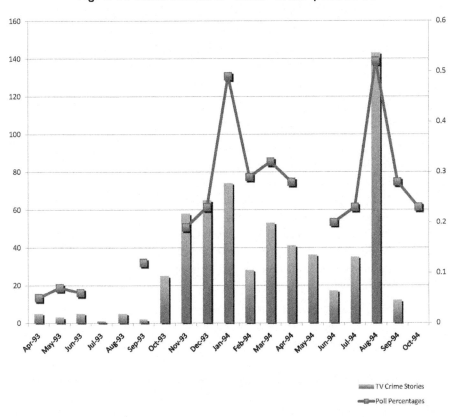

TV Crime Stories
Poll Percentages

Borrowing *Time*'s August 23, 1993 cover headline, NBC entitled its violent crime series in January 1994 "America the Violent." This was NBC's successor to its "Society Under Siege" series of October and November 1993. NBC's Tom Brokaw began the nightly national news broadcast of January 21, 1994, for instance, with the words: "Crime and violence. The focus of so much attention across the country these days. Next week, all of our NBC news broadcasts will focus on the problem and solutions, what can be done about it. Tonight, NBC Chief Financial Correspondent Mike Jensen sets the stage by adding up the staggering cost of violent crime."

The other two networks also featured their own versions of a crime focus that week. The CBS January 28, 1994 broadcast began this way:

CONNIE CHUNG. In Washington, President Clinton today delivered his first speech since...his State of the Union address this week, and it was no accident that Mr. Clinton decided to show up for this one. White House correspondent Rita Braver reports why.

RITA BRAVER. In Miami this week, a drug agent and a police officer wounded by a drug dealer. In Cleveland, a stabbing at a high school, and in Washington today, over one hundred mayors met to talk about the subject that's uppermost in their mind: crime.

Peter Jennings introduced ABC's January 28, 1994 broadcast with:

We're going to begin tonight with law and order and politics and perceptions. It is the perceptions driven by all the headlines about guns and sensational murder trials and conspiracy that are driving much of the political agenda. Today, the Menendez murder trial is over in California. The Tonya Harding saga in Oregon continues to fascinate. Most Americans tell us crime is out of control, and that's why politicians are having another meeting in Washington today.

In that same week—a week that fell between poll samplings taken between January 20-23, 1994 and January 28-30, 1994—public concern about crime rose by eighteen points, from thirty-one percent to forty-nine percent.

From January through September 1993, the three networks together averaged about three crime issue stories per month.[46] In October 1993,

---

46 These figures are taken from the Television News Index and Abstracts, known generally as the Vanderbilt Index. The dramatic increase in late 1993 and 1994 in network stories about crime as a general and distinct category reflects a shift in network treatment rather than a shift in Vanderbilt's procedures. In a personal conversation with the Vanderbilt Index's staff in April 1995, I was informed that they attempt to classify stories according to the story's own "bucket" (i.e., if they can categorize a story specifically, for example, "O. J. Simpson," as opposed to "crime" or "murder" they will do so.) Thus, the figures cited in Figures 6 and 7 do not include, for example, any stories on O. J. Simpson.

I double-checked each of the daily broadcast entries in the abstracts portion of the Vanderbilt Index to verify the numbers displayed in the Vanderbilt monthly index. These daily entries list all stories presented on that day's nightly news broadcasts, and the exact times they were presented within the broadcasts. Thus, the numbers I use herein of stories concerning the crime issue are all accounted for individually and are not an artifact of the Vanderbilt Indexer's indexing system. In a small number of cases, the Vanderbilt Indexers missed some crime issue stories in their monthly subject category totals. I have corrected these errors in the data shown in this article. As another cross check, I used the Internet version of the Vanderbilt Index, employing a search strategy of keyword "crime." The pattern of very low numbers of crime stories prior to the coverage wave compared to the very high

300

the three networks broadcast twenty-five crime issue stories; fifty-eight stories were broadcast in November 1993, sixty-five stories in December 1993, and seventy-four stories in January 1994. January 1994's coverage of the crime issue was up, therefore, by a factor of more than twenty-four over the level of crime coverage in the first nine months of 1993.[47]

In October 1993 when the networks and newspapers launched their part of the coverage wave, political actors' statements played a secondary role in the news stories about crime. Of the twenty-five stories concerning the crime issue on national network nightly news that month, only three specifically concerned the crime bill and one covered "Three Strikes, You're Out." The remaining twenty-one stories concerned crime as a general issue, with the youth angle being uppermost. These stories appeared primarily on NBC's *America Close Up* series, CBS's *Eye on America*, and ABC's *American Agenda*. NBC's *America Close Up* series, for example, was entitled "Society Under Siege" and began in October 4, 1993.

Originally scheduled for a five-day run, NBC's "Society Under Siege" ended up being extended into a two-month run. The series focused on violence among young people, with reports of incidents in cities such as Salt Lake City, New York City, Sacramento, Topeka, Portland, San Francisco, Raleigh-Durham, Buffalo, etc. Each segment led with crime statistics (with the main body of each story being about a specific city), and ended with references to violent incidents in other towns or cities. NBC's technique of stringing references to other places at the end of each report created the image of an epidemic of violence gripping the nation. Needless to say, the title for their series—"Society under Siege"—employed warlike imagery, as if crime were threatening to overrun society.

After January 1994, the number of television stories about the crime issue subsided somewhat, though the number of stories remained very high by pre-October 1993 standards. Poll levels also dropped when the media dropped their overall level of crime coverage. In August 1994,

---

numbers of crime stories during the coverage wave was also very evident using that alternate search strategy.

47 The February, 1994, Tyndall Report (cited by Extra! (FAIR's magazine), May/ June 1994, Vol. 7, No. 3, p. 10) reported that in the three years ending in January 1992, the three major television networks spent sixty-seven minutes per month on crime stories in their nightly network news. By comparison, between October 1993, and January 1994, they devoted 157 minutes per month to crime stories. This represents a greater than 234 percent increase in crime stories on network television national news.

network crime issue news hit an all-time high of 143 stories. Out of those 143 stories, fifty-four were devoted to covering the Clinton crime bill. Thus, while the explosion of stories in August 1994 can certainly be attributed in part to the crime bill, the majority of stories were not about the crime bill.

In that same month of August 1994, poll-measured crime concerns also reached an all-time high of fifty-two percent.[48] In Figure 4, I have also included the MIP poll results contemporaneously. Notably, this un-paralleled leap in newspaper and television crime issue news was not as-sociated with any specific preceding or contemporaneous crime events.

Intra-media Influence

Were the newspapers and television responding to the newsmagazines when they increased their crime coverage in October 1993? How could the newsmagazines have evoked such a powerful response from news-papers and television news organizations? In the absence of significant criminal events and/or changes in the crime rate in September and Oc-tober 1993, the reason for the extraordinary leap in newspaper and tele-vision news coverage begs for explanation. There are compelling reasons to suggest that the newsmagazines triggered the other major media's coverage wave.[49]

Intra-media influence is not solely, or even mainly, measured by size of audience share. The fact that the newsmagazines have in recent times suffered decreases in readership, therefore, does not undercut their intra-media influence. In fact, they have adjusted their strategies to accommo-date their declining readership:

> Time and Newsweek send faxes to key executives every Sunday, boasting of the stories in the forthcoming issue of their magazines, "increasingly trying to show that they're not just rehashing the news

---

48 Did other factors such as the prevalence of "reali-TV" crime shows such as *COPS*, have something to do with this attention to crime in late 1993-94? Undoubtedly. These shows, however, cannot account for the volatile polls given the timing. These "docu-cop" shows began with *Unsolved Mysteries* in 1987, followed in 1988 by *American Detective* and *America's Most Wanted. COPS* began broadcasting in 1989, *Top Cops* and *DEA* in 1990, and *FBI: The Untold Stories* in 1991.

49 Skeptical readers might not be convinced by this specific hypothesis, but the major thrust of this case study does not require its acceptance.

but that they're breaking it," in the words of Evan Thomas, assistant managing editor of Newsweek....

Equally important, newsmagazines want to beat the competition on trend and social issue stories, stories that first identify or put into perspective an emerging subject or problem."[50]

Indeed, their August 1993 cover stories on crime were researched weeks ahead of publication in an effort to name an alleged trend—random, violent crime, especially among youth.[51]

An alternative interpretation of the above is that the TV and newspaper outlets were responding to some factor other than the newsmagazines. Perhaps they noticed the mid-September 1993 polls, decided that the public was now more concerned about crime, and expanded their coverage in response. To answer this question, let us look at the four polls taken that month. See Table 2.

Table 2: Most Important Problem Polls—Sept. 1993

Date of Sample	Poll Sponsor	Percent citing "crime"
9/9-15/93	L.A. Times	15
9/10-12/93	Gallup	16
9/16-19/93	CBS/NYT	10
9/25-28/93	L.A. Times	6

Source: Roper Center

The first two polls in September 1993 show nearly identical fifteen and sixteen percent readings, which conforms to what one would expect since the polling dates were almost identical. The last two polls in September 1993 showed a decline in crime being mentioned, from ten percent in the September 16-19, 1993 sample down to six percent in the September 25-28, 1993 sample, the latter being the same reading as June 1993. This

---

50 "New Media Playing Field Opens Way to More Errors," *Los Angeles Times* online, August 6, 1998, http://articles.latimes.com/1998/aug/06/news/mn-10609, accessed February 28, 2011.

51 In the case of *Time*'s August 2, 1993 cover story "Big Shots: An Inside Look at the Deadly Love Affair between America's Kids and their Guns," the principal author, Chicago bureau chief Jon Hull, spent five weeks in Omaha preparing the story.

pattern is consistent with some factor causing a temporary bump up of crime concerns in the first two weeks of September 1993 and with crime concerns then settling back to their previous level of six percent. Note further that this bump up to fifteen and sixteen percent, with the exception of a single poll in 1977,[52] was the first spike in crime concerns since 1968. This doubling of crime concerns in September 1993 should not, therefore, be treated as random "noise."

This pattern supports the hypothesis that the four August 1993 newsmagazines crime cover stories had a temporary effect on public crime concerns, inasmuch as there was no outstanding criminal event or government action that coincided with this jump in the polls in that time period. If the Los Angeles Times was following its own polls here and made decisions based simply on popular sentiment, then it would likely have decreased its crime coverage based on the fall in public concern at the end of September 1993. Instead it increased its coverage. While the news media had ready access to the Los Angeles Times polls and to the CBS/NYT poll, Gallup's September poll was not published until December 1993. So the only poll data readily available to the media indicated that public interest in crime was actually declining through September 1993.

If one compared the September 1993 polls to the June 1993 polls and prior levels of six percent or below, one would see a momentary jump in September 1993. But it is highly unlikely that all four major newspapers and the three major television networks noticed this shift in the polls. Even if they had noticed it, the available evidence indicates that journalists do not in general take their cues for what stories to cover and how to cover them from the public.[53] Rather, they generally make news judgments based on what they think will please their superiors, and look to other media to judge whether they are covering the right stories.[54]

Because audience feedback is difficult to obtain (other than the occasional phone call and letters to the editor which Gans found journalists universally dismiss), public feedback tends to consist of the opinions of family members, friends, and neighbors. Time Managing Editor James R. Gaines, for example, explains the magazine's conclusion in 1993 that Americans were fed up with crime as coming from "talk over the

---

52　The fifteen percent reading in 1977 was only in one poll. It occurred coincident with a plethora of news stories on crime and law and order issues across major local papers.

53　Gaye Tuchman, "Professionalism as an Agent of Legitimation," *Journal of Communications* (Spring1978), 106-113. Michael Schudson, *Discovering the News* (New York: Basic Books, 1978).

54　Gans, 1979; Winerip, 1998.

barbeque. It is a gut thing, a sense that, though maybe it's from a middle-class commuter's perspective, this craziness has even invaded the sacred precinct of a 5:33 p.m. commuter train."[55]

In fact, Herbert Gans points out that journalists generally reject feedback from the public and are particularly suspicious of polls, generally judging the public unfit to make decisions about what stories should be covered and how those stories should be covered.[56] The media simply do not decide what they will cover on the basis of polls. Even if they did, in the case of the September 1993 polls, a fifteen to sixteen percent reading is not very high, compared to the higher levels of concern being registered for other issues in the same polls. "Health Care" was named by twenty-eight percent of respondents, the "Economy" by twenty-six percent, "Unemployment and Jobs" by twenty percent and the "Federal Budget" by fifteen percent.

Other Crime Coverage Waves?

Have there been other times in US history when news attention to crime was very high that did not result in elevated concerns in the polls, thus casting doubt on my hypothesis that media acted as an extraneous variable to poll responses? As I have already indicated, as far as the newsmagazines are concerned, there is no precedent for the level of their attention to crime coverage in the 1990s. Figure 5 displays the level of television crime news stories between 1968 and 1994[57] and shows that the network nightly news broadcasts' attention to the crime issue in late 1993-94 had no precedent.

---

55 Stephen Braun and Judy Pasternak, "A Nation with Terror on Its Mind," *Los Angeles Times*, February 13, 1994, A16.

56 Compare Tuchman, 1978.

57 The scale on this Figure 5 is slightly different than that on Figures 3 and 4 because the search strategy looked for crime stories as opposed to crime *issue* stories. Thus, the magnitude of Figure 5 is greater than the magnitudes in Figures 3 and 4.

Fig. 5: No. of TV Crime Stories

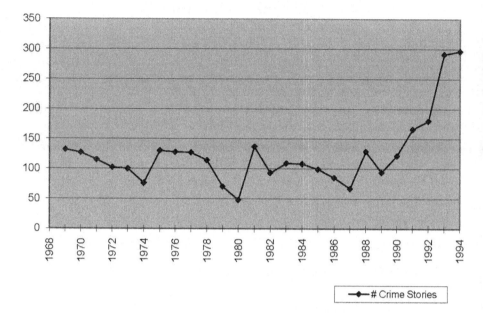

It is not possible to reproduce with the same methods a comparison of crime news in the four newspapers I selected for this study for the period prior to 1982.[58] The television data, however, are probably the most indicative and persuasive by themselves, since television is the most heavily consumed news form of the three media forms. Employing the Information Access Company's index of articles from January 1, 1982 through December 31, 1994 in the *Los Angeles Times* (home edition), *The New York Times* (late and national editions), *Wall Street Journal* (eastern and western editions), and *Washington Post* (final edition), one finds, with the partial exception of *The New York Times*, a generally uniform and parallel pattern of rising crime coverage for the four papers between 1987 and 1994. As can be seen from Table 3 below, the number of crime stories increased dramatically in 1994 for all four surveyed newspapers and for three of the papers from 1993.

---

58   This is because the Information Access Company whose indexing system I have used herein does not index these papers earlier than 1982. It would be possible to use *The New York Times'* own index for earlier years, but it is not comparable to the search and indexing system employed by the Information Access Company's that I employed for the rest of my newspaper data.

Table 3: Crime Stories in the *L.A. Times,*
New York Times, Washington Post and *Wall Street Journal*

Year	L.A. Times	N.Y. Times	Wash. Post	Wall Str Jrnl
1982	20	229	30	19
1983	82	111	42	25
1984	42	101	41	35
1985	43	98	47	19
1986	29	88	28	19
1987	19	70	23	14
1988	21	45	29	9
1989	33	60	48	10
1990	47	118	30	14
1991	46	82	69	12
1992	58	63	74	13
1993	116	81	105	26
1994	239	231	231	75

Source: Newspaper Articles Database in Melvyl, indexed by Information Access Company, covering 1/1/82 through 3/01/95, using exact subject search term: "crime."

Conclusion

The prevailing models for explaining the crime issue's prominence in the 1990s—generalized public anxiety and attention to rising crime rates—fail to adequately account for this revealed pattern of polls and media activity. The evidence adduced here for a media effect is very strong. It would, of course, be reductionist to assert that simple shifts up or down in media attention to an issue automatically result in a corresponding shift in poll results.

In this case study, the poll shifts that occurred related to both the coverage wave's magnitude (the sheer number of stories and the diversity of outlets involved) and the story themes emphasized. The levels of juvenile violence actually began to drop off before this coverage wave began and cannot, therefore, be seen as proportionately responsible for the coverage

307

wave's magnitude or timing. Public officials' statements, linked primarily to pending proposed legislation such as "Three Strikes" played an important secondary role in this coverage wave. Key overall was the news outlets' exceptional attention to the problem of youth violence that focused public attention, leading to the historic spikes in the polls. The polls were not a simple reflection of public sentiment. Rather, media activity, together with official public statements, acted as extrinsic variables vis-a-vis the public and the polls.

Media reach and influence more people, hold our attention longer, pervade our social and physical environments more extensively, and impact public policy more than ever. Not only do the media *not* principally mirror public sentiment, but they have become a surrogate electorate, effectively supplanting any semblance of the electorate's influence.

What is more, the outlook of the right-wing today dominates the media. The Right's ambitions to take over the society and govern have thus been highly successful, even though their victory is not yet complete. If this were a basketball game, the Right would be up by twenty points at the start of the fourth quarter. For the other side, the side of the people, the situation is desperate, though not utterly hopeless. In our case, the stakes are not just the outcome of a basketball game. The stakes are the entire world and its fate.

I now turn to Chapter Seven to consider in more depth the prospects for change.

CHAPTER SEVEN

The Prospects for Change

If one acquires the habit of contemplating vast horizons, overall views and fine generalizations, one can no longer without impatience allow oneself to be confined within the narrow limits of a special task. Such a remedy would therefore only make specialization [the division of labor and existence of classes] inoffensive by making it intolerable and in consequence more or less impossible.

EMILE DURKHEIM[1]

Look up at the night sky, and you get the impression of stability, serenity, a fixed eternity. Nothing could be further from the truth. The universe is hugely dynamic and everything is moving. Supernovae go off, galaxies collide, black holes devour anything that approaches. Stars are constantly dying and being created.

JULIA STEELE[2]

If you have had a chance to see the world as it really is, there are profoundly different roads you can take with your life. You can just get into the dog-eat-dog, and most likely get swallowed up by that while

---

1 Emile Durkheim, "The Division of Labor in Society," in *Classical Sociological Theory: A Reader*, ed. Ian McIntosh (New York: New York University Press, 1997), 200.

2 Julia Steele, "View from the Top," *Hana Hou Magazine*, June 2010, 60.

trying to get ahead in it. You can put your snout into the trough and try to scarf up as much as you can, while scrambling desperately to get more than others. Or you can try to do something that would change the whole direction of society and the whole way the world is.

BOB AVAKIAN[3]

Durkheim presumed that the 1800s' social, economic, and political hierarchies, based as they were upon industrial society's division of labor, would continue indefinitely. He believed that capitalism's extensive specialization of tasks, rather than atomizing people, reinforced social solidarity because everyone depended more upon each other for their joint survival. By contrast, because the people in pre-industrial societies were more self-sufficient, and therefore less interdependent, their social solidarity represented something less evolved.

Durkheim described tribal societies as characterized by "mechanical solidarity": people bound together because they *do* similar things. In his comparison between tribal and industrialized societies, however, he overlooked the fact that while tribal societies' division of labor is scant, the tribe's survival rests upon everybody's participation. Every able body is counted upon to help secure the group's material needs, and malingering is unthinkable. Social solidarity thus plays a no less vital role in tribal/pre-industrial societies than it does in industrialized societies. In fact, maintaining modern society's classes requires, as Durkheim candidly admits in the quote that begins this chapter, that most of the working class be denied a higher education because a higher education would only fill them with dissatisfaction with their constrained role. Translated into today's American mores—Let them have their beer, burgers, and *Monday Night Football.*

The sense of normlessness and alienation that the division of labor can foster, therefore, can only be avoided by depriving many of societies' members of the finest that humanity has created—"the vast horizons, overall views, and fine generalizations."[4] Durkheim, notably, did not say

---

3   Bob Avakian, *From Ike to Mao and Beyond: My Journey from Mainstream America to Revolutionary Communist* (Chicago: Insight Press, 2005), 442.

4   Durkheim held that the division of labor itself does not cause anomie (anomie = a sense of normlessness, not knowing what is expected of you and where you belong). Rather, anomie occurs only when people are blocked from the opportunity to seek a different class position and the "terms of the struggle" are unequal—where there is, in effect, unequal opportunity—that they will become unhappy. If they believe that

that workers who are exposed to these "overall views" and "vast horizons" would be incapable of grasping the meaning of these larger vistas. Despite his belief in the inherent inequality of people,[5] Durkheim recognized that workers are capable of appreciating these grander understandings if exposed to them, which is why such exposure must be avoided. Workers' position in the division of labor requires that they be barred from seeing vast horizons; otherwise they will be unhappy with their lot. Learn too much and you cannot willingly go back to unknowingness. Take the red pill, as in the film *The Matrix*, and there is no returning to (not so) blissful ignorance.

In any population of people, it is true, there are going to be those who are better at specific things than others. Having incompetents handling critical matters such as medicine, or people in charge of disaster prevention and relief who know nothing about emergency management, violates most people's expectations of a good society. Not everyone can become a physician, and only qualified individuals should take key posts. But this obviously sensible policy differs from excluding the working class, oppressed minorities, and/or women from learning about the grander vistas that humanity has achieved. To understand how the political system really works, to be exposed to the best in art and science, to be introduced to humanity's key philosophical questions, the varying answers to those questions historically, and to be steeped in history and its lessons and so on in this fashion should be the norm for virtually everyone in a society,

---

they have been given a reasonable chance for upward mobility, therefore, and if they are given a sense of how their work contributes to something larger than themselves, then they will be satisfied with their lot in life. How valid is Durkheim's argument? The "free market," as I have analyzed in this book, enriches those who are already wealthy and increasingly diverts resources away from those with less. Equal opportunity, to the extent that it has ever existed, has becomes less and less equal for this reason. Moreover, policy-makers have been eliminating equal opportunity programs, describing them as "reverse discrimination" and interfering with "market forces." Even if equal opportunity *were* operating, however, the existing division of labor and hierarchies would remain, with many restricted to menial tasks and others condemned to overwork because the existing class structure does not allow for the full expression of people's talents. Knowing that your labor is contributing to your employers' enrichment does not offer a salve for growing inequities.

5   "[I]f the institution of classes or castes sometimes gives rise to anxiety and pain instead of producing solidarity, this is only because the distribution of social functions on which it rests does not respond, or rather no longer responds, to the distribution of natural talents..." from *The Division of Labor in Society* by Emile Durkheim, cited in Laura Desfor Edles and Scott Appelrouth, *Sociological Theory in the Classical Era* (Thousand Oaks: Pine Forge Press, 2005), 104.

regardless of what they end up doing as an occupation. Specialized skills and area specific knowledge are not the same as these kinds of lessons. It does not take exceptional intelligence or talents to benefit greatly from that manner of education.

So why exclude people from these arenas? The only reason can be that the existing division of labor and hierarchy of prestige demean and diminish many people in comparison to their capabilities and the regard they deserve as human beings. Were this not the case then there would be no necessity to conceal so many arenas of knowledge from people. The problem here, in other words, lies with the stratification of society and the differential material and non-material rewards attached to the different strata. The shortcomings here do not lie mainly with the people; the populace's ability to understand exceeds the capacity of a highly stratified society to accommodate them and their fullest roles.

Durkheim treats specialization, by contrast, as an unalloyed good. "It is the need for happiness that may impel the individual to specialize more and more."[6] And, "far from being trammeled by the progress of specialization, individual personality develops with the division of labor."[7] What he overlooked, however, was that Taylorization's[8] sharp reduction of work on an assembly line to a set of simple repetitive movements was only partly carried out to enhance efficiency. A key objective of Taylorization is social control and profitability—to fragment working class jobs as much as

---

6   Emile Durkheim, *The Division of Labor in Society* (New York: The Free Press, 1984), 180.

7   *The Division of Labor in Society* by Emile Durkheim, cited in Edles and Applerouth, *Sociological Theory in the Classical Era* (Thousand Oaks: Pine Forge Press, 2005), 105.

8   Taylorization is named after American mechanical engineer Frederick Winslow Taylor (1856-1915). Taylor created "scientific management," an attempt to reduce every action by workers on an assembly-line process to their most "efficient."
     "It is only through *enforced* standardization of methods, *enforced* adoption of the best implements and working conditions, and *enforced* cooperation that this faster work can be assured. And the duty of enforcing the adoption of standards and enforcing this cooperation rests with *management* alone." From Frederick Winslow Taylor, *Scientific Management: Early Sociology of Management and Organizations* (New York: Routledge, [1947] 2003), 83. [Emphases in original.]
     'I can say, without the slightest hesitation,' Taylor told a congressional committee, 'that the science of handling pig-iron is so great that the man who is . . . physically able to handle pig-iron and is sufficiently phlegmatic and stupid to choose this for his occupation is rarely able to comprehend the science of handling pig-iron." From David Montgomery, *The Fall of the House of Labor: The Workplace, the State and American Labor Activism, 1865-1925* (New York: Cambridge University Press, 1989), 251.

possible so that anyone could be easily replaced (thus driving down the cost of their labor) and ensuring that capital could exercise more power over workers who are rendered thereby even more disposable. This was the secret that turned McDonalds into a multi-billion dollar business—dumbing down the jobs into increments so that management could replace any worker readily. Since capitalism ensures what Marx called the "Reserve Army of the Unemployed," any worker can be readily replaced, thereby cutting the cost the owners have to pay labor.

Though Durkheim recognized that workers could understand the "vast horizons" and "fine generalizations," he argued that to avoid too much anomie among them, it was sufficient that they be informed that their work contributed to a larger goal. He correspondingly believed that it was enough that people be "charitable and just" to each other and that each should aim "to fulfill the function he performs best."[9] The idea that differences among people could be narrowed, that their roles could be shared, and the pay and income gap diminished, exceeded what Durkheim was willing to imagine.

All of which prompts a question: Why do the less desirable jobs in any society, such as picking crops or cleaning bathrooms, have to be reserved for a certain class of people who must do these jobs their whole lives, while others are exempted entirely from having to participate in these socially necessary tasks? Why cannot these tasks, the putatively lowly, but indispensible, as well as the highly esteemed, be shared by everyone? Of course, someone who has exceptionally specialized skills such as brain surgery should not be doing things that would endanger their hands and eyes, but they could certainly spend some of their time doing more humble tasks. They and the society would be the better for it.

In the network show *The Undercover Boss*, the boss learns what those in his or her employ go through, things that the boss has become insulated from because of his or her elite position. At the end of each show the boss makes some paltry adjustments to the lower-level jobs, thereby reinforcing how much more could and should be done than such paltry window dressing.

Functionalist theory assumes that societies require a hierarchy for their overall welfare. The people who occupy leading and disproportionately-rewarded positions do so because they perform exceptionally

---

9   "[The collective conscience] requires us only to be charitable and just towards our fellow-men, to fulfill our task well, to work towards a state where everyone is called to fulfill the function he performs best and will receive a just reward for his efforts." Emile Durkheim, "The Division of Labor in Society," in *Classical Sociological Theory: A Reader*, ed. Ian McIntosh, (New York: New York University Press, 1997,) 204.

important functions and they are particularly worthy due to their skills; to get them to fill these crucial posts they must be disproportionately rewarded; others who are less talented cannot fill the elites' shoes and therefore occupy the less well-rewarded positions; if people are doing what they are most suited for, then the whole society benefits.

This argument seems plausible, but functionalists conflate several different factors in justifying social inequality. To begin with, they equate incentive with material rewards. While people obviously differ in their abilities, the people who assume leadership posts do not necessarily have to be materially rewarded more substantially for what they do. Teachers, for example, carry out exceedingly important tasks for a society, as do parents, yet they are not well compensated. They do what they do for reasons other than the material rewards. The American dictum that implicitly celebrates moneymaking, "Those who can, do, those who can't, teach, and those who can't teach, teach teachers," overlooks the fact that if everyone avoided teaching because they were all so good at other jobs, there would be no one *to teach* the young and the untrained. Would all children and teens be autodidacts then? Is not outstanding teaching one of the critical skills in any society at any time in human history? How does the accumulated knowledge and experience over millennia get passed along otherwise? Is everyone who home schools their children the best teacher for all subjects? Where do these home school parents get the materials such as books for their children to read if not from people who are writing books in order to teach?

While everyone needs to be motivated to work and to excel, the nature of the reward does not necessarily have to be material. A society that equates material rewards with success and that relies upon material success to motivate people is also saying—and must say—that success equals having things that others do not have. This turns society into a zero sum game of winners and losers and structurally encourages a sense of entitlement among the "winners" that they are better than the "losers" and that they merit goodies and respect that should not be granted to the less deserving hoi polloi. Is this the meaning of a good society: the leaders think of themselves as so much better than everyone else? Because there is only a finite amount of monetary and material incentives to go around, more for a few people means less for most others. Moreover, if the incentive must always be external to the job or activity itself, then something is wrong with the work or activity; what makes it not rewarding intrinsically? Perhaps the activity needs to be changed so that those who do it gain satisfaction from the act of doing it. Not all jobs are amenable to that change, which is why the less desirable activities such as cleaning up need to be shared.

I work at a university in which teaching is valued more highly than research. At Research 1 (R-1) universities, the opposite is true; at R-1 institutions, a great deal of friction typically exists among faculty within the same discipline because they are competing for slices of a finite pie for their research, another zero sum game. At non-R-1 universities, being a good teacher is something everyone can achieve; it is not a zero sum game. Consequently, relations among faculty members at teaching-focused universities are characteristically far more collegial.

Material rewards as *the* incentive means that social solidarity, what functionalists value more than anything else, is actually undermined by the structure's inherent logic that people participate in a zero sum game in which many must be deprived so that a few may benefit a great deal. Rewarding people with non-material incentives, on the other hand, does not function as a zero sum game if what is being honored is cooperation and dedication to the group. Physicians in the US customarily make much more than the average worker. People will commonly cite doctors' expertise and the importance of what they do as the reason for this inequity. In countries outside of the US, physicians perform equally important work for their patients but are not paid nearly as much. Is this because people in the US need more incentive to become physicians? Is it because physicians outside of the US are not valued as much as within the US?

If we stopped paying brain surgeons as much as they now earn, would that mean that everyone now performing brain surgery would put down their scalpels and say: "Well, I'm not doing *this* any more." Would the people who are paid well now and/or honored for their work refuse to do their jobs if they were paid less? If outlandish salaries were no longer paid to TV network anchors (such as the $20 million per year that CBS pays Katie Couric) and if CBS, for example, paid their anchorperson, say $200,000 per year, would this mean that they would not be able to find a good person to anchor their nightly news broadcast? I should imagine that there are some people for whom the reward of fame, exposure, influence or service to the society would mean that they would be willing to do the job for a relative pittance in dollars. Not that CBS would have to do this, but the point here is obvious.[10] These jobs would continue to be done because the monetary compensation is not the only reason why people do such jobs. (The President of the United States makes $400,000 a year. Do

---

10 Major corporations like CBS are also paying their front people such as Couric for other factors such as being able to project a credible image and for protecting the major players without having to be told directly how to do this. On a purely financial basis, hiring Couric has not paid off for CBS because since she assumed the anchor position, CBS's nightly news program has lost audience share.

people run for the presidency because of the material incentives? Are we not getting the best people for the job because we are not offering more money for them? If we had paid a higher salary to the person who was president from 2001-08, would we have gotten someone better?). Certain jobs such as prostitution *would* disappear, if people having sex under hazardous conditions with strangers were not getting paid lots of money and better alternatives were available for prostitutes. Indeed, the nature of virtually all working class jobs would have to be transformed.

Functionalists believe that societies function best when they operate as a meritocracy, where those who have the most merit fill the most desirable positions. If a society rewards people materially and disproportionately as *the* social incentive, then the capital, both literal and social, that accrues to those who are most highly rewarded rebounds to their offspring, relations, and friends who are not necessarily more meritorious. These others get the benefit of their connection to the highly paid by virtue, in the case of the children, of having chosen their parents well.

Durkheim believed that it was necessary to reduce the barriers as much as possible and provide people with as much equality of opportunity as possible.[11] But if a hierarchical society is governed by those who already have the most and if the norm for that society is that material wealth is the measure of success, then it can only be expected that those in high positions would work to preserve the advantages (both for themselves and for those they favor, such as their relatives and friends) against those who do not have their connections, even if the others are more meritorious. The net result of this is that the most meritorious often do not rise to the positions that they should. The whole society suffers as a result. This contradicts the key stated principle of functionalism—the welfare of the whole society.

Even if a perfect meritocracy were possible, the results would still be problematic because the disparities it would generate would over time confer advantages and inequities by family and class and by other invidious criteria such as gender, race/ethnicity, regional advantages, or sexual orientation. In other words, even if Durkheim were granted even more than he wished and all of the barriers to equal opportunity were eliminated,

---

11   "[The division of labor] not only supposes that individuals are not consigned forcibly to performing certain determined functions, but also that no obstacle whatsoever prevents them from occupying within the ranks of society a position commensurate to their abilities. In short, labour only divides up spontaneously if society is constituted in such a way that social inequalities express precisely natural inequalities." Emile Durkheim, "The Division of Labor in Society," in *Classical Sociological Theory: A Reader*, ed. Ian McIntosh (NewYork: New York University Press, 1997), 204.

the gaps between the people would widen due to the practice of materially rewarding the most meritorious; this would create a class that reproduced its advantages for its family members and friends within two generations, undercutting the meritocracy and thereby sabotaging the putatively core values of the general welfare and solidarity.

I am reminded, when thinking of the functionalists' celebration of the allegedly non-antagonistic relations among all of the society's classes, of the Disney movie *The Lion King*'s opening scene. The newborn male lion Simba's proud parents hold him up while standing on a cliff overlooking the wide African plain. Arrayed in concentric circles on that plain are all of the animals of the kingdom—giraffes, water buffalo, gazelles, and so on—bowing down before the new lion king. "The Great Circle of Life," the film's thematic score, rises in this grand happy scene in which the prey of lions celebrate the newest member to join the ranks of their predators, who will one day happily eat them.[12]

Having the forbidden realms opened to the working class would immensely enhance the degree of social solidarity felt by people who are now barred from accessing society's prized tasks and rewards. The ideas, leadership, and other artistic contributions that the oppressed bring to the planet would enrich the society, were their gifts properly valued. And yes, this would undermine the existing division of labor. Would this not be a good thing? It would only be a bad thing for those who now enjoy the lion's share of society's resources and who would have to give up some of what they now monopolize. This is a novel notion certainly, although it is one that the Chinese under Mao Zedong implemented before his death in 1976 and capitalism's subsequent restoration. Under Mao the leading and most celebrated class was the proletariat. They were the heroes of the revolution, path-breakers in transforming China. On the eve of and during the 1989 Spring Uprising, workers articulated their deep dissatisfaction at Deng Xiaoping's moves to restore capitalism to China:

This government favors every social group except the working class. The so-called "leading class of the society" has been consigned to limbo. Not only has the government not showed any kindness to workers, it has further tried in various ways to abuse us.—Chinese worker, *Zoomlens*, December 6, 1988

---

12 To avoid making this truth apparent, the movie depicts Simba during his exile as eating bugs—a decidedly non-leonine activity—instead of feasting upon his animal companions.

All bosses are the same—they're only there for making money. God damn it, I've worked for thirty years and still have to serve dishes to capitalists! I still do not understand why we have to enter into joint ventures with bosses and that the masters of our country, the workers, have to work for capitalists.—Restaurant worker, Shenzhen Special Economic Zone, China, 1987

Although the official media still call the working class the leading class of the nation, workers seem to know well that it is nothing but a cliché. For instance, from 1984 to 1987, the NCTU conducted a series of surveys in many cities. The results showed that 56 percent of workers thought that the social status of the worker was declining (Xiao & Shi 1989: 18). Workers' frustration grew even stronger as time went on. A survey of 33 cities . . . in late 1987 found that 71.6 percent of the worker interviewees believed that, rather than being the leading class, the working class was now at the bottom of society, because workers had no political power, no money, and no higher education, the things the [sic] Deng's regime highly valued. What they can offer is only manual labor, which was less compensated for those days. A more recent survey showed that those who felt that workers' social status was declining had gone up to 83 percent.[13]

Today in China the capitalists, both foreign and domestic, are the celebrated and leading class, with the proletariat now consigned to working endlessly for micro-wages under inhuman conditions. A rising tide of violent clashes with authorities numbering at this point in the tens of thousands of incidents annually, along with a rash of suicides and desperate, murderous acts against children by profoundly alienated individuals, have accompanied China's "modernization" campaign. They make up the seamy underside of the bright, shiny, elegant capitalist toys such as gold-plated Mercedes Benzes and iPhones for the nouveau riche in today's China.

---

13   Dennis Loo, "China 1989 First Installment," from "Exorcising the Ghost of Mass Political Activism: Deng Xiaoping, Workers, Peasants and the 1989 Spring Uprising," DennisLoo.blogspot.com, February 5, 2007, http://dennisloo.blogspot.com/2007/02/china-1989-first-installment.html, accessed March 4, 2009.

This is the Way Things Are

The only kinds of fights worth fighting are those you are going to lose, because somebody has to fight them and lose and lose and lose until someday, somebody who believes as you do wins.

I.F. STONE[14]

Those who want to see neoliberalism repudiated and replaced by a system that safeguards the planet and its denizens as precious confront immense obstacles. Some people, in fact, think that such a goal represents the height of idealistic folly. "Human nature," these folks declare, "makes your objective impossible. Venality, corruption, and narrow self-interest mean that those with power and privilege will always prevail. Even if you could displace those with the power now, even if you start out determined to prevent exploitation and oppression from reasserting themselves, and even if you could assemble strong leaders for your ends, all of which are doubtful, you would surely fail eventually. The masses of people are too stupid, gullible, and philistine. Your high-minded objectives would shrivel and die in the face of the public's apathy and narrowness. And your leaders, even if they start out as altruistic and high-minded, will eventually deteriorate into new oppressors and self-serving exploiters. This is the way it has always been and always will be because humans are unequal in endowments and effort, and they are fallible and selfish."

The shortest retort to these objections is: "The present system certainly works awfully well, don't you think?" And of course, the longer retort is the rest of this book. In contrast to those who argue that society's faults stem from the shortcomings of "human nature," the structuring of society as it is presently constituted deserves the principal blame.

Even conservative intellectual James Kurth in the *American Conservative* in 2006 warned of the dire consequences of continuing society's present trajectory:

> In the course of the 20th century, there were several eras of growing economic inequality. On a few occasions, they came to an end in a relatively gentle way, with democratic elections and more egalitarian legislation. More often, however, they were ended by a catastrophe,

---

14   I. F. Stone, famous journalist, as quoted in David Swanson, *Daybreak: Undoing the Imperial Presidency and Forming a More Perfect Union* (New York: Seven Stories Press, 2009).

such as the Great Depression, a violent social revolution, or a world war. When the rich went out, it seems, they normally did so with a bang, and not with a whimper. The way things are now going, it is likely to be so in the future.[15]

While the status quo becomes increasingly intolerable and alarming for growing numbers of people and for the planet, our hypothetical person's litany of objections about the feasibility of fundamental social change deserves serious consideration, regardless of the person's motives in raising these points. Having said that, I first need to make a distinction between two groups: First, there are the people who say that they agree with change but nevertheless argue strenuously that any efforts to achieve fundamental change will not work, resulting in their rejecting one plan after the other. "Revolution will never happen," they say. When people say, "It will never happen," what they are really doing is justifying their own inaction by saying that everybody else will not do anything. Their apathy is justified by everybody else's apathy. Their emphatic disagreements about the feasibility of attempts at change are premised more upon their belief that no fundamental change is really necessary or desirable, than upon a genuine wish that more promising strategies be employed to bring about change. If you do not wholeheartedly agree that a goal is worth pursuing, then quibbling over tactics and strategy to achieve that goal is just a distraction.

To people in that boat I say, proceed along as you are and let those of us who are aware and willing to stare into the face of peril do what must be done. When a bus is careening out of control and the driver is not paying attention but is screwing around with someone in the front so that he does not notice or discounts the reality that the bus is heading for a precipitous cliff, someone else has to step forward and take control for the sake of the entire busload of people. Someone in that situation could decline to take action, saying to himself and others that he would never succeed in wresting control of the bus from the bus driver, and that trying to do so would only get him ridiculed, hurt or killed; but in such a situation, inaction represents a cowardly and ultimately fatal choice.

The second group of people, those who have attempted to organize other people around a worthwhile cause, know nonetheless that the difficulties of doing so provide more than ample grounds for frustration. Changing the existing system requires not only mass involvement; it

---

15   James Kurth, "The Rich Get Richer," *American Conservative* online, September 25, 2006, http://www.amconmag.com/article/2006/sep/25/00006/, accessed October 2, 2010.

demands extraordinary leadership. Why should we expect that dramatic positive change should take anything less than tremendous effort? Is anything really worthwhile in any arena achievable without protracted and determined effort?

The very notion that real change requires mass participation in ways that far exceed voting and supporting the leaders and/or party you believe in, that what is called for requires serious engagement with the cardinal questions of the day and of society and nothing less, will seem to many people to be surpassingly strange and far-fetched. To begin with, it violates the commonsense view of what "democracy" entails—that the vote equals democracy. Voting, however, as I argued in Chapter Five, does not mean very much or even anything at all in this system.

It does means something, however, when large numbers of people start to insist on direct participation in public policymaking—witness what the world saw erupt from seemingly out of nowhere in Egypt in early 2011. Bureaucracies shun such eruptions of actual mass democratic participation. The two major American political parties love large crowds, but only if those crowds are there to cheer on the designated party speakers, and not if the crowds are skeptical, too thoughtful, or demanding of answers beyond promises that the party officials have the general welfare in mind. "Leave the details to us," these august party leaders say. "Thank you very much, and keep those donations rolling in" or, they do as Hillary Clinton did when delivering a February 15, 2011 speech in DC extolling the virtues of non-violent popular protest and free speech as carried out by Egyptians against their despotic government. During her speech seventy-one year old former senior CIA analyst Ray McGovern in the audience silently stood up and turned his back on her, uncovering his T-shirt that said "Veterans for Peace" with a white dove on it. Within thirty seconds three security guards demonstrated upon Mr. McGovern the American way to deal with those who exercise non-violent free speech—assaulting him and roughing him up while handcuffing him until he was bloodied.[16] During

---

16 "As Secretary of State Hillary Clinton spoke in Washington, D.C., on Tuesday about the failures of foreign leaders to respect people's freedoms, a 71-year-old U.S. veteran Army officer, a man who spent 27 years in the CIA and delivered presidential daily briefs, a peace activist and proponent of nonviolence, the man who famously confronted Donald Rumsfeld for his war lies, the man who drafted our letter to Spain and delivered it to the Spanish Embassy on Monday, our friend Ray McGovern turned his back in silence. As Clinton continued to speak about respecting the rights of protesters, her guards—including a uniformed policeman and an unidentified plain-clothed official—grabbed Ray, dragged him off violently, brutalized him, double-cuffed him with metal handcuffs, and left him bleeding in jail. As he was hauled away (see video), Ray shouted 'So this is America?' Clinton

this assault on Ray McGovern, Hillary kept on talking, not missing a beat, contrasting the terrible countries' leaders who use violence against non-violent demonstrators to the wonders of US standards. "The rights of individuals to express their views freely," she said, "these rights are universal, whether they are exercised in a public square or on an individual blog." [17]

"They Fight Their Way, We'll Fight Our Way" [18]

While those who despise the Left like to invoke the noxious nostrum, "Do you consider that the ends justify the means?" (as if the extreme Right's own ends and means were not utterly shameful), the genuine Left regards the means as inextricably tied to the ends. The means you choose must correspond to the ends you seek, or the ends you seek you will never see. The Left seeks a society in which authentic popular rule is increasingly realized, and for that to happen, educating people about what is really going on, treating people as ends in themselves rather than as spectators who cheer on the real actors and real leaders, and getting people involved in the political process directly—as well as in every other arena of human existence including science and art—are both necessary and desirable.

You cannot undermine social inequities and you cannot hope to begin to dismantle and rebuild on an entirely different basis the existing institutions and bureaucratic structures unless the people are involved in that process in a living and ongoing way. How do watching TV soap operas and reality shows, playing video games, reading the *National Enquirer* (or its more "highbrow" imitators like *People*) and watching *Entertainment Tonight*, even begin to compare to that? How much more bracing, enlivening, and empowering would it be for people to be grappling with real issues and real people instead of confined to the fabricated and poor imitations of reality that pass for too much of entertainment and news today?

---

went right on mouthing her hypocrisies without a pause." David Swanson, "Police Brutalize Ray McGovern as Hillary Clinton Talks Free Speech," Truthout.org, February 17, 2011, http://www.truth-out.org/police-brutalize-ray-mcgovern-hillary-clinton-talks-free-speech67888, accessed February 19, 2011.

17   Allen Abell, "Funny Things Happen on Way to Free Speech Forums," *Winnipeg Free Press*, February 19, 2011, LexisNexis.com, http://www6.lexisnexis.com/publisher/EndUser?Action=UserDisplayFullDocument&orgId=574&topicId=100007429&docId=1:1364250878&start=17, accessed February 21, 2011.

18   Mao Zedong on the manner in which reactionaries wage war versus the way revolutionaries wage warfare.

There is a sports adage that the winner in a game is the one who sets the tempo and style of the contest. If the other person or other team sets the pace, they have the initiative, and if you adopt the pace that most suits your opponent's strengths, you will almost certainly lose. This applies to political contests and wars as well: framing the terms of the contest and choosing the terrain on which the battle is fought essentially determines the outcome from the very start, unless the contest is reframed during the course of the fight. This is what Mao meant when he said in reference to guerrilla war, "They fight their way, we fight our way." Revolutionary armies that seek to defeat a larger and better-equipped army by engaging in the style of battle that favors their opponent will be crushed.

As an illustration of what this means, in a 2002 military exercise, the largest war game ever conducted, the US simulated an invasion of Iraq. Retired Marine Lieutenant General Paul Van Riper played "Saddam Hussein" in the exercise. Employing unorthodox techniques, Van Riper ripped apart the US forces at the very start of the game. Embarrassed by their devastating "defeat," the brass overruled Riper's "victory," ordered their "sunken" ships and "killed" soldiers resurrected, and demanded that Van Riper ignore the brass's amphibious landings and behave like the US military would in order to ensure a US victory.

> Van Riper had at his disposal a computer-generated flotilla of small boats and planes, many of them civilian, which he kept buzzing around the virtual Persian Gulf in circles as the game was about to get under way. As the U.S. fleet entered the Gulf, Van Riper gave a signal—not in a radio transmission that might have been intercepted, but in a coded message broadcast from the minarets of mosques at the call to prayer. The seemingly harmless pleasure craft and propeller planes suddenly turned deadly, ramming into Blue boats and airfields along the Gulf in scores of al-Qaida-style suicide attacks. Meanwhile, Chinese Silkworm-type cruise missiles fired from some of the small boats sank the U.S. fleet's only aircraft carrier and two marine helicopter carriers. The tactics were reminiscent of the al-Qaida attack on the USS Cole in Yemen two years ago, but the Blue fleet did not seem prepared. Sixteen ships were sunk altogether, along with thousands of marines. If it had really happened, it would have been the worst naval disaster since Pearl Harbor.
>
> It was at this point that the generals and admirals monitoring the war game called time out.

"A phrase I heard over and over was: 'That would never have happened,'" Van Riper recalls. "And I said: 'nobody would have thought that anyone would fly an airliner into the World Trade Centre...' but nobody seemed interested."

In the end, it was ruled that the Blue forces had had the $250m equivalent of their fingers crossed and were not really dead, while the ships were similarly raised from watery graves. . . .

"You are going to have to use cellphones and satellite phones now, they told me. I said no, no, no—we're going to use motorcycle messengers and make announcements from the mosques," he says. "But **they refused to accept that we'd do anything they wouldn't do in the west.**"

Then Van Riper was told to turn his air defences off at certain times and places where Blue forces were about to stage an attack, and to move his forces away from beaches where the marines were scheduled to land. "The whole thing was being scripted," he says.[19] [Emphasis added.]

I am reminded here of games played with very young children who yell "No fair! You cheated!" when they lose. This war games' debacle had previously been enacted in real life during the US defeat in Vietnam, where the Vietnamese so annoyingly refused to play by the same rulebook as the US. I am reminded here too of Conway's Law. Conway's Law states that organizations' designs (e.g., their software products) will copy the communication structures of the organization itself. While Conway's Law is intended to apply to the nature of designs created by organizations, I believe it can be usefully applied more broadly: organizations tend to see others, including other organizations, as mirrors of themselves, because their own internal organizational structure affects how the organization sees the world, how it receives information, and how it processes and interprets that information.

The US, for examples, tried vainly throughout the Vietnam War to find the headquarters (HQ) for the Viet Cong underground. They were convinced it would look like a Vietnamese version of the Pentagon with large, interconnected buildings. They never found such a complex because the Vietnamese did not create an HQ the way the US would have.

When the 2009 Christmas Day bomber Umar Farouk Abdul Mutallab (aka Abdulmutallab) failed to ignite his exploding underwear on board

---

19   Julian Borger, "Wake-up Call," *The Guardian* online, September 6, 2002, http://www.guardian.co.uk/world/2002/sep/06/usa.iraq, accessed September 2, 2010.

the Northwest flight bound for Detroit, *The New York Times* reported in the aftermath,

Qaeda operatives in Yemen were caught discussing an "Umar Farouk" who had recently been in contact with Mr. Awlaki about volunteering for terrorist operations, one official said. American intelligence officials learned of the conversation in November, although it had been intercepted by a foreign intelligence service in August, an administration official said. [*They had his first name and knew this Umar Farouk was going to carry out a terrorist action.*—DL]

The National Security Agency intercepted a second phone conversation in November involving Qaeda members in Yemen, in which they discussed an unnamed Nigerian man who was being groomed for an operation. (Mr. Abdulmutallab is Nigerian.) The next month, intelligence officials eavesdropped on Qaeda operatives who talked of sending a militant toward the West to carry out a strike. [*They also knew, mentioned in previous news stories, that Umar Farouk Abdul Mutallab's father, a prominent banker, had urgently told the US embassy in Nigeria that his son was involved with terrorists and had told the family that they would not see him again.*]

Other intercepted conversations mentioned a significant event on Christmas Day, although it was unclear if the event concerned a strike against an American target or a movement of Qaeda backers, perhaps motivated by the deadly raids that Yemeni forces began in mid-December, officials said. [*Corroboration that a terrorist incident would happen on Xmas.*]

In the final weeks of the year, American intelligence officials, using spy satellites and communication intercepts, were intently focused on pinpointing the location of Qaeda fighters so the Yemeni military could strike them. By doing so, the American officials hoped to prevent attacks on the United States Embassy in Yemen, personnel or other targets in the region with American ties. [*They thought that the best way to deter this Xmas attack was by a military strike upon Qaeda fighters, if they could find out where they were concentrated, **not** by trying to locate and detain Umar Farouk Abdul Mutallab, a Nigerian identified by his father as a terrorist.*]

Yet they had unwittingly left themselves vulnerable, American officials now concede. **Counterterrorism officials assumed that the militants were not sophisticated or ambitious enough to send operatives into the United States.** And no one shifted more intelligence analysts to the task, so that they could have supported the military assaults by Yemen while also scrutinizing all incoming tips for hints about future attacks against Americans, one administration official said.

So, though intelligence analysts had enough information in those days before Christmas to block the suicide bomber on the Northwest flight, they did not act.

"We didn't know they had progressed to the point of actually launching individuals here," Mr. Brennan said on Jan. 7 at a White House briefing.

An administration official added, "The puzzle pieces were not being fitted to any type of homeland plot."[20] [Emphasis and italicized commentary added.]

Counterterrorism officials' conclusion that no terrorists were "ambitious" enough to send operatives to the US can be countered simply by saying two things, (1) 9/11, remember that one? and (2) sending operatives into the US is as ambitious as buying a plane ticket. Some people reading the reports of this intelligence debacle conclude, understandably, that US officials cannot possibly be as stupid as they appear to be and that therefore they must have knowingly allowed this incident to occur. That is not, however, how I read the data, even though certainly false flag attacks do occur.

People now in charge possess hubris in the classic meaning of the term—they do not believe that their adversaries are capable of being imaginative, ambitious, or brave, even in the face of dramatic and repeated evidence to the contrary. This is a blind spot on their part, not one which every single person in charge is guilty of, but one that pervades and dominates the institutional culture; empires tend to think in these ways. Why would you, if you were the top dogs after all, ascribe admirable attributes to your adversaries, whom you regard as your inferiors? This is one of empires' central weaknesses; it is also one of the reasons why even those people who are not in favor of revolutionary change need to think very carefully about which side they are choosing to support. The empire does not really care about your individual fate and is doing things daily that jeopardize people's lives and the planet's welfare and viability.

Defeating the empire is not something that occurs only on the literal battlefield. It is also something that is determined throughout the

---

20   Eric Lipton, Eric Schmitt, and Mark Mazzetti, "Review of Jet Bomb Plot Shows More Missed Clues," NYTimes.com, January 18, 2010, http://www.nytimes.com/2010/01/18/us/18intel.html, accessed January 18, 2010.

continuum of battles over many issues, including: ideas; philosophy; forms of organization and leadership in economy, politics, and other realms; ways of arguing; ways of responding to and respecting empirical data; interest in truth as opposed to expedience; how people and the environment should be treated; the nature of relations among people (e.g., between women and men, different races and ethnicities, rich and poor countries, etc.); ways of responding to criticism and ideas that are not your own; ways of handling one's own errors and those of others; and more, all the way up through how warfare is carried out. The contrast between the methods and goals of the neoliberals and those of us who seek an entirely different world is stark.

Some people try to win over others by not seeming to be too different from what is already the conventional way of thinking, but the starker we show the contrast to be, the better. Highlighting those differences rather than narrowing those differences reflects objective reality—there is an enormous difference in values, methods and goals. Drawing out those differences also illuminates the need for and contributes to the necessary and indispensible revolutionary changes that must occur.

Yes, But…

The difficulties to be surmounted while carrying forward the vision I am suggesting are enough to cause some of the people who are actually trying to do something admirable to give up the attempt, either temporarily or permanently, or to seek easier paths, including accommodating themselves to what they had previously considered unacceptable. As someone who had once considered himself a communist once said to me when I ran into him at the Hawaii State Legislature Building one evening, describing his own accommodation to the system upon being appointed to a high administrative post: "The system's been all right to me." Oh, I see. So revolution is all about what it does for *you* as an individual?

While mass movements are made possible by people who participate with all degrees of commitment—with some choosing the role of misdirecting the police and/or reactionaries when they come chasing after the activists, "They went *that* a' way"—those who would lead others in embarking on the long journey of dramatically transforming the existing power relations in society must be willing to endure unpopularity, ridicule, danger, hardship, and sacrifice. They must, moreover, be doing it for reasons that far surpass and indeed render insensible the narrow ends of only trying to better one's own personal situation, both before and especially after they succeed in overthrowing the powers they seek to unseat.

Why should we expect any less from the leaders of major social change? Easy answers and quick "solutions," or replacing one set of dominators with another set of dominators, is for those who do not really desire change as much as they crave the semblance of change and being comfortable themselves. Major social change has always involved spending more than a few weekend hours at demonstrations or in personal pursuit of high office in the establishment while leveraging as your street "cred" forevermore the years you spent as a community activist and/or your humble beginnings. It has required not just the risking of jobs, careers, and livelihoods, but people putting their lives on the line with some of them losing their lives in the effort. Anyone telling you otherwise is lying to you, and perhaps to himself or herself as well.

This is what the history of the labor movement, the civil rights movement, and any other major change movements, including of course revolutions here and worldwide, tells us. Nothing worthwhile has ever happened because a lot of people said, "I'll let so and so take care of it." As I wrote in Chapter Five, one of democracy's unspoken flaws is the notion that democratic participation and rule by the people consist of voting for someone to take care of things for the rest of us. This is not democracy in its highest expression; this is passing off responsibility for matters that should be—and are—the concern of everyone. This limited vision of democracy is particularly pronounced in the US. In Europe, for example, street demonstrations are far more common and much larger, with the concessions made by government to the people's demands much greater for that reason. As an expatriate American explains in Michael Moore's film *Sicko*, "in Europe governments are afraid of the people; in America people are afraid of the government." If people do not regard as their personal business what is going on in the larger society, then let them cease their claims of allegiance to "democracy" *and* let them openly endorse oligarchy because that is what they will get; such people are not suited for authentic popular rule.

It is for these precise reasons that some say that the kinds of movements and kinds of change of which I am speaking here are impossible: there are too many free riders—those who will take advantage of the work that others do.

Let us consider this problem.

This issue is like an artichoke with multiple layers that need to be peeled back. To base ourselves on a theory that consigns the masses of people to a backseat in politics (with their only roles being to vote every few years for candidates who are preselected by the two major parties' leaders and approved as "legitimate" by the mass media) means that authentic popular rule has been judged "off the table" from the start. A foundational theory for authentic popular rule must include a means by which broad popular participation in actual governance is progressively achieved.

Classical democratic theory involves two invalid and conflicting assumptions: (a) that the very most the people can do is limit the degree to which they are being taken advantage of by their leaders,[21] and (b) that everyone of adult age has the necessary knowledge—largely provided by mass media—to govern.[22] Stated slightly differently, (a) the people cannot govern themselves, and (b) they already govern.

Well, gentlemen and ladies of democratic theory, which is it?

Democratic theory cannot solve this conundrum because it conflates the role of leaders and led. Any alternative theory that is worth its salt has to address this problem head on. To resolve this contradiction requires that we understand the roots of the problem. This gap between leaders and led exists for two major reasons. The first has to do with the very exigencies of social life.[23] The second has to do with the historical divisions of society in two ways: first, there is the division of society into various classes; and second, the division of people into those who live mainly by their minds (mental laborers) and those who live mostly by their hands (manual laborers).

The Nature of Social Life

In any given group and around any given activity there are inevitably a small number of people who are more advanced in their understanding (more farseeing, more insightful, more inclusive in their vision of the roles of others); most individuals in any group are intermediate; and some are

---

21 As cited in Chapter Five, Karl Popper put it this way: "[D]emocracy, the right of the people to judge and to dismiss their government, is *the only known device by which we can try to protect ourselves against the misuse of political power*; it is the control of the rulers by the ruled." [Emphasis added.]

22 As I discussed in the Introduction and Chapter Five, functionalist theory (aka the Consensus Perspective) holds that mass sentiment (aka the "conscience collective" in Durkheim's works) determines what public officials and the media do because elites serve at the pleasure of and/or reflect the shared values/sentiments of the people.

23 I say "social life" and not human life because this principle actually applies among other animals outside of Homo sapiens. Among social animals there are leaders—for example, among apes, wolves, etc.

relatively backward by comparison.[24] Groups of people do not move into action as a block with everyone marching to the same beat and responding at the same pace to the same precipitating factors. Moving groups into political action requires triggering the advanced individuals first and foremost. When a car is stuck in mud, getting it unstuck involves giving the leading tires some traction so they can pull the entire vehicle out of the mud.

Preventing movements from being mobilized requires neutralizing and paralyzing the subject group's advanced individuals. Mass sentiments cannot be mobilized and become real unless they are focused and organized; for that to happen leadership is required, as I underscored in Chapter One. Leadership and masses of people are necessary complements to each other; leaders must have a social base and a following, and the masses cannot express themselves without their leaders. This gap between the leaders and the led has always been with us, predating even the appearance of castes and classes, and will never go away.

Leaders can play either a facilitating role toward good ends or they can hinder what should be done. Their actions or inactions reverberate powerfully on those who follow them. The Democratic Party's refusal, for example, to pursue Bush and Cheney's impeachment, prosecution for their crimes, and removal from office, and its refusal under Obama to hold anyone accountable for the Bush regime's confessed crimes has had a disorienting and destructive impact on the sentiments and outlooks of the people who still look to the Democrats for leadership. Some of the people who, a few years ago, would have blanched at the very idea of torture and indefinite detentions and condemned them roundly can now be seen justifying them. The fault here does not lie primarily with Democratic Party followers. People who still follow the Democratic Party, just as those who follow the GOP's lead, are doing what can be expected: they are conforming to the groups that they consider the legitimate political authorities.

In any society the mainstream is going to conform to mainstream values, institutions, ideas, and leading figures. In a feudal society the mainstream supports feudal values and norms. In a socialist society the mainstream support socialist values and norms. In a capitalist society the mainstream supports capitalist values and norms.

---

24 Advanced, intermediate and backward here refer to individuals' stance and abilities relative to the goals of the group and situation. The most advanced members of a team, for example, are those who best grasp and are most effective in implementing a new game plan. Who is advanced and so on in a group will vary depending upon the context, goals and other factors.

If the existing authorities embark on a radical turn in policy but mask the magnitude of their actions with persuasive rhetoric, and if the mass media go along, then how can we reasonably expect society's mainstream to break with the leading authorities? Is the average person, or are even the most highly informed citizen, going to be ready to break with both the leading political parties and the mass media by concluding that their reading of the situation trumps that of the leading institutions and individuals? The mainstream will not do so unless and until a powerful enough alternative political and moral authority emerges that contends against the existing authority. Such an unusual scenario happens, when it happens at all, in part because the alternative authority does its work very well; but it mainly happens because the existing authorities become unable to hold things together. As a rule, people in any society are reluctant to break with convention. Conventional ways of doing and thinking must be at or near the breaking point, while simultaneously beset by a major challenge from an alternative path and alternative leadership, in order for a significant portion of the people to rupture from the existing system and its leaders. This is not a process that happens slowly and gradually, even if there are some building actions involved. It is a process that occurs in a concentrated span of time, in an accelerated fashion, under conditions of crisis.

This is what happened for a time in the 1960s when the existing authorities suffered from a "credibility gap" and the Left exercised broad influence, even though its actual numbers were small. As one indicator of this, during the high tide of the 1960s, a large majority of college students endorsed the idea of a revolution. The way that people defined revolution varied widely, but the mere fact that eighty percent (in at least one poll) believed that revolution was necessary was indicative of the mood of the times, the degree of crisis of the system, and the strength of the Left relative to the Right.

The problem in the US today, in brief, is not mainly that the people are bad or indifferent or gullible or immoral or consumed personally in pleasurable pursuits, though these elements exist in abundance. The main problem is that the established and widely recognized opinion leaders upon whom people rely and from whom they receive their overall orientations have been installing neoliberal policies in the driver's seat. The American psyche's degradation, to the point where Americans in all too many instances are going along with explicit and monstrous violations of international and national laws and widely and readily understood principles of morality and decency, is not primarily a product of average Americans forsaking their consciences. Leaders are primarily responsible. The soldiers guilty of committing atrocities at places like

Abu Ghraib, Guantanamo, and Bagram do not commit their acts because they are particularly depraved individuals; they were and are doing what they were and are expected to do and are ordered to do by their superior officers. This does not make those frontline soldiers guiltless of awful crimes; it does, however, make them relatively less guilty than their superiors.

Social psychologists have shown in experiments designed to measure people's willingness to go against the group that most people will adopt the group answer, even when they know indisputably that the answer given by everyone else around them is wrong. In experiments, for example, where five people sit around a table and are asked to answer very simple questions (such as which straight line is longer even though both lines are obviously the same length), and when four of the respondents have been secretly instructed by the experimenters to give the same wrong answer, about eighty percent of the time the fifth respondents adopt the group's wrong answer. Most people do not wish to be socially isolated and will do what they know is wrong, even deeply immoral things, rather than be isolated from the group. Breaking with the group not only means possible social isolation, the consequences for which can range from being made fun of to being killed, but it also means that you have to be willing to stand out and say to the others that they are wrong and you are right. Most people are not comfortable assuming that stance.

When people come into a group and see that everyone else is behaving in a particular way, they assume—erroneously—that everyone else is acting that way because they have all consciously decided to act in such a manner. Not wanting to assume that they know better, most people will then adopt the group's behavior. Social psychologists call this process of reasoning "pluralistic ignorance." It is more commonly seen in the story of the "Emperor's New Clothes" in which the only person in the crowd willing to point out that the emperor is stark naked is a little boy; all of the adults are too embarrassed and afraid to point out the powerful emperor's obvious nakedness and instead celebrate his (nonexistent) marvelous new clothes.

People are first and foremost social beings. While Descartes' famous dictum, "I think, therefore I am," captures something critical about what it means to be human, an even more accurate descriptor would be "I adapt, therefore I am." Most people in any situation go along with the group norms not primarily because they agree with those norms but because they are adapting themselves to what they see most of the others around them doing. This rule of human behavior exists not primarily because people are sheep but because we all recognize that our survival depends on being in good standing with others. In a recent study that reproduced the famous Solomon Asch conformity experiment (with the difference that in the recent study MRI's were taken of the participants' brain activity), when people gave answers that agreed with the group, even though the group's answer was obviously wrong, their brains showed no emotional distress. When they gave the right answers but those answers differed from the group, however, their emotions were triggered. In other words, when we are doing the wrong thing, so long as that wrong thing agrees with what the group is doing, our brains do not evidence emotional distress. But doing the right thing when it means departing from the group's actions is emotional. The study further found that the group's stance actually influences people's individual *perceptions*.[25]

As social beings, we also follow leaders' examples. When recognized leaders provide examples that are egregious, those examples set a negative tone for most people. When leaders set a positive tone, they have a similarly powerful impact on those who follow them, this time in a positive direction. How far a leader can go, it is true, depends on what his or her social base is capable of handling. A leader does not have unilateral power to determine what a group will do. But the initiative rests with leaders to determine which of the contradictory aspects of his/her group come to the fore. Stanley Milgram found that in a particular variation of his famous obedience experiment:

> The rebellious action of others severely undermines authority—In one variation, three teachers (two actors and a real subject) administered a test and [electrical] shocks [to the subject in another room]. When the two actors disobeyed the experimenter and refused to go beyond a certain shock level, thirty-six of forty subjects joined their disobedient peers and refused as well.[26]

---

25 Sandra Blakeslee, "What Other People Say May Change What You See," NYTimes. com, June 28, 2005, http://www.nytimes.com/2005/06/28/science/28brai.htmL, accessed June 30, 2008: "The researchers found that social conformity showed up in the brain as activity in regions that are entirely devoted to perception. But independence of judgment—standing up for one's beliefs—showed up as activity in brain areas involved in emotion, the study found, suggesting that there is a cost for going against the group."

26 Stanley Milgram, "The Perils of Obedience," *Harper's*, December 1973, 62-77. The article can be found also at "The Perils of Obedience," http://home. swbell.net/revscat/perilsOfObedience.htmL, accessed February 14, 2011.

That is a variant of the Milgram Experiment that has not received the amount of attention it richly deserves.[27] I discuss the Milgram Experiment further later in this chapter.

One measure of the difference between admirable leaders and those who are not is whether they appeal to the better, higher sentiments of the people or to lower sentiments and narrower concerns. In either instance the leaders are resonating with some strain of their social base, but the direction in which the whole group moves depends upon the leaders' initiating actions. Rather than spending their energy bemoaning the backwardness of Americans, people would do better by actively engaging themselves in providing leadership and setting examples for others to follow. The so-called problem with "the people" always primarily involves the role being played by those in leading positions, whether they are the official authorities or those leaders among the groups who are trying to change the direction of the group/society.

One evening many years ago I was standing on a sidewalk in Honolulu with my significant other at the time. We were out for a stroll and had just come out of an event nearby. We stopped to observe a fire raging in a commercial building right in front of us. The fire had just started up and no fire fighters were around yet. We were standing on the sidewalk facing an empty parking lot in front of the building on fire, and a crowd of people was around us on the sidewalk also watching the fire. After a few moments of this I turned to my partner and said, "I'm going to take a couple of steps closer to the fire to get a better look." She said, "No, do not do it." I said, "Why not?" She replied, "Because nobody else is doing it." Despite her advice, I stepped forward two or three steps. Of course, you know what happened next: the other people immediately did the same, breaking the invisible line that had initially held us all back.

As I discussed in Chapter Five, the failure to impeach Bush and Cheney and remove them from office for their crimes was widely ascribed (by those who bothered to remark on it) to the failings of the American public. However, had even one person of prominence such as John Kerry, or a single very high-profile mass media outlet such as *The New York Times*

---

27 Subjects administered electrical shocks to a stranger in another room when the stranger failed to answer a question correctly. The experiment was to see if subjects would follow authority's injunctions to continue the shocks or refuse to obey. Milgram was pilot-testing his 1960 experiment in the US, planning to take it to Germany to test Germans who he thought were particularly obedient because of their allowing the Nazis to rule in the 1930s and 1940s. Milgram never did go to Germany because he found his answer right here at home: Americans, just like the Germans, were all too willing to follow authority.

or *Washington Post* called for their impeachment or even for an earnest inquiry into the grounds for a possible impeachment, the outpouring of popular support would have been immense. There would not have been any more wondering about why the American people had been so quiescent in the face of the crimes of Bush and Cheney.

Had Gore or Kerry insisted with tenacity on a recount and an investigation into the extensive evidence of fraud in their election battles with Bush, the resulting revelations would have likely prevented Bush from being "elected" in the first instance and "re-elected" in the second instance. To those who cite the Supreme Court's decision in the 2000 contest, I would note that if Gore had called upon everyone who supported counting all of the votes to show up with signs for a peaceful but mass demonstration outside of the Supreme Court while the Supreme Justices were deliberating, that we might very well have seen a different ruling from the Supreme Court.

When Kerry was asked in a September 17, 2007 open forum at the University of Florida about why he did not challenge his "loss" to Bush in the 2004 election given that Kerry actually won the election, security guards proceeded to manhandle and eventually taser the student (Andrew Meyer) raising this very legitimate question. If Kerry had told the guards to stop what they were doing, the guards would have stopped; this was, after all, a US senator, and if Kerry as the speaker had made this demand, far more of the audience would have joined him in persuading the guards to desist, creating a very different atmosphere in the room.

The gap between leaders/led can be narrowed in the sense that new people can be brought forward as leaders and the group's overall knowledge and ability can thereby be advanced. The experience of any good teacher, social movement leader, good coach, or mentor bears this truth out: leaders who raise the consciousness, knowledge, performance, and ability of those they lead are reducing the gap between the leaders and the led in the sense that the led are becoming better leaders themselves. Those who come forward in every generation to take over the reins from their elders, and who have been taught and learned well, are taking over leadership roles. Leaders who bring their followers forward are in turn able to move even further forward because of the advancement of those they lead. As this applies to politics, leaders who help others understand the actual dynamics of political affairs—a topic that I address a bit later in this chapter—are helping to bridge the gap.

The Mental/Manual Divide and the Existence of Classes

Being knowledgeable about, and being trained to participate fully in the workings of, society's leading institutions—whether in the fields of politics, economics, science, art, literature, sports, warfare, or others—so that these arenas are no longer mysteries out of most people's reach—is something that since the Agricultural Revolution (aka the Neolithic Revolution) has been restricted to society's elites. The distinction between mental and manual labor is evident in the concrete form of social classes. While there was some limited division of labor prior to the Agricultural Revolution (when with the advent of cultivation, it became feasible for populations to stay in one place), that division of labor did not take the form of an entire class being relieved of the harshest physical tasks, leaving the "dirtier" but critically necessary work to the rest of society. Mental laborers have also been remunerated disproportionately well both materially and non-materially (with prestige being attached to their work), while manual laborers were (and are) looked down upon and deprived of what should have been (and are) rightfully theirs based upon both their indispensable contributions to society's welfare and their status as fellow human beings.

Defenders of "free enterprise" say that people get what they deserve, and that if you impede market forces you will quash people's initiative, inventiveness, and creativity. How can it be seen as a proper reward for work when billions are paid in bonuses even though the corporation (e.g., Wall Street investment banks) has actually been losing money? Is this not rather an example of the logical consequence of a system that rewards owners and deprives workers who are already disadvantaged based on lopsided power differentials?

Free market fundamentalists claim that without material incentives innovation and creativity would cease and people would become lazy. Every society that has ever existed, it is true, has had to find a means to motivate people to work because the survival of the group depended upon it. In the US, the American Dream—becoming materially rich—performs that ideological function. In order for the American Dream to work, there must be a very large disparity between those who strike it rich and those who do not; if the gap between rich and poor is not big, then there is little incentive to try to become rich. Thus, the American Dream and the Horatio Alger myth require inequality, and in large amounts. As Robert Merton, who first pointed out this contradiction, observed, the American Dream is criminogenic—that is, it promotes more crime; this is because most people cannot achieve the American Dream of wealth legally, and some of them (at the very least) resort to illegal activities and deception to realize their dreams of material riches.

Inventions prior to the Industrial Revolution were shared either immediately or eventually among the populace, without their inventors having to become billionaires. Somehow many people still managed to invent things despite not being promised enormous riches. Somehow their curiosity and desire to find new paths weren't stifled. Einstein did not develop the theory of relativity because he was motivated by greed. The inventor of the first working telephone was not Alexander Graham Bell, but Antonio Meucci, a radical Italian immigrant whose goal was to provide a free service so that people would be able to communicate more readily with each other, fostering a sense of community.

Since the Industrial Revolution, inventions that could be harnessed to profit, such as the assembly line, have become the standard. Other inventions, however, such as panty hose that do not run and light bulbs that last forever, have been bought up by competing companies whose profits depended upon their items' planned obsolescence, with the long-lasting versions promptly buried, never to see the light of day. Los Angeles, the city with the nation's worst traffic congestion, once had a mass transit system nicknamed the "red cars" coursing through the city. General Motors and major auto-related industries bought the red cars system and then shut it down, forcing most Angelenos to drive cars. The vast majority of inventors have not seen the main rewards from their inventions. Instead, bankers and financiers have nearly always been the prime beneficiaries.

In the world of mass media entertainment and news, enormously talented and creative individuals find it a daunting task to bring their abilities and best creations before a mass audience unless their work conforms to mass media's gatekeepers' tastes and primary goal of moneymaking. Great works that criticize the existing system are especially unlikely to be funded, promoted, and/or distributed widely.[28] News stories of great importance that could be told in gripping ways are rarely told. Instead, we learn who is the "most provocative celebrity" of the week, what Brangelina are doing now, how bitchy the Kardashian sisters are to each other, and about the internecine fights between the GOP and the Democrats (fights which skirt or distort the fundamental questions and focus on public policy as if the alpha and omega of it were the equivalent of two sports teams' rivalry): Lakers and Celtics, the Democrats and the Republicans—who will win the contest this time?

---

28   The gigantic hit *Avatar* represents an outstanding exception to this rule.

Meanwhile, in 2010 ABC promoted over and over as its biggest new show, something called *Wipe Out*, in which people were whacked and dumped into the water. If the people being whacked had been British Petroleum and Goldman Sachs executives or Bush and Cheney, the audiences for those shows would have been record setting. "On ABC tonight, we try waterboarding out on its greatest promoters, Bush, Cheney, Yoo, and Bybee in a game of Truth or Consequences. See how long they last! What deeds will they confess to? Will they tell us where Jimmy Hoffa's body can be found?"

Unfortunately, such shows may never air. . .

Individual Inequalities and Class Inequalities

Durkheim believed that social classes mirrored individual differences. While he did not believe that classes exactly matched individual differences, as he was not so out of touch with reality as to ignore the fact that inequalities of opportunity existed, he steadfastly believed that class differences fundamentally reflected different individual endowments. Social Darwinists likewise believe that the extant social hierarchies exist because some people are fitter and better than others.

Why should those whose only contribution to society is to buy and sell derivatives and who are therefore contributing nothing of real value to the society, or people who through either accident or a single brilliant insight have positioned themselves to receive gargantuan profits for the rest of their lives, pass on this booty to their children and succeeding generations; why should people whose talent lies in fooling people be given a lion's share of society's resources? Money and resources, after all, are not unlimited; more resources given to some mean less can be given to others. Why should some tens of thousands of people die every single day because they cannot get clean water to drink, while other people profit from this daily crime?

When BP executives decided that failure was impossible and proceeded (like the geniuses behind the Titanic) to drive a giant stake to unprecedented depths and pressures into the heart of the Gulf of Mexico, causing the worst human-caused environmental disaster in at least American history, is their incredible hubris evidence of their fitness? As Naomi Klein explained in June 2010:

> A year ago, [BP CEO] Hayward told a group of graduate students at
> Stanford University that he has a plaque on his desk that reads: "If

338

you knew you could not fail, what would you try?" Far from being a benign inspirational slogan, this was actually an accurate description of how BP and its competitors behaved in the real world. In recent hearings on Capitol Hill, congressman Ed Markey of Massachusetts grilled representatives from the top oil and gas companies on the revealing ways in which they had allocated resources. Over three years, they had spent "$39bn to explore for new oil and gas. Yet, the average investment in research and development for safety, accident prevention and spill response was a paltry $20m a year."

These priorities go a long way towards explaining why the initial exploration plan that BP submitted to the federal government for the ill-fated Deepwater Horizon well reads like a Greek tragedy about human hubris. The phrase "little risk" appears five times. Even if there is a spill, BP confidently predicts that, thanks to "proven equipment and technology", adverse affects will be minimal. Presenting nature as a predictable and agreeable junior partner (or perhaps subcontractor), the report cheerfully explains that should a spill occur, "Currents and microbial degradation would remove the oil from the water column or dilute the constituents to background levels". The effects on fish, meanwhile, "would likely be sub-lethal" because of "the capability of adult fish and shellfish to avoid a spill [and] to metabolize hydrocarbons". (In BP's telling, rather than a dire threat, a spill emerges as an all-you-can-eat buffet for aquatic life.)

Best of all, should a major spill occur, there is, apparently, "little risk of contact or impact to the coastline" because of the company's projected speedy response (!) and "due to the distance [of the rig] to shore" about 48 miles (77km). This is the most astonishing claim of all. In a gulf that often sees winds of more than 70km an hour, not to mention hurricanes, BP had so little respect for the ocean's capacity to ebb and flow, surge and heave, that it did not think oil could make a paltry 77km trip. (Last week, a shard of the exploded Deepwater Horizon showed up on a beach in Florida, 306km away.)[29] [Emphasis added.]

When Obama, in response to the BP catastrophe, claimed that the government would make the Gulf "better than it was before," an assertion

---

29 Naomi Klein, "Gulf Oil Spill: A Hole in the World," Guardian.co.uk, June 19, 2010,
    http://www.guardian.co.uk/theguardian/2010/jun/19/naomi-klein-gulf-oil-spilL,
    accessed June 21, 2010.

that belies the record of the far smaller Exxon Valdez disaster's ruin-
ation of ninety percent of Alaskan habitat still with us decades later, is
this not evidence of irresponsibility by leaders of a disastrous system on
a grand scale?

Threats of Context and the Future Prospects Under the Present System

When a Pentagon think tank document, as I discussed in Chapter Three,
concludes that "threats of context"—the very workings of the system as it
is—will surely produce at least some of the worst disasters of all, then the
notion that mere reforms are not enough is really the most realistic assessment that can be made. What does the BP Deepwater Horizon Oil Rig
catastrophe represent if not the ordinary workings of the system itself?
Even if scads of safety measures are observed (which they were not in
the case of the BP disaster), even if multiple back-up systems are put into
place (which also was not done), the statistical probabilities of at least one
catastrophic failure during drilling at depths of more than 20,000 feet in
oceans where pressures are enormous are simply too great to permit deep
water drilling at all; the ramifications of even one such disaster on the
ocean and the marshlands are too horrific to consider.

If a ship is headed for a huge iceberg, don't the people who see the
impending disaster have a responsibility to convince enough of the others
of what is ahead? If you refuse to take on that responsibility because you
might be ridiculed or might be risking "your career," then what kind of
meek soul are you?

The measures being implemented by the powers that be are not addressing these "threats of context." Indeed, the measures being implemented are actually contributing mightily to exacerbating the dangers and
the damage. Bureaucracies are resistant to even considering change, much
less envisioning and properly preparing for catastrophic events. The modern world is, in substantial degree, a very large, highly ramified, interlock-
ing, overlapping, and redundant set of bureaucracies.

Neoliberalism represents capitalism and imperialism in their more
naked expressions (fascism would be capitalism in its most naked form).
Neoliberalism emerged when it did and has come to the fore to dominate
public policy making for two reasons: first, since the fall of socialist rule
the capitalist camp has been able to have its way, dictating its own terms;

and second, because neoliberalism is the specific expression of capitalism/imperialism in a period when it has no real rivals.

For those who hope that the solution could be getting rid of neoliberalism and restoring the welfare state, some less ruthless version of capitalism, I remind them that the problem, as I laid out in Chapter Two, is that imperialism is the natural and inevitable outgrowth of capitalism's fundamental nature. The top one to two percent will continue to suck up most of the spoils so long as no sufficiently powerful contending force pushes in the other direction. The New Deal's regulatory regime to mute the negative effects of "free market" forces—forces responsible for the 1929 Stock Market Crash—came about not because FDR was an enemy of capital, but because his hand was forced by the crisis and most especially by the threat of revolution from the Left, both domestically and internationally. (Whether an actual revolution would have ensued or not is not the question here; the question is whether the prospect of that revolution was a reality.) Any serious discussion of the manner in which the unfettered forces of capital could possibly be reined in sufficiently, therefore, must take into account the fact that it took a revolutionary movement to force even the New Deal's regulations to be instituted. Lobbying for reforms and backing candidates who promise "change" do not even begin to cope with the immensity of the problems that we face now in a time when, to take just one example, corporations, foreign and domestic, are declared "persons" by the US Supreme Court and permitted to now spend in concealed ways unlimited amounts of money on political races.[30]

But, one might still object, it may be necessary to bring about revolutionary changes, but it is still not possible. The question of feasibility is a fair question, and I will address that in the upcoming pages, but first, an even more important question: what if major change is not possible at all? Does that mean that one should not speak up and act on behalf of what is right, fair, and rational? Does one stand up for the moral high ground, the rule of law, and the rule of reason and science only if one can guarantee success? Certainly moral codes and the rule of reason were not obtained by taking the low or easy road historically. Science from the start has had to battle for recognition. It continues to do so. Civil liberties, constitutional rights, the rule of law, and humanitarian codes of conduct were only established through struggle and through fighting against conventional wisdom. There have ever been those who counsel that change is not possible in the face of power and popularity. It will always be so. *It is simply not*

---

30   This is the January 20, 2010 *Citizens United v. Federal Election Commission*, No. 08-205, decision.

possible to be for justice in the face of injustice and not have to battle against the odds to achieve it. The most advanced understanding gains its footing only through struggle. If it were not the most advanced understanding then obtaining it would be easy: just do what the lowest common denominator wants to do.

In the German concentration camps, the Nazis were able to recruit some Jews who, in return for being protected from being gassed themselves, helped the Nazis control and herd their fellow prisoners to the gas chambers. Prisons, likewise, are run through the assistance of trustees, prisoners who act like guards. Every single population has within it individuals who will betray their own people in return for petty or not so petty privileges for themselves. The easy paths have always been the low roads. The best interests of humanity and of the planet have always rested in the hands of those relative few willing to lead others onto the high road.

Some people insist that real change is not possible. "Revolution will never happen," they say authoritatively, declaring that those who disagree with them are either starry-eyed dreamers or opportunistic manipulators, or even worse, both, wolves in sheep's clothing. People who make flat assertions as to the impossibility of revolutionary change are wrong on principle to do so. They are not wrong to say this because they are wrong about their declaration, even though they are wrong about that, as any reasonably long view of history tells us: human history is full of changes, including revolutionary changes. No, our no-nonsense, dead certain cynics are wrong to insist that change is impossible because their stance seeks to rationalize not doing things that should be done. What should be done on moral and/or legal grounds must be done, whether or not you can guarantee success for your actions. If it were otherwise and you should only stand up for principle when you know that you are going to win, then expedience would be the only principle governing humanity. If the criterion for doing the right thing were whether or not you could guarantee success beforehand, then the right thing would never have been done. Societies would have remained stuck at the stages in which slaves were the norm, or when women were entirely the property of men, or when being from the wrong tribe or region meant that you could be sacrificed, raped, and enslaved at will. None of history's rebellions or revolutions would have happened, because those who fought for them to happen would have never done so because there was no guarantee ahead of time that they would succeed. The odds they faced in launching their fights were long and only the brave dared press forward in the face of the dangers ahead.

There is a very big difference, parsing this question further, between asserting that change is impossible and raising the question of how it can be done. The courageous souls who first pushed off from familiar shores to embark on long sea voyages to find other lands, with the lengths of those voyages unknown and uncertain, and knowing full well that they might perish in the effort, did not say: "It is impossible to find land. Stay here where it is safe and secure." The people who made such declarations, of course, stayed home. The ones who made history sailed into the unknown. The latter are the kind of people that humanity has always relied heavily upon: the ones willing to do what other more fearful and/ or self-interested individuals regard as too difficult. The actions of such leaders are indispensable for stirring others into action and drawing upon their best selves.

Some people recognize the need for fundamental change but are stuck on the question of strategy: can what needs to be done actually be done? If we look back over history we can see numerous examples of fights that many people thought were impossible to win. When slavery was the prevailing system, the common wisdom, even among many of the slaves, was that ending slavery would never happen. When women first stepped forward to call for the end of the oppression of women, many men expressed puzzlement or opposition, and many women, even those who dearly wished it could come about, thought it could not happen. When Copernicus and later Galileo determined that the earth revolved around the sun and not the other way around, they faced persecution for their views. When Darwin proposed his theory of evolution, he knew that his conclusions would be extremely controversial and that powerful institutional forces would resist his revolutionary conclusions. When the theory of continental drift was first proposed by Alfred Wegener in 1915, the reaction to his theory was "almost uniformly hostile, and often exceptionally harsh and scathing."[31]

When quantum mechanics first revealed the truly bizarre behavior of subatomic particles that make up the foundation of our universe, none other than Einstein refused to believe it. "God," he said, "does not play dice with the universe." Ah, but God *might* play with an infinite number of universes. The Many World's theory—that there exist an endless number of universes folded into each other—exerts a powerful influence on theoretical physics today. This unexpected and bizarre—to conventional thinking—theory would account for otherwise absurd, confounding, and unexplainable results in quantum mechanics. What might seem impossible sometimes turns out to be true. Speaking more broadly of social

---

31 University of California Museum of Paleontology, UCMP.Berkeley.edu, http://www.ucmp.berkeley.edu/history/wegener.html, accessed June 7, 2010.

change, a number of things that began by appearing impossible to bring into being have been achieved.

To win a fight such as the one that provoked this book means that we have to begin with a deep understanding of what we face. Ordinary tools of perception and analysis will not do. Surface appearances and even personal experiences can be very deceptive. Personal experiences are, by necessity, partial snapshots of reality and therefore incomplete. To understand and change economic, social, and political dynamics presents a complicated challenge, one not to be undertaken superficially, and one not to be pursued without being grounded by a sober, serious, and ongoing reading of history, social science, philosophy, and so on. Much of conventional wisdom, it turns out upon closer examination, is false and/or misleading.

The common belief, for example, that the natures of the systems we live in are due to the individual choices, values, and personalities of the people in those systems is wrong. It is not merely slightly wrong; it is fundamentally wrong. Systems operate according to system logic. That is why we call them systems. In the famous Milgram Experiment, Stanley Milgram created a mini-system of authority and subjects.

The authority figure was the man in the gray coat holding a clipboard—the setting, coat and clipboard all symbols of his authority.[32] Imagine another person bursting into the Milgram Experiment room. The intruder exclaims to the subject, "You do not need to follow his orders. You are torturing the person in the other room. Resist! Walk out with me." To make this scenario more realistic the man with the clipboard could call upon guards outside the room to come in and seize the interloper and shut her up, telling the subject at the controls that he or she should ignore the intruder and continue with their duties. At this point the person who has been administering the shocks has to ask him or herself what they should do and what it means that the person from whom he or she has been following orders has now revealed himself to be something more troubling than just a man in a gray coat.

The person who burst into the room is attempting to create what social psychologists call a new social proof—a new standard for behavior, a new norm. Innovators create new norms and innovators must fight for the new standards.[33] What shapes the mores of an era are not primarily

---

32   Milgram used gray instead of a white coat so as to lessen his authority.

33   These innovators are sometimes unknown individuals. New fashions, for example, can start within groups of young people with the person or persons who started it hard to determine after the fact. But we know that whoever started the new trend was admired by those around them.

the actions and values of the mainstream. There is in fact never any truly undifferentiated mass of people. There are leaders at all levels and in all settings. The temper of the times is set by the actions of those who establish the norms from which others take their cues. When greed, material riches, and selfishness are the norm and when the law becomes whatever the leaders say it is, then the whole society suffers. When a society's system endangers the lives of its people and the viability of the planet, and when that system's leaders refuse to take the steps that must be taken to avoid disaster, then new leaders, representative of a different system, must step forward and create a new norm. They must set the standard and call on other people to adopt and adhere to that new standard.

It is not a question of having to get everyone to stop being selfish or expecting everyone to become heroes; it is not a question of advising everyone to "do their own thing"; it is a question of what standard is being set by the society's opinion-makers. It is the standard-setters and the system's logic that determine what most people will do and which end of the behavioral spectrum is favored. If the standard setters are adhering to an altruistic position, this does not eliminate the presence of greedy or otherwise antisocial and pathological individuals; it just makes them outré for the majority of the society. What we have now is the opposite situation, with most of the leading individuals in the political and economic arena moved by greed and personal advancement and with a system in place that is based upon promoting these antisocial behaviors and attitudes.

Sociology's central premise is that social structures—that is, social systems—are overall more important and powerful than the individuals who occupy them. As Durkheim correctly put it, society and social facts are *sui generis*—they exist independent of the people who make them up. Social facts have two characteristics: they exist external to the individual, and they exert a coercive force over the individual. Examples include gender, language, and "race." The Office of the President of the United States, for example, exists independently of whoever is president at any given time. As the Stanford Prison Experiment famously demonstrated, the roles of prison guard and prisoner exist separately from the particular individuals filling those roles. If the individuals filling those roles are Stanford undergraduates and they are in a Stanford University building's basement without any real bars, they will nonetheless behave eerily like actual prison guards and prisoners.

This sociological premise grows out of the fact that people behave differently in groups than they do on their own, and that group life requires norms for people to follow, or at least for the mainstream of the group to follow. The role that Durkheim's description of social facts plays in sociology is equivalent to the role that Darwin's theory of evolution plays in biology, the role that "show me, don't tell me" plays in acting, the role that the paint (or lane) and rebounding play in basketball, the role of the net and the lines in tennis, the role that garlic occupies in Chinese and Italian cooking, and the role that E = MC2 and the laws of thermodynamics play in physics. That is to say, it is indispensable.

While we all have autonomy in the sense that we can choose different paths at any given moment, we are fundamentally social beings who survive because we are interdependent; we acknowledge and sustain that interdependence by following norms. Most of these norms are not written down but are virtually universally understood and subscribed to (consciously or unconsciously); only the insane and extremely immature violate these rules on a consistent basis. We exist as a collectivity. We always have and always will.

Even those who were hermits began life and became viable human beings because adults raised them from birth, caring for them lovingly and teaching them what they needed to know in order to survive. The skills that hermits used to live in the wilderness—the ability to hunt, gather, grow food, start and maintain a fire, build and protect a shelter—were all passed on to them through others who in turn learned these indispensable skills through the collective and historical experience of human societies.

Even the most "rad" individuals (such as those who wear outrageously big and spiky Mohawk haircuts) have others who share their look, behavior, and so on; or else they are social outcasts who can only remain alive because they abide by at least some of the necessary social rules, because someone loves them unconditionally and feels obligated to them, or because they possess some highly valued skill so that others tolerate their idiosyncrasies in exchange for what they can offer. Furthermore, all individual human beings are in fact products of, and could not exist without, internal *systems* within our bodies: the neuromuscular *system*, the cardiovascular *system*, the digestive *system*, the skeletal *system*, and so on. As I argued in Chapter One, individuals and groups are different manifestations of the same fundamental process. Groups need individuals as a means for the group to express and advance itself; and individuals require groups to survive and exist in the first place.

Neoliberalism's advocates want all of us to believe that there is no such thing as society and that we are all solitary individuals whose only significant social units are the family and the nation. Systems, they would say, are simply the sum total of the actions of all of the individuals; none of us decide what we will do with regard to any visible or invisible system rules because there are no system rules, since systems do not exist in the first place. We all, according to them, seek to maximize our individual material gains without regard to the interests of the group. As I pointed out in Chapter One, if this neoliberal axiom were true, then humanity would never have survived and we would have long ago died away as the dinosaurs did.

Neoliberalism's central philosophical premise represents a sleight of hand trick. The people who follow neoliberal principles, cheerleaders for individual freedom and autonomy, do so by adapting themselves to the *system* logic of the organizations and institutions that promote neoliberalism. In other words, neoliberalism's true believers operate as *a collective* with a kind of group mind and spirit. The "talking points" discipline of the most fervid neoliberals, those found in the GOP, is followed religiously to the letter. No room here for autonomy or people rebelling at the very idea of someone telling them what to do. It is much too important that they all advocate in concert for the ideology and rhetoric of independent thought and action to have actual independence of thought interfere with group desires and plans.[34]

The persistence of the idea that the systems that we live in are simply the product of the personalities and choices of the individuals within them represents an obstacle in the path of effective social action aimed at social change. If we recognize that people are part of structures and forces larger than themselves at all times, then the question of bringing about social change means that we need to understand how group dynamics operate and how the most important systems function. The postmodern idea that we are only what we imagine and that nothing exists outside of that social construction leads people away from directly confronting the very real objective realities of the present and future worlds and the dominant systems of that current reality.

The foremost system that sets the political and economic context for all that I have discussed and analyzed in this book is the system of capitalism/imperialism. This system has certain particular and outstanding features that shape the way it operates and the processes that it sets in

---

34   For example, in March 2010, David Frum, former George W. Bush speechwriter famous for creating the term "axis of evil," was forced out of the American Enterprise Institute for daring to publicly criticize the GOP's opposition to the Obama Health Care bill. As described by fellow conservative Bruce Bartlett: "Frum told him AEI staffers 'had been ordered not to speak to the media' about health care 'because they agreed with too much of what Obama was trying to do. . . . The donor community is only interested in financing organizations that parrot the party line.'" Howard Kurtz, "Conservative David Frum Loses Think-Tank Job After Criticizing GOP," WashingtonPost.com, March 26, 2010, "http://www.washingtonpost.com/wp-dyn/content/article/2010/03/25/AR2010032502336.html, accessed May 31, 2010.

motion. Everything in capitalist/imperialist systems are subordinated to the pursuit of profit, including people's lives, welfare, and the planet's very viability. Public officials say otherwise, and in some instances some of them mean otherwise, but any one who attempts to put other concerns above the pursuit of profit and the continued viability of a system that rests upon profit is fighting an uphill battle in which victories are few, temporary, and trumped by the nature of the system itself. It is rather like trying to use a fork to transport water. It does not matter how frantically you keep trying, the thing just will not do what you need it to do.

Capitalism and its highest stage, imperialism, are in turn part of a larger dynamic of the progressive development of different modes of production (forms of organizing the economy) over the course of human history. What most people were never told, or do not believe, is that the particular manner in which humanity organizes itself to secure the means to survive at any point in time is not everlasting in nature; nor is the division of labor tied to those means of production, or the corresponding social relations, ideas, values, beliefs, or institutions that rest upon that mode of production everlasting in nature. Up until the last five percent of the duration of human existence, humanity lived in pre-class and pre-state formations, with the degree of social inequality scant and the notion of private property and individualism (in the sense of the individual bearing no responsibility for the group) non-existent.

If "human nature," that ghost that so many people believe in earnestly and steadfastly, were real, then the first ninety-five percent of our existence should prove that our human nature dictates that we should live without social classes. But, some object, we do not live in hunting and gathering societies any longer. Technological developments and large populations preclude pre-class societies, and the division of labor that accompanies advanced industrialized societies dictates that classes will remain with us forever. We cannot go back to those earlier days, they say. The thirst to consume and to live materially richer lives make competition for the choicer spots in the social hierarchy something that will characterize human society indefinitely. So we are told, and so, many of us believe.

Dog eat dog; every man for himself. *This* is what society is? It is not true of dogs, by the way, since dogs are social creatures and travel in packs. It is true of those dogs trained by their handlers to kill other dogs (and potentially people), but such dogs can no longer get along with their fellow dogs and are a threat to other people. It does not take long to recognize that society is a social collectivity that can only exist based on co-operation and mutual interdependence. Even in sports or games in which winning by beating the other person or team is the objective requires teams of people. This is even true in the so-called individual sports or games such as tennis or chess. Individual competitors become winners only through the support system that sustains the individual combatants.

The view that societies are in essence mainly (or wholly) characterized by individual competition represents a convenient fiction, useful for those who currently rule society since it makes their obligations to the rest of the society seem discretionary as opposed to obligatory. Individuals who perform in surpassingly extraordinary ways—the Michael Jordans, the Albert Einsteins, the Yo Yo Mas, the Malcolm Xs and so on—represent the cutting edge of their groups and of society, both in the times in which they lived, and as extensions of what came before them historically. They are the ones pushing the envelope, but they are connected to that envelope; without it they would not be able to do what they do. Leaders in their fields are sustained by the support systems that nourish them, both from within their own times and through the efforts and accomplishments of those who came before them historically.

This description of the relationship between the individual and the group also differs from the functionalist view, the latter perspective holding that individual leaders are simply doing the group's bidding (representing the collective conscience) based upon values held in common by the public and by those who lead them. The functionalist perspective, however, overlooks the diversity and clash of values within the body of society. For Durkheim, society's members share nearly all the same values. Can it be said, however, that British Petroleum, Goldman Sachs, Halliburton, and Walmart executives share the same values as the mass citizenry of the US? Rush Limbaugh and Cindy Sheehan cannot agree on virtually anything. They each, in turn, have a following. How can they be said to be part of the same "conscience collective?"

If competing values exist within the society, then individual leaders and the groups of which they are part represent and fight for these different values. The outcome of that ongoing fight determines which values and which groups hold the dominant position at any given time. Just as the quality of coaching makes a difference in sports (determining to a large extent whether a given competitor wins or loses when the competitors are roughly equal in talent and desire), so leaders play a disproportionately important role in the fortunes of those they lead. A better coach, armed with a smart game plan, can take an inferior squad and lead it to victory over a stronger team with a less able coach. Correspondingly, a stronger team can lose to a much weaker foe when the better team is poorly coached or when their morale is low. Likewise, a much larger and far better equipped army can fall to an adversary that is better led, highly motivated, and that enjoys the noncombatant population's support.

This provides us with a much more dynamic and accurate picture of how public policy is made and how cultural trends come into being than the much more static and empirically inaccurate conventional understanding that public policy and trends are products of "*the* public" or "*the* culture." Obviously, culture and politics are products of the public in the sense that everyone—leaders as well as those they lead—are all members of the public. But leaders and those they lead play different parts and unequal roles in the process. The question society faces now is what values will be the leading ones, since different values exist within the body politic and the values that lead set the overall tone for everyone. Which values will people emulate—selfishness and xenophobia, or altruism and a view of others as equals? Regardless of which values dominate, a spectrum of attitudes and corresponding behaviors will persist, but which one sets the standard and therefore the minimum ground rules will make all of the difference.

When the necessity and advantages of social interdependence for humanity are recognized explicitly, then advocating that some or all people be freed of any obligations to the rest of society and the environment can be seen for what it is—a profoundly antisocial, unsustainable, and inherently dangerous fraud. It is not merely a bad idea. It is a disastrously wrong idea that is running our society and an idea that is endangering life on the planet. It is an idea that needs to be roundly exposed and thoroughly repudiated.

How Do the People Learn That They Are Not the People and How Do They Learn To Be the People?

The people do not actually rule; the present system of elections and, even more importantly, the present economic organization do not allow them to rule. Continuing to try to achieve authentic popular rule within the present structures and processes will only produce agony and repeated failure. Persistence by those of good intentions in that doomed enterprise grows out of continuing faith in the "democracy at work" thesis: the view that this *is* democracy and we just need to adjust and reform what has not been working, for the fundamental theory is sound. This mistaken belief interferes with people's ability to recognize what has actually been going on and will continue to go on as long as this system remains intact. Just as the neoliberals have waged a fierce and highly successful fight to win people to their theory and ideology of how things work and ought to work, those who seek a different world than the neoliberal nightmare need to wage a fierce fight for an alternative worldview and theory. You cannot defeat the empire employing the belief and value system of that empire. That is the reason why I have stressed foundational philosophical issues in this book.

What we have now is democracy for the ruling circles and their oppressive rule over the rest of us: "Love it or leave it" with tons more money to the richest, celebrity circuses as "news," and let-them-eat-toxic-waste prescriptions for the people and other living beings. If some people do not like it, threaten them and lock them away as suspected terrorists. Even the reasonably fair fights within the ruling circles of the past are turning more and more into iron rule over those who stray the least bit from the most extreme orthodox neoliberal faith. Democrats who dare to even faintly criticize any of 21st century America's litmus tests for loyalty (such as the "War on Terror;" massive, warrantless surveillance without suspicion; and the abrogation of civil liberties) have been condemned by the GOP and their media mouthpieces as treasonous. Any Republicans who break ranks with the GOP leadership are also treated as apostates.

As for We the People, we can have our say, as long as what we say does not get much attention and does not directly affect the making of public policy.

Neoliberals believe that popular opinion determines what is true; if a lot of people believe something, this makes it true. This is like respecting the views of one of a group of people yelling on cell phones based on who is the loudest. Certainly all too many of the talking heads on TV and on talk radio adopt this principle. Truth, however, is not—and should not be—determined by popularity or how loudly it is shouted. So how can we determine what is true in current events, since there are so many different opinions and reports about what is going on?

Here is where facts and what is treated as true interpenetrate with one's desires. Like a group of people riding a bus to a series of destinations, some people want to go further than others. Some people, once they get "theirs," once their social and economic position is secured and they are comfortable, want to get off the bus. They also think that their stop is suitable for everyone else and that the bus should end its journey there, even if this destination does not provide justice or fairness for the vast majority of people. Reactionaries such as Rush Limbaugh, who appeal to the people's worst sentiments and desires to scapegoat, scoff at the desires of minorities/nationalities and women to undo centuries of oppression. "Get over it!" Rush says in effect. "Quit your bellyaching! The way things are is fine and dandy. I've got mine, why are not you content with what you've got? What's wrong with *you*?"

While truth exists independently of any individuals' or groups' perceptions of truth and advocacy of what they think is true, the connection between the politics and ideology of different groups—their version of where the bus should end its journey—and their views and stands are crucial to recognize, for they play central roles in the configuration of the political arena. In any major political battle, different individuals express differing group interests (whether or not they do so consciously) and those different groups have different attitudes about how to proceed and where we should go.

As I wrote in Chapter Five, convincing people that their choice was limited to the Democratic nominee or the Republican nominee and nothing else, is like persuading a child that they are *in charge* when they decide whether they will eat the peas or the carrots. Breaching the framework of what the self-interested elites of our society present to the people as their only choices must occur if any actual change is to occur.

Unleashing the actions of the more politically advanced who are, by definition, smaller in number but key to the behavior and attitudes of others since they set the standard for others, is central to bringing about genuine and fundamental change. Even though both matter and neither should be overlooked, conformity matters more than consensus in determining the tenure of a given political system. That is, it is not people's beliefs that hold systems together as much as the inertial forces of the system itself. People do not trade the status quo for something radically different unless the status quo is no longer the status quo. When the existing authorities are in profound trouble and they can no longer hold things together, and if an alternative leadership with sufficient influence and size (with its roots and influence having been established during the period preceding the full eruption of the crisis) is present and contending in the midst of this crisis, then a fundamental shift can potentially occur.

The neoliberals with their neoliberal vision are proving themselves unable and unwilling to act as superintendents of this planet. They are wracked by crises, and while they are still in power and in command of huge resources, they face immense contradictions for which they have no real answers. The magnitude of the problems and the absence of a powerful and influential alternative force to that of the existing system are having a paralyzing effect on most people, leading some to various versions of despair, wishful thinking, or false sanctuaries in faith-based movements.

An alternative to the neoliberal nightmare exists. Will humanity take it? At this point that is a decision to be made by a relatively small number of people. Revolutions—as well as fashion and musical trends—begin among a very small group of people and spread to another relatively small group, in total a mere one percent of the people, equivalent to roughly three million in the US. The popular uprisings in Egypt et al offer gusts of powerfully fresh winds, a dramatic demonstration of how mass actions can be brought into being and what determined masses who will not be denied can accomplish.

While not everyone or even many people are able to become *the* leaders of such change, many people are capable of becoming *a* leader, even on a modest level among their friends and family. Moreover, the logic and premises of the dominant forces today are extremely vulnerable to counterarguments and actual facts. Very many people are also capable of providing financial and other forms of support for those who are willing now to step forward as leaders. Even very modest financial support from many different people adds up to a lot of money. Those people and organizations who are committed to revolutionary changes can do a tremendous amount with what are comparatively modest sums relative to the vast sums being spent by the forces who benefit from the existing terribly distorted state of affairs.

To paraphrase Archimedes, give us one percent and we can lift this country and this world.

What Then To Do?

The challenge we face is extraordinary, daunting, and multifaceted. Anyone claiming otherwise misrepresents the difficulties and complexities. Accomplishing this feat of dramatically restructuring society is only possible in times of great strife, because it takes a crisis to bring about the necessary magnitude of indomitable energy and the level of intolerance for the status quo that are needed. But you cannot wait for such times to arrive to lay the requisite and difficult groundwork. No matter how dissatisfied people might be with the existing leaders, the majority will continue to follow them until the existing leaders can no longer hold things together *and* there is another, alternative leadership that they know of and become willing to follow. People will seek and are seeking other more palatable options: "Can't we just vote for the right person?" Well, no, you cannot. It does not work that way.

If you want to see a different world than the present one and/or you are disturbed by the trajectory of things, then what can you do? I started this book citing the fundamental truth that what people do is based upon how they see the world. Thus, the battle over truth and over perception—what is true and what needs to be taken into account given its objective reality—are central to any attempts at social change.

Unlike the literal textualists who believe that perception equals truth (what you think is true makes it true), the two are not synonymous. Believing something to be true does not make it so. The idea that you can will something into being by faith and that one's adversaries are by definition not to be believed (since they see things differently from you) represents a radical rejection of the possibility of truth independent of subjectivity. One of the ways that this stance gets expressed by literal textualists and those who respect power more than truth is in their ad hominem attacks on those with whom they disagree: "Those who differ with me are biased and cannot possibly be believed. Whatever they say is suspicious. I do not have to take what they say seriously because of that."[35]

When the fact that their criticisms are ad hominem is pointed out to such people, some of them flatly deny that they are employing an ad hominem argument—because they know enough to recognize that ad hominem is a bad thing to be doing—but they have not the faintest idea what ad hominem means. When I first encountered this I was puzzled. How could they not see that they were relying on an ad hominem argument? Why did they so loudly protest that I am wrongly accusing them of what is so obvious? I finally realized that this was not a matter of simple ignorance, curable by a visit to the dictionary to read that an ad hominem argument is dismissing what someone says because of who that person is rather than because of the content of what they have said. If you do not think that objective reality exists independent of perception, then all that exists is opinion and perspective. Hence, one's adversaries must be wrong because they do not see things the way you do. Ergo, they cannot have any purchase on any truths; otherwise this would mean that you yourself are wrong, which cannot be.

It also follows from this epistemological stance that the way to deal with those who disagree with you is not to try to reason with them, since

---

35 This is also an unfortunately all too common argument made among some on the Left as well: that you have no right to say anything about, for example, sexism, if you are not a woman, or that you have no right to talk about race if you are not of that particular race. This view is, while perhaps understandable, nonsense. If someone is right in their observations, it does not matter who they are, and it does not even matter what their motives are.

reasoning involves appeal to independent criteria. Instead, the way to deal with those who disagree with you is to try to twist their arms, suppress them, or attempt to undermine their reputations, in other words to use deception and/or coercion. This accounts for the egregious behavior of those who do not respect truth and who abide by might—violent words and violent acts, intimidation and character assassination, the culmination of which are beatings, torture, and/or murder.

Objective truth and perception are related; if you are not aware of what is true, then your ability to shape events is profoundly compromised by your ignorance of the truth. Truth is not, however, something that is unchanging in nature. The leaders of the US Empire like to believe, for example, that their high tech wizardry makes them invincible, that their military might means that they are unbeatable. In a direct confrontation between military forces it is true that the US would win. But that is not the nature of the ongoing wars in Afghanistan and Iraq.

Let me illustrate this further: The truth that someone is physically stronger than someone else does not necessarily mean that the weaker person cannot beat the stronger person in a fight. It does mean, however, that the weaker person has to take the fact of the other person's greater physical strength into account in order to have a chance to win. You cannot just plunge into such a fight heedless of what the conditions are. To have a chance you have to adopt a game plan and choose a battleground that neutralizes or even turns the other person's greater physical strength into a weakness. This is what martial arts such as Aikido do—use their opponent's strength against them.

In other words, first of all we need to know what is going on in order to have a chance to affect the course of present and future events. Having access to good information and good analysis is therefore indispensable. Otherwise you are operating blindly or under illusions. If you are preparing a meal to eat, then your ingredients matter a great deal. You cannot make a good dish if your raw materials are poor. Someone can be given the very best ingredients to make a meal in the world, but if they do not know how to cook, then what they make will, in all probability, not be all that good. They could even ruin it entirely. So the ingredients matter, but what you do with those ingredients also matters.

Good intentions are not enough to guarantee good results. Where, then, does one go to get good information, and how does one develop reliable analytical skills?

In Appendix 1 that follows, I list some sources that are useful places to get information. The list is not intended to be exhaustive, since the places from which one can get information and analysis these days are substantial.[36]

Any account that you read, view, or hear has been framed interpretively. This is inevitable; choices must be made as to what to highlight and what to leave out. This is as true of news reporting and any nonfiction endeavor as it is of fiction and art. The question then comes down to what facts are *relevant* and what those facts add up to. It is not possible to provide a cookbook recipe on how to decide what is relevant and what their meaning is in any given process, but it is possible to lay down certain principles.

The first principle is that any social process involves the dynamic interplay between what sociologists call structure and agency. Structure refers to the social context, the rules stated and unstated for the system in question. (The most commonly articulated manifestation of structure in laypersons' language is the power and reality of institutional or organizational culture.) Agency refers to individuals' choices within that larger system context. In this process the overall more determining factor is structure because (a) we are social beings not individuals, and (b) social structures' persistence depends upon social rules being followed and those who ignore or violate those rules being sanctioned. As social beings we rely upon social structures, and we can only continue to exist because we exist within them. Structure and social rules exert a constant and powerful force over us.

We need structure and networks to survive. But those structures can be overall hindrances. The solution to a problematic structure is not lack of structure. The solution is not to call upon people to follow their own paths (telling them to disregard peer pressure and other forms of social suasion) and expect that this is an avenue they will adopt. The solution, instead, is a different structure. News stories or analyses that elevate the individual and individual choices above the actual de facto rules of structures are misrepresenting the actual situation. So that is the first thing to keep in mind when you read or see accounts of social issues. Efforts to change must rest principally upon individual and group efforts to replace the problematic structures with different structures.

Second, as I have stressed throughout this book, public policies, corporate behavior, and any other group behavior are not the product primarily of the values, personalities, or choices of the individuals within them. They are primarily the product of the *standards* being set by the leading

---

36   This includes consulting what the other side is saying too, for there are important things to be learned from them and the way they are constructing "reality."

individuals in those groups and organizations and the *governing logic* and rationale of those organizations and groups. Changing the behavior and nature of public policy, et al requires a structural change, and said structural change must be led by individuals who enlist the support of others to supplant the existing leaders *and* the existing structures. Change, in other words, requires leadership and groups of people acting in concert with each other and under that leadership.

Third, different classes and different groups have different material interests, and those material interests are reflected in ideologies, values, beliefs, and their pursuit of their group's interests. Recognizing the parameters of different ideologies and how they serve different classes and groupings within those classes is critical to developing an ability to see beneath the surface to the essence of any social issue and social struggle. Put in more common parlance, there are vested interests, and those interests are expressed or articulated by the leading spokespeople for those groups. The bottom line, the fundamental division in our society, is between, on the one hand, those whose interests rest upon dominance and the drive towards monopolizing the society and planet's resources and, on the other hand, those whose interests lie in the husbanding of those resources for the good of the whole rather than the part. The startling evidence of the neoliberals' bankruptcy surrounds us everyday, and grows starker as time moves on. Their attacks on the people grow more vociferous and damaging by the day. The prospect of a radically different future from that spreading nightmare exists in embryonic form today.

Which path will be taken? The world awaits. The future beckons. Who will answer the call?

APPENDIX 1

Resources

A website adjunct to this book can be found at http://dennisloo.com. The site provides further materials for those reading this book, with guides to the various chapters, highlighting certain core themes and elaborating on certain points. The site also offers an opportunity to converse with other readers of the book and with the author—a moderated forum for people to comment on developments, conditions, and situations they see as worthy of note.

Finding a place where lively, principled, sophisticated, and in depth commentary and discussions take place on a consistent basis is hard to find. Yet such a place—a salon in the best sense of the term—is needed more than ever. All topics will be considered and strenuous debate and inquiry are encouraged, but with civility, reason, and evidence at all times.

Truth does not need to be kept in a temperature-controlled room, isolated from the winds and storms of the world. If what someone says is true, then they have nothing to fear from those who disagree with them; truth grows in the context of vigorous debate. Debate, however, is not for showing off or trying to bully those who disagree with you. Debate works if and when it is for the purpose of getting at the truth. Being open to other viewpoints and wanting to wrangle over the truth is a hallmark of a wise person. Truth always needs to be struggled for because it represents the most advanced understanding at any point in time.

The following very short list is deliberately designed to be brief because I do not want to inundate the reader. I have thus left out many excellent sites. Any one of these sites below, however, will refer you to other very useful sites. The perspectives of the listed sites below range from liberal to revolutionary.

If you are not already acquainted with any of those on this list, you will find them helpful. Most of them will allow you to set up automatic free emails to you on a frequent basis of their newest postings. If you spend ten or fifteen minutes a day with any one of these sites, you will be better informed than most of the rest of the US. While they each contain breaking news, they are not on this list primarily because of their news breaking character but because they do extremely good news analysis. Most of these sites will also help you to keep track of what the mainstream and right-wing extremists are saying and doing, an important thing to do in its own right.

Besides your becoming better informed by reading these sites, nearly all of them could use more substantial financial support. Because most of them operate on a shoestring budget, your individual donation/sustainer can make a disproportionately large difference. If you encourage others in your circle of friends and family to do likewise, you can single-handedly make a significant difference in the ability of these groups to get their word out.

As I have argued in this book, good intentions based upon an incorrect understanding of what is going on and why it is going on will not get you where you need to go. It is for that reason that changing what people know and how they analyze the world will have a material impact on the world.

Aljazeera	http://english.aljazeera.net/
Black Agenda Report	http://blackagendareport.com
Consortium News	http://consortiumnews.com
Counterpunch	http://counterpunch.org
Dennis Loo	http://dennisloo.com
FAIR	http://fair.org
(Fairness and Accuracy in Reporting)	
Glenn Greenwald	http://www.salon.com/news/opinion/glenn_greenwald/index.html
Media Matters	http://mediamatters.org
OpEd News	http://opednews.com
Project Censored	http://www.projectcensored.org/
Revolution Newspaper	http://revcom.us
World Can't Wait	http://worldcantwait.net

APPENDIX 2

Polls on the Possible Impeachment of Bush and/or Cheney, 2005-2007

These polls occurred in the context of opposition by both the GOP and the Democratic Party leadership and nearly the entire mass media, with the exception of *Harper's*, to the idea of impeachment. Given the major parties' and mass media's nearly universal opposition to impeachment, the numbers recorded in these polls in favor of initiating an impeachment process are remarkable. The polls are listed in reverse chronological order.

	Poll	Question	Support	Oppose
11/13/07	American Research Group	**Impeach and Remove Bush:** "President Bush has *abused his powers* as president which rise to the *level of impeachable offenses* under the Constitution and he should be **impeached and removed** from office." "November 13, 2007—Impeachment," http://americanresearchgroup.com/impeach/, American Research Group, Inc, retrieved on April 9, 2010.	34%	36%

11/13/07	American Research Group	**Impeach and Remove Cheney:** "Vice President Cheney has *abused his powers* as vice president which rise to the level of impeachable offenses under the Constitution and he should be **impeached and removed** from office." "November 13, 2007—Impeachment," http://americanresearchgroup.com/ impeach/, American Research Group, Inc, retrieved on April 9, 2010.	43%	30%
11/12/07	Rasmussen	**Impeach and Remove Cheney** —Regina Sass, "Poll: 31% Believe Vice President Dick Cheney Should Be Impeached," http://www. associatedcontent.com/article/445349/ poll_31_believe_vice_president_dick. html?cat=62, retrieved on April 9th, 2010.	31%	40%
9/6/07	Zogby	**Impeach Bush or Cheney or Both** "Some groups on both the right and left are now petitioning Congress to impeach the President and/or the Vice President. Based on your own knowledge of George Bush's and Dick Cheney's conduct regarding war policy, detainee treatment, domestic surveillance, the 9/11 attacks and Congressional investigations, which one of the following comes closest to your opinion? 1. Congress should start impeachment proceedings against George 2. Congress should start impeachment proceedings against Dick C 3. Congress should start impeachment proceedings against both 4. Congress should take no action on impeaching Bush or Cheney" "Zogby America Likely Voters 8/23/07 thru 8/27/07 MOE +/- 3.1 percentage points," http://www.911truth.org/ images/ZogbyPoll2007.pdf, retrieved on April 15, 2010.	32%	66.8%

7/8/07	Demo crats.com	**Begin impeachment hearings for Bush which could lead to removal**	43%	50%
7/8/07	Demo crats.com	**Begin impeachment hearings for Cheney which could lead to removal**	45%	43%
7/8/07	USA Today/ Gallup	**Begin impeachment hearings for Bush which could lead to removal:** "As you may know, impeachment is the first step in the constitutional process for removing a president from office, in which possible crimes are investigated and charges are made. Do you think there is or is not **justification for Congress to begin impeachment proceedings** against President Bush **at this time?**" "USA Today/Gallup poll results," http://www.usatoday.com/news/washington/2007-07-09-bush-poll-results_N.htm, retrieved on April 10, 2010.	36%	62%
7/7/07	Rasmussen	**Impeach and Remove Bush**	39%	49%
7/6/07	ARG	**Impeachment proceedings against Bush:** "Do you favor or oppose the US House of Representatives **beginning impeachment proceedings** against President George W. Bush?" "November 13, 2007—Impeachment," http://americanresearchgroup.com/impeach/, American Research Group, Inc, retrieved on April 9, 2010.	45%	46%
7/6/07	ARG	**Impeachment proceedings against Cheney** "Do you favor or oppose the US House of Representatives **beginning impeachment proceedings** against Vice President Dick Cheney?" "November 13, 2007—Impeachment," http://americanresearchgroup.com/impeach/, American Research Group, Inc, retrieved on April 9, 2010.	54%	40%

5/8/07	Insider Advantage	**Impeach Bush and Cheney:** "Would you favor or oppose the **impeachment** by Congress of President **George W. Bush and Vice President Dick Cheney?**" Matt Towery, "Bush-Cheney Impeachment Might Be Idle Talk, But Numbers Show True Trouble," http://townhall.com/columnists/MattTowery/2007/05/08/bush-cheney_impeachment_might_be_idle_talk,_but_numbers_show_true_trouble, retrieved on April 12, 2010.	39%	55%
1/25/07	Newsweek	**Wish Bush Presidency Was "Over"**	58%	37%
1/3/07	Harris	**Investigations**	56%	34%
10/25/06	USA/ Gallup	**Major investigations (by Democrats)** "Suppose the Democrats win control of both houses of Congress in this year's elections and try to do each of the following after they take control in January. Please say whether you would approve or disapprove of that action: Conduct **major investigations** of the Bush administration" "USA Today/Gallup poll," http://www.usatoday.com/news/polls/tables/live/2006-10-25-poll.htm, retrieved on April 12, 2010.	51%	47%
10/21/06	Newsweek	**Impeach (by Democrats)**	51%	44%
9/2/06	CNN	**Impeach and Remove**	30%	69%
5/22/06	FOX (RV)	**Impeach (by Democrats):** "Regardless of how you plan to vote, if the Democrats win this year's Congressional elections do you think it would **be right for them to try to impeach President Bush over the Iraq war and weapons of mass destruction,** or not?" "**Polls & Research:** Few Americans Expect Bush Impeachment," http://www.angus-reid.com/polls/view/11956, retrieved on April 12, 2010.	30%	62%

4/24/06	Democracy Corps (LV)	**Censure**	46%	45%
4/12/06	LA Times	**Impeachable offense:** "If George W. Bush **broke the law** when he authorized government agencies to use electronic *surveillance to monitor American citizens without a court warrant*, **do you think that is an impeachable offense**, or not an impeachable offense?" "Hard Times For Bush and GOP" http://latimes.image2.trb.com/lanews/media/acrobat/2006-04/22915725.pdf, retrieved on April 12, 2010.	36%	56%
4/12/06	LA Times	**Censure:** "As you may also know, a U.S. Senator has called for a Senate resolution to censure George W. Bush, which is a **formal expression of disapproval**, but **does not carry any legal consequences**. The Senator **claims** it was illegal for Bush to authorize government agencies to use electronic surveillance to monitor American citizens without a court warrant. What do you think? Do you think that George W. Bush should be **censured** by the Senate for this, or not?" **"Hard Times for Bush and the GOP,"** http://latimes.image2.trb.com/lanews/media/acrobat/2006-04/22915725.pdf, retrieved April 15, 2010.	46%	45%
4/10/06	WashPost/ABC	**Impeach and remove:** "Democratic Congressman John Conyers has called for **creation of a committee to look into** impeaching Bush and removing him from office. Do you think Congress should or should not **impeach Bush and remove him from office?**" **"Washington Post-ABC News Poll,"** http://www.washingtonpost.com/wp-srv/politics/polls/postpoll_immigration_041006.htm, retrieved on April 15, 2010.	33%	66%

4/10/06	WashPost	**Censure:** "As you may know, Bush authorized **wiretaps** on telephone calls and e-mails of people *suspected of involvement with terrorism*, **without first getting court approval** to do so. Democratic Senator Russ Feingold has called for Congress to censure or officially reprimand Bush for doing this. Do you think Congress should or should not **censure** or **officially reprimand** Bush for authorizing these wiretaps?" **"Washington Post-ABC News Poll,"** http://www.washingtonpost.com/wp-srv/politics/polls/postpoll_immigration_041006.htm, retrieved on April 15, 2010.	45%	53%
3/27/06	Democracy Corps (LV)	**Censure**	44%	51%
3/27/06	Democracy Corps (LV)	**Censure**	41%	56%
3/18/06	Newsweek	**Impeach and remove:** "Do you think Congress should take **action to IMPEACH** President Bush and **consider removing** him from office, or not?" "President Bush and the Bush Administration," http://www.pollingreport.com/bush_ad.htm, retrieved on April 10, 2010.	26%	69%
3/18/06	Newsweek	**Censure:** "As you may know, Senator Russ Feingold has called for Congress to censure or formally **reprimand President Bush over the issue of his warrantless wiretapping program**. Censure is a way for Congress to **express strong disapproval** of a President's actions without going so far as impeachment. Would you support the **CENSURE** of President Bush by Congress, or not?" "President Bush and the Bush Administration," http://www.pollingreport.com/bush_ad.htm, retrieved on April 10, 2010.	42%	50%

3/15/06	ARG (LV)	**Impeach:** "Do you favor or oppose the United States House of Representatives voting to impeach President George W. Bush?" Bob Fertik, "New ARG Poll on Censure & Impeachment," http://www.democrats.com/node/8219, retrieved on April 15, 2010.	43%	50%
3/15/06	ARG (LV)	**Censure:** "Do you favor or oppose the United States Senate passing a resolution censuring President George W. Bush for authorizing wiretaps of Americans within the United States without obtaining court orders?" Bob Fertik, "New ARG Poll on Censure & Impeachment," http://www.democrats.com/node/8219, retrieved on April 15, 2010.	48%	43%
2/1/06	MyDD (RV)	**Hold accountable through impeachment and removal:** "If it were determined that President **Bush broke the law**, do you support the U.S. Congress **holding him accountable** through **impeachment and removal** from office?" Chris Bowers, "Polling Project, Sixth Release," http://mydd.com/2006/2/1/polling-project-sixth-release, retrieved on April 15, 2010.	50%	39%
1/16/06	Zogby	**Hold accountable through impeachment:** "If President Bush **wiretapped** American citizens **without the approval** of a judge, do you agree or disagree that Congress **should consider holding him accountable** through impeachment." Bob Fertik, "Poll: Americans Support Bush Impeachment for Wiretapping," http://www.democrats.com/bush-impeachment-poll-2, retrieved on April 15, 2010.	52%	43%
12/14/05	Rasmussen	**Impeach and remove Bush**	32%	56%

367

12/14/05	Rasmussen	**Impeach and remove Cheney**	35%	53%
11/4/05	Zogby	**Consider impeaching:** "If President Bush **did not tell the truth** about his reasons for going to war with **Iraq**, Congress should consider holding him accountable through **impeachment.**" David Swanson, "New Poll: Majority of Americans Support Impeachment," http://www.afterdowningstreet. org/?q=node/4421, retrieved on April 17, 2010.	53%	42%
10/11/05	Ipsos	**Consider impeaching:** "If President Bush did **not tell the truth** about his reasons for going to **war with Iraq,** Congress **should consider holding him accountable** by impeaching him." Bob Fertik, "Poll: Americans Favor Bush Impeachment If He Lied about Iraq," http://www.democrats.com/bush-impeachment-poll-1, retrieved on April 9, 2010.	50%	44%
6/30/05	Zogby (LV)	**Hold accountable through impeachment:** "If it is found that President Bush did **not tell the truth** about his reasons for going to war with **Iraq**, Congress **should hold him accountable** through impeachment." "No Bounce: Bush Job Approval Unchanged by War Speech; Question on Impeachment Shows Polarization of Nation; Americans Tired of Divisiveness in Congress—Want Bi-Partisan Solutions—New Zogby Poll," http://www.zogby.com/news/readnews. cfm?ID=1007, retrieved on April 10, 2010.	42%	50%

This chart is based upon material assembled by Bob Fertik for "Demand More Polls on Bush Impeachment," August 24, 2005, http://www.democrats.com/bush-impeachment-polls, retrieved on April 9, 2010. Ellie Wood, who constructed this chart, added additional material.

368

APPENDIX 3

Methodological Issues in the 1990s Crime Wave Study in Chapter Six

Note: I have pulled these passages that belong within Chapter Six's discussion into this appendix because the main audience for this book will not be scholarly and therefore will find this particular material more technical and possibly less interesting. For those readers who are interested, however, here are most of those deleted passages:

The field of Communications Studies has been more active in attempting to identify media effects (defined as media's effect on public opinion) than has the field of social problems theory. Historically, three strains within media effects research can be identified. These are the following: (a) media effects as persuasion (changing attitudes), (b) media effects as framing (defining or interpreting conditions), and, more recently, (c) media effects as priming (foregrounding certain events and associated issues). Priming sees media as priming consumers by calling attention to specific events and conditions and foregrounding issues associated with those events.[1] News media must, of course, select their stories from among the welter of events and conditions present in the world—after all, only so much space exists in a broadcast and only so many inches on the front page. Priming is, therefore, necessary and inevitable.

Showing that priming *actually affects* public opinion, however, has proven very difficult in prior research. Inconclusive results litter the

---

1   Ray Surette, *Media, Crime and Criminal Justice: Images and Realities*, 2nd ed., (Belmont, CA: Wadsworth Press, 1998).

landscape of media effects studies. The failure to decisively demonstrate media effects makes it impossible to resolve the ongoing debate over how "maximal" or "minimal" media effects actually are. Communications Studies by itself lacks the methodological toolkit to frame media effects within a larger social arena. Joining Communication Studies with social problems theory, therefore, makes sense for tracing the process by which one issue emerges as a social problem and other issues are discarded.

Demonstrating a "strong" media effect would contribute to resolving the "minimal" versus "maximal" media effects debate and would install media in a more central place within social problems theory. Failure to do this would mean underestimating media's power to affect public policy and further distort the public policy process. Media's coverage of the 1993-94 "crime wave" in the US offers an opportunity to demonstrate a "strong" media effect.

. . .

The dominant variant within social constructionism recognizes and even highlights media-induced distortions of a social problem's seriousness. However, social problems theory would be better off adopting a model that situates media (and/or public officials) in a position more in line with their actual social power. Such an approach would recognize media's (and public officials') pronounced ability to act as *primary* claims-makers.[2] That approach would more fundamentally question a specific social problem's legitimacy than would simply noting that media have "hyped" an issue.

Most media effects studies have employed either a cross-sectional or panel approach. However, neither strategy adequately addresses the causality issue. Cross-sectional approaches do not provide a heuristic model that allows for the determination of underlying relationships, thus making it impossible to establish with confidence whether a public agenda actually originated from a media agenda; furthermore, cross-sectional studies are

---

2   The dominant social problems model defines a primary claims-maker as an entity that makes the initial claim that an issue should be treated as a social problem and acts as its strongest advocate throughout the course of a social problem's life history. A secondary claims-maker reacts to primary claims-makers' advocacy and either propagates the primary claims-makers' claims or ignores them. According to the dominant model, media and the state are seen as nearly always secondary claims-makers. Joel Best, *Damned Lies and Statistics: Untangling Numbers From the Media, Politicians, and Activists* (Berkeley: University of California Press, 2001), 15 describes media's role as that of conduit for interest groups' claims: "Successful activists attract support from others. The *mass media* – including both the press. . . and entertainment media. . . **relay** activists' claims to the general public." [Emphasis added.]

snapshots in time, and therefore cannot account for longitudinal media lag effects. Panel studies are a better tool for making a case for media effects, but problems remain in determining the possible duration of time-lag effects and in controlling for alternative casual factors outside of media effects.[3]

Excluding those studies that have adopted cross-sectional methods (and, therefore, have simply assumed that the causal order runs from media to the public), the only studies that have shown fairly clear indications of media effects are Beckett[4], MacKuen and Coombs,[5] Iyengar[6] and Iyengar, Peters, and Kinder.[7] In both the Beckett study and the MacKuen and Coombs study, the demonstration of a media effect used regression analysis because the data compiled did not lend themselves to an obvious interpretation.[8] In the Iyengar study and the Iyengar, Peters, and Kinder study, an experimental approach was employed.

---

3 Fay Lomax Cook, Tom R. Tyler, Edward G. Goetz, Margaret T. Gordon, David Protess, Donna R. Leff, and Harvey L. Molotch, "Media and Agenda Setting: Effects on the Public, Interest Group Leaders, Policy Makers, and Policy," *Public Opinion Quarterly* 47 (1983):16-35.

4 Beckett, "The Politics of Law and Order."

5 Michael MacKuen and Steven L. Coombs, *More Than News: Media Power in Public Affairs* (Beverly Hills: Sage, 1981).

6 Shanto Iyengar, "Television News and Citizens' Explanations of National Affairs," *American Political Science Review*, Vol. 81 (1987), No. 3: 815-831.

7 Shanto Iyengar, Mark D. Peters, and Donald R. Kinder. 1982. "Experimental Demonstrations of the 'Not-So-Minimal' Consequences of Television News Programs." *American Political Science Review*, 76 (1982): 848-858.

8 I do not use statistical techniques such as regression or time series analysis on these data because they are unnecessary. Regression, and similar statistical methods, are necessary when the data are more oblique than those presented here. As Paul Tracy, "Prevalence, Incidence, Rates and Other Descriptive Measures," in *Juvenile Delinquency*, eds. Joseph Weis, Robert Crutchfield, George Bridges (Thousand Oaks, CA: Pine Forge Press), 77 argues:

> There is a tendency in social science research today . . . to apply very sophisticated statistical models and multivariate analytical procedures to research data. In many instances, these highly advanced procedures are desirable, if not absolutely necessary. Despite this tendency, there is no substitute for a thorough descriptive analysis of one's data accompanied by a well-conceived presentation of tables and figures. The most simple analyses, effectively displayed, are often the most convincing and communicative to the reader.

My study corrects for some of the methodological limitations of prior studies by incorporating data drawn from over several decades. Examining data over time compensates for the restrictions and potential errors inherent in cross-sectional studies and panel studies. This study looks at three factors in determining media effects vis-à-vis the 1993-94 crime wave: (1) "Most Important Problem in the Nation" (MIP) data from national public opinion polls; (2) crime incidence and prevalence data; and (3) quantitative and qualitative measures of crime news coverage.

The MIP poll provides researchers with a powerful tool for examining longitudinal shifts in public opinion (or at least public attention) because it has been administered for several decades in precisely the same format. It thus serves as an appropriate instrument for measuring possible agenda-setting effects. For researchers, one of the distinct virtues of the MIP polls is that the question "What do you think is the most important problem facing the country today?" has been posed in precisely the same way since 1935.[9] This obviates framing effects problems that would compromise the reliability of longitudinal data comparisons.

The MIP data used in this analysis were drawn from the entire polling record (unpublished and published polls) available through the Roper Center. (These polls' questions were all asked in a closed format. In some instances, pollsters offered first, second, and third choices to respondents. The results used in this study were restricted to first choice answers.) Using the entire polling record has proved valuable for two reasons. First, it permitted the rigorous implementation of a controlled, repeated, cross-sectional methodology—indispensable in a media effects study. Second, it showed that the published record of poll results was not only incomplete, but that it was also at times inaccurate. Without a database as complete as this, it simply cannot be determined with any reliability whether media attention or shifts in public attention/interest came first. (An important caveat is that because individual-level media consumption is not available—outside of the confines of an experimental study—researchers cannot truly distinguish media effects from self-selection by individual consumers. Traditionally, nearly all media effects studies have employed aggregate-level data. This study follows that tradition.)

There remains the problem of selecting resources of the appropriate type and quantity from which to measure media activity. An inappropriate or incomplete data source can instantly sabotage a study's validity. For example, the *Reader's Guide to Periodical Literature* has been a popular

---

9   I used all MIP polls conducted by all major polling organizations housed at the Roper Center.

index for media researchers, but it does not index newspapers or television news broadcasts. While the index has the virtue of a long publishing history and does track some of the major newsmagazines, its content focus is on popular literature, not on news sources, and therefore it has limited use in analyses of news media effects. A news wave could splash across major media outlets and raise hardly a ripple in the *Reader's Guide*.

Another problem with data sources occurs when researchers focus on too few outlets. Classically, for a media effect to be demonstrated, a media coverage wave must precede shifts in public attention. But nearly every prior media effects study has confined itself to one, or at most two, media outlets. In part, the decision to choose one or two outlets has been driven by practical considerations—that is, which outlet has an available index. In part, too, the implicit assumption has been that an outlet such as the *New York Times* can be treated as *exemplary* of the rest of the news media. If, however, the coverage wave began with a media outlet other than the one(s) used in the study, the media effects study's identification of the coverage wave's timing will be inaccurate. By their nature, coverage waves embrace a wide variety of news outlets. One cannot adequately examine a coverage wave without including the major players.

. . .

Despite scholarly recognition of media work's self-referential nature, oddly no media effects studies have previously incorporated this element into their study design. This study addresses this shortcoming by incorporating the three truly major media outlets. These are four major "national" newspapers (the *Los Angeles Times*, the *New York Times*, *Washington Post*, and the *Wall Street Journal*), the three major newsmagazines (*Newsweek, Time* and *US News and World Report*),[10] and the nightly national news broadcasts on the three major networks (ABC, CBS and NBC).[11] Major news media are hence treated herein as a differentiated whole. This makes

---

10   Because I was interested in major media impact, I chose to concentrate on crime cover stories in the newsmagazines instead of the sum total of their crime-related articles. My decision to select newsmagazine cover stories was based in part on a shift in recent years in newsmagazines' marketing strategy. In retrospect, an analogous strategy of concentrating on front-page newspaper stories only, rather than their sum total of stories, would have been possible and probably desirable.

11   In part, my decision to use these national broadcasts, as opposed to more local or regional broadcasts, was due to the fact that national broadcasts are indexed whereas local broadcasts are not, and because tapes of those broadcasts are more available than are tapes of local broadcasts that are almost impossible to obtain. In addition, the national broadcasts were generally a better source of information about national

it possible to investigate the collective impact of the different major media as well as the potential interactive effects among the different media. By comparison, the customary technique of sampling an exemplary media source cannot, except by chance, apprehend a news coverage wave's inception and course of development.

In summary, this study incorporates a number of unique methodological features, the most important of these being the use of the entire polling record as a primary source and the inclusion of all major news outlets and their treatment as a differentiated whole. By using this technique, a straightforward finding could be arrived at that is highly suggestive of a media effect. In the absence of a direct measure of individual-level media consumption, completely ruling out alternative hypotheses is, of course, impossible. Nonetheless, in light of the state of the art in media effects studies, and given the equivocal nature of past media effect studies, this study's findings are significant. In light of the salience of crime as an issue in the public arena, and the common presumption that crime's salience can more or less simply be attributed to broad public sentiment, the findings here are pertinent. This case study further carries with it substantive theoretical implications with respect to social problems theory and public policy debates.

---

crime initiatives. At the time of this study, cable news did not yet have the large audience that it now has.

INDEX

Note: an italicized *f*, *n* or *t* following a page number indicates a figure, footnote or a table, respectively.

underdeveloped countries, 80–81

underdogs, 11

Uniform Crime Reports (UCR),
95n23, 289, 298

Union of Soviet Socialist Republics
(USSR/Soviet Union), 66n2, 75n11,
84, 87–88, 90, 125, 183, 206

unions, labor, 128

United Arab Emirates (UAE), 131

United Kingdom, 47, 270

United Nations, 11–12, 61n46, 270

United Nations (UN) Charter, 264

United States, 29–31, 87. *see also entries
beginning US ...*

unity, 144, 186

Universal, 267n8

University of California, 5

unlawfulness, 188

unpopularity of, 141–142

Unsolved Mysteries (TV show), 302n48

US Air Force, 132

USA Patriot Act, 57, 189–190, 209, 211

US combat deaths, 213

US Congress, 70, 140, 175, 177, 203,
244. *see also* bailouts

US Defense Department, 133, 135, 146,
167, 191–196

US Department of Homeland
Security (DHS), 136, 149, 150

US Department of Veterans Affairs
(VA), 12n15

Useche, Benardo, 51n25

US embassy (in Iraq), 242n28

use value, 78–79, 81

US executive branch, 178, 184,
203n21, 237

US government. *see also* the state;
individual groups and leaders;

specific branches:
corporations and, 52;
Israel and, 61–62;
legitimacy and, 119, 120;
neoliberalism and, 3, 10, 59;
oppression by, 11–12;
revolutions (rebellions) and, 146,
192–196, 226;
terrorism and, 188–189;
War on Terror and, 196–197

US House of Representatives, 70

US Justice Department (DOJ), 208–
209

US National Security Administration
(NSA), 30n3, 160, 242, 325–326

US News and World Report (magazine),
100–101, 291–292, 295, 296, 373

US Pentagon, 340

US Presidents, 52, 81, 315–316. *see
also* executive branch of US
government; *individual presidents*

USS Cole, 146, 323

US Senate, 70

USSR (Union of Soviet Socialist
Republics/Russia/Soviet Union),
66n2, 75n11, 84, 87–88, 90, 125, 183,
206

US State Department, 160, 188–189

US Supreme Court, 184, 335, 341

V

VA (US Department of Veterans
Affairs), 12n15

values, 21–22, 24–25, 27–28, 99, 349. *see
also* morality

values, economic, 78

Vanderbilt Index, 300n46

Van Riper, Paul, 323–324

Ventura, Jesse, 232–233